ELITES, NONELITES, AND POWER

POLITICAL POWER AND SOCIAL THEORY

Series Editor: Julian Go

Political Power and Social Theory is a peer-reviewed journal committed to advancing the interdisciplinary understanding of the linkages between political power, social relations, and historical development. The journal welcomes both empirical and theoretical work and is willing to consider papers of substantial length. Publication decisions are made by the editor in consultation with members of the editorial board and anonymous reviewers. For information on submissions, and a full list of volumes, please see the journal website at www.emeraldgrouppublishing.com/tk/ppst

Recent Volumes:

Volume 22:   Rethinking Obama, 2011

Volume 23:   Political Power and Social Theory, 2012

Volume 24:   Postcolonial Sociology, 2013

Volume 25:   Decentering Social Theory, 2013

Volume 26:   The United States in Decline, 2014

Volume 27:   Fields of Knowledge: Science, Politics and Publics in the Neoliberal Age, 2014

Volume 28:   Patrimonial Capitalism and Empire, 2015

Volume 29:   Chartering Capitalism: Organizing Markets, States, and Publics, 2015

Volume 30:   Perverse Politics? Feminism, Anti-imperialism, Multiplicity, 2016

Volume 31:   Postcolonial Sociologies: A Reader, 2016

Volume 32:   International Origins of Social and Political Theory, 2017

Volume 33:   Rethinking the Colonial State, 2017

Volume 34:   Critical Realism, History and Philosophy in the Social Sciences, 2018

Volume 35:   Gendering Struggles Against Informal and Precarious Work, 2018

Volume 36:   Religion, Humility, and Democracy in a Divided America, 2019

Volume 37:   Rethinking Class and Social Difference, 2020

Volume 38:   Global Historical Sociology of Race and Racism, 2021

Volume 39:   Trump and the Deeper Crisis, 2022

Volume 40:   Marxist Thought in South Asia

SENIOR EDITORIAL BOARD

Ronald Aminzade
University of Minnesota, USA

Eduardo Bonilla-Silva
Duke University, USA

Michael Burawoy
University of California-Berkeley, USA

Nitsan Chorev
Brown University, USA

Diane E. Davis
Harvard University, USA

Peter Evans
University of California-Berkeley, USA

Julian Go
The University of Chicago, USA

Eiko Ikegami
New School University Graduate Faculty, USA

Howard Kimeldorf
University of Michigan-Ann Arbor, USA

George Lawson
London School of Economics, UK

Daniel Slater
University of Michigan, USA

George Steinmetz
University of Michigan, USA

Maurice Zeitlin
University of California-Los Angeles, USA

POLITICAL POWER AND SOCIAL THEORY   VOLUME 41

ELITES, NONELITES, AND POWER: THE CRITICAL LEGACY OF ELITE THEORY FROM MARX TO LACHMANN, AND THEN BEYOND

EDITED BY

REBECCA JEAN EMIGH
University of California, Los Angeles, USA

AND

DYLAN RILEY
University of California, Berkeley, USA

United Kingdom – North America – Japan
India – Malaysia – China

Emerald Publishing Limited
Emerald Publishing, Floor 5, Northspring, 21-23 Wellington Street, Leeds LS1 4DL

First edition 2025

Editorial matter and selection © 2025 Rebecca Jean Emigh and Dylan Riley.
Individual chapters © 2025 The authors.
Published under exclusive licence by Emerald Publishing Limited.

Reprints and permissions service
Contact: www.copyright.com

No part of this book may be reproduced, stored in a retrieval system, transmitted in any form or by any means electronic, mechanical, photocopying, recording or otherwise without either the prior written permission of the publisher or a licence permitting restricted copying issued in the UK by The Copyright Licensing Agency and in the USA by The Copyright Clearance Center. Any opinions expressed in the chapters are those of the authors. Whilst Emerald makes every effort to ensure the quality and accuracy of its content, Emerald makes no representation implied or otherwise, as to the chapters' suitability and application and disclaims any warranties, express or implied, to their use.

British Library Cataloguing in Publication Data
A catalogue record for this book is available from the British Library

ISBN: 978-1-83797-584-6 (Print)
ISBN: 978-1-83797-583-9 (Online)
ISBN: 978-1-83797-585-3 (Epub)

ISSN: 0198-8719 (Series)

Printed and bound by CPI Group (UK) Ltd, Croydon, CR0 4YY

INVESTOR IN PEOPLE

To Richard Lachmann, our brilliant colleague and friend

CONTENTS

About the Editors   *xi*

About the Contributors   *xiii*

Acknowledgments   *xvii*

SECTION 1: THE POWERS OF ELITES AND NONELITES

Chapter 1   Introduction: Relational Power Theory: Elites and Nonelites   *3*
Rebecca Jean Emigh and Dylan Riley

Chapter 2   Streets and Elites: Corruption Grievances in Contemporary Revolutions   *45*
Colin J. Beck and Mlada Bukovansky

Chapter 3   Asian Art Patronage: Race, Ethnicity, and Cultural Legitimation   *71*
Patricia A. Banks

Chapter 4   Decolonizing Porto? Thinking on the Portuguese "Unfinished" Decolonization Process From a Collaborative Action-Research Project With the City's Black Communities   *85*
Lígia Ferro, Beatriz Lacerda, Lydia Matthews and Susan Meiselas

SECTION 2: ELITES AND SOCIAL TRANSFORMATIONS

Chapter 5   Elite Conflict and Industry Regulation: How Political Polarization Affects Local Restriction and State Preemption of the US Hydraulic Fracturing Industry   *113*
Lori Qingyuan Yue and Yuni Wen

Chapter 6   Elite Politics and Economic Crisis: Hyperinflation in Argentina, 1989–1990   *141*
Tod S. Van Gunten

Chapter 7   Elites, Colonialism, and Property Rights in Historical Perspective   *175*
Abhishek Chatterjee

Chapter 8   Do Events Shape Race? A Comparative-Historical Examination of the Catholic Irish in 17th-Century Barbados and Montserrat   *211*
Caroline Virginia Reilly

Chapter 9   Historical Trajectories of Official Information Gathering in India   *239*
Patricia Ahmed, Rebecca Jean Emigh and Dylan Riley

Index   *285*

ABOUT THE EDITORS

Rebecca Jean Emigh is a Professor of Sociology at UCLA. She authored numerous prize-winning books and articles on comparative and historical sociology, focusing on long-term processes of social change in topics such as capitalism, knowledge, music, news, and censuses. Her article, "The Power of Negative Thinking" (*Theory and Society* 26:649–684), was recently translated into Chinese. She was chair of the Comparative/Historical Section of the American Sociological Association and was a coeditor of *Social Science History*. She is the incoming chair of the Theory Section of the American Sociological Association. She is currently editing *The Oxford Handbook of Comparative and Historical Sociology* and writing a book on epochal analysis.

Dylan Riley is a Professor of Sociology at the University of California, Berkeley. He studies capitalism, socialism, democracy, authoritarianism, and knowledge regimes in broad comparative and historical perspective. He has authored or coauthored six books and has published articles in the *American Journal of Sociology*, *American Sociological Review*, *Catalyst*, *Comparative Sociology*, *Contemporary Sociology*, *Comparative Studies in Society and History*, *Social Science History*, *The Socio-Economic Review, Theory and Society,* and the *New Left Review* (of which he is a member of the editorial committee). His work has been translated into German, Portuguese, Russian, and Spanish. He is also at work on two larger book projects: a collection of essays provisionally entitled *Science, Ideology, and Method* and a comparative-historical analysis of democratization in Germany, Italy, Japan, France, the United Kingdom, and the United States from c1200 to c1950 provisionally entitled *Special Paths*.

ABOUT THE CONTRIBUTORS

Patricia Ahmed is an Assistant Professor of Sociology and criminology at South Dakota State University. Her research interests include comparative/historical sociology, cross-cultural sociology, globalization, and deviance. Her recent publications include works on census categorization in Puerto Rico and the sociology of knowledge (with Rebecca Jean Emigh and Dylan Riley), and on interdisciplinary collaboration (with Erin Miller et al.) published in the *Journal of the American Pharmacists Association.*

Patricia A. Banks (Harvard University PhD and A.M./Spelman College BA) is the Co-Editor-In-Chief of *Poetics* and Professor of Sociology at Mount Holyoke College. Banks is the author of four books, including *Black Culture Inc: How Ethnic Community Support Pays for Corporate America* (Stanford University Press 2022); *Race, Ethnicity, and Consumption: A Sociological View* (Routledge 2020); *Diversity and Philanthropy at African American Museums* (Routledge Research in Museum Studies 2019); and *Represent: Art and Identity Among the Black Upper-Middle Class* (Routledge 2010). Banks is the Chair of the Section on the Sociology of Consumers and Consumption at the American Sociological Association and serves on the boards of the *American Sociological Review*, *Cultural Sociology*, *Ethnic and Racial Studies*, the Black Trustee Alliance and the Mount Holyoke College Art Museum. She has been in residence at Stanford University as a Fellow at the Center for Advanced Studies in the Behavioral Sciences (CASBS) and at Harvard University as a Sheila Biddle Ford Foundation Fellow at the Hutchins Center for African & African American Research. In 2023, Banks' book *Black Culture, Inc.* received three national awards.

Colin J. Beck is a Professor of Sociology and affiliate of the International Relations Program at Pomona College in Claremont, California. He is the author of *Radicals, Revolutionaries and Terrorists* (Polity, 2015) and coauthor of *On Revolutions: Unruly Politics in the Contemporary Era* (Oxford University Press, 2022). His prior works on revolutionary waves in *Social Science History* and *Theory & Society* have won article awards from the American Sociological Association. He has also published articles in *Sociological Theory, Mobilization, Socius, International Sociology,* various edited volumes, and other venues.

Mlada Bukovansky is a Professor of Government at Smith College, Northampton, Massachusetts. She is the author of *Legitimacy and Power Politics: The American and French Revolutions in International Political Culture* (Princeton University Press, 2002), a coauthor of *Special Responsibilities: Global Problems and American Power* (Cambridge University Press, 2012) a coauthor of *On Revolutions: Unruly*

Politics in the Contemporary World (Oxford University Press, 2022), and coeditor of *The Oxford Handbook of History and International Relations* (Oxford University Press, 2023). She has published articles in the journals *International Organization*, *Review of International Studies*, *Review of International Political Economy*, and *International Politics*, and contributed to a number of edited volumes in the field of international relations.

Abhishek Chatterjee is an Associate Professor of political science at the University of Montana. His research interests include the origins of states and markets, and the philosophy of the social sciences, especially the relationship between ontology and research methods. He is the author inter alia of *Rulers and Capital in Historical Perspective: State Formation and Financial Development in India and the United States.*

Lígia Ferro teaches at the Sociology Department, Faculty of Arts and Humanities – University of Porto. She has received her European PhD from the University Institute of Lisbon, ISCTE-IUL (2011). She was a Visiting Scholar at several universities in Europe, the United States, and Brazil. Lígia Ferro is the President of the European Sociological Association and is a member of the board of the European Network of Observatories in the Fields of Arts and Cultural Education – ENO. She is the author and editor of several publications in Portuguese, English, Spanish, and French. Lately, she has been working on cultural practices, arts education, migrations, and action research, especially in urban contexts.

Beatriz Lacerda has a degree and a master's degree in Sociology from the Faculty of Arts and Humanities of the University of Porto. She has experience in artistic and community intervention projects in the city of Porto, where she crosses the fields of sociology and cinema, using ethnography and participatory visual methodologies. Among the projects in which she has participated are "Travessia" (2021), "Campanhã Cinema Club" (2021–2023), "Rising Cinema" (2023), and "Inflatable Cinema" (2021–2023). She is currently on a PhD scholarship for the "Pericreativities" project, coordinated by Otávio Raposo (ISCTE) and Lígia Ferro (IS-UP), where she will have the opportunity to deepen her research in the areas of territory, youth and creativity, migration and colonialism, ethnography, and processes of co-participation.

Lydia Matthews is a Brooklyn- and Athens-based critical writer, contemporary art curator, educator, and cultural activist who currently serves as a Professor of Visual Culture in the Fine Arts program of Parsons School of Design and Director of the Curatorial Design Research Lab at The New School. Trained as a contemporary art historian at the University of California, Berkeley, and the University of London's Courtauld Institute, her work focuses on the intersection of current art/craft/design practices, diverse local cultures and global economies. Thus far, she has been invited to design participatory curatorial ventures in New York, Greece, Turkey, Georgia, Kazakhstan, Portugal, and the Czech Republic. https://www.lydiamatthews.com/

ABOUT THE CONTRIBUTORS

Susan Meiselas is a New York-based documentary photographer and President of the Magnum Foundation. As the author of *Carnival Strippers* (1976), *Nicaragua* (1981), *Kurdistan: In the Shadow of History* (1997), *Pandora's Box* (2001), *Encounters with the Dani* (2003), *Prince Street Girls* (2016), *A Room of Their Own* (2017), and *Tar Beach* (2020), Meiselas is well known for her documentation of human rights issues in Latin America. Her awards include a MacArthur Fellowship (1992), a Guggenheim Fellowship (2015), the Deutsche Börse Photography Foundation Prize (2019), and the first Women in Motion Award from Kering and the Rencontres d'Arles. *Mediations*, a survey exhibition of her work from the 1970s to present, was recently exhibited at the Fundació Antoni Tàpies, Jeu de Paume, San Francisco Museum of Modern Art, the Instituto Moreira Salles in São Paulo, Kunst Haus Wien, among other international venues. https://www.susanmeiselas.com/

Caroline Virginia Reilly is a PhD student in Sociology at the University of California, Los Angeles and has earned MAs in Sociology from the University of Memphis (2020) and the University of California, Los Angeles (2022). Her interests include comparative-historical sociology, gender, and race, ethnicity, and racialization. She is the first author of "Critical Mass and Critical Representation: Economic Transition, Workplace Cultures, and Women CEOs in China" (with Dr Junmin Wang, University of Memphis) in *Sociology of Development* and the second author of "Gender Bias, Institutional Predicaments and Innovativeness of Female CEOs in China" (with Dr Wang [first author] and Kaniz Fatema, PhD student, University of Iowa) in the *Journal of Developmental Entrepreneurship*. Reilly is currently working on her dissertation project, which examines income and ethnoracial disparities in access to and quality of prenatal and postpartum care in the United States.

Tod S. Van Gunten is Senior Lecturer in Sociology at the University of Edinburgh (Scotland, United Kingdom) and held previous positions at the Max Planck Institute for the Study of Societies (Cologne, Germany) and the Carlos III-Juan March Institute (Madrid, Spain). He received his PhD in Sociology from the University of Wisconsin-Madison. His areas of research include Latin American political elites, the social and political role of the economics profession, and social processes in financial and other markets. Current research projects include the effect of elite networks on career processes in the 20th century Mexican state.

Yuni Wen is a Teaching Fellow in the International Business Group at Oxford Saïd Business School. Her research focuses on the regulatory challenges arising from digital innovation and the reputation risks associated with artificial intelligence.

Lori Qingyuan Yue is an Associate Professor at the Management Division in Columbia Business School. Her research focuses on the relationship between business and society, especially regarding how organizations respond to contentious social environments and regulation uncertainty.

ACKNOWLEDGMENTS

We would like to thank Michelle Marinello and Johanna Hernández Pérez for their research assistance. Funding from the UCLA Dean of the Social Sciences and a UCLA Faculty Senate Grant supported this work.

SECTION 1

THE POWERS OF ELITES AND NONELITES

CHAPTER 1

INTRODUCTION: RELATIONAL POWER THEORY: ELITES AND NONELITES

Rebecca Jean Emigh[a] and Dylan Riley[b]

[a]University of California, Los Angeles, USA
[b]University of California, Berkeley, USA

ABSTRACT

In this chapter, we review the historical development of elite theory, and then we propose a way forward beyond it. Elite theory emerged as a critique of democracy in the late 19th century. Although it used historical materials illustratively, it tended to be ahistorical theoretically because its primary aim was to demonstrate the perdurance of elites even in conditions of mass suffrage. Lachmann was the first scholar to develop elite theory as a truly historical and explanatory framework by combining it with elements of Marxism. Even Lachmann's theory, however, remained inadequate because it did not rest on a fully articulated theory of power. In this introduction, we suggest a "relational power theory" as a remedy to this situation, and we use it to formulate a general heuristic for the study of elites, nonelites, and their interrelationships. To illustrate its utility, we show how it can illuminate the chapters in this volume (though they were not necessarily written for these purposes).

Keywords: Power; elites; nonelites; dialectical realism; comparative historical sociology

In this volume, we make two bold claims: First, it is time to overcome elite theory! Although this tradition contains many important insights, it is insufficiently historical: Elite theory never historicized its own conditions of applicability, nor did it develop a satisfying account of historical change. We argue that

---

Elites, Nonelites, and Power
Political Power and Social Theory, Volume 41, 3–43
Copyright © 2025 Rebecca Jean Emigh and Dylan Riley
Published under exclusive licence by Emerald Publishing Limited
ISSN: 0198-8719/doi:10.1108/S0198-871920240000041001

elite theory needs to be recast as "relational power theory," which emphasizes the mutual constitution of elites and nonelites through the power relations that connect them. Second, we argue that resource mobilization theory and political process theory, two predominant ways of considering when nonelite social movements are successful, are special cases of our relational power theory. Our intervention is not only theoretical but political. Because elite theory has always been insufficiently historical, it has failed to explain the conditions under which social life could be organized in a cooperative as opposed to hierarchical mode. This is true even of the venerable tradition of progressive uses of the theory. However, resisting and transforming elite and nonelite relations is key, in many ways, to the survival of humanity. It is for this reason that a historically and theoretically informed internal critique of the theory has a political import.

Accordingly, by drawing attention to these conditions, we try to give hope to humanity. In a world of vertiginous inequality, escalating ecological disaster, endless wars, and extraordinary political and economic turbulence generated by a winner-take-all society seemingly designed to concentrate privilege and power in the hands of a very few, the central question that faces social science – and indeed the world – is whether social protest will change anything or whether elites will continue to lead the planet and its population to disaster. All the important topics of contemporary social science – including racial justice, environmental change, immigration, economic inequality, and education, to name a few – turn around this issue. The question of the power of elites and nonelites, and the conditions under which that power might be tamed and turned to the benefit of humanity, thus lies at the heart of social science today.

This multidisciplinary volume brings together a cutting-edge set of chapters on power, elites, and nonelites that weigh in on these central issues of the world and social science. Furthermore, we consider these topics in a new, inclusive way by drawing in researchers who deal with topics central to elite theory, but who might not be represented in more classic statements of it. We envision this volume as the key "go to" piece for several generations of scholars. This volume discusses elite theory, but, more broadly, we consider the relationship between elites, nonelites, and power.

Elite theory has been useful in identifying single or multiple elites that have a lot of social influence. Elite theory, however, draws on a narrow definition of elites and power and cannot explain how elites are able or unable to bring about social transformations. Furthermore, elite theory does not consistently conceptualize elites and nonelites relationally. The theory thereby falls into the trap of attempting to describe elites through their intrinsic or inherent characteristics. To address these issues, we make several theoretical interventions. First, we conceptualize power more broadly than classic elite theory. We understand that power – in its multiple manifestations – is constituted relationally between elites and nonelites. To think about this relationality, we draw on Marxist theory. While Marxist theory is inherently relational, it often focuses on the relation of exploitation between capitalists and laborers. In doing so, however, Marxist theory often misses other relationships: more generally, the ones that affect elites and nonelites outside of relations of surplus extraction. Thus, we use Marxism as a particular theoretical instantiation of a more general process of how society is relational but extend this idea outside of the economic sphere. For example, Tilly and Tarrow (2015, p. 97) analyzed contentious politics as an interaction between challengers and their opponents (among others). We expand on this idea more generally to note that power is dialectically constituted between elites and non-elites in social spheres beyond the economic one to create our "relational power theory."

We understand our approach as a dialectical realist one that analyzes social reality as composed of dialectical relationships (Emigh et al., 2024, pp. 295–297; Riley et al., 2021, pp. 331–334). Because social reality is complicated, pieces of these relationships – not the social whole – must be analyzed. However, the combination of different sets of relationships always provides a more accurate and insightful analysis. Thus, as we suggest, while elites and nonelites may be studied separately, and this contributes to sociological knowledge, considering the relationship between them, and, more generally, between multiple elites and nonelites, provides much more social knowledge.

This volume pays tribute to Richard Lachmann, who was our much-admired colleague who died unexpectedly during the pandemic (but not from COVID-19) in 2021. Elite theory has a long history, but before Lachmann, elite theory was mostly a set of descriptors that pointed to elites' characteristics but did not develop theories of what they could do, to what effect, and where. In contrast, Lachmann developed a Lakatosian (Lakatos, 1970, p. 132) research programme out of these descriptions. He defined elites and developed a few guidelines for specifying their effect: (a) look for the configuration of elites (e.g., single, double, or multiple); (b) look for the balance of power among these elites; (c) where there is only one elite, look at their capacity to extract surplus from nonelites; and (d) look at where elites then are obliged to transform social relations (Lachmann, 1990, pp. 402–404). This formed a research programme that made it possible to explain how elites could change – or not change – social reality. It set up these heuristics for finding interesting problems as well as specifying empirical parameters for evaluation. And in doing so, Lachmann established a whole new way to do research where little previously existed. We recognize the genius in his approach.

When Lachmann took his particular path of defining and evaluating elite configurations, however, he necessarily excluded others. As we note in our dialectical realist approach, reality is complicated, so researchers necessarily select some aspects over others, as did Lachmann (Emigh et al., 2024, p. 297; Riley et al., 2021, pp. 331–334). In particular, Lachmann focused on elite and nonelite relations, but on one social category (class) and one form of power (organizational). While this created a useful research programme with a lot of explanatory power, the question is, is it possible to extend this to other relations and axes of power, and if so, how? Here, then, we explore these possibilities of the relationship between elites and nonelites along multiple lines of power.

The topical focus is also important. Lachmann was mostly looking at economic resources. Using this definition, however, it is difficult to see how race, gender, sexual orientation, ableism, and other important social phenomena link to elite theory, and indeed Lachmann's theory does not address these issues. Thus, in this volume, we address other dimensions of social stratification as they also produce elites and nonelites, as society is relational in many ways other than just along the lines of the traditional Marxist theory of class. Lachmann was always interested in engaging in real dialogue – thus, we believe that he would approve of our extending his research, even if we go in a different direction than he probably would have. Of course, he is not now here to discuss this with us, but we think he would have encouraged the exchange.

In this introduction, then, we review the classic statements of elite theory from Pareto to Bourdieu and place Lachmann's contribution within this context (Section, "The Tradition of Elite Theory: From Pareto to Lachmann"). We also use this review to point out a couple of basic weaknesses of elite theory, even with Lachmann's improvements. We then use these critiques as the basis for a new multidimensional view of power (Section, "Conceptualizing Power") and apply this view to develop a theory of the relationship between elites and nonelites. Next, we apply this scheme to a discussion of the relative powers of elites and nonelites (Section, "The Relational Power of Elites and Nonelites"). Finally, Section, "Elites, Nonelites, and Historical Change," discusses how elites and nonelites transform society. We introduce the chapters in this volume in Sections, "The Relational Power of Elites and Nonelites," and "Elites, Nonelites, and Historical Change."

THE TRADITION OF ELITE THEORY: FROM PARETO TO LACHMANN

Richard Lachmann's fundamental contribution can be stated simply enough. By combining elite theory with elements of Marxism, he developed a distinctive account of historical change. This is in many ways an impressive and surprising achievement because elite theory in its origins was profoundly hostile both to theories of historical development and to Marxism in particular (even though all elite theorists borrowed heavily, either implicitly or explicitly, from Marxisant theories, especially theories of ideology; Pizzorno, 1972, pp. 15–16). Thus, in combining these theoretical traditions (elite theory and Marxism), Lachmann was bridging a deep conceptual and political divide. To show this, we place his work in the context of elite theory as a theoretical tradition, starting with the initial trio of elite theorists (Pareto, Mosca, and Michels).

Elite theory emerged among a group of Italian (or at least Italian by adoption) thinkers: Vilfredo Pareto (1848–1923), Gaetano Mosca (1858–1941), and Roberto (or Robert) Michels (1876–1936). Their terminology, substantive foci, methodologies, and sometimes their specific arguments were quite different, and they never formed a school, such as the Durkheimians did in France. However, there is an obvious similarity among them, as was recognized at the time of their writing, and the three rather quickly came to be regarded as varieties of a common species of thought (Pizzorno, 1972, p. 13).

Pareto (1848–1923)

Using a conceptualization of ranking individuals according to their "capacity" to denote elites, Pareto (1916b, pp. 470, 599) painted a somber portrait of democracy, which had little to do with popular sovereignty.[1] The sorts of political regimes termed democracies in the modern world (essentially, for Pareto, Europe and the United States, in addition to, bizarrely, Turkey and Russia) were those in which "the power of making laws belonged to a great degree to an assembly elected by at least part of the citizenry" (Pareto, 1916b, p. 598). Pareto, anticipating Schumpeter, thus defined democracies narrowly in terms of institutions, not as a form of self-government by the demos. But even with this very restricted definition, the concept could not really identify types of regimes. France, Pareto, (1916b, p. 599) pointed out, accorded the greatest power to parliament, but there were important restrictions on elected assemblies in the United Kingdom, the United States, Italy, and Russia.

Social reality, Pareto (1916b) then suggested, differed sharply from official ideology because in all the major states there was a small governing class that "maintained itself in power partly through force and partly through the consent of the governed class" (p. 599). In short, the rhetoric of democracy obscured the reality of rule by a small elite (Pareto, 1916b, pp. 598–599). The concept of popular sovereignty was one species of "derivation," a post hoc justification of social reality, not an explanation of it (Bobbio, 1969a, pp. 101–107; Pareto, 1916a, p. 433; Pizzorno, 1972, p. 31). The real difference between regimes was whether they relied primarily on the consent of the governed class or on force.

Pareto focused on two types of elites: foxes and lions. Pareto associated lions and foxes with two different styles of rule. He portrayed lions as specialists in the use of force, and foxes as experts in "cleverness, fraud, and corruption" (Pareto, 1916b, p. 553). Pareto conceived of these as alternative strategies for rule. Governing classes typically had both lions and foxes, and Pareto held that stable social orders reproduced themselves by balancing the two types. This would produce a balance between the techniques of consent based ultimately on material concessions (corruption) and ideological trickery (fraud) and the techniques of force based on violence (Pareto, 1916b, pp. 602, 614–617). Governments with too many foxes were too reluctant to use force, producing "an unstable equilibrium, and revolutions follow such as that of Protestantism against the men of the Renaissance, and of the French people, in 1789, against its governing class" (Pareto, 1916b, p. 589). For Pareto, however, the most important point was that revolutions never increased popular sovereignty but led only to new structures of elite rule. Because of this argument, Pareto (1916b, p. 586) often used cyclical or wave-like metaphors when discussing historical change. To conclude, Pareto interpreted history as an oscillation between elite foxes and lions. Their proportion within the governing class explained when governments would be primarily based on force or consent, which Pareto interpreted as the successful application of corruption and trickery.

8 *Introduction*

Mosca (1858–1941)

Mosca (1896, p. 64) defined elites simply as organized minorities who possessed some quality that society recognized as socially valuable. Both aspects (restricted number and social recognition) were important. Mosca (1896, p. 64) thought that elites were able to pursue their interests effectively precisely because they were minorities, and in this way could overcome collective action problems. Elites could rule because, being organized, they could always outflank the majority, which, according to Mosca (1896, p. 64), was inherently disorganized. Elites, however, were never content to rule simply by virtue of their organizational superiority. They also always made a claim to be qualified by fulfilling either a real or a socially recognized function (Mosca, 1896, p. 65).

Like Pareto, Mosca used this observation to unmask the ideology of democracy. For Mosca, the problem was the distinction, which had its roots in classic political philosophy, between monarchies, aristocracies, and democracies. This distinction, from political philosophy, grouped together highly dissimilar regimes, such as – at the time of Mosca's (1896, p. 62) writing – Italy and the United Kingdom, France and the United States, or Russia and Turkey. For Mosca, the problem with the distinction was that neither a single person nor a whole population ruled. Absolute monarchs required a cooperative staff and an aristocracy to transmit their commands. Democratic pressures, in contrast, must be channeled by an organized minority to have an effect (Mosca, 1896, pp. 61–64). Thus, he concluded instead that minority rule was a "constant and natural fact" (Mosca, 1896, p. 63). In a sense, therefore, there was only one type of government: aristocracy (Mosca, 1896, p. 62; Pizzorno, 1972, p. 42).

Mosca developed his understanding of elites in two ways that went decisively beyond Pareto. First, he argued that inter-elite conflict and cooperation could have an important impact on political regimes. While elites generally governed in all regimes, in some regimes there was only one such elite governing according to a single program, while in others a plurality of elites existed. When there was a single elite, the political regime was likely to be despotic and to be unrestrained by law. Where, in contrast, there was a plurality of elites, they tended to compete with and check one another, thereby creating a system of laws that regulated their relations (Mosca, 1896, p. 132). Thus, legal regimes emerged not from the constitutional division of powers, but from elite conflict itself (Mosca, 1896, p. 146).

Second, Mosca (1896) accorded ideology – in his terminology, "political formulas" (p. 85) – a more central role than did Pareto. Instead of seeing political ideas as post hoc rationalizations of basic psychological dispositions, as did Pareto, Mosca argued that these formulas were not psychological but historical, and played a positive role in the exercise of power. The role of the political formula is somewhat analogous to Weber's (1921, p. 398) concept of legitimacy or Gramsci's (1971, p. 12) concept of hegemony. These political formulas, or doctrines and beliefs, crystalized in a political formula that "philosophers of law generally call a principle of sovereignty" (Mosca, 1896, pp. 84–85). Thus, although in a given society multiple elites and multiple political formulas could coexist, each elite was organized around a main formula that justified its rule by explaining the basis on which it held power.

These political formulas were crucial to elite rule and, despite their substantive content, masked the reality of rule by a limited elite (Mosca, 1896, pp. 85–86). Indeed, Mosca argued that the main threat to elite stability was when the elite and the masses were organized according to differing political formulas. He described this situation in terms of the survivals of older "social types" in empires that had expanded to incorporate pre-existing societies (Mosca, 1896, p. 108). The problem of different social types was also highly relevant to modern societies. Unlike under feudalism, where the elite lived among its following in what Mosca (1896, p. 116) called "bureaucratized societies," cultural and educational differences between the elite and the mass could become accentuated. These cases of intellectual isolation could lead to the emergence of a "true state within a state" in which a new counter-elite, organized according to a new political formula, challenged the legal government (Mosca, 1896, p. 122). The primary reference for Mosca was Italian socialism.

Mosca, to summarize, had an organizational concept of elites, a theory of how plural elites shaped political regimes, and a fairly well-developed account of ideology. Thus, he developed a much more subtle and historically specific account of elite rule than Pareto. Moreover, Mosca, to explain historical change, distinguished between different types of elites in different historical epochs; in particular, he distinguished between elites in feudal and bureaucratic regimes. Under feudal regimes, elites combined economic, judicial, and military functions (Mosca, 1896, pp. 97–98). Under bureaucratic states, a salaried officialdom, the division of administrative labor, and a high level of discipline emerged (Mosca, 1896, p. 101). Importantly, in the latter case, the elites themselves could not be equated with those who controlled the government since there was now a relative separation between the economy and politics (Mosca, 1896, p. 104). Thus, Mosca, like Pareto, was aware of the need, especially in modern society, to distinguish between a social elite and the governing class in a narrower sense. However, what drove the transition from the feudal to the bureaucratic state remains somewhat unclear in Mosca's analysis. We return to this point below.

Michels (1876–1936)

Michels' general concept of elites resembles Mosca's in its focus on organization. Yet, he developed this argument in a more trenchant and focused way than Mosca because he showed how the formation of organized minorities was a consequence of modern democracy. Thus, he did not just claim that elites in general ruled in all times and places. He made the more specific argument that regimes with extensive suffrage tended to produce elite rule by their internal workings. Democracy, he suggested, faced not only external obstacles – for example, resistance from conservative elites – but also internal ones produced by itself (Michels, 1911, p. vii).

Michels developed this basic idea by focusing on the intimate relationship between mass organization and democracy. Here, he identified a paradox. While democracy required organization, organization tended to undermine democracy, thereby producing oligarchy. Thus, the ideal of democracy was everywhere violated by the reality of contemporary political life. The implication of Michels' argument, then, was that democracy was an internally contradictory project. As it took on more and more of a mass character, it would become ever more dominated by oligarchy (Michels, 1911, pp. 350–381).

Michels sought to demonstrate this argument by investigating the most democratic parties of his day: the German and Italian socialist parties. By establishing oligarchic tendencies within these parties that explicitly demanded democracy, he suggested that the development of oligarchy was connected to the structural tendency of democratic society, not to particular features of specific political parties (Michels, 1911, p. 12).

Michels accepted the Marxist idea that modern politics is basically a class struggle. But classes, he argued, could pursue their aims only when *organized*. Organization created the necessary "collective will" (Michels, 1911, p. 21) by which classes obtained their aims. Although organization was a necessity for all classes, it was especially necessary for those at the bottom of the social hierarchy: the proletariat. Organization "is the weapon of the weak in their struggle with the strong" (Michels, 1911, p. 21). Michels' argument suggested that as suffrage expanded, organization would also increase.

The spread of organization was precisely what undermined democracy through the production of elites. Organizations, and particularly political parties, were, for Michels, fighting organizations. To be effective, they must be able to make decisions, process information, and pursue tactics and strategy. Michels argued that even the most basic of these procedures was technically impossible through a deliberative assembly. Once an organization had more than about 10,000 members, it could no longer be constituted as an effective deliberative body because persons in large aggregates were irrational and incapable of deliberation (Michels, 1911, p. 25). Thus, organizations would inevitably be hierarchical (Michels, 1911, p. 69). There was, then, a strong tendency for political parties to develop as systems of delegation and representation in which the mass of the party membership turned over the day-to-day control to the party hierarchy.

As a result, this representation became increasingly detached from the mass. The party leadership would seek to entrench its superiority over the mass by constituting itself as an *elite* (Michels, 1911, p. 31). In Michels' argument, then, there was a close and paradoxical relationship between democracy and oligarchy. As democracy expanded, so did organization, but as organization spread, it undermined democracy (Michels, 1911, pp. 22–23). Michels thus claimed that democracy produced elite rule.

Michels, like Mosca, argued that ideology played an important role. In a general sense, the idea of democracy was a kind of false consciousness that disguised the real character of modern political life (Michels, 1911, pp. 8, 12). But more specifically, it constrained all political parties to make their claims in popular terms. Political struggles in modern democracies always underwent a process of ethical embellishment because every political force "speaks in the name of the people, of the totality" (Michels, 1911, p. 16).

Michels also had a distinctive vision of historical change. His basic point was that human history was not so much a struggle between classes seeking to establish alternative principles of economic organization, as a struggle between rising and declining elites seeking to entrench their political power. He began with the example of the bourgeoisie. This class in its initial struggle with the landed aristocracy presented itself as the bearer of the "rights of man" (Michels, 1911, p. 17) but, in reality, the bourgeoisie either established itself as a new aristocracy, as in the United States, or fused with the old aristocracy, as in France and Germany (Michels, 1911, p. 15).

Michels extended this point to socialism. He suggested that the socialist claim to represent the interests of the whole of humanity was basically the same as the bourgeois claim. This claim was merely an "ethical embellishment" (Michels, 1911, p. 13) – an argument that served the interests of a new socialist elite. The reason for the cyclical process of the rise and decline of elites stemmed from the requirements of class struggles. Since every class rising to power, and particularly the modern proletariat, needed an organization to pursue its aims, class struggle in fact tended to become a struggle between organizational elites rather than a struggle between autonomously organized social groups. Socialism embodied not the rise of the proletariat to political dominance, but the latest version of aristocracy: the rise of a new political class (Michels, 1911, pp. 16–17).

It is hard to overstate the importance of elite theory, especially that of Michels and Pareto, for the development of US sociology in the mid-20th century, and an exhaustive review would be beyond the scope of this introduction. The most important elite theorist for understanding Lachmann's project, though, is Charles Wright Mills, to whose work we now turn.

Mills (1916–1962)

Mills restated the main macro-historical concerns of elite theory. Mills (1956, p. 242) challenged the reigning pluralist consensus that a shifting congeries of interest groups, none of which had any greater influence than the other, was the basis of US politics. Mills (1956, pp. 266, 268) suggested that while the notion of competing interest groups was a somewhat adequate view of what he described as the middle and lower levels of power, at its apex a consolidated "power elite," made up of a political, military, and economic segment, was becoming increasingly dominant in the post-World War II era. The rise of these three elites connected in the political sphere to the increasingly formal and thin character of US democracy, in the military sphere by the increasing importance of US military might, and in the economic sphere by the emergence of the giant corporation in place of smaller firms (Mills, 1956, p. 275).

The other side of the process of elite rule was the disintegration of a public, which debated issues into an atomized and fundamentally passive mass. Anticipating an argument that Habermas (1962/1989, pp. 160–161) would make later, Mills pointed out that early democratic theory was based on the idea of public opinion as a source of rational discussion. Increasingly, however, the public was

12   *Introduction*

manipulated by giant parties, interest associations, and big media (Mills, 1956, p. 300).

Mills, like Michels, suggested that the extension of mass democracy itself was one of the mechanisms tending to produce large organizations, and thereby paradoxically mass impotence: "Mass democracy means the struggle of powerful and larger-scale interest groups and associations, which stand between the big decisions that are made by state, corporate, army, and the will of the individual citizen as a member of the public" (Mills, 1956, p. 307). Accordingly, mass democracy paradoxically disempowered individual citizens.

Intellectually, Mills' accomplishment was rather paradoxical. He deployed a set of conservative critiques of democracy to unmask the pluralist consensus of the post-war US order, but from a left-wing perspective. He thereby suggested that its democracy was largely a sham.

Bourdieu (1930–2002)

Bourdieu is a central referent for contemporary elite theory (Eyal et al., 1998, pp. 17–45; Khan, 2012, p. 365). His sociology reprises Michels' argument that mass democracy was associated with the expropriation of means of political expression from most of the population (Bourdieu, 1981a, p. 4). Furthermore, just as Michels had argued before, Bourdieu (1981a, pp. 4–5) emphasized that the monopoly of the means of political representation was greatest in precisely those parties that were challenging the monopoly of the means of production: namely, the parties of the left. This view of political representation led Bourdieu to a specific conception of politics. For him, political struggle unfolded in an autonomous political field in which the stances taken by different political actors were determined more by their relationship to other actors in the field than by their relationship to their bases – an idea that Michels had anticipated although not fully developed (Bourdieu, 1981a, p. 6). Thus, very much like the classic elite theorists, Bourdieu saw politics as a matter of intra-elite position-taking masked by the false democratic ideology of representation (Bourdieu, 2012, p. 60).

To sum up, elite theory began as a conservative critique of democracy; it then migrated to the left, where it was used to unmask the self-satisfied images of democracy put forward by state managers in the United States and elsewhere. Although not often read in social theory courses today, the indirect influence of elite theory is hard to overstate.

Elite theory, however, was unable to overcome several difficult problems. The first is a simple conceptual problem: None of the elite theorists was ever able to give a satisfying definition of what an elite is. Pareto (1916b, p. 470) relied on the idea of an ahistorical distribution of talents. Mosca's argument is more sophisticated as it refers to a social fact, "organization." But, like Pareto's, it is ahistorical since organized minorities were said always to rule (Mosca, 1896, p. 64). Michels (1911, p. 12), like Mosca, seemed to think that organized minorities were always more effective than masses, but he did not explain where they came from historically. Mills (1956, p. 266) seemed to have a historical narrative about the linked process of elite consolidation and massification, but he did not explain what was driving this process; in particular, he did not link it to elite conflict itself. Bourdieu (1981a, p. 6) had a seemingly more adequate view since he was very concerned with establishing a relational sociology. But his relations were always among elites, never between elites and nonelites. Furthermore, although he connected the emergence of the elite to the rise of an autonomous political field, he never adequately explained the origins of fields, and thereby never explained the origins of elites. This general problem derives from the conceptual approach of all the elite theorists, for all of them tried to conceptualize elites by defining them as stand-alone groups, rather than understanding elite positions as products of specific types of power relationships between elites and nonelites. This is even true of Bourdieu's seemingly more relational view, as the relationships he focused on were exclusively among elites, not between elites and nonelites.

The second, closely related, problem of elite theory is its inadequate account of historical change. History was a central topic of all these theorists: the rise of foxes for Pareto, the transition from "feudal" to "bureaucratic" rule for Mosca, the "oligarchic tendencies" of mass democracy for Michels, the rise of a power elite combined with a passive and atomized population for Mills, and the emergence of autonomous fields for Bourdieu. However, none of them developed an adequate account of these changes *in terms of elite theory*. In the absence of this, these theorists usually invoked various untheorized processes – such as Mosca's transition from feudal to bureaucratic states or Mills' emergence of mass society – operating in the background of the theory and forming the crucial, yet unexamined, context for elite formation and elite conflict. To move forward, then, elite theory needed to be both *relational* and historical, and indeed, it needed to be historical *because* it is relational.

Lachmann (1956–2021)

Lachmann was born the year Mills' *Power Elite* was published and was in his early 20s just as the renaissance of comparative and historical sociology in the United States was taking off in the mid-to-late 1970s. He attended Princeton as an undergraduate, and then went to Harvard to study with Theda Skocpol. His political outlook, like that of Mills himself, was basically on the left; he was always more radical and iconoclastic than his mentor, having published, for example, an early piece using Gramsci, Hebdige, and Hall to analyze the commodification of graffiti art in the New York City subways (Lachmann, 1988, pp. 229, 231). Those political commitments would re-emerge particularly in his last work, *First Class Passengers on a Sinking Ship*, which came out with Verso in 2020.

Lachmann's theoretical project, however, was somewhat autonomous from these political concerns. We could construct his contribution this way. Lachmann began with the hard core of elite theory that elites who derive their power from their position in organizations are the key actors in explaining historical change. But he noted immediately a problem with elite theory. It had not been able to explain qualitative changes in the relationships between elites and nonelites. In short, as we pointed out above, it had not been able really to offer a convincing

14 *Introduction*

account of historical change. This was Lachmann's point of departure. To address this weakness, Lachmann turned to Marxism, with its focus on the transfer of surplus from producers to appropriators. This was an original move since none of the elite theorists had discussed appropriation in any serious way. From this position, Lachmann was able to use elite theory to critique Marxism for its assumption that class conflict was primary, and to use Marxism to critique elite theory for its assumption that the relationship between classes and elites was always the same.

Lachmann (2000) defined elites "as a group of rulers with the capacity to appropriate resources from nonelites and who inhabit a distinct organizational apparatus" (p. 9; see also Lachmann, 1990, p. 401). This definition is obviously closely related to the Marxist notion of class because it defines elites partially in terms of their ability to appropriate resources. However, Lachmann used elite theory, especially Mosca's, to point out that elite interests were defined not only with respect to their relations to direct producers, but also with respect to rival elites. Thus, elites' basic interest was to reproduce themselves in relationship to direct producers and to preserve "the capacity to extend ... organizational reach against rival elites" (Lachmann, 2000, p. 9; see also 1990, pp. 400–402). Thus, Lachmann synthesized the strongest element of elite theory (its focus on horizontal conflicts among elites) with the strongest elements of class theory (its focus on conflicts between elites and nonelites).

This scheme, however, makes it very difficult to distinguish between elites and class fractions. For Marxists, too, it would seem, analyze both class and inter-class conflicts in a way that is strictly analogous to what Lachmann said about elites. Lachmann (2000, p. 10) insisted that some elites were not class fractions because they were "not distinguishable by their relations to production." What Lachmann seemed to mean by this is that nonclass (or class fraction) elites were to be distinguished from other elites in terms of features that did not refer to their position in the relations of production. Elites with common positions in relations of production might nevertheless have different interests because of the specific organizations they inhabited. For example, Lachmann emphasized the important role of the clergy as a separate rival elite to the gentry in the transition to capitalism in England. But their possession of property and their relationship to direct agrarian producers was fundamentally similar to that of the gentry. Thus, their class interests did not distinguish them. Members of the church hierarchy, however, had interests flowing from the particular organization they inhabited (the church) that distinguished them from the gentry. In the case of England, it was only after the clergy were eliminated as an autonomous elite through the Reformation and their organization was merged with that of the gentry that agrarian capitalism could emerge (Lachmann, 2000, p. 190).

On this basis, Lachmann was able to construct a highly original and ambitious theory of the transition to capitalism and also a theory of elite decline. First, Lachmann critiqued existing accounts of the transition from feudalism to capitalism. Dobb, in an argument that had a long subsequent life, argued that the Black Death of 1348 created a fundamental divide between Eastern and Western Europe. In the West, the decline in population allowed peasants to escape from serfdom and force the commutation of their dues into money rents. However, the same population decline in the East led to a second serfdom as lords were able to reimpose feudal obligations on agrarian direct producers. What emerged in Western Europe, in both England and France, was a "petty mode of production" in which self-sufficient peasants now paid money rents to lords (Lachmann, 2000, p. 19). Lachmann (2000) suggested, however, that Dobb could not explain why "there was a two-century lag from the abolition of servile labor after the Black Death to the development of private property in land and the proletarianization of a plurality of peasants in the century following the Henrician Reformation" (p. 19). He suggested that elite theory could solve this problem by focusing on how conflicts among elites could lead to transformations in relations of production.

Lachmann's second contribution was to use elite theory to explain the decline of US hegemony. In *First Class Passengers*, Lachmann (2000) investigated the connection between the structure of elite relations and the durability of a hegemon, understood as a "polity ... able to enforce a system of geopolitical and economic relations that advantages it over all other polities" (p. 49). Lachmann argued that a hegemon could rule where there existed plural elites combined with a low level of elite conflict. Where, in contrast, elites were singular (as in the Nazi or Napoleonic empires) or where there was a high level of conflict (as in the absolutist cases), rule by a hegemon was impossible. In the first sort of case (Nazism and the Napoleonic empire), elites simply dominated the lands that they conquered to extract resources without gaining any local allies. In the second case (absolutism), elites entrenched their own interests at the expense of the general interest; they thus became autarkic, and their own interests split apart from the general interest.

To demonstrate his argument, Lachmann focused on five main cases: absolutist Spain and France, treated as militarily dominant powers that lacked hegemony; the Netherlands, a power that was briefly hegemonic; Britain, the most durable hegemon so far; and the United States, whose hegemonic period, Lachmann (2020, pp. 99–240, 251–260) suggested, had been relatively brief (1945–2008) and was rapidly coming to a close.

Lachmann's analysis of US hegemony is particularly interesting. US hegemony was based on an alliance between national firms linked together through cross ownership and tied to large commercial banks and

> regional and local banks and firms that were shielded from competition with bigger rivals thanks to federal and state regulations that local elites had the political muscle to sustain through influence on their congressional delegations and in their state governments. (Lachmann, 2020, p. 288)

So, elites were differentiated between local and relatively protectionist elites and large, multinationally oriented elites, but despite this differentiation they were not antagonistic. Beginning in the Nixon administration, "waves of mergers in sectors such as banking, telecommunications, media, utilities, retail sales, and agriculture" created "elite consolidation within major industries" (Lachmann, 2020, pp. 288–289). These new concentrated elites "do not use their financial and organization muscle to push for broad national policies. ... Rather, they use their leverage over legislators and regulators to win privileges that can best be described as autarkic" (Lachmann, 2020, p. 292). Thus, the United States was slipping back toward a pattern of rule somewhat closer to that of the absolutist period, except perhaps with a more unified elite. The emergence of this autarkic self-interested elite would undermine US hegemony, just as it had Spanish and French hegemony in the early modern period.

Lachmann's work, to sum up, extended elite theory in two crucial ways. First, it developed a rigorous conceptualization of elites (groups with the capacity to appropriate resources through organizational control over the means of production from nonelites and to hold off rival elites; Lachmann, 1990, p. 401), and for the first time explained their relationship to the concept of class. Secondly, it transformed elite theory into a comparative research program aimed at explaining different macro-historical outcomes such as the rise of capitalism and the rise and decline of hegemony.

Lachmann moved quite far in the direction of having a relational theory of elites and nonelites. Power was relational, so nonelites and elites coconstituted whatever power elites held. For example, when a single elite ruled, its ability to shape society, as Marx (e.g., 1867/1977, p. 784) predicted, was determined by the relative class capacity of elites and nonelites (Lachmann, 1990, p. 401). Therefore, elites and nonelites were mutually constitutive: An elite could only be an elite with respect to some nonelite, and vice versa. Another example is when there were multiple elites: While the relation among the various elites was key, the relations between each elite and its nonelites could also be important (Lachmann, 1990, p. 401).

Even in this expanded form, however, some of the characteristic problems remained, and, in particular, forms of power were never clearly specified. Lachmann's work implied that elites' and nonelites' levels of power may vary. However, it is clear that they vary across social dimensions. For example, feudal lords held considerable juridical power over serfs, but they had little capacity to shape the productive process. In contrast, capitalists and workers are typically equal in the sphere of formal politics, but owners can determine the details of how work is performed in a way that feudal lords never did. Thus, it is not clear which elite (lords or capitalists) should be considered more powerful as their relative levels of power have varied across these social dimensions. Finally, elites and nonelites may hold power with different forms and characteristics. For example, elites may have more visibly coercive and symbolic power, yet nonelites may have deeper, longer lasting, cooperative power (such as the power that derives from nonelites' knowledge of how work is done or how information collected; Emigh et al., 2019, p. 420; Mukerji, 2009, pp. 11–12). Conversely, nonelites can under some circumstances have a great deal of cultural power, while elites must rely exclusively on material power. These situations were rarely discussed in classic elite theory, although Mosca at least hinted at their possibility. The crucial point is that elite and nonelite relations need to be specified across a range of different types of power relations. However, because Lachmann did not have a fully developed theory of power, he was never fully able to analyze adequately either qualitative changes in relations between elites and nonelites, or the transformations in the structure of inter-elite relations.

The Current State of Elite Theory

Elite theory has enjoyed a recent resurgence, particularly in the past decade or so, because there are certain similarities between contemporary society and the ones described by the classic elite theorists. While inequality in advanced capitalist countries has substantially increased since the 1980s (Gautney, 2022, pp. 10–11; Piketty, 2014, pp. 308–312), it is also true that formal democracy continues to be the modal governmental form of such societies (for how long is an open question). Furthermore, there is increasing demographic diversity in elite social institutions (Khan, 2012, pp. 362, 371–373). Thus, in contemporary society, rhetorical and ideological commitments to equality combine with vast and increasing substantive, especially economic, inequalities. This sharp separation between an apparent consensus around equality or equity and the social reality of elite rule is analogous to the situations to which Pareto, Mosca, and Michels were reacting.

One product of this contemporary social situation is a focus on explaining the elite origins of liberal democracy. For example, Ansell and Samuels (2014, p. 11) argued that political transitions emerge from intra-elite conflict between, on the one hand, a group that controlled the state and, on the other, a wealthy group that did not control the state. New economic groups emerge that have a growing fear of expropriation by the established elite, and this established elite fears that the growth in the size and political power of the new economic groups will threaten its power, making it costly or difficult to repress (Ansell & Samuels, 2014, p. 11). The outcome of such conflict depends on the different elites' resources and bargaining power (Ansell & Samuels, 2014, p. 11). Another line of analysis considers elite capture, especially as it pertains to identity politics. Both Táíwò (2022, pp. 69–72) and Haider (2018, pp. 31–35) developed critiques of the substitutionist ideology, in which a particular elite member of a group speaks for or represents the putative interests of the whole group, which allows for diversity among elites without addressing the yawning chasm of economic inequality. In this way, what began as an initially universalist critique focused squarely on economic questions has been transformed into a series of upper middle-class rituals. By focusing on political legitimacy, however, current accounts lack understanding of elite entrenchment at the local level (Musgrave & Wong, 2016, p. 93).

However, basic conceptual – especially definitional – problems remain. For Lachmann (1990, p. 403), as we have seen, actors are members of an elite if they are central to the elite's organization and if they are free to leave and create their own organization. An elite's capacity, and therefore this organizational ability, depends primarily on its position relative to other elites (Lachmann, 1990, p. 401). Khan (2012, pp. 362, 365–371), on the other hand, defined elites as those who have control over or access to a resource (political, economic, cultural, social network ties, or knowledge). He combined a Weberian definition of elites based on the possession of power and resources with a more Marxist definition based on a dominant social position (Haboddin & Afala, 2022, p. 61; Khan, 2012, p. 362).

These conceptualizations are useful, but not fully satisfying. For example, elite theory needs a more nuanced and sophisticated understanding of power to define elites (Musgrave & Wong, 2016, pp. 91–93). Similarly, elite capacities are usually more assumed than illustrated empirically. Elite capacity vis-à-vis other elites is generally underspecified and often evaluated only post hoc (i.e., when an elite is victorious, it is assumed to have had greater capacity in comparison to its rivals). Furthermore, it is rarely clear exactly what roles elites play in organizations, how central they are, and how and when they might be able to form new organizations. In addition, it is not clear whether this organizational definition of elites encompasses all elites. For example, are some elites *disorganized?* Race, gender, sexual orientation, and a host of social characteristics pose such questions in a particularly acute form (e.g., Sall & Khan, 2017, p. 512). How are men or Whites understood as elites if their status derives from broad categorical frameworks and resources attached to those frameworks, rather than from the occupation of a position in an organizational hierarchy? How do inequalities along some dimensions interact with inequalities along others? For example, as Du Bois (1935/2007, p. 353) pointed out, Whiteness may bring perceived psychological benefits to nonelite Whites, yet harm their economic interests. Yet elite theory rarely specifies any social characteristics other than interests and capacity. Such characteristics, however, must be key as organizations are racialized and gendered (Acker, 1990, p. 139; Ray, 2019, pp. 27–28). Thus, virtually all elite theory needs to be reevaluated with these issues in mind. To redress these weaknesses, we first discuss power before linking this back to elite theory.

CONCEPTUALIZING POWER

There is considerable debate about how to conceptualize power, for example, whether it is analytical or normative, relational or possessive, negative or positive, repressive or productive, constraining or enabling, intentional or unintentional, or structural or agentive (Stör, 2017, p. 142). In his classic definition, Hobbes (1651/1985, p. 150) said that power is the "present means to obtain some future apparent good." Weber (1921/1978, p. 53) defined power as "the probability that one actor within a social relationship will be in a position to carry out his own will despite resistance, regardless of the basis on which this probability rests." But more recent discussions about power have moved beyond the narrowly agentic and subjectivist views embodied in the Weberian and Hobbesian accounts to consider the possibilities of doing and not doing in more detail. Lukes (2021, pp. 20, 27, 45), for example, drawing on pluralist and behavioralist understandings, noted that power has a tripartite characteristic: the power to make decisions, the power to not make decisions, and the power to shape what kinds of options can be envisioned. Yet, as Mau (2021/2023, p. 38) noted, power need not be based on human agency. Power can be held by people (Weber, 1921/1978, pp. 954, 1112), but also in language (Sewell, 1992, p. 23), material objects (Latour, 1991, pp. 105–110), and organizations (Acker, 1990, pp. 144–146; Ray, 2019, p. 27). Nonagentive power can be exercised by the emergent properties of social relations among human agents or subjects (Mau, 2021/2023, p. 44). Thus, in the Marxist sense, power refers generally to the influence of social forms on the life of society (Mau, 2021/2023, p. 24).

Even agentive and nonagentive powers, however, have multiple forms (Mann, 1986, pp. 24–25). For example, Etzioni (1961, p. 5) suggested three forms of power: coercive, remunerative, and symbolic; Mann (1986, p. 2) referred to four forms: ideological, economic, military, and political. Winters (2011, pp. 13–20) defined five types of power resources as formal political rights, official positions, coercion, mobilization, and material power. These formulations are useful, but they are not consistent across the authors (for example, Etzioni described symbolic but not organizational power, Winters the reverse). Some conceptualizations also merge social mechanisms that make the deployment of power possible (e.g., organizations) with expressions of power (e.g., visibility) and the social spheres in which power is found (e.g., politics, economics).

In sum, then, these theorists of power illustrate that it is more complex than elite theory's simple conceptualizations suggest. Elite theorists before Lachmann generally understood power as domination. Lachmann extended Marx's understanding of appropriation to consider how organizational elites control resources. These simple understandings of power, however, are not in keeping with its complexity, as is clear from our short review of theories of power above.

While a fully developed new theory of power is beyond the scope of this introduction, we distinguish here two aspects of power (a) the relational (e.g., elite and nonelite) social mechanisms that make possible its operation, and (b) how the mechanisms express themselves socially. To illustrate, we give two examples. First, under capitalism, the class power of the owners of means of production might express itself conflictually, when laborers are disciplined to extract additional surplus, or cooperatively, when owners band together in organizations to influence the state. Thus, in this case the same underlying mechanism (ownership of the means of production) manifests itself in two quite different ways. Second, the power that derives from the control of a media outlet could manifest itself either visibly, as producing stories with a particular political and topical bent, or invisibly, not covering certain topics or events. Here again a single underlying mechanism can manifest itself in different ways.

A further layer of complexity arises from the fact that various social mechanisms can combine. For example, a class may have both material power, deriving from ownership, and ideological power. In addition, the expressions can combine in various ways (for example, power might be expressed visibly and conflictually or, in contrast, invisibly and cooperatively). Finally, the mechanisms and expressions can also combine in multiple ways (for example, power may be held visibly through assets and invisibly through hegemony). Thus, multiple combinations of mechanisms of power and their expressions are possible.

In addition, these combinations can change over time. We suggest a few concrete ones. First, changing combinations of the mechanisms might create different forms of power. For example, organizational and ideational power, over time, might combine with coalitional power. Second, the expressions of power might shift (for example, from informal to formal or invisible to visible). Third, both the mechanisms and expressions may change (for example, associational power might wane but become more formal, while material power might increase but become more invisible). Thus, unlike previous elite theories, we propose a relational theory of elites and nonelites, a subtle understanding of power, and a way to understand historical transformations.

To give an introductory, illustrative example of how our approach to power might better account for historical change than existing theories, we return to Marx. Marx (1867/1977, pp. 283, 320) considered that capitalists' ownership of the means of production, and correlatively the working class's lack of access to those means, allowed capitalists to exploit labor since workers had to accept a wage contract as their condition for access to their means of social reproduction. That is, capitalists had a relative monopoly over the material resources – the means of production – that constituted the objective preconditions to produce use values. This monopoly made it possible to employ laborers, appropriate the surplus as the condition for according workers access to those means of production, valorize the surplus as profit in markets, and reinvest this profit, thus accumulating capital. Capitalists' monopoly over access to these material assets gave capitalists power because the social monopoly over these assets was, for Marx, the social mechanism that underlay exploitation. Of course, for Marx, capital was not a thing but an expression of social relations, and thus we emphasize that material assets entail social processes created through accumulation and human labor. The social mechanism of power for Marx was based on social control over these material assets.

Marx considered the capitalist system of ownership, described above, as an outcome of class power. However, how that power has expressed or manifested itself has varied historically. For example, for Marx (Marx & Engels, 1845–1846/1977, pp. 89–90), exploitation and appropriation in precapitalist societies was visible. Landlords and peasants lived in close proximity and were not bound to one another through a wage labor contract but through other customary and legal arrangements. As a result, the violence directed towards peasants was inflicted purposely in a visible way, and the transfer of the surplus was also a public event. As Marx (1867/1977, p. 170) characterized the situation under feudalism, "the social relations between individuals in the performance of their labour appear at all events as their own personal relations, and are not disguised as social relations between things." Under capitalism, however, exploitation and appropriation were obscured and invisible because they occurred in a domain of absolute private property and under the cover of the exchange of equivalents in the labor contract (Marx, 1867/1977, pp. 164–167). Furthermore, because of the complex division of labor and the centralization of labor activity in factories, it became difficult to observe directly the social processes that created and sustained power. Indeed, the power of capital appeared simply as a technical prerequisite to carrying on production in general (Marx, 1867/1977, pp. 480–491). This obfuscation becomes ever more dramatic in postindustrial societies (though Marx of course did not observe it): The division of labor dramatically increases, and globalization separates production processes themselves, the observation of them, and the consumption of goods ever further and further apart. Thus, for Marxist theory, the social mechanism that creates power, exploitation, and appropriation based on material resources can be visible or invisible. This example shows that the expression or manifestation of power is different from the mechanism that creates and sustains it.

Because the different mechanisms and expressions of power change and recombine, we argue that this conceptualization of power is key to understanding historical transformations. In Marxist and Gramscian theory, making exploitation and appropriation visible undergirds social transformations: Unveiling hegemony does not necessarily or immediately change the social mechanism of power, but it may make it possible to challenge it. Furthermore, Marx did not consider solely material power. He was deeply concerned with the power of ideas as well as organizational structures such as the state. Thus, for example, how these material resources combined with state and ideological power, and how these changed over time, were also crucial to his analysis (Marx & Engels, 1845–1846/1977, pp. 79–81, 94–95). Gramsci (1971, p. 12) continued with this analysis to argue that intellectuals per se were key to maintaining or changing the material conditions of capitalism. Thus, these examples show that the social mechanisms of power combine with each other, as well as with the various expressions of power, to create forms of power that are not static, but that have the potential to shift, recombine, and change.

To develop this idea, first, we specify the social mechanisms of power. We draw inspiration from "power resources" theory, though in many ways we also depart quite dramatically from it (review in Refslund & Arnholtz, 2022, pp. 1959–1961). Power resources theory grew out of Marx's (1867/1977, p. 283) idea of labor as a form of power and Wright's (2000, p. 962) distinction between structural and associational power. This power is intrinsically relational: The power of the capitalists and that of the laborers depend on each other (Refslund & Arnholtz, 2022, p. 1963; Wright, 2000, p. 962), and we extend this relational perspective. Wright's two forms of power have in turn been extended into five forms: organizational, associational, structural, coalitional, and ideational (Refslund & Arnholtz, 2022, p. 1962; Schmalz et al., 2018, p. 115). Organizational power stems from positions and rules that set down established patterns of action (Refslund & Arnholtz, 2022, pp. 1963–1964; Schmalz et al., 2018, p. 121); associational power stems from collectivities that form when individuals link up to pursue aims (Refslund & Arnholtz, 2022, p. 1963); structural power derives from a social position or location (Refslund & Arnholtz, 2022, p. 1962); coalitional power stems from the power to create alliances among organizations (Refslund & Arnholtz, 2022, p. 1965); and ideational power stems from normative, cognitive, and cultural ideas (Refslund & Arnholtz, 2022, p. 1964). From the power resources perspective, then, these five elements are all resources (riffing on the Marxist idea of material resources), but we reconceptualize them all here as mechanisms through which power works.

To these five, we explicitly add a sixth mechanism, control over material resources, which is explicit in Marx but not in power resource theory. Power resource theory developed initially to consider the relative power of laborers and capitalists (review in Refslund & Arnholtz, 2022, pp. 1959–1961). For example, Wright (2000, p. 962) defined power in terms of the capacity of individuals and organizations to realize their class interests. Power resources theory, then, focuses on economic power, and thus the power that flows from control over a particular type of material resources is subsumed into – but not analyzed separately from – the explicit analysis of the other five power resources. However, we want to apply the five power resources more broadly, beyond just the economic sphere, to understand power. To do so, we therefore have to consider control over material resources explicitly as a sixth social mechanism (not as a mechanism that undergirds the other five mechanisms, as in power resource theory per se).

These six social mechanisms, we argue, can be expressed or manifest differently. We discuss five of them here, as polarities around visibility (visible or invisible), formality (formal or informal), depth (deep or surface), consensuality (conflict or cooperation), and directionality (bottom-up or top-down). The first expression is visibility. Power can be spectacular, or invisible, anonymous, and knowledge-based (Foucault, 1975/1979, pp. 8, 171, 176–177, 192). The expression shapes appropriate strategies of resistance. Spectacular power demands counter spectacle, whereas knowledge or expertise may call for knowledge-based forms of resistance. Making a social mechanism of power visible, for example, can be a form of resistance, and thus science and politics are closely related, as Gramsci (1971, p. 138) suggested.

The second polarity is formality. Power can be explicitly delegated or invested; alternatively, it may be held implicitly or informally as influence or persuasion (Gramsci, 1971, p. 12; Weber, 1921/1978, pp. 956, 1006, 1112). This also has consequences for forms of struggle. When power is held formally, social and political movements can explicitly target and attempt to transform it. When power is exercised informally as influence or persuasion, different strategies are required to transform it. In the latter case, social actors must first identify its existence to render it tangible before struggling against it.

The third polarity concerns the depth of power. Power can be superficially or deeply held. For example, language holds power deeply, while states hold power superficially (cf. Sewell, 1992, pp. 23–24). Language is commonly spoken by many individuals across time and space; membership in a community of speakers requires no official act. It is a consequence of anonymous social processes. In contrast, holding a position of power in a state requires an official act or state procedure. The power that derives from mastery of a language is therefore in a sense deeper than the power deriving from incumbency in office. These differences are also reflected in patterns of historical transformation. States often undergo rapid political transformations (e.g., the French and Russian revolutions and the unification of Germany) within cultural areas that have remained relatively fixed. Accordingly, the history of language communities and the history of states do not perfectly overlap.

The fourth polarity, consensuality, concerns the degree to which power is cooperative or conflictual (Gramsci, 1971, p. 12; Hegel, 1821/1991, p. 343; Weber, 1921/1978, pp. 956, 1006, 1112). For example, the division of labor might increase the ability of a given human group to reproduce itself, thereby increasing its power over nature, or even over other human groups, even though the relations within the group may not be marked per se by conflict. Such a transformation would be consensual. At the other extreme, power might work through the application or threat of violence.

Finally, directionality is another polarity of power (see Emigh et al., 2016, pp. 36–39). Power can flow in different ways, from the bottom-up or from the top-down (Emigh et al., 2016, pp. 38–39; Tilly, 1999, p. 332). We conceptualize power relationally, so elites' and nonelites' power is always connected, and not always in a zero sum way. For example, an increase in a peasant's ability to cultivate land (thus an increase in his power over nature) might lead to an increase in surplus for a lord. In addition, although along some dimension there must be a sharp asymmetry in power in favor of elites (otherwise they would not be elites), along other dimensions elites and nonelites may be relatively balanced, or the nonelites may dominate. The cultural power of African American music and style is an example. Thus, the mechanism of power might work from the nonelites upwards to elites, or downwards from elites to nonelites. These different polarities, then, create a jagged terrain of struggle and cooperation that must be studied empirically.

We do not claim here to have captured all aspects of power. Importantly, however, we note that what are commonly called forms of power are combinations of the different social mechanisms and expressions. Mechanisms and expressions can combine in multiple ways: Combinations of mechanisms can combine with each other and with different combinations of expressions; furthermore, different combinations of expressions can also combine with each other and with combinations of mechanisms. For example, what is typically called economic power is a quite complex combination of mechanisms and expressions. It entails the control of material resources. It also entails control over the arrangement of the material conditions of social reproduction. This is usually understood as the distribution of property that, particularly in capitalism, forces people to produce surplus value through economic necessity (Mau, 2021/2023, p. 323). These features take organizational form as laws and bureaucratic practices. It also may entail associational practices such as unions. Capitalism is also supported by ideologies of labor, individuality, and reification. Thus, economic power combines material resources, organizational power, and ideational power. As Marx noted, its workings can be visible or invisible. Similarly, what is typically called political power commonly combines organizational power, coalitional power, and ideational power, and it can be visible as well as invisible.

While Lachmann focused on formal, organizational power and how elites formed around this, we understand that if we broaden the understanding of power, we can view multiple elites who can hold different forms of power and deploy it in different ways. We argue that elites form around these social mechanisms, relationally, to nonelites. For example, capitalists exist only in relationship to wage labor; lords exist only in relationship to serfs; and Whites exist only in relationship to non-Whites. Furthermore, relations among elites differ largely according to the character of the relations between elites and nonelites. For example, intralordly relations have a qualitatively different character from intracapital relations. Thus, as the various forms of struggle between elites and nonelites need to be specified historically, so to do the struggles among elites. Accordingly, the theory of power needs to be linked to the theory of elites. We do this next by discussing the six mechanisms of power to show how elite and nonelites hold power relationally.

THE RELATIONAL POWER OF ELITES AND NONELITES

Material Resources: The Control Over Assets

Control over tangible material resources, such as means of production, coercion, worship or salvation, or intellectual resources, such as books and laboratories, provide elites and nonelites with power (cf. Sewell, 1992, pp. 13, 22; Weber, 1921, p. 397; 1922, p. 526; 1921/1925, pp. 69–79, 241–242).[2] Marx noted that capitalists owned the means of production, whereas laborers did not, thereby linking the two sides of the situation (ownership and nonownership). For him, capital was a social relation of power that implied the existence of a propertyless but juridically free working class (Marx, 1867/1977, pp. 271–273). The concentration of resources among capitalists (itself an outcome of accumulation) in turn determined how they could exploit laborers, appropriate their surplus, and use the profit from it to accumulate more assets and wealth (Marx, 1849/1922, pp. 27–28). Importantly, capitalists as an elite could not exist outside of a class of propertyless workers. To use the language of elite theory, in Marx's view elites and nonelites were internally related.

Of course, claims over wealth and income can coconstitute elites and nonelites more generally in capitalist societies in multiple ways (Kristal, 2010, p. 739; Winters, 2011, p. 18). Cash, a highly flexible form (Winters, 2011, p. 18), can be obtained directly as personal income or indirectly as organizational income, creating a potential division between those with access to liquidity and those who lack such access.

The distribution of wealth, which is generally much more unequal than the distribution of income, has become more concentrated since the 1980s, creating another division (Piketty, 2014, pp. 13, 51). Highly concentrated wealth, even if it originates in entrepreneurship, creates oligarchs and oligarchies, based more often on rent collection than on investment in production (Piketty, 2014, p. 562; Winters, 2011, p. 18).

Forms of economic power can combine. Bradlow (2021, pp. 198, 204, 208), for example, showed how economic elites (in this case South African, who were White racial minorities and legacy elites) subverted the imperatives of political majorities by using their resources, in particular revenue hoarding and selective spatial investment, to retain their power. Material resources are highly versatile – for example, they make it possible to buy defense, protection, and security (Winters, 2011, pp. 18–19). Wealth can also buy the sustained engagement and participation of others (Winters, 2011, p. 18). Economic power also intersects with gender. Women can be elites; they may be wealthy because of their own or others' income or assets, and even in households with traditional work and domestic labor arrangements, they may be influential (Keister et al., 2022, pp. 150–151).

Elite and nonelite relations can also form around concrete resources, goods, and services other than income or wealth. Generally, elites have more access to economic resources, both direct and indirect, but nonelites too have economic power, depending upon the form of relationship. Employment, compensation, and productivity influence workers' bargaining power (Kristal, 2010, p. 737). Bargaining is only possible, however, where labor has some juridical rights (such as under capitalism). Monetary resources can be boosted by public provisions such as education, health care, and other such goods and services (Kristal, 2010, p. 739). The amount of resources devoted to such public goods depends partially on the fact that typically workers act not only as workers but also as citizens through the vote (Przeworski, 1985, p. 11).

The broader point is that property – material power – is a social relationship (Haboddin & Afala, 2022, p. 62; Winters, 2011, p. 21). It can be extended to areas that are not often thought of as property. For example, Whiteness as racialized privilege, historically, was legally valuable and had material benefits, and therefore it was treated legally like a property interest (Harris, 1993, pp. 1740–1741).

Organizational Power: Powers to Direct and Coordinate

Organizational power, like material resource power, is a staple of elite theory. As we noted, Lachmann (1990, pp. 401, 404–408) defined elites in terms of the organizational apparatus in which they were embedded, and thus elites could be located in economic, political, or religious organizations (to name a few). Organizations allow individuals in high-level positions, such as managers and bureaucrats, to control resources and the labor of others within the organization through a mechanism of command rather than a claim to ownership (Weber, 1921/1978, pp. 973–975; Wodke, 2016, p. 1379; Wright, 1985, pp. 83, 88). High-level positions control "organizational assets" that can be used to exploit laborers (that is, to benefit from their labor) in a way analogous to the way that physical assets make exploitation possible (Wright, 1985, p. 88). But organizations primarily work through domination, not through the control of resources as such (Weber, 1921/1978, p. 942; Wodke, 2016, p. 1380). Organizations as institutions of domination structure the division of labor, time-management rules, informal rituals about interaction, and locations in physical space, and thus entail power relations (Acker, 1990, p. 146; Ray, 2019, pp. 29, 32).

We emphasize, however, that elites and nonelites hold positions within organizations relationally. For example, the leadership often depends on information embedded in lower levels of the organization that can be hard to extract

(Weber, 1921/1978, pp. 1417–1418). Elites' powers can only be understood in terms of their positions within the organizations and how much control they have. Gaining the cooperation of the entire organizational staff is never easy nor assured, hence the constant attempt to specify rules, procedures, and spheres of competence (Weber, 1921/1978, pp. 956–958).

Organizations are durable and thus they generally embody past power relations while shaping present and future ones; they thereby enable in a path-dependent way some actions while constraining others (Refslund & Arnholtz, 2022, p. 1964; Therborn, 1978, p. 35). In organizations, therefore, there is always a disjuncture between the present distribution of power and the past distribution of power that organizational structures embody. For example, even when nonelites gain power, they may be constrained in what they can do by the very structure of the organization in which that power has been gained (Marx, 1871/1996, p. 181). For example, a bureaucracy set up for war planning must be used entirely differently for peaceful social and democratic purposes (Devine, 1988, pp. 29–34).

Economic and political power derive, to a large extent, from organizational power. Economic organizations, especially ones common to capitalist economies, are set up hierarchically so that managers direct the actions of those below them in the hierarchy, with the purpose of pursuing profit (Weber, 1921/1978, p. 974). In the phase of US-dominated capitalism, corporations – effectively globe-spanning, bureaucratic planning organizations – are the quintessential economic units (Arrighi, 1994, p. 281). Political power also, to a large extent, derives from politicians' locations within political organizations that give them power to legislate, and thus to shape enforcement directly. Political organizations span political action committees, formal political parties, legislative bodies, and enforcement agencies. Of course, modern societies are replete with hierarchical, bureaucratic organizations that give power to those at the top of the organizations (e.g., universities, neighborhood organizations, religious bodies), as Michels (1911, pp. 21–23) originally understood.

Associational Power: Capacities to Mobilize

Associational power derives from individuals' ability to form ties with others in similar social positions and with similar interests. It is located generally neither in the state nor in the economy, but in civil society (Bobbio, 1969b, pp. 85–87; see review in Riley, 2010, pp. 6–8). It is often easier for elites than nonelites to develop associational power because they have greater free time and greater access to the institutions that associational power is directed toward (Almeida & Chase-Dunn, 2018, p. 190). To challenge prevailing power relations, nonelites must solve collective action problems and organize (Acemoglu & Robinson, 2006, p. 25; Boix, 2003, p. 3). Collective action is easier when it is institutionalized, that is, where groups and their leaders have the capacity to coordinate and assure the actions of group members (Keefer, 2009, p. 662). Such groups include political parties, unions, religious organizations, and cooperatives (Keefer, 2009, p. 662). Accordingly, associational power can be deployed by nonelites – for example, when laborers organize collectively (Garrett, 1998, pp. 9–10, 13; Kristal, 2010, p. 737; Wright, 2000, p. 962). So, social movements often, but not always (Riley, 2010, pp. 51–55), come from below (Almeida & Chase-Dunn, 2018, p. 190).

Associational power is necessarily relational, entailing both elites and nonelites. For example, Wright (2000, p. 960) argued that the relationship between the power of the working class and capitalist class was curvilinear: When the associational power of the working class was low, the power of the capitalist class to realize its interests was high. At intermediate levels of working-class associational power, the power of the capitalist class was low. However, when the associational power of the working class was high, then the power of the capitalist class was also high. Where both classes were powerful, class compromise benefited both parties (Wright, 2000, p. 960). Analogously, Riley (2010, pp. 47–55) showed how the party form of socialism was taken over and imitated by the Italian fascists: Without a radical insurgency deeply rooted in civil society, there would have been no radical right-wing reaction.

Associational power influences the political as well as economic sphere. For example, nonelites' demands for democracy generally succeed only at low or moderate levels of inequality, when they have the means and incentives to mobilize (Boix, 2003, pp. 10, 13; Haggard & Kaufman, 2016, p. 12). When the poor overcome collective action problems – for example, by organizing unions and political parties – elites' costs of repression rise and elites prefer moderate concessions (Boix, 2003, p. 13; Gramsci, 1971, p. 243). Nonelites are unlikely to succeed at high levels of inequality (Haggard & Kaufman, 2016, p. 12). Elites generally maintain better access to formal institutional channels and resources than nonelites, but elites also use informal modes of mobilization to influence and contend with each other and to mobilize nonelites (Almeida & Chase-Dunn, 2018, p. 190). Elites and nonelites hold power relationally: As either elites or nonelites develop associational power, it changes the terrain on which struggle unfolds, thus forcing the development of new techniques of struggle.

Structural Power: Social Systems and Locations in Them

Structural power stems from individuals' locations in social relations more generally. Its presence does not require organization, association, or ownership as such. Instead, it derives from the occupation of a strategic position. For example, Wright (2000, p. 962) considered two types of economic structural power; Silver (2003, p. 13) labeled them as marketplace bargaining power, that is, power stemming from tight labor markets, and workplace bargaining power, that is, stemming from the location of workers in an industry. Structural power also depends on the particular sector of the economy (e.g., Silver, 2003, pp. 38–40). For example, services have generally been much more difficult to offshore than manufacturing.

Similarly, international competition for goods, capital, and labor may affect elites' and nonelites' structural power (Kristal, 2010, p. 740). The entry of less-developed countries into the world market, for example, deprived laborers in more developed countries of bargaining and income power (Kristal, 2010, p. 740). Globalization thus shifted structural powers of labor by undermining them in the global north, but strengthening them in the global south (e.g., Silver, 2003, p. 33). It also creates internal turbulence as governments seek to balance the long-term and short-term consequences of trade (Garrett, 1998, p. 10).

The economic system is not the only point of structural power. For example, elites often control coercive means (Acemoglu & Robinson, 2006, p. 25). In fact, the main thrust of political process theory or theories of the political opportunity structure of social movements is a structural one. In these theories, the structural elements considered include the degree of openness of the institutionalized political system, the degree of consolidation or fragmentation of elites, alliances within elites, and the state's ability and inclination to inflict punishments (review in Foryś, 2023, p. 80). Thus, nonelites often have a structural opportunity to act where the state is either open or weak and where there are fractures and weaknesses among the elites. Social structural and political changes, for example, shift opportunities for different elites as well as nonelites to secure power (Haboddin & Afala, 2022, p. 64).

Economic and political structures often intersect with cultural ones (see more about this in ideational power below) to give differential power to actors. For example, political opportunity structures affect political identities (Tilly & Tarrow, 2015, p. 13). These political opportunity structures affect what claims resonate with individuals, what established political actors are available, what claim-making activities are prescribed or proscribed, and what repertoires are available to shape claims (Tilly & Tarrow, 2015, pp. 111–112). Structural changes can determine the composition of elite economic, sociocultural, and educational resources (Haboddin & Afala, 2022, p. 63).

Disruption is also a form of structural power that often combines economic and political structural power (Schmalz et al., 2018, p. 116; Tilly, 1973, pp. 429–430; Usmani, 2018, pp. 669, 672–673). Elites, in general, have more power than nonelites because they have greater capacities to disrupt economic life (Usmani, 2018, pp. 672–673). However, the gap between elites' and nonelites' disruptive capacities narrow or widen depending on the character of their economic roles (Usmani, 2018, p. 673). If elites withdraw resources, it creates an immediate crisis (Usmani, 2018, p. 674). But nonelites, the majority, can withdraw in large numbers, creating mass disruption and social turbulence that threatens elites' power; however, they have to coordinate such action, which is difficult to accomplish (Acemoglu & Robinson, 2006, p. 25; Usmani, 2018, pp. 669, 674). Thus, nonelites that work in essential industries, are difficult to replace, have specialized or scarce skills, or live far from population centers have more leverage (review in Usmani, 2018, p. 675). Tight labor markets mean that laborers can pull out of their current jobs to create widespread disruption. A strategic location in the production process, such as ports in a highly globalized economy, means that laborers' refusal to participate can create widespread disruption (Silver, 2003, p. 13). The state may side either with elites or nonelites; if the disruptive capacities of elites are large, then the state may side with them (Usmani, 2018, p. 675). However, states cannot ignore nonelite grievances in the long run, and so may take a middle path of trying to appease both elites and nonelites (Usmani, 2018, p. 675).

Disruption can take the form of strikes, sit-ins, sabotage, and slow-downs (Schmalz et al., 2018, p. 116). Wright's two forms of structural power (Silver, 2003, p. 13) suggest that marketplace bargaining power makes it possible for laborers to pull out of the labor force altogether, while workplace bargaining power makes it possible to engage in work stoppages (Silver, 2003, p. 13; cf. Usmani, 2018, p. 667). Looting, another form of disruption, stems from elite and nonelite interaction and, in particular, ties between the nonelites and officials who are semicorrupt or turn a blind eye (Auyero, 2007, p. 27). Structural opportunities for looting can be opened or closed through, for example, brokerage between political party brokers and the police, the implicit legitimation of violence by state elites signaling spirals by political party brokers, and broken negotiations (Auyero, 2007, pp. 27, 153). Protest also causes disruption. Piven and Cloward (1977, p. 24) argued that protest by the poor and marginalized had a more disruptive effect when the protesters played a central role in the institution, and so, the disruption was likely to have broad political reverberations. Structural conditions – electoral stability, nonelites' organizational positions, and elite alliances – were crucial in establishing the parameters for disruption to succeed (Piven & Cloward, 1977, pp. 19, 29–32). Finally, Scott (1985, p. xvi, 29) pointed out that "weapons of the weak," such as foot dragging, dissimulation, and false compliance, are everyday forms of resistance that fall just short of outright collective defiance so as not to provoke authorities. These sorts of disruptive behavior slow down economic and social processes necessary for elite domination and are difficult to prevent or address by elites who depend on nonelites.

Other approaches combine an analysis of material resources, associations, and structures. For example, Korpi (2006, p. 168) tied individuals' life-course risks and resources, stemming from different locations within socioeconomic structures, to opportunities for class-based collective action. Employers and other major interest groups that control many economic resources favor market solutions where they can control the outcome with these economic resources (Korpi, 2006, p. 173). In contrast, employees, generally with limited economic resources, organize collectively in unions and political parties and often strive for social citizenship that makes possible state-provided welfare benefits (Korpi, 2006, p. 173). Thus, organized labor can successfully defend its interests through collective mobilization (Schmalz et al., 2018, p. 113). The general point is that, just as is true of the other forms of power discussed here, structural power mutually constitutes elites and nonelites.

Coalitional Power

Coalitional power stems from the ability to link organizations, groups, or collective actors together to form alliances (Refslund & Arnholtz, 2022, p. 1965).

This capacity depends in part upon the other forms of power such that the group initiating the coalition can provide benefits to its potential allies. Most people have access to multiple networks through neighbors, communities, religious associations, educational institutions, and politics (Brookes, 2013, pp. 191–192). Thus, organizational coalitions can be built across different dimensions. Successful coalitions were built, for example, in Sydney's public educational system, around Chicago's living wage campaign in Chicago, and in Toronto's health care system (Tattersall, 2010, pp. 12–14).

Labor unions typically try to gain strength by forming such coalitions. Community–union coalitions, for example, form ties between labor unions and immigrants, minoritized groups, or other excluded groups (Brookes, 2013, p. 192). Coalitions can advance union goals as well as create new forms of social change (Tattersall, 2010, p. 2). Such coalitions are usually most effective when they are deep, that is, long-term, reciprocal, positive sum, and face-to-face (Brookes, 2013, p. 192). However, coalition building often happens at the local level and in response to specific issues and campaigns (Refslund & Arnholtz, 2022, p. 1966). Labor may also gain strength by associating with leftist political organizations and parties (Kristal, 2010, p. 739). Domestic social movements are more likely to mobilize when they are tied to international organizations (Almeida & Chase-Dunn, 2018, p. 195).

Such coalitions extend beyond labor organizations. For example, the pushes for and against same-sex marriage in California were shaped not only by the possibilities of coalitions between court-centered strategies, LGBT-rights movements, and private and state elites, but also by the ways that these actors undercut these coalitions (NeJaime, 2011, pp. 175–177). When the various actors were not aligned, elite support did not necessarily produce increased support for same-sex marriage (NeJaime, 2011, p. 193). Prominent and openly gay political actors also took varying positions (NeJaime, 2011, p. 194).

Coalitional power can also be deployed among elites, or between elites and nonelites. Indeed, the history of US political parties is largely that of a shifting congeries of coalitions linking particular groups of US owners to particular nonelites, thus largely blocking an open political expression of class conflict (Bensel, 2000, pp. xviii–xx; Davis, 1980, p. 23). Like the other forms of power, coalitional power constitutes elites relationally. Coalitions bring forth counter coalitions. The precise way in which coalitional power is deployed will thus shape the character of elites and nonelites.

Ideational Power

Both nonelites and elites hold ideational power, and both may create and alter it. But elites have a different relationship to ideational power. Elites generally benefit from the obviousness of existing social relationships. In a general sense, elite ideologies tend to be positivist because they equate the possible with the fully realized (Riley, 2022, pp. 101–103). To exercise ideational power, nonelites must call into question prevailing cultural or social arrangements, typically by uncovering their historical roots. Gramsci (1971, pp. 12, 428–429) noted that hegemony sustains power relations by making them appear factual. Thus, consent to those relations is a spontaneous bowing to reality. The economic structures of capitalism are held in place not only by interests, but also by their taken-for-grantedness. For Gramsci (1971, p. 10), however, this spontaneous consent is less automatic than it might seem. The dominant realism must be created by intellectuals, and thus elites (Gramsci, 1971, p. 6).

When nonelites can call into question hegemonic assumptions, they create counter hegemony, which may undermine this spontaneous consent. Indeed, Hebdige (1979, p. 2), Willis (1977, p. 3), and Hall (1997/2007, p. 271) provided extensive examples of how nonelites developed counterhegemonic practices, which eventually also bolstered hegemonic ones, through punk style, acting out in school, and movies.

Marxist theory contrasts the idea of unspoken consent to ideology, which consists of cultural beliefs that are widely and openly discussed and debated (though they can be conceptualized as rooted in material practices, e.g., Althusser, 1970, pp. 158, 162, 165). Ableism, for example, has both hegemonic and ideological elements; thus, disability is a relationship to power, not just an identity (Schalk & Kim, 2020, p. 38).

From the Weberian perspective, following any authority at least in part depends on the belief in its legitimacy (Weber, 1921/1978, p. 213). Schoon (2022, pp. 478–503) argued that legitimacy is the co-occurrence of expectations that define a relationship, the assent to that relationship by the audience, and conformity to those mutual expectations. Regime collapse or change, at least in part, may occur because of a crisis of legitimacy, especially in democratic regimes. For example, Slater (2009, p. 208) pointed out that democratic oppositions, especially to authoritarian regimes, generally have symbolic, but not coercive or remunerative, power. This symbolic power is wielded through a message that resonates with many people and motivates them emotionally to join a movement (Slater, 2009, pp. 223–224). Thus, capacities for mass collective action depend on the resonance of the message that is path dependent (Slater, 2009, p. 220; Usmani, 2018, p. 672). For example, immigrant laborers and imperial expansion spread a transnational discourse about laborers' and citizens' rights, and claims to these rights helped legitimate labor movements (Silver, 2003, p. 33). These are examples of cultural diffusion from below (laborers) and above (imperial expansion), respectively (Silver, 2003, p. 33).

These cultural processes also can operate at the global level through a world society (Meyer et al., 1997, p. 145; review in Almeida & Chase-Dunn, 2018, p. 195). International organizations often serve as avenues that spread these ideas (Almeida & Chase-Dunn, 2018, p. 195). Access to public media can serve as a resource and can be especially useful for nonelites to spread ideas (Artz, 2020, p. 1398). A similar idea can be found even in rational choice theory: Nonelites' belief in victory may encourage collective action (Boix, 2003, p. 14).

Ideological power is linked to, or sets the stage for, the other mechanisms of power (cf. Ray, 2019, p. 30; Sewell, 1992, p. 13). For example, a combination of the mechanisms of organization, structure, and ideation applies to information gathering. Nonelites are not as powerful as elites. While individual nonelites have little direct influence over information gathering, elites depend on nonelites as repositories of commonsense knowledge and lay categories (Emigh et al., 2016, p. 27). Nonelites can also apply direct pressure to elites to collect information or collect it in particular formats, as well as influence when and where these lay categories are deployed as information categories; nonelites can also be extremely uncooperative or even sabotage such attempts, rendering elites' efforts unsuccessful or meaningless (e.g., Bulmer, 1986, p. 474; Emigh et al., 2016, p. 26; Starr, 1987, pp. 12–13; review in Higgs, 2004, pp. 16, 20–21; cf. Loveman, 2007, pp. 8–9).

Another example is that organizations are both gendered and racialized, so they have cultural schemas about race and gender that support Whiteness and masculinity (Acker, 1990, p. 139; Ray, 2019, p. 33). These cultural schemas are embedded into the distribution of concrete economic resources that give men and racial majorities (generally Whites) more power. They also link to abilities to make ties with others, either within (associational) or outside (coalitional) the organization. For example, time spent in organizational activities (like hours worked or hours spent waiting for services) is carefully monitored among non-Whites, making it difficult for them to access economic resources or create network ties (Ray, 2019, p. 37). Organizations are also intrinsically gendered: Assumptions about gender underlie their rules, procedures, and contracts (Acker, 1990, p. 139). Sexual harassment is not an exception to organizational structure, but a component of it (review in Acker, 1990, p. 142). Similarly, the concept of a job assumes a particular gendered organization of domestic life and social production – that a job can be detached from all other social, domestic, and personal needs – that inherently favors men and gives them more opportunities to accumulate economic resources and make social ties (Acker, 1990, p. 149). Women, and especially Black women, do unpaid household and community work (Banks, 2020, p. 343). Cultural schema also becomes embedded into social structures, and in particular in legal rules, processes, and procedures. For example, racial ideologies of Whiteness – Whiteness as property – ties cultural ideas about White identity to ownership of property, which in turn is incorporated into a legal system that upholds the rights of Whites (Harris, 1993, pp. 1713–1714; Ray, 2019, p. 30).

Ideational elites and nonelites are coconstituted through ideational power, just as in all other mechanisms of power. While elite ideational power may initially appear as an unquestioned common sense or doxa, a counterhegemonic heterodoxy may force elites to justify existing social arrangements (Bourdieu, 1981b, p. 69; 2012, p. 185). Furthermore, elite ideologies often appropriate elements from counterhegemonic ideologies, as occurred with the incorporation of elements of Marxism into high culture in the 1920s or with feminism in the 1980s (Fraser, 2013, pp. 209–226; Gramsci, 1971, pp. 388–399).

In some sense, much of social movement theory combines these six mechanisms of power. Resource mobilization theory looks at how nonelites create social movements based on structural political opportunities; material resources; organizational, coalitional, and associational capacities; and ideologies that support framings of grievances into actions (Benford & Snow, 2000, p. 611;

Tarrow, 1994/2011, p. 16; review in Almeida & Chase-Dunn, 2018, pp. 190–191). Both resource mobilization theory and political process theory examine how nonelites gather resources and find structural openings in the political system to create social change (cf. review in Almeida & Chase-Dunn, 2018, pp. 190–191). From these perspectives, mobilization depends on movements' access and ability to accumulate collective resources and then associationally use them for collective action (McCarthy & Zald, 1977, p. 1216; review in Schmalz et al., 2018, p. 114).

Combining Mechanisms and Expressions of Power

In sum, while Marx looked relationally at capitalists and laborers, we note that other social categories – such as gender, race, sexual orientation, and ableism – also are relationally constructed by elites and nonelites. To illustrate more generally this relational point, we considered six mechanisms of power (material resources, organizations, associations, structures, coalitions, and ideation) that can create multiple sets of elites and nonelites around a variety of social categories. We also considered five expressions of power: visibility, formality, depth, consensuality, and directionality. These mechanisms and expressions combine to create forms of power, as we illustrate with the chapters in our volume.

Colin J. Beck and Mlada Bukovansky combine an analysis of structural and coalitional power. They argue that street-level corruption (e.g., the police) creates a potential for mobilization, while institutionalized corruption facilitates anger towards the state regime. Depending on the power of competing blocs of elites and nonelites, elite corruption can enable or disable social reform movements. Structural mechanisms create opportunities for nonelites and for coalitions of cross-class alliances. Thus, Beck and Bukovansky show – as we have argued is necessary – that elite and nonelite power must be considered relationally. Furthermore, their chapter is an illustration of how mechanisms of power combine with each other and with expressions of power to explain social outcomes. In their chapter, for example, the social struggles entail nonelites trying to make the power surrounding corruption visible as opposed to invisible so as to hold officials accountable. Furthermore, the actors are engaged in conflictual or cooperative behavior, depending on the particular patterns of corruption, coalitions, and structural opportunities.

Patricia A. Banks provides an example of an analysis of racial elites and, in particular, how Asian elites provide high levels of support for Asian art. Such racial or ethnic elites hold power through their monetary resources, ideological power through their support of cultural institutions and cultural objects, organizational power through their participation in artistic institutions, and coalitional power through their ability to link organizations together. While racial and ethnic elites may be less powerful vis-à-vis ethnic and racial majorities in some ways, by combining power across these different forms, they may have substantial influence. In some sense, their power, like their identity, is intersectional. Importantly, elites support the museum with their economic resources through formal monetary donations. These elites, however, as donors, hold organizational power in the cultural institutions informally through their support and donations, although they may not have any formal organizational power. Finally, these elites hold cultural power through the material cultural objects that they donate (of course, they may also shape these cultural systems ideologically as well through the physical art).

Lígia Ferro, Beatriz Lacerda, Lydia Matthews, and Susan Meiselas explicitly look at how ideational and structural power work, and, in particular, how to make their invisible aspects visible. They explicitly look at how nonelites challenge the ideological discourse about the positive aspects of Portuguese colonialism. Like colonialism everywhere, the Portuguese used violence to rule, yet in Portugal there is a persistent idea of a soft colonialism that was relatively peaceful and pedagogically oriented. This form of denial, however, perpetuates structural racism and inequality. Black individuals and communities in Portugal are often disadvantaged and invisible. While this sort of work is not generally included in studies of elite theories, this sort of study is key to understanding the relative power of elites and nonelites. Ferro et al.'s study follows the tradition of Hebdige and Hall by looking at how art and style challenge hegemony. They show how art and culture are tools and contexts for identity construction, and how artistic strategies illuminate a counterhegemony to tackle and undermine the power of White Portuguese elites. Thus, this chapter investigates the possibilities of making the structural and ideational power of Whiteness visible.

ELITES, NONELITES, AND HISTORICAL CHANGE

Finally, we arrive at our discussion of how elites and nonelites transform societies. Elite theory, in fact, does not specify well when elites are able to transform – or not – social relations (Emigh, 2000, p. 833). In part, this is because classic elite theories rejected the idea of social progress in one way or another, favoring instead a cyclical view of history in which social forms repeated in a standardized sequence (Pizzorno, 1972, p. 13). It also stems from the fact that most classic elite theories – for example, Mosca (1896, p. 146) and Pareto (1916a, p. 143) – focused on the composition and influence of elites, not their roles in social transformation. Nor did they generally considered nonelites relationally, so missed any influence they might have.

Lachmann was the first to try to tie theories of social change to elite theory by specifying first the necessary composition of elites – one elite needed to gain power – and second the necessary outcome – that a single elite had to transform social relations. But neither of these conditions are well specified. First, the conditions under which a single elite comes to power are hard to specify as elites' capacity is often apparent only after they have gained power. Second, it is hard to specify when and why elites transform social relations. Elites' actions are often assumed to transform social relations when they have the power to extract resources from nonelites in line with their interests in some novel way. Yet, it is rarely clear what their interests are before the transformation. Furthermore, whether interests – often contradictory – are long-term or short-term is also not well specified. Lack of transformation is even harder to explain. It generally occurs because a single elite comes to power yet fails to make any transformation.

Another possibility is that an elite gains power, makes transformations, but then gets stuck and misses the opportunity for further changes while other elites take advantage of it. However, it is quite difficult to judge whether transformations occur or not and whether such transformations stem from elites' actions or inactions. Finally, empirical examinations of any of these features – of the relative strength of elites and the nonelites, of the variable levels of power across social dimensions, or of the determinative role of conflict among groups of elites as opposed to conflict between elites and nonelites – are rarely examined. One additional issue with elite theory is that power differentials among elites and nonelites are not always assessed separately from their outcomes. Thus, more power of either elites or nonelites is often conflated with a successful outcome for them. The amount of power is rarely determined in advance. Thus, much of elite theory underspecifies the mechanisms that make transformations possible. This quandary points to another set of issues that our volume can address.

Here we point epistemologically to how it is possible to look at transformations by looking not for elites and whether they hold power, but by looking at the relationship between elites and nonelites and how they hold differential amounts of power, in terms of the six mechanisms outlined above. These differential social mechanisms combine in different ways that can in turn create transformations. Mechanisms of power combine and intersect, reinforcing or undermining each other, as we noted above. These different combinations can shift over time as the strengths of the mechanisms change. Furthermore, the expression of power explains different ways that the mechanisms may change. Where mechanisms are invisible, informal, and cooperative, quite different strategies are needed than where they are visible, formal, and conflictual. Moreover, the time frame of the study may be quite important, for example, if elites have more power in the short run but less in the long run. What may appear quite stable in the short run may be quite unstable in the long run. Again, we turn to the chapters in our volume to address these issues of social transformation. Although not explicitly employing the typology of power we develop, each can be positioned within our broader framework.

Lori Qingyuan Yue and Yuni Wen concentrate on four main mechanisms of power: material resources, associations, structure, and coalitions. These mechanisms are expressed mainly in formal and conflictual ways. Yue and Wens' elites are economic elites who formally hold large assets of material resources (the owners of fracking firms) and political elites who hold formal roles in political organizations (the heads of local and state governments). These elites' positions derive primarily from their organizational positions in firms and governments and are thus held formally. Yue and Wen analyze how conflicts between frackers and those who would regulate them are articulated in the US political system as a conflict between state-level and municipal-level governments. As such, they can influence politics both directly by financing, particularly conservative, politicians, and indirectly by promising economic growth. Yet, they do not hold formal political power, so they try to influence political outcomes by combining their economic power with associational power (lobbying) and coalitional power (the alliance with conservative political elites).

The structural configuration of the US political system (federalism), combined with an increasing polarization of the population between urban and rural areas, has two consequences. Polarization pushes urban elites to attempt to impose fracking regulations, while federalism allows fracking companies to focus on state-level governments to preempt local attempts to regulate them. The major historical transformation, the consequences of which they describe, is the rise of geographically based political polarization in which cities became bastions of liberalism, and the countryside becomes ever more conservative. If either of these factors differed (if the population was not polarized along rural–urban lines, or if the United States was a more centralized state), this set of strategies would not work. Thus, an implication of their work, although one that remains implicit, is that those who might seek to constrain elite power in the fracking industry should work either (a) to build coalitions across the urban and rural divide or (b) to reform federalism or do both.

Tod S. Van Gunten's chapter combines three mechanisms of power – material resources, associational ties, and organizational position – with three expressions of power, visibility, formality, and conflict. Van Gunten uses these analytical tools to analyze the absence of the emergence of an elite coalition. He thereby uses elite theory to solve a puzzle generated by both state-centered and distributionalist accounts of hyperinflation. The fundamental puzzle imposed by the Argentinian experience is that hyperinflation occurred in the absence of a major political crisis. The case, therefore, presents an unexpectedly positive outcome ("unexpected present") in the sense that it addresses an outcome that occurred in the absence of its putative causes (Emigh et al., 2024, pp. 307, 310). Such cases are generative of theoretical development. State-centered theories suggest that this outcome of hyperinflation reflects an institutional weakness of the Argentine state; fiscalist theories point to latent distributional conflicts. But, as Van Gunten points out, the outcome remains unexplained by both theories because Argentinian hyperinflation was financial, not a fiscal, phenomenon. Van Gunten argues that an account based on elite fragmentation can explain the outcome. The inability of Argentinian elites to overcome their coordination problems meant that they could not address hyperinflation. These elite relations were generally expressed visibly in formal political and economic organizations and engendered considerable distributional conflict.

Abhishek Chatterjee's chapter focuses on the material mechanisms of power and their conflictual expressions. He asks a classic question of historical sociology, namely, why did private property rights in land largely fail to emerge in 18th- and 19th-century British India despite the deep commitment of many colonial administrators to establishing them? Chatterjee explains this outcome by focusing on the information asymmetries between rulers as specialists in the means of coercion and cultivators. Rulers are interested in extracting the maximum amount of resources possible from cultivators by threatening cultivators' (and thereby rulers') social reproduction. However, an information asymmetry exists between rulers and cultivators. Cultivators have a much better sense than rulers of what the maximum ability to pay (MAP) is. Furthermore, rulers are *aware* of their relative ignorance in this regard. Rulers therefore tend to subcontract collection rights to subrulers who have better knowledge of MAP than central rulers. These intermediaries play a central role in explaining the development, or nondevelopment, of property rights. The position of these intermediaries, however, is tenuous. It depends on coercion wielders' continuing conviction of not having sufficient information. In India, the fundamental obstacle to the emergence of private property in land was that ruling elites were too powerful vis-à-vis both the intermediaries and the cultivators.

Caroline Virginia Reilly's chapter – focusing on structural and ideational power – investigates a case in which an ethnoracial group (in this case the Irish in the Caribbean) experienced upward mobility but without emulating the dominant group. In both Barbados and Montserrat, the Irish occupied a kind of intermediate position between Black enslaved persons and White plantation owners. This intermediate position was common to almost all slave societies. Because of the threat of the French invasion of 1667, however, the Irish of Montserrat were able to increase their social status without assimilating to the dominant English elite. In Barbados, though, no such shift in status occurred, and the Irish continued to occupy an intermediate position between the two main racial/class groups. This chapter takes elite theory in a new direction because it deals with how ideational power intertwines with structural power to produce, or not, novel forms of ethnoracial hierarchy.

Finally, Patricia Ahmed, Rebecca Jean Emigh, and Dylan Riley's chapter, with its broad historical sweep, in various ways, touches on most of these mechanisms and expressions of power. Yet, perhaps the most interesting for our introduction is how historical trajectories themselves are structural elements that constrain or enable the deployment of ideational categories of identities by political organizations seeking to create enumerative categories. The chapter considers the relative power of elites and nonelites to implement information-gathering categories. Where and when state elites, social elites, and nonelites prevail depends on the structure of the power relations as enabled or constrained by long-term historical trajectories. Analyses often begin with the state actors' explicit calls for information, but in reality the success of information gathering and its outcomes structurally depend on the interaction and relative power of state and social actors (Emigh et al., 2020, pp. 299–300, 304).

Ahmed et al. use the relative power of elites and nonelites to consider explicitly changes in social classifications and whether they might possibly stem from changes in information categories, which is not usually considered as an outcome in elite theory. They show that state elites (organizational power) are generally too weak to collect information and thus rely on social elites to do so. In turn, however, such social elites must draw on nonelite repertoires of ideational power. Thus, the transformative effect of elite information gathering should not be overdrawn. Elites in fact are rarely able to create information categories that have a transformative effect, as the categories generally stem from social sources in a bottom-up way. To show this, a long durée structural perspective is required. In this case, the visible actions of the state and social elites may be less powerful than the invisible ones of nonelites.

CONCLUSION

In this volume, we honor Lachmann and his work on developing elite theory as a research programme. We also suggest the need to overcome elite theory per se, and instead propose the development of a new research programme, which we call "relational power theory," that considers the relationship between elites and nonelites, their relative power, and their effect on social transformations. Elite theory and social movement theory face two similar problems: They both fail to recognize all of the characteristics and mechanisms of power, and they fail to fully recognize that elites and nonelites are coconstitutive.

Classic elite theory in a general sense was an attempt to "out-Marx Marxism." All three of its major exponents took the Marxist observation of the merely formal character of contemporary democracy as their starting point. They then pushed this argument forward, claiming that a restricted elite ruled in all times and places. Mills applied these ideas to the case of the United States, where they took on an entirely different political meaning from what the classics had accorded them. In Mills' hands, elite theory became a weapon for unmasking the complacent pluralist self-image of Eisenhower's America. In a different way, Bourdieu deployed elite theory as a critical tool for understanding the structure of political representation in advanced democracies. But elite theory, from its very beginnings to its later uses, had difficulty in accounting for social change, and particularly for the origins and possible transformations of elite power. Of course, these theorists recognized social change, but they could not explain it using the tools of elite theory itself. Lachmann's intellectual contribution was to link (or relink) elite theory to Marxism precisely to redress this weakness. This put elite theory on much firmer empirical and methodological ground. But Lachmann's effort fell short in developing a fully relational account of elites and nonelites, largely because he did not develop an adequate theory of power.

In contrast, we formulate a general theory of power and then look dialectically at the relationship between elites and nonelites. We expand on Marx's point that society is composed of relationships, but while Marx focused on relations of exploitation, we extend this to other social relationships. We argue that forms of power have (at least) two aspects. First, they are composed of a social mechanism that positions elites and nonelites relationally (material resources, social structures, associations, organizations, coalitions, and ideation) and an expression (visibility, formality, depth, consensuality, and directionality). With the examples of the chapters in this volume, we illustrate how these social mechanisms and expressions combine and transform. In doing so, we draw on our agenda of dialectical realism that suggests that by drawing together different partial accounts of reality, we can develop better accounts of it (Emigh et al., 2024, pp. 295–297; Riley et al., 2021, pp. 331–334).

We also argue that two prominent ways of looking at the possibilities of nonelite social movement mobilization – resource mobilization theory and political process theory – are special cases of our more general relational power theory of elites and nonelites. For example, resource mobilization theory is just a special case of our power relational theory applied to, at least in large part, nonelite social movement mobilization. The theories are special cases of our theories because, as they have developed historically, they have come to incorporate the six mechanisms (material resources, social structures, associations, organizations, coalitions, and ideation) of power that we discuss here. The historical development of resource mobilization theory and political process theory, however, means that the combination of mechanisms has been somewhat ad hoc as the research has cumulated findings and theorizations. Here, instead, we explicitly discuss these mechanisms in a systematic way so as to draw them together.

Contemporary society paradoxically combines a thoroughgoing rhetorical commitment to equality with vertiginous and growing substantive inequality along many dimensions. Never have tiny elites had so much social influence, yet rarely have they paid such lip service to flat hierarchies, networks, casualness, and equity. Andrew Carnegie's bowler and bow tie has been replaced by Mark Zuckerberg's hoody and T-shirt, but the social power wielded by the latter is, if anything, greater than the former. In a sense, this is an intensification of the belle epoque hypocrisy to which the initial elite theorists responded with their pitiless critique of the ideologies of popular sovereigny and democracy. And it explains the current attraction of elite theory today. Yet today's elite theorists are in some danger of making the same mistake as their classic forbears. For the goal cannot be simply to describe elites, but rather to lay bare the historically specific conditions for elite emergence and decline. Thus, we call for a thoroughgoing historization of elite theory and social movement theory. The goal of the relational power theory is to describe the conditions under which restricted groups have massively inordinate influence in society. By identifying those conditions, we hope to begin the conversation of how to change them. In our view, it is both intellectually and politically inadequate to remain at the level of descriptive positivism in this domain. Uncovering the qualitatively distinct character of elite and nonelite relations, as these have been constituted by different forms of power, is one step toward transforming them.

NOTES

1. All the translations in this text are our own.

2. We agree with Sewell (1992, p. 13) that structures have a dual nature, composed of schemas (virtual) and resources (material). However, Sewell (1992, p. 22) mistakenly associated depth with the virtual aspect of structures and power with the material aspect of structures. We resolve the problem by showing that ideas and depth are entailed in power in different ways.

REFERENCES

Acemoglu, D., & Robinson, J. A. (2006). *Economic origins of dictatorship and democracy*. Cambridge University Press.

Acker, J. (1990). Hierarchies, jobs, bodies: A theory of gendered organizations. *Gender & Society, 4*(2), 139–158.

40   *Introduction*

Almeida, P., & Chase-Dunn, C. (2018). Globalization and social movements. *Annual Review of Sociology, 44*, 189–211.

Althusser, L. (1970). *Lenin and philosophy and other essays* (B. Brewster, Trans.). Monthly Review Press.

Ansell, B. W., & Samuels, D. J. (2014). *Inequality and democratization: An elite-competition approach.* Cambridge University Press.

Arrighi, G. (1994). *The long twentieth century: Money, power, and the origins of our times.* Verso.

Artz, L. (2020). A political economy for social movements and revolution: Popular media access, power and cultural hegemony. *Third World Quarterly, 41*(8), 1388–1405.

Auyero, J. (2007). *Routine politics and violence in Argentina: The gray zone of state power.* Cambridge University Press.

Banks, N. (2020). Black women in the United States and unpaid collective work: Theorizing the community as a site of production. *The Review of Black Political Economy, 47*(4), 343–362.

Benford, R. D., & Snow, D. A. (2000). Framing processes and social movements: An overview and assessment. *Annual Review of Sociology, 26*, 611–639.

Bensel, R. F. (2000). *The political economy of American industrialization, 1877–1900.* Cambridge University Press.

Bobbio, N. (1969a). *Saggi sulla scienza politica in Italia [Essays on political science in Italy].* Editori Laterza.

Bobbio, N. (1969b). Gramsci la concezione della societá civile [Gramsci's conception of civil society]. In P. Rossi (Ed.), *Gramsci e la cultura contemporanea. Atti del Convengo internazionale di studi gramsciani tenuto a Cagliari il 23–27 aprile 1967* (pp. 75–100). Editori Riuniti.

Boix, C. (2003). *Democracy and redistribution.* Cambridge University Press.

Bourdieu, P. (1981a). La representation politique: Éléments pour une théorie du champ politique [Political representation: Elements for a theory of political fields]. *Actes de la recherche en sciences sociales, 36–37*(1), 3–24.

Bourdieu, P. (1981b). Décrire et prescrire: Note sur les conditions de possibilité et les limites de l'efficacité politique [Describe and prescribe: Note on the conditions of possibility and the limits of political effectiveness]. *Actes de la recherche en sciences sociales, 38*(2), 69–73.

Bourdieu, P. (2012). *Sur l'état. Cours au Collège de France (1989–1992) [On the state. Courses at the Collège de France (1989–1992)].* P. Champagne, R. Lenoir, F. Poupeau, & M-C Rivière, (Eds.). Raisons d'agir/Seuil.

Bradlow, B. H. (2021). Weapons of the strong: Elite resistance and the neo-apartheid city. *City & Community, 20*(3), 191–211.

Brookes, M. (2013). Varieties of power in transnational labor alliances: An analysis of workers' structural, institutional, and coalitional power in the global economy. *Labor Studies Journal, 38*(3), 181–200.

Bulmer, M. (1986). A controversial census topic: Race and ethnicity in the British census. *Journal of Official Statistics, 2*(4), 471–480.

Davis, M. (1980). Why the US working class is different. *New Left Review I, 123*, 3–44.

Devine, P. (1988). *Democracy and economic planning: The political economy of a self-governing society.* Routledge.

Du Bois, W. E. B. (2007). *Black Reconstruction: An essay toward a history of the part which Black folk played in the attempt to reconstruct democracy in America, 1860–1880.* Oxford University Press. (Original work published 1935).

Emigh, R. J. (2000). Review of Capitalists in spite of themselves: Elite conflict and economic transitions in early modern Europe by Richard Lachmann. *American Journal of Sociology, 106*(3), 832–834.

Emigh, R. J., Riley, D., & Ahmed, P. (2016). *How societies and states count: Vol. 1. Antecedents of censuses from medieval to nation states.* Palgrave Macmillan.

Emigh, R. J., Riley, D., & Ahmed, P. (2019). Toward a sociology of knowledge of land surveys: The influences of societies and states. *The Journal of Historical Sociology, 32*(4), 404–425.

Emigh, R. J., Riley, D., & Ahmed, P. (2020). The sociology of official information gathering: Enumeration, influence, reactivity, and power of states and societies. In T. Janoski, C. de Leon,

J. Misra, & I. W. Martin (Eds.), *The new handbook of political sociology* (pp. 290–320). Cambridge University Press.

Emigh, R. J., Riley, D., & Ahmed, P. (2024). The dialectical comparative methodology. In N. H. Wilson & D. Mayrl (Eds.), *After positivism: New approaches to comparison in historical sociology* (pp. 284–330). Columbia University Press.

Etzioni, A. (1961). *A comparative analysis of complex organizations: On power, involvement, and their correlates.* The Free Press.

Eyal, G., Szelényi, I., & Townsley, E. (1998). *Making capitalism without capitalists: Class formation in post-communist Central Europe.* Verso.

Foryś, G. (2023). The political opportunity structure and the evolution of the organizational base of peasants' and farmers' protest activity in Poland in the twentieth and twenty-first centuries. *East European Politics and Societies and Cultures, 37*(1), 77–102.

Foucault, M. (1979). *Discipline and punish: The birth of the prison* (A. Sheridan, Trans.). Vintage Books. (Original work published 1975).

Fraser, N. (2013). *Fortunes of feminism: From state-managed capitalism to neoliberal crisis.* Verso.

Garrett, G. (1998). *Partisan politics in the global economy.* Cambridge University Press.

Gautney, H. (2022). *The new power elite.* Oxford University Press.

Gramsci, A. (1971). *Selections from the prison notebooks of Antonio Gramsci* (Q. Hoare & G. N. Smith, Eds. & Trans.) International Publishers.

Habermas, J. (1989). *The structural transformation of the public sphere: An inquiry into the category of bourgeois society* (Thomas Burger, Trans., with the assistance of Frederick Lawrence). MIT Press. (Original work published 1962).

Haboddin, M., & Afala, L. M. (2022). Formation of local elite power base in local politics: "The emerging" and "the surviving." *Jurnal Politik, 8*(2), 59–89.

Haggard, S., & Kaufman, R. K. (2016). *Dictators and democrats: Masses, elites, and regime change.* Princeton University Press.

Haider, A. (2018). *Mistaken identity: Race and class in the age of Trump.* Verso.

Hall, S. (2007). The spectacle of the "other." In S. Hall (Ed.), *Representation: Cultural representations and signifying practices* (pp. 223–290). SAGE. (Original work published 1997).

Harris, C. I. (1993). Whiteness as property. *Harvard Law Review, 106*(8), 1709–1791.

Hebdige, D. (1979). *Subculture: The meaning of style.* Routledge.

Hegel, G. W. F. (1991). *Elements of the philosophy of right* (A. W. Wood, Ed.; H. B. Nisbet, Trans.). Cambridge University Press. (Original work published 1821).

Higgs, E. (2004). *The information state in England: The central collection of information on citizens since 1500.* Palgrave Macmillan.

Hobbes, T. (1985). *Leviathan* (C. B. Macpherson, Ed.). Penguin Books. (Original work published 1651).

Keefer, P. (2009). Inequality, collective action, and democratization. *PS: Political Science and Politics, 42*(4), 661–666.

Keister, L. A., Thébaud, S., & Yavorsky, J. E. (2022). Gender in the elite. *Annual Review of Sociology, 48*, 149–169.

Khan, S. R. (2012). The sociology of elites. *Annual Review of Sociology, 38*, 361–377.

Korpi, W. (2006). Power resources and employer-centered approaches in explanations of welfare states and varieties of capitalism: Protagonists, consenters, and antagonists. *World Politics: A Quarterly Journal of International Relations, 58*(2), 167–206.

Kristal, T. (2010). Good times, bad times: Postwar labor's share of national income in capitalist democracies. *American Sociological Review, 75*(5), 729–763.

Lachmann, R. (1988). Graffiti as career and ideology. *American Journal of Sociology, 94*(2), 229–250.

Lachmann, R. (1990). Class formation without class struggle: An elite conflict theory of the transition to capitalism. *American Sociological Review, 55*(3), 398–414.

Lachmann, R. (2000). *Capitalists in spite of themselves: Elite conflict and economic transitions in early modern Europe.* Oxford University Press.

Lachmann, R. (2020). *First-class passengers on a sinking ship: Elite politics and the decline of great powers.* Verso.

Lakatos, I. (1970). Falsification and the methodology of scientific research programmes. In I. Lakatos & A. Musgrave (Eds.), *Criticism and the growth of knowledge* (pp. 91–195). Cambridge University Press.

Latour, B. (1991). Technology is society made durable. In J. Law (Ed.), *A sociology of monsters: Essays on power, technology and domination* (pp. 103–131). Routledge.

Loveman, M. (2007). Blinded like a state: The revolt against civil registration in nineteenth-century Brazil. *Comparative Studies in Society and History, 49*(1), 5–39.

Lukes, S. (2021). *Power: A radical view* (3rd ed.). Macmillan Educational Limited.

Mann, M. (1986). *The sources of social power: Vol. 1. A history of power from the beginning to A.D. 1760*. Cambridge University Press.

Marx, K. (1922). *Lohnarbeit und Kapital [Wage labor and capital]*. (K. Kautsky, Ed.). J. H. W. Dietz Nachfolger. (Original work published 1849).

Marx, K. (1977). *Capital: Vol. 1* (B. Fowkes, Trans.). Vintage Books. (Original work published 1867).

Marx, K. (1996). The civil war in France: Address of the General Council of the International Working-Men's Association to all the members of the Association in Europe and the United States. In T. Carver (Ed. & Trans.), *K. Marx, Later political writings* (pp. 163–207). Cambridge University Press. (Original work published in 1871).

Marx, K., & Engels, F. (1977). The German ideology. In C. J. Arthur (Ed.), *The German ideology* (pp. 39–95). International Publishers. (Original work published 1845–1846).

Mau, S. (2023). *Mute compulsion: A Marxist theory of the economic power of capital*. Verso. (Original work published 2021).

McCarthy, J. D., & Zald, M. N. (1977). Resource mobilization and social movements: A partial theory. *American Journal of Sociology, 82*(6), 1212–1241.

Meyer, J. W., Boli, J., Thomas, G. M., & Ramirez, F. O. (1997). World society and the nation-state. *American Journal of Sociology, 103*(1), 144–181.

Michels, R. (1911). *Zur Soziologie des Parteiwesens in der modernen Demokratie: Untersuchungen über die oligarchischen Tendenzen des Gruppenlebens [On the sociology of party systems in modern democracy: Studies on the oligarchic tendencies of group life]*. Verlag von Dr. Werner Klinkhardt.

Mills, C. W. (1956). *The power elite*. Oxford University Press.

Mosca, G. (1896). *Elementi di scienza politica [Elements of political science]*. Fratelli Bocca.

Mukerji, C. (2009). *Impossible engineering: Technology and territoriality on the Canal du Midi*. Princeton University Press.

Musgrave, M. K., & Wong, S. (2016). Towards a more nuanced theory of elite capture in development projects. The importance of context and theories of power. *Journal of Sustainable Development, 9*(3), 87–107.

NeJaime, D. (2011). Convincing elites, controlling elites. *Studies in Law, Politics, and Society, 54*, 175–211.

Pareto, V. (1916a). *Trattato di sociologia generale [Treatise on general sociology]* (Vol. 1). G. Barbèra.

Pareto, V. (1916b). *Trattato di sociologia generale [Treatise on general sociology]* (Vol. 2). G. Barbèra.

Piketty, T. (2014). *Capital in the twenty-first century* (A. Goldhammer, Trans.). The Belknap Press of Harvard University Press.

Piven, F. F., & Cloward, R. A. (1977). *Poor people's movements: Why they succeed, how they fail*. Pantheon Books.

Pizzorno, A. (1972). Sistema sociale e classe politica [Social system and political class]. In L. Firpo (Ed.), *Storia delle idee politiche, economiche e sociali. Vol 6. Il secolo ventesimo* (M. Giovana, S. Lombardini, D. Marucco, A. Passerin D'Entrèves, A. Pizzorno, A. Ronchey, M. L. Salvadori, G. Sartori, P. Scoppola, and V. Zanone, [Eds.]; pp. 13–68). UTET.

Przeworski, A. (1985). *Capitalism and social democracy*. Cambridge University Press.

Ray, V. (2019). A theory of racialized organizations. *American Sociological Review, 84*(1), 26–53.

Refslund, B., & Arnholtz, J. (2022). Power resource theory revisited: The perils and promises for understanding contemporary labour politics. *Economic and Industrial Democracy, 43*(4), 1958–1979.

Riley, D. (2010). *The civic foundations of fascism in Europe: Italy, Spain, and Romania 1870–1945*. The Johns Hopkins University Press.

Riley, D. (2022). *Microverses: Observations from a shattered present*. Verso.

Riley, D., Ahmed, P., & Emigh, R. J. (2021). Getting real: Heuristics in sociological knowledge. *Theory and Society, 50*(2), 315–356.

Sall, D., & Khan, S. (2017). What elite theory should have learned, and can still learn, from W. E. B. Du Bois. *Ethnic and Racial Studies, 40*(3), 512–514.

Schalk, S., & Kim, J. B. (2020). Integrating race, transforming feminist disability studies. *Signs: Journal of Women in Culture and Society, 46*(1), 31–55.

Schmalz, S., Ludwig, C., & Webster, E. (2018). The power resources approach: Developments and challenges. *Global Labour Journal, 9*(2), 113–134.

Schoon, E. W. (2022). Operationalizing legitimacy. *American Sociological Review, 87*(3), 478–503.

Scott, J. C. (1985). *Weapons of the weak: Everyday forms of peasant resistance*. Yale University Press.

Sewell, W. H., Jr. (1992). A theory of structure: Duality, agency, and transformation. *American Journal of Sociology, 98*(1), 1–29.

Silver, B. J. (2003). *Forces of labor: Workers' movements and globalization since 1870*. Cambridge University Press.

Slater, D. (2009). Revolutions, crackdowns, and quiescence: Communal elites and democratic mobilization in Southeast Asia. *American Journal of Sociology, 115*(1), 203–254.

Starr, P. (1987). The sociology of official statistics. In W. Alonso & P. Starr (Eds.), *The politics of numbers* (pp. 7–57). Russell Sage Foundation.

Stör, L. (2017). Theories of power. In C. L. Spash (Ed.), *Routledge handbook of ecological economics: Nature and society* (pp. 141–151). Routledge.

Táíwò, O. O. (2022). *Elite capture: How the powerful took over identity politics (and everything else)*. Pluto Press.

Tarrow, S. G. (2011). *Power in movement: Social movements and contentious politics*. Cambridge University Press. (Original work published 1994).

Tattersall, A. (2010). *Power in coalition: Strategies for strong unions and social change*. Cornell University Press.

Therborn, G. (1978). *What does the ruling class do when it rules? State apparatuses and state power under feudalism, capitalism and socialism*. NLB.

Tilly, C. (1973). Does modernization breed revolution? *Comparative Politics, 5*(3), 425–447.

Tilly, C. (1999). Survey article: Power–Top down and bottom up. *The Journal of Political Philosophy, 7*(3), 330–352.

Tilly, C., & Tarrow, S. (2015). *Contentious politics* (2nd ed.). Oxford University Press.

Usmani, A. (2018). Democracy and the class struggle. *American Journal of Sociology, 124*(3), 664–704.

Weber, M. (1921). *Gesammmelte politische Schriften [Collected political writings]*. Drei Masken Verlag.

Weber, M. (1922). *Gesammelte Aufsätze zur Wissenschaftslehre [Collected essays on scientific theory]*. Verlag von J. C. B. Mohr (Paul Siebeck).

Weber, M. (1925). *Grundriss der Sozialökonomik. III. Abteilung: Wirtschaft und Gesellschaft [Outline of social economics. Vol. 3: Economy and society]*. Verlag von J. C. B. Mohr (Paul Siebeck). (Original work published 1921).

Weber, M. (1978). *Economy and society: An outline of an interpretive sociology* (G. Roth & C. Wittich, Eds.). University of California Press. (Original work published 1921).

Willis, P. (1977). *Learning to labor: How working class kids get working class jobs*. Columbia University Press.

Winters, J. A. (2011). *Oligarchy*. Cambridge University Press.

Wodke, G. T. (2016). Social class and income inequality in the United States: Ownership, authority, and personal income distribution from 1980 to 2010. *American Journal of Sociology, 121*(5), 1375–1415.

Wright, E. O. (1985). *Classes*. Verso.

Wright, E. O. (2000). Working-class power, capitalist-class interests and class compromise. *American Journal of Sociology, 105*(4), 957–1002.

CHAPTER 2

STREETS AND ELITES: CORRUPTION GRIEVANCES IN CONTEMPORARY REVOLUTIONS

Colin J. Beck[a] and Mlada Bukovansky[b]

[a]*Pomona College, USA*
[b]*Smith College, USA*

ABSTRACT

While oft-ignored, grievances remain a central part of revolutions. We argue that the theorization of grievances requires conceptually unpacking specific complaints and relating them to mobilizing mechanisms. We thus focus on one set of grievances – corruption – that is especially prevalent in 21st century revolutionary episodes. Drawing on prior conceptualizations of corruption, we hypothesize that four different configurations of corruption influence five different mechanisms of contention. First, everyday street-level corruption creates the potential for sudden and spontaneous protest and creates the basis for widespread, coalitional mobilization. Second, institutional corruption focuses attention on the regime to make it a target of revolutionary claims. Third, competition among elites creates the potential for cross-class alliances but may forestall durable sociopolitical change and, in some cases, even allow for authoritarian consolidation of power through anti-corruption drives. We illustrate these dynamics through one clearly successful case of revolution in Tunisia in 2011, one case of mixed results from political revolution in Ukraine from 2004 to 2014, and a negative case of revolution in China since 2013.

Keywords: Revolution; corruption; protest; Tunisia; Ukraine; China

---

Elites, Nonelites, and Power
Political Power and Social Theory, Volume 41, 45–69
Copyright © 2025 Colin J. Beck and Mlada Bukovansky
Published under exclusive licence by Emerald Publishing Limited
ISSN: 0198-8719/doi:10.1108/S0198-871920240000041002

INTRODUCTION

It is no secret that much of revolution theory privileges structural causes of mobilization and success. Grievances are held to be an insufficient cause of mobilization and assumed to be relatively constant under exclusionary regimes (Goodwin, 2001; Skocpol, 1979). Yet as Snow and Moss (2014) observed, grievances are always at the heart of movements. In this article, we argue that it is time for scholars of revolution to re-examine grievances as anger at elites is a necessary condition for revolutionary mobilization (Lachmann, 2020). We define revolutions simply, following Tilly (1993) who in turn followed Trotsky (1932), as situations of dual power where two or more blocs that command the loyalty of a segment of the population claim to be or control the state. In the contemporary world, revolution commonly takes the form of nonviolent contention, oriented towards individual freedom rather than social transformation, and informed by global standards for governance (Beck et al., 2022). Contemporary revolutions are thus based in individual experiences more than cohesive ideological or political programs. Grievances, often imposed by the actions of the state or unresolved by its agents, therefore create the potential for revolutionary claims to develop. We focus on one type of grievance that is common to contemporary revolutionary mobilizations – corruption – and analyze its impacts through comparative case studies of Tunisia, Ukraine, and China.

In contrast to our approach, prior research conceptualized grievances differently. Even before Skocpol's (1979) state-centered account, individual motivations and complaints were argued to be secondary to structural conditions. For instance, mid-20th century strain theorists (e.g., Davies, 1962; Gurr, 1970; Johnson, 1966) saw the frustrations of the masses as products of rapidly changing social structures. Grievances were thus a mediating mechanism between macro-level forces and the outbreak of protest against a regime. Even Marxist accounts, which took class-based grievances seriously (e.g., Boswell & Dixon, 1993; Paige, 1975), spent little effort in theorizing their role and focused on socioeconomic positions to explain rebellion.

Developments of the so-called "fourth generation" of revolution theory also have largely ignored grievances. Rather, the focus has been on movement strategy and tactics, particularly the role of nonviolence (Chenoweth & Stephan, 2011), leaderships (Selbin, 1993), and conjunctures of agency and structure (Foran, 2005). Here, the antithesis of structure is agency – the capacity of groups to act in a revolutionary situation – rather than individuals' motivations. Yet scattered across the last few decades of revolution research are hints that grievances actually do matter. For instance, Dix (1984) argued that revolutionary movements are only successful to the extent that they unite disparate claims under a negative coalition that can, at least, agree on the overthrow of the regime if not the reasons why or solutions to come. Kurzman (2004) also drew attention to individual perceptions and the choice to join protests or not. And Beissinger (2013) has attempted to map out the motivations of protestors in the street. Yet how specific grievances matter, or do not, remains largely unexplored terrain.

We contend that grievances are best brought back into the study of revolution as objects to be theorized, not merely catalogued. Grievances are more than mediating factors that allow for mobilization; they can be intrinsic to the revolutionary process and a necessary component of protest. To theorize grievances, however, means that they should be unpacked. There is little reason to assume that any given grievance will lead to the same sort of protest. Rather, specific types of complaints can lead to different actions, targets, and claims.

In the 21st century, one type of grievance against elites stands out – economic and political corruption (Lachmann, 2020). Informed by Johnston's (2005, 2014) "syndromes of corruption" typology, we suggest that rather than simply midwifing revolution, corruption grievances can be both an opportunity and an obstacle for revolutionary movements. Shared grievances regarding corruption may not only mobilize people and trigger revolutionary action but also become a way for elites to block political opportunities for mobilization. We hypothesize that there are five distinct mechanisms by which corruption grievances shape revolutionary movements, three of which enable or accelerate revolutionary mobilization, one of which is indeterminate, and one of which directly contributes to regime resilience, neutralizing revolutionary movements. We identify these mechanisms by triangulating between the levels at which corruption is experienced by social actors and articulated as a grievance on the one hand and the incentive structure shaped by the form of corrupt practices on the other. In this manner, the dynamics of corruption and mobilization engage questions about the power and structure of elites and nonelites in transformational conjunctures that were at the heart of Richard Lachmann's (2000, 2020) work.

Since the prevalence of street-level corruption can explain the flaring up of sudden protest, our first mechanism simply links the experience of everyday corruption to spontaneous protest. Perceptions that corruption reaches beyond the street and manifests as systemic, institutional corruption can provide a platform for more widespread, coalitional mobilization, which is our second mechanism. Prevailing liberal, market-friendly governance norms transmitted through international institutions amplify this effect by offering benchmarks and other resources by which protestors may explicitly challenge the legitimacy of corrupt regimes. The second mechanism thus links systemic corruption to a more structured and focused form of mobilization, involving coalitions of actors. Third, the perception of institutionalized corruption narrows people's focus on the corrupt governing regime. This articulates with more focused demands for regime change and, like the second mechanism, draws in a broader coalition of actors.

Our fourth and fifth mechanisms focus on the political opportunity structure facing actors with revolutionary grievances. If systemic corruption takes the form of power blocs jockeying for the spoils to be had when in control of governing institutions, competing elites generate different incentives and opportunities for revolutionary actors. On the one hand, a populist leader may tap into mass grievances in order to eliminate rivals for power, allying one power bloc with the revolutionary movement. Revolutionaries may thus gain elite allies interested in toppling a rival-dominated regime. This is why corruption involving competing power blocs within a state may have indeterminate effects on revolutionary mobilization: a cross-class coalition could further the revolutionary movement on the one hand (our fourth mechanism). But on the other hand, competition between the power blocs may trigger either consolidation or overthrow of a governing regime *without* a cross-class coalition with revolutionary actors. In such cases, corruption may facilitate institutional retrenchment. While our fourth mechanism involves a cross-class coalition challenging a regime, our fifth mechanism thus identifies conditions where anticorruption campaigns become means to eliminate political rivals and consolidate authority, deflecting revolutionary grievances without changing the system.

In the following sections, we show how corruption grievances can be conceptually unpacked into their specific components and related to mobilizing mechanisms. First, we review how corruption has been deployed as a revolutionary grievance and also how it has stymied revolutionary transformation. We then demonstrate the utility of the approach through three cases. The 2011 Revolution in Tunisia shows the role that street-level corruption plays in accelerating protest and how institutional corruption focuses attention on the regime. Beyond the impacts of street-level and institutional corruption, Ukrainian mobilizations from 2004 to 2014 illustrate how elite corruption can both stimulate and curtail the possibilities of revolutionary transformation. Finally, the negative case of China since 2013 exemplifies how targeted anti-corruption drives can consolidate power and curtail protest against a regime.

CORRUPTION AND REVOLUTIONARY MOBILIZATION

Corruption has long been taken for granted as a routine part of politics, and the articulation of corruption as a grievance and critique of authority is traceable back to biblical times (Noonan, 1984). Artists, preachers, and pamphleteers have deployed the concept in many ways, seeking a response from audiences who would readily relate to the dilemma and possible tragedy of a bribe paid to pervert a judgment or a divine indulgence sold to the undeserving. Political philosophers have deployed the term polemically as well as descriptively, though attempts to assess the causes and consequences of corruption in an empirical, social scientific way did not emerge until the mid-to late-20th century, often as part of the study of how developing societies "modernize" (Heidenheimer, 1970; Huntington, 1968; Nye, 1967). Since the 1990s, international institutions such as the World Bank and nongovernmental organizations such as Transparency International have made anti-corruption concerns a part of their "good governance" prescriptions, adding a layer of incentives to support reformist (but not revolutionary) mobilization against corruption. The focus of anti-corruption research has also broadened to include the "supply side" of corrupt transactions, and corruption has come to be seen as something more than a problem plaguing "developing" countries of the global south (Bukovansky, 2006; Bullough, 2019; Findley et al., 2014).

Michael Johnston (2005, 2014) showed persuasively that institutional orders that limit access to political participation and economic opportunity experience corruption differently than those with relatively more open access. But corruption plagues even well-established electoral democracies, just in different forms (Johnston, 2005; Mungiu-Pippidi, 2015). Access to political and economic opportunities may be blocked in different ways, by different power configurations, leading Johnston (2005) to posit four distinct "syndromes" of corruption: official moguls, oligarchs and clans, elite cartels, and influence markets. The syndromes are a typology based on a cluster of variables specifying which groups have access to wealth and power, how many distinct cadres are competing for resources, and the extent to which access to the levers of wealth and power is denied to ordinary citizens.

In a second book, Johnston (2014) argued that anti-corruption reform efforts should be tailored to the specific corruption syndrome prevalent in any given society. The overall aim of reform should be to achieve "deep democratization," which he defined as "processes whereby citizens become able to defend themselves and their interests by political means" (Johnston, 2014, p. 29). These processes involve self-interested political contention, coalition-building, and the development of institutions ensuring access to participation and ability to restrain arbitrary power. Johnston did not identify revolution as a possible path to deep democratization; in fact, the term "revolution" does not even appear in Johnston's index. Despite this, his admonition to link reform efforts to the specific "syndrome" of corruption is suggestive.

We build on Johnston's insight that corruption may be present in different configurations of politics and society and hypothesize that such differences may influence the form of revolutionary mobilization and the likelihood of revolutionary transformation. We concentrate on three configurations in which the experience of corruption shapes revolutionary grievances: at the street level, where the need to pay bribes is a part of people's everyday lives; at the broader institutional level, where an entire political system is seen to operate as a rent-seeking machine; and at the level of competing power blocs, where a divided elite competes for control of institutions which serve as their main source of spoils or rents – this last configuration approximates Johnston's (2005) "oligarchs and clans" or "elite cartels" syndromes. In the oligarchs and clans syndrome, access to power blocs in competition for state spoils or rents is more constrained than in elite cartels, the latter being more permeable to citizen involvement in a context of more diverse opportunities for wealth accumulation.

Street-Level Corruption and Sudden Protest

Corruption is not something people necessarily need experts to explain to them; it is a lived experience that people easily recognize and identify with. This makes it a potentially potent mobilizing idea. The type of corruption most experienced by ordinary people has been called street-level or "bread-and-butter" corruption. When such corruption is common, then there are common negative experiences of the regime, even if they are not obvious. For instance, under autocratic regimes, individuals often hide their true beliefs about the legitimacy of the regime, fearing repression (Kuran, 1995). This creates a normative pressure for all to conform. Yet, street-level corruption is a moment that exposes this falsification. Few enjoy the process of bribery, and routine exposure to it creates the potential for complaints to emerge. Such complaints can take the form of spontaneous individual or small group collective action. Thus, protest against corruption can emerge unexpectedly even though it has been germinating for a long time in the shared experiences of street-level corruption.

Sudden protest creates an immediate decision for bystanders – do I join, support, or ignore this action? The answer to this question is also informed by street-level corruption. Pervasive corruption creates pervasive experiences, and people begin by telling stories about their experiences. Such stories, shared furtively among trusted friends or publicly through parody or encoded performances, carry revolutionary potential (Selbin, 2010). As stories are created and shared, grievance becomes a collective process. This creates a desire for change if not a coherent political platform. Thus, in contrast to more abstract grievances about political processes or ideals, corruption diffuses protest more quickly than other motivations. Corruption grievances also spread protest by potentially involving large numbers of people that may constitute the basis of coalition formation. Individuals and groups do not need to agree on much if they can agree that the system is rigged against them (Dix, 1984). This process of acceleration of protest is our second mechanism of corruption and revolution.

In short, individual experiences of street-level corruption can lead to spontaneous protest, and pervasive corruption creates the potential for larger mobilization and the basis of a revolutionary coalition. Whether such protests build and are threatening to a regime is informed by the degree and form of institutional corruption, as discussed next.

Institutional Corruption and Mass Mobilization Against Elites

Like concerns about the injustice of bribes, concerns about a rigged system point to a second set of mechanisms connecting corruption and revolution: the concern not with individual bribes but with an entrenched, corrupt system. In situations where corruption is seen to be widespread and endemic to the political system as a whole, elites and "the system" become the key targets of protest. Further, corruption heightens economic inequality between elites and masses (Lachmann, 2020). Desires for economic security are affected by the experience and perception of corrupt officials. This chains material circumstance to discontent with the regime. Corruption is thus, in our third mechanism, a grievance that focuses attention on the governing regime.

Anti-system grievances expressed as a concern with corruption have a long history in political thought. For ancient philosophers, evoking corruption entailed a moral judgment regarding not just the integrity of political leaders but also of the polity as a whole. Aristotle's distinction (Aristotle, 1984, Book 4, Chapter 2) between aristocracy and oligarchy hinges on corruption: while both forms share a basic structure (rule of the few), the difference between them depends on whether the elite governs in the public interest (aristocracy) or its own private interest at the expense of the public good (oligarchy). The 17th-century English thinker Thomas Hobbes also saw corruption as a problem, one that could lead to the dissolution of government and civil war. Hobbes was suspicious of corruption as a political grievance, however, both because such grievances had the capacity to undermine the government and ignite civil war and because people often rendered judgments from improper cognitive foundations – that is, they did not reason properly about corruption, confusing emotional preferences for facts (Blau, 2009; Euben, 1989). Hobbes' unease about deploying corruption as a political critique highlights its ubiquity as a revolutionary grievance.

By contrast, the arguably more influential Lockean liberal tradition was more sanguine about revolution, even as it moved away from a reliance on civic virtue and concentrated instead on constitutions and institutional design (Pocock, 2003). In the liberal tradition, revolutions occurring against corrupt regimes signaled progress toward a more representative and legitimate government; their outcomes were anticipated to be liberal in the sense of instituting restraints on arbitrary and tyrannical power (Blau, 2009; Euben, 1989). Although abuse of power can take many forms, once liberal prescriptions regarding good governance had stabilized into a model of representative government combined with the rule of law grounded in protection of property rights so that a market society could flourish, political corruption came to be firmly identified as a deviation from liberal norms of governance (Euben, 1989). Liberalism thus seems to take for granted that the purpose of revolution is to bring about a representative, democratic government. Revolution, in this tradition, is more about getting to democracy than getting rid of corruption, though often the implication is that the two are linked (Mungiu-Pippidi, 2015).

For students of comparative political development, the path toward liberal norms was initially construed as a process of "modernization." Samuel Huntington (1968) cast corruption as an inevitable by-product of modernization. Modernization brings on a questioning of traditional ways of organizing social and political life. Traditionalists bemoan the corruption of old values by new practices and, importantly, the new elites who bring modern values into the "traditional" society. Established modes of patronage, in turn, are seen as corrupt in contrast to the modern merit-based bureaucracy some elites (trained abroad) are attempting to institute. This clash of values is likely to breed crises of regime legitimacy. Huntington also suggested that corruption can actually be functional for regimes in the absence of strong institutions, a point advanced by Nye (1967). Nye saw the relationship between corruption and revolution as uncertain, which perhaps it was in the context of the mid-20th century. But the repeated occurrence of protests against corruption throughout the first decades of the 21st century suggests that it may no longer be so.

In the contemporary world, corruption is a signal that institutions are inaccessible and/or unresponsive to their publics and thus susceptible to maximalist demands for change (Goodwin, 2001). And corruption reveals the lack of alignment between global, rationalized discourses of good governance and local practices. This challenges the legitimacy of regimes and makes them susceptible to revolutionary challenges (Beck, 2014; Lawson, 2015). When the regime itself, particularly narrow cliques at the top, are participants in corruption, its position is particularly tenuous. Corruption thus narrows the focus of protest quickly – remove corrupt actors and life will improve.

Elite Power Competition, Anti-corruption, and Revolutionary Potential

Corruption also affects revolution through the dynamics of elite power competition. Elites may join revolutionary movements or they may stymie them (Goldstone, 1991; Lachmann, 2000). If elites owe their positions to endemic corruption, then it is unlikely that they will join a revolutionary movement unless the source of their corrupt gains will not be threatened by revolution or unless they see better opportunities in joining the revolutionary cause. The presence of corrupt competing power blocs thus has an important, but indeterminate effect on revolutions.

One reason for this indeterminacy is that elites are not always a single class. Johnston's (2005) "oligarchs and clans" syndrome highlights elite competition for spoils of a corrupt system in a relatively binary class structure, where political power means economic opportunity and vice versa. But if wealth and access to political power flow from different streams, such that one does not automatically translate into the other, things get more complicated. If economic elites operate in a domain somewhat shielded from political influence, as is the case in many liberal market societies, does this inhibit popular revolutionary mobilization targeting corrupt elites in general, or does it merely help to channel grievance toward politicians rather than the wealthy (or vice versa)? Our analysis thus suggests two possible mechanisms of anti-system grievances: those amplified by an elite cadre which joins the revolutionary coalition and those deployed by contending elites to curb each other's influence without instigating systemic change. Twenty-first century populist leaders thus have learned to tap into corruption grievances to mobilize large groups. Here, corruption is a grievance that does not in itself generate a political platform. In fact, any political platform may be manipulated by elites in such a way as to evade measures, such as redistribution, that would materially address popular grievances. Moreover, corruption may enhance the resources available to entrenched elites to help them stem the revolutionary tide through, for example, "buying off" the opposition or simply by enhancing their repressive capacities. It helps that the resources may themselves be transnational and so in many cases out of the immediate reach of ordinary citizens.

Many of the enabling conditions for elite corruption are to be found not only in the "global south," "transitioning economies," or "emerging markets" but rather also in the core economies and the structures of global capitalism, and particularly finance (Bullough, 2019; Findley et al., 2014). This is the "supply-side" of corrupt incentives, long neglected in the literature that rendered corruption as largely a developing country problem. Money laundering and tax evasion have come under increasing scrutiny, particularly in the context of US and allied efforts to track down and limit the financing of terrorist networks and to impose sanctions on so-called rogue regimes. A by-product of such efforts has been casting light on at least some of the major financial players enabling corruption. As revelations such as the Panama Papers have shown, corruption can be pervasive in many countries no matter their location (see especially Sharman, 2017).

The ability of elites to stash corrupt gains offshore, making such resources untraceable by ordinary citizens because of the patchiness of the international legal framework applying to shell companies and banking, also poses significant challenges to revolutionary mobilization around the corruption issue. Initiatives such as the World Bank's Stolen Asset Recovery Initiative attempt to address this issue but are probably only chipping away at the tip of an iceberg. The financialization of the core economies involved in capital account liberalization and the proliferation of offshore wealth networks has also contributed to populist backlashes against cosmopolitan, detached elites (Lachmann, 2020).

All this suggests that the proliferation of offshore wealth networks, alongside the expansion of an international regime attempting to curb corruption and incentivize better governance, creates a complex set of incentives and disincentives when it comes to revolutionary mobilization against corruption. On the one hand, the "good governance" agenda proffered by the World Bank, Organization for Economic Cooperation and Development (OECD) aid donors, NGOs such as Transparency International, and other institutions serves as a resource for citizens mobilizing against corrupt elites in their own countries. On the other hand, the offshore world is itself a resource for concealing corrupt gains (Sharman, 2017). If elites are able to access such resources during times of revolutionary mobilization, such resources may be brought to bear in their struggle to remain in power. The "supply side" of corrupt transactions, especially the financial infrastructure permitting the offshoring of assets, draws our attention to the more nuanced incentive structures facing status quo elites and revolutionary coalitions. In the context of elite power competition, then, corruption can either accelerate or forestall wider mobilization.

Finally, our fifth mechanism of the interplay of corruption and mobilization lies in the emergence anti-corruption norms and their use as a tool of power consolidation. Transparency International (founded by Peter Eigen, a former World Bank official) published the first of its now annual Corruption Perceptions Index (CPI) in 1995. The index provided a "measure" of corruption, which then enabled analyses of the relationship between the CPI score of a given country and other variables, such as foreign direct investment or gross domestic product (GDP) growth (Transparency International, 2021). A parallel development that reinforced this trend was the growth of an international legal regime aiming to curb corrupt practices, beginning with the OECD Anti-Bribery Convention, and culminating in the United Nations Convention against Corruption (UNCAC) (Abbott & Snidal, 2002; Bukovansky, 2006; Mungiu-Pippidi, 2015). Following in Transparency International's footsteps, the World Bank got into the rankings game with its World Governance Indicators, also designed to provide more quantifiable measures of corruption. Other indices and modes of measurement have since followed (Cooley & Snyder, 2016), the most recent being a draft attempt by the United Nations to generate a series of quantitative benchmarks through which to assess compliance with the UNCAC (see Messick, 2023).

Thanks to these developments, social scientists strongly influenced by economics now treat corruption as a measurable problem amenable to modification via rational, instrumental institutional reform or redesign (Johnston, 2005, 2014; Mungiu-Pippidi, 2015; Rose-Ackerman, 1999). Developing this work, scholars such as Rose-Ackerman and Palifka (2016) focused on the legal and institutional underpinnings of liberal market societies to generate propositions about how to alter institutional incentive structures in order to lessen the likelihood of corrupt practices by public officials. The early (and in some cases continuing) recommendations inspired by this work often involved constraining the discretion of officials in areas of procurement, tax collection, and public service delivery and recommending that public office and administrative salaries provide adequate livelihoods so as to lessen the incentive to take bribes. Becker and Stigler's (1974) influential work from the Chicago school of economics inspired sustained focus on incentive structures, but without much attention to political processes, let alone revolutionary mobilization. This approach to corruption and its control reinforced the "Washington Consensus," which advocated a larger role for market forces in allocating resources, with a concomitant curtailing of the discretion of public officials in developing countries. Such an approach made international financial institutions the purveyors of policy advice which essentially involved shrinking the public sector. Technocratic blueprints for improving a country's balance of payments position had little to say, however, about the necessary political changes that would be needed to implement such advice (Bukovansky, 2006).

Despite these developments in internationalizing a "good governance" agenda, international anti-corruption efforts, ironically, may give authoritarians the opportunity to consolidate their hold on power. It is not only opposition populists who can use corruption as cudgel against their elite opponents, regimes can, too. Painting a competing power bloc as corrupt is one method for eliminating rivals: officials can be dismissed, investigated, and imprisoned. And the public may accept an anti-corruption cover story or even demand it as a way of ameliorating its own corruption grievances. Anti-corruption campaigns may thus help legitimate a central regime and delegitimate contenders against it.

We thus argue that pervasive corruption has complex effects on the revolutionary process. On one hand, it can sort elites and constituencies into competing power blocs, one of which might ally with a revolutionary movement. And on the other, it can provide the cover needed for one authoritarian group to consolidate power over others. Corruption can thus be entangled with elite power competition, and revolutionary potential may be the casualty. Fig. 1 summarizes the interplay of these four corruption dynamics and our five mechanisms of revolution.

In the sections that follow, we examine these five mechanisms in the context of recent cases of corruption and revolution that represent the possible variation of the phenomenon. First, we examine how street-level corruption accelerated successful revolutionary protest in Tunisia in 2011, through sudden protest and widespread, coalitional mobilization. Second, we show how oligarchical corruption and competition weakened the state in Ukraine and made it susceptible to protest movements that succeeded in changing regimes but not elites. Finally,

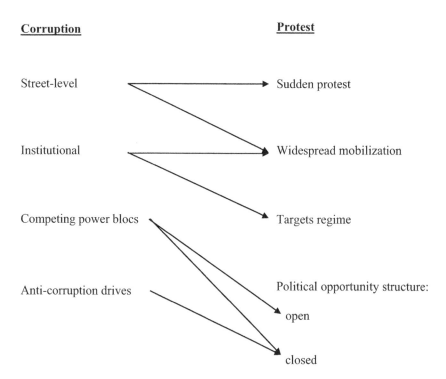

Fig. 1. Corruption Grievances and Mechanisms of Revolutionary Protest.

we consider how anti-corruption protests and campaigns have been a sphere of elite power consolidation in 21st century China that forestalls the potential for transformative protest movements.

FROM CORRUPT STREETS TO STREET PROTESTS: TUNISIA 2011

While the general story of the beginning of the Tunisian Revolution of 2011 is well-known – a street vendor sets himself on fire to protest police mistreatment and sparks nationwide protests against the regime – the details reveal intersections with two different types of corruption. First, it was the existence of street-level corruption that created the moment of confrontation, which was catalyzed by official indifference to corrupt practices. Second, mass protests began in a region of Tunisia that was plagued by institutional corruption that had allowed the Ben Ali regime to enrich itself, creating a target for popular grievance.

Mohamed Bouazizi originally began selling produce from a cart in the streets of Sidi Bouzid in central Tunisia after a bank had foreclosed on his family's agricultural land (Bayat, 2017). Mid-morning on December 17, 2010, he was accosted by police for not having a permit. This was a routine affair – officials often confiscated street vendors' wares only to return them in exchange for bribes. But in this instance, a municipal official, who also was a woman, allegedly slapped Bouazizi while taking his produce scale. Bouazizi immediately went to the governor's office to complain and have his property returned but was met with indifference. Bouazizi's cousin recounted that he replied to the official "If you don't see me, I'll burn myself." Within the hour, Bouazizi stood in the center of the road, poured gasoline on himself, and lit a match while shouting "How do you expect me to make a living?" (The Australian, 2011). Bouazizi was transported to the hospital but would die from his injuries on January 4, 2011.

Soliciting bribes is classic street-level corruption, routine and usually tolerated. It accelerated to grievance in this case partially because of the humiliation of having been slapped by a woman in a patriarchal society (Pearlman, 2013). But it was the fact that this grievance, clear and public, was not addressed by a corrupt system that catalyzed Bouazizi's protest. Suicide by self-immolation is one of the most attention-grabbing and effective repertoires of individual protest (Biggs, 2013). It is effective precisely because it involves almost unthinkable spectacle, manifesting internal pain as external display of defiance. Bouazizi literally wanted to be seen by the authorities that had done him injustice. His final words grieve a lack of economic opportunity and are a protest of how corruption and indifference had made him unable to work, even in such a limited venture as street vending.

The rage that Bouazizi felt was shared by his fellow citizens. Protests began in Sidi Bouzid that same day. By December 19, 2010, police in Sidi Bouzid had begun arresting protestors. In the next few days, two protestors in the city also committed suicide, while others were killed or injured by an increasingly repressive police. On December 27, the first demonstration in the capital Tunis took place, in solidarity with Sidi Bouzid. Ben Ali denounced the protests the following day, but a tipping point had been reached. Protest diffused quickly across the country, fueled in part by the new tools of social media (Howard & Hussain, 2013). The regime then tried conciliation, shuffling cabinet appointments, and promising job creation. Ben Ali visited Bouazizi, still in a coma, in the hospital, but this backfired and enraged family members and protestors (Ritter, 2015). By the first week of January 2011, labor unions, lawyers' and teachers' associations, and trade guilds had begun to organize protests against the regime. On January 10, the government closed all schools and universities, and Ben Ali promised to step down from power by 2014. It was too late. Protests wracked the country, Ben Ali called upon the military to restore order, which it refused to do, and he fled into exile in Saudi Arabia on January 14. A revolution barely a month old had toppled a seemingly secure regime.

While a full accounting of the Tunisian Revolution marries structural conditions and trajectories of protest (see, e.g., Bayat, 2017; Ritter, 2015), the grievance of corruption is central to the success of the protests that became revolution in January 2011 (Alianak, 2014; Levey, 2011). To understand how corruption set off a protest cascade, two dimensions are relevant. First is the setting of the initial act by Bouazizi. Sidi Bouzid lies in rural, central Tunisia at a remove from the more developed and industrialized areas around Tunis. As a relatively underdeveloped hinter region, corruption by local authorities was pervasive and routine (Thorne, 2011). Sidi Bouzid, like other rural locales in the country, was also disadvantaged structurally by 21st century development policies (Bayat, 2017). This local environment, where a lack of economic opportunity combined with official corruption, was fertile ground for a protest against the regime to start. From this viewpoint, Bouazizi's suicide protest is as much an example as a cause of mobilizing grievances. A similar act in, say, Tunis would likely have had much less of an effect.

The same policies that created the situation in Sidi Bouzid also allowed the ruling elite to exploit the public sector for personal enrichment. US diplomatic cables, released by WikiLeaks in November 2010, attested to the corruption of the Ben Ali family. While the release of this information certainly fueled protests the next month, encounters with a corrupt system were already a common experience. Ben Ali's personal corruption was merely a target for widely shared grievances. Based on an analysis of public opinion data, Beissinger et al. (2015) find that corruption was the second most popular reason given by protestors for mobilizing, coming only behind economic concerns and definitively ahead of political concerns like freedom and democracy. As the case of Bouazizi demonstrates, it is also difficult to disentangle economic concerns and corruption grievances – the two are consistently entwined.

Thus, corruption was a mass shared grievance that helps explain the speed of the Tunisian Revolution. Protestors had a shared experience of everyday corruption and institutional corruption. This made a startling act like Bouazizi's easy to self-identify with, which is key to the diffusion of protest (Beck, 2015). This also helps explain the unexpected success of spontaneous and mostly leaderless protest, which is a key feature of the revolution (Bayat, 2017). In the absence of formal organization, shared experience and disruption of everyday life are the scaffolds of movements (Piven & Cloward, 1977). No other grievance could have set off the cascade that resulted from Bouazizi's suicide protest. Tunisia thus illustrates how street-level corruption feeds two mechanisms of revolution – sudden protest and widespread mobilization – and that institutional corruption can focus attention on the regime, instead of other targets.

The phenomenon of corruption creating sudden and widespread protest is certainly not limited to Tunisia in 2011. In two recent examples, similar dynamics have been at play, even if neither has led to a full-fledged political revolution. In 2022, Sri Lankans began to stage demonstrations against the government of President Gotabaya Rajapaska. Since 2019, the country had been in an economic slump. As in Tunisia, the economic situation was exacerbated by perceptions of the Rajapaska family's corruption, revealed by reporting in 2021 in the "Pandora Papers" which is a leaked database of offshore financial holdings by global elites (Alecci, 2022). Over the next few months, protest and repression escalated in a tit-for-tat fashion, with protestors calling for Rajapaska to resign. On July 9th, protestors gathered outside the presidential house, overwhelmed its security, and occupied the building (Restrepo & Shapiro, 2022). Within days, Rajapaska had resigned and fled into exile in the Maldives. Similarly, the 2022 protests in Mongolia show how corruption grievances can quickly escalate demonstrations.

In December, it was revealed that billions of dollars' worth of government coal exports had been stolen. Protestors demanded that the names of the accused officials be released and attempted to break into government offices in Ulaanbaatar (Reuters, 2022). Mongolian authorities quickly announced investigations and arrested the suspected thieves within days. This conciliation was effective and forestalled a protest cascade.

The cases of Sri Lanka and Mongolia confirm the Tunisian lesson – corruption is a grievance that can mobilize large numbers of protestors quickly. But it also suggests the limits to a grievance-based account of successful revolutions. Sri Lankan protests changed who was in power but did not institute a new form of governance, and Mongolian protests ended quickly due to government concessions. Revolution is only one possible outcome of the interplay of mobilization and elite corruption. Another possibility is that corrupt institutions become an arena for elite competition and conflict, as the case of Ukraine demonstrates.

FROM CORRUPT ELITES TO CORRUPTED REVOLUTIONS: UKRAINE, 2004–2014

From his in-depth analysis of recent revolutions, Beissinger (2022, p. 318) concludes that "urban civic revolutions are better understood not as revolutions for democracy, but as revolutions against a corrupt and predatory political class." Perhaps no case better exemplifies this than the Ukrainian revolutions of 2004 and 2014. However, Ukraine's last two decades also demonstrate that while revolution can topple regimes and reorient societies, it can also fail to change entrenched elites engaged in corrupt struggles for power and resources.

The road to revolution in Ukraine lies in the immediate aftermath of its independence from the Soviet Union in 1991. Like other postcommunist states, the new Ukrainian government privatized state assets in a transition to capitalism and a haltingly democratic future. This had the unintended effect of creating a capitalist class – the oligarchs – whose primary interests lay outside of building a functioning state (Radnitz, 2010). In fact, Ukrainian politics became a place where different elite networks competed for economic power through political cover, influencing public opinion through media holding, regional party formations, and local patronage structures. As Onuch and Hale (2022) recount, Volodymyr Zelensky's television show before he became president satirizes the situation:

Oligarch 1: Friends, we didn't gather here for the scenic view.

Oligarch 2: Gentlemen, aren't you tired of pointlessly wasting money? First, we spend millions to bring our candidates to the political forefront, and then we spend twice as much to ruin our competitors.

Oligarch 1: Those are the rules. You want to install your own president? Then back him.

While corruption being the glue that binds together economic and political elites is not unique to Ukraine, it certainly found an apogee in its competitive politics.

The corruption of the system was well-known and as in Tunisia, Sri Lanka, and Mongolia created a shared mobilizing grievance for protest. In 2000 and 2001, activists demonstrated against President Leonid Kuchma, whose notorious venality led to the corrupt system being nicknamed *Kuchmizm*. The protests were sparked by a recording of Kuchma seemingly ordering the killing of a journalist. While these protests were unsuccessful in dislodging Kuchma, they did set the stage for the 2004 Orange Revolution.

The Orange Revolution, nicknamed for the color of the opposition's coalition, was a mobilization against electoral fraud in 2004's presidential election. Government authorities had rigged the election to be favorable to Kuchma's designated successor, Viktor Yanukovych. His challenger, Viktor Yuschenko, had even been poisoned with dioxin while on the campaign trail (Beck et al., 2022). Protests began immediately on the second round of voting as exit polls and official tallies sharply diverged. Demonstrations in Kyiv attracted half a million participants, with the central square occupied around the clock (Onuch, 2015). The national election commission declared Yanukovych the winner, while parliament passed a no confidence vote against him in his role as prime minister. With a muted response by security services and negotiations between the camps, the Supreme Court of Ukraine broke the deadlock and ordered a new election, which Yuschenko's Orange coalition won.

The year 2004 had two notable features. First, while it was truly an electoral revolution – a mobilization that takes advantage of fraud in an election to press political claims – corruption was a central grievance (Beissinger, 2022; Bunce & Wolchik, 2006). The revolution can very much be seen as a reaction to *Kuchmizm* and a rejection of the status quo that Yanukovych represented. However, second, the revolution was only accomplished through elite negotiation and mutual accommodation (D'Anieri, 2006; Onuch & Hale, 2022). Yuschenko agreed to constitutional changes that would divide executive authority between the president and prime minister. This created further competition among elite networks and had the result of fracturing the coalition as Yuschenko and his prime minister, Yulia Tymoshenko, jockeyed for power. The competition allowed for an unlikely comeback for Yanukovych and his patronage network (Gerlach, 2014; Hale, 2010), first returning to the prime minister's office in 2006 and then winning the presidency outright in 2010.

As in 2004, Yanukovych's corruption set the stage for the 2014 Euromaidan revolution, also known as the Revolution of Dignity. The proximate spark for protests in 2014 was the sudden decision to not sign an association agreement with the European Union, but as in 2004, the continued competition between corrupt elites had generated widespread frustration (Beck et al., 2022; Onuch, 2015). Demonstrations began in November 2013 in Kyiv, occupying central squares of the city. Unlike 2004, however, protestors were met with a repressive police response. This had the immediate effect of intensifying the demonstrations and attracting wider participation, a cycle repeated four times until February

2014 (Onuch, 2015). By then, many members of Yanukovych's party had fled the capital, and the opposition parties were able to form a quorum without them in parliament and promptly removed Yanukovych from office.

The immediate aftermath saw a Russian invasion of eastern Ukraine and Crimea and the election of Petro Poroshenko – another oligarch and politician – to the presidency. While Poroshenko's administration was able to forestall a catastrophe in the war for the Donbas region and promote Ukrainian nationalism, it was largely seen as a failure. The economy failed to prosper, and it seemed as if the country had again just traded one elite corruption network for another. It is against this backdrop that Zelensky, a comedian with a popular television show, announced his run for the presidency. In a case of life imitating art, Zelensky not only resoundingly won the presidency, but he also proved himself an effective leader in the war launched by Russia in 2022. Still, corruption is pervasive in Ukrainian society, with officials in the defense ministry accused of embezzling funds during the war.

The politics of Ukraine since its independence and its intersection with revolutions in 2004 and 2014 display a different configuration of elites, corruption, and mobilization than the Tunisian case. Elite corruption can become endemic, and when not centered on a single ruling clique, it becomes the basis of competing patronage networks – an example of Johnston's (2005) oligarchs and clans syndrome. Influence over the state thus becomes the ultimate patronage prize, and the state itself becomes the arena for competition. In contrast to the expectations of classic state-breakdown theory (Goldstone, 1991; Goodwin, 2001; Skocpol, 1979), however, even a successful revolution that supplants a regime is unable to dislodge the pattern. Rather, state and society quickly return to the status quo, trading one corrupt clique for another or even reviving a prior competitor. That any progress towards governance has been made is due in large part to war with Russia and the coalescing of a civic national Ukrainian identity (see Onuch & Hale, 2022).

Ukraine is not the only case of endemic corruption as the basis for elite competition. South Africa and Brazil also display similar patterns, with varying intersections with protest. In South Africa, recurrent charges of corruption have stalked high-level officials and none more so than Jacob Zuma. Zuma has been indicted three times for corruption, and his family made an appearance in the Panama Papers archive (Cowell, 2016). The first indictment in 2005 followed on then president Thabo Mbeki dismissing Zuma from the deputy presidency. The second indictment was withdrawn after evidence of illegal surveillance and spying by prosecutors was uncovered. While charges from the third reinstated indictment are pending, his successor Cyril Ramaphosa had hundreds of thousands, if not millions, of dollars in cash stolen from his farm in 2020. When the story emerged in 2022, his political rivals seized on it as evidence of corruption and tried, but failed, to impeach him (McKenzie, 2022). The corrupt competition for power has also yielded popular protest, such as in 2021 when Zuma was jailed for contempt of court. On the same day Zuma was taken into custody, riots broke out in his party's traditional stronghold of KwaZulu-Natal. Over the course of two days, the riots turned into looting and violence, killing at least 354 people

(The Presidency of South Africa, 2021). As police were unable to contain the unrest, the South African military was deployed within the week and mobilization subsided.

In Brazil, too, corruption is wielded as a weapon between competing power blocs. Most notably, Lula da Silva's first presidency was plagued with corruption. Corruption was also endemic in his successor and political ally Dilma Rousseff's, administration (Balán, 2014). In 2015, a large series of protests took place over a bribery scandal in the state-owned oil company Petrobas. Demonstrators were able to mobilize millions of citizens in national demonstrations in March, April, and August. Federal authorities had also begun investigating Lula's post-presidency influence peddling. In March 2016, authorities raided Lula's home, and large protests ensued, with nearly seven million demonstrating nationally (Reuters, 2016). In response, Rousseff appointed Lula her chief of staff, which would have provided legal immunity. The appointment, however, was set aside by the Supreme Court, and Rousseff was impeached and removed from the presidency. Lula was convicted the following year of accepting bribes. He spent almost two years in prison before being released while his case was appealed. The Supreme Court later annulled his convictions on procedural grounds, which cleared Lula to again run for the presidency against Jair Bolsonaro, whose administration was similarly dogged by corruption allegations. When Bolsonaro lost re-election to the presidency to Lula, his supporters created roadblocks, demonstrated, and finally ransacked federal buildings in Brasilia, copying the January 6th attack on the United States Capitol.

In both of these cases, corrupt cliques of elites competing for political power created mass protests, as it did in Ukraine. However, both South Africa and Brazil escaped full-fledged revolutionary regime change partially because of contingency and partially because of the resilience of institutions and democratic mechanisms. South Africa and Brazil also reveal a different way that corruption intersects with mobilization – anti-corruption efforts can be a political tool of power consolidation, as the next case of China shows.

FROM ANTI-CORRUPTION TO POWER CONSOLIDATION: CHINA 2013–2022

As in Ukraine, the transition to market capitalism in China created opportunities for corruption at both personal and institutional levels. China, unlike Ukraine, however, maintained an authoritarian political system. Until recently, a hallmark of China's state capitalist system was a remarkable degree of decentralized power, what Lieberthal (2004) terms "fragmented authoritarianism." Under this system, cliques of local and regional officials connected to more powerful central party members were able to create networks of corruption, particularly through control of state-owned enterprises (Pei, 2016). This created two potential dangers for the Chinese Communist Party. On one hand, corruption and decentralized power could threaten China's rise to the status of a global power (Hung, 2015), and on the other, popular grievances over corruption could delegitimate the state (Lee, 2014).

In response to these challenges, when Xi Jinping assumed power in 2012, he quickly announced an anti-corruption campaign against "tigers and flies." The campaign targeted both high-ranking officials and state-owned enterprise managers (tigers) and local officials (flies). By 2014, it became clear that the anti-corruption drive was a serious endeavor as Politburo members, high-ranking party officials, and a general were indicted and stripped of party membership. This initial campaign seems to have been equally a sincere effort to control corruption and a way to consolidate power around Xi. For example, Wedeman (2017) argued that the campaigns did not resemble the factional purges of the cold war era and were oriented towards larger institutional problems of corruption than any one clique alone. And there is substantial evidence that investigations did indeed target corrupt officials and networks (Gao & Pearson, 2022; Lorentzen & Lu, 2018). It is thus possible that anti-corruption campaigns in authoritarian settings can truly be that – efforts to weed out graft and personal enrichment. However, there remains a degree of targeting in the campaigns, which suggests that elite competition for power is at play (Zhu & Zhang, 2017). Top officials were likely to have shorter investigations (Gao & Pearson, 2022), and those who have personal ties to Xi himself appear to have been protected from investigations (Lorentzen & Lu, 2018). From the perspective of the present, where Xi has extended his presidency for an unprecedented third term, it is safe to conclude that anti-corruption can consolidate power no matter its initial motive. In contrast to Ukraine, corruption as a tool of power competition did not lead to fragmentation of elite authority due to the regime's success in eliminating rivals.

It is easy to assume that the campaigns would be popular with the public as protests are often about corruption (Hess, 2013; Lee, 2014). However, corruption, anti-corruption, and elite competition in China interact with the public sphere differently than in the prior cases. Protest in China is a common but a highly managed affair – a way of making grievances known to officials and resolvable by the legal system (Lorentzen, 2017; Michelson, 2007). This is not to say that protest is always ineffective or unthreatening to the regime. Take, for example, the wave of anti-COVID policies in the fall of 2022. Popular frustration with recurrent lockdowns, quarantines, mandatory testing, and other attempts at eradicating COVID outbreaks had grown steadily. The implementation of such policies also revealed that local officials were often unprepared to logistically manage challenges like assuring delivery of food and medicines. Popular anger grew sharply after a building fire in Xinjiang in November 2022 killed 10 who were reportedly confined in a lockdown. The resulting "white paper" protests – so named for the act of holding blank sheets of paper to point out government censorship of discontent – took off quickly and spread across the country. By December 7th, the government announced the end of zero-COVID policies, and protest subsided.

The difference between these protests and anti-corruption protests lies in one key feature. Anti-corruption protest in China is rarely about systemic corruption. Rather, it tends to focus on local officials and their abuses (Lee, 2014). Routine contention is also carefully managed by the state (Lei, 2018; Michelson, 2007). From this view, anti-corruption drives might be about managing the expression of grievances as much as resolving them. Accordingly, Zhu et al. (2019) find that the campaigns have not increased support for anti-corruption in general. Instead, anti-corruption efforts seem to have led to more favorable public opinion of the central regime. Thus, corruption grievances are managed in such a way that they do not lend themselves to national mobilization. This contrasts with Tunisia, where local grievances were not managed by the central regime at all, and revolution resulted.

China stands somewhat apart for its effective anti-corruption drives as well as elite power consolidation through them (see Carothers, 2022). This is due, in no small part, to effective management of the campaigns as well as effective management of potential contention from below. As such, there really is no parallel case to examine. A possible case comparison to draw might be one of time period. If a future anti-corruption drive takes place, its similarities and differences to Xi's campaigns of the 2010s can validate the utility of our framework.

CONCLUSION: THE POSSIBILITIES AND LIMITATIONS OF CORRUPTION GRIEVANCES

We have argued that grievances in general remain a source of popular mobilization against regimes. Specifically, we have shown through our case analysis that corruption grievances, in the contemporary world, have unique features that can crystallize mobilization into a revolutionary situation. We hypothesized that corruption interacts with revolutionary processes through five different mechanisms: street-level corruption that creates the potential for sudden collective action and widespread mobilization, institutional corruption that focuses mobilized anger on the regime, elite corruption that may enable revolutionary movements or constrain them depending on the interests of competing power blocs, and anti-corruption drives as a form of power consolidation and contention-proofing of a regime.

Our cases suggest that these mechanisms can combine in different ways to yield different trajectories. Table 1 illustrates the cases comparatively across configurations of corruption and the five mobilizing mechanisms. To summarize, corruption is a widely shared grievance than can transcend other differences and accelerate revolution. Corruption grievances quickly bring people to the streets once protest has begun. In Tunisia, it is striking how quickly mass protest began locally after Bouazizi's self-immolation, and how quickly protests spread across the country in the first days after. Similarly, in Ukraine during both revolutions, occupation of the Maidan accelerated quickly once the regime responded with stonewalling or repression. Ordinary people protesting corruption is easy to identify with and easy to join as its demands are hardly maximalist or extreme, as recurrent local protest in China suggests. In the case of Ukraine, dissatisfaction with elite corruption and oligarchical rivalry was also able to bridge other political divides. In the Orange Revolution, participants came to the streets

Table 1. Corruption Grievances and Protest in Tunisia, Ukraine, and China.

		Tunisia	Ukraine	China
Corruption Grievance	**Street-level**	Spontaneous self-immolation of Bouazizi (1) Shared grievance for national protest (2)	-	-
	Institutional	Focused attention on Ben Ali regime (3)	Basis of mobilizing coalitions (2) Delegitimates incumbent president (3)	Common grievance in local protests (2)
	Competing power blocs	-	Made elections political opportunities for protest (4)	Distinction between local and central authorities (4)
	Anti-corruption drive	-	-	Consolidated central authority (5)

Note: Numbers in parentheses refer to mobilizing mechanisms: (1) sudden protest, (2) widespread mobilization, (3) regime targeting, (4) open political opportunities, (5) closed political opportunities.

united for free elections and good governance, no matter where they stood on other social divides. By 2014, corrupt competition for power had exhausted the populace and discredited many of the major political players, including the regime. This again led to revolutionary mobilization, the election of a political outsider as president, and a solidifying national identity. Because institutional corruption affects the functioning of state and society, it is able to unify different constituencies into a revolutionary coalition, as occurred in Tunisia, in a way that few other grievances can. Corruption thus allows protest to diffuse more quickly than more specific political claims might.

However, corruption also has particular downsides for revolutionary movements. As corruption grievances are diffusely held and minimalist in orientation, they are unable to substitute for a true political program. It is not enough to just desire a more just political and economic world; a movement must also establish plans to build it. This lack of radical envisioning lies at the failure and moderation of many revolutionary challenges of the past few decades (Beck et al., 2022). Tunisia exemplifies the pattern. The sudden displacement of the regime allowed for a democratic transition but one that was not planned for or even anticipated. As such, Islamists quickly won electoral power and then lost it to competitors who have moved away from democracy. Ironically, a lack of radical envisioning may partly be caused by the plethora of "good governance" advice coming from aid donors, international financial institutions, and NGOs. If a potentially revolutionary coalition outsources its political platform to the thick layer of foreign advisors eager to assist them, this may neuter its revolutionary potential. Grievance-based mobilization also cannot substitute for true organizing (Tufekci, 2018). Broad grievances build coalitions of convenience rather than coalitions of coordination and alliance. While differences among mobilizing actors can be papered over by a focus on corruption, they can easily re-emerge when the moment of protest is over. This is the dynamic that played out in Ukraine in 2004. Once power had changed hands, it became clear that there was no true ideological platform or strategy for the future. As a result, the Orange coalition splintered and elite competition for power resumed. Corruption is also a cudgel for authoritarians. In China, anti-corruption drives suppress opponents and contain popular mobilization. Even today in Ukraine, corruption investigations have been a political tool as much as a progressive one. Corruption grievances and mobilization is thus a two-sided sword for revolutionary challenges. It can enable a mass movement, but it can also give an excuse for elites to repress alternatives.

Attentiveness to systemic, supply-side corruption facilitated by offshore wealth networks may shed light on structural features of institutions that are not always visible to enthusiastic modernizers and reformers. Neoliberal recommendations geared toward limiting the discretion of corruptible public officials and enhancing the scope of market allocation of resources pay little attention to the possibilities of political and social mobilization. However, international institutions can sometimes learn. The turn towards "good governance" in global regimes can be seen as a reaction to the political instability brought about by prior policy programs. Protests during the Latin American debt crises of the 1970s–1980s, in the East Asian financial crisis of the late 1990s, and during the Eurozone crisis in the mid-2000s, all targeted austerity policy prescriptions, and the major international financial institutions slowly took notice. As a result, contemporary revolutions now take place in a climate thick with prescriptions and financial incentives geared toward improving governance and reducing corruption in the developing world, post-Soviet transition countries, and, at least since the Eurocrisis of the early 2000s, southern Europe. Yet these same prior examples suggest that the development of an anti-corruption technocracy may have unintended effects on political instability if elites manage to tap offshore wealth networks and deploy anti-corruption drives in a way that shores up their own position. Corruption can be a potent grievance, but corrupt networks may in turn render the problem of creating a more just, equitable, and accessible political and economic system much more difficult than simple overthrow of a given regime. Corruption may introduce a very undesirable form of resilience into political regimes.

Overall, we have theorized that corruption is a central feature of contemporary revolutions, either as a mobilizing mechanism or a tool of elites. Given that political corruption, economic inequality, and popular frustration are only likely to build in the coming decades as world economy and geopolitics shift (Lachmann, 2020), it is far past time for revolution studies to recapture grievances. Grievances should not be analyzed monolithically but unpacked and related to specific mobilizing processes. Only in this way can the complex interplay of grievance, structure, agency, and contingency be understood.

ACKNOWLEDGEMENTS

We thank Rebecca Jean Emigh and Dylan Riley for their insightful feedback, participants of the Global Affairs and Human Security Workshop at the University of Massachusetts, Amherst for their comments, and our coauthors of *On Revolutions* – Erica Chenoweth, George Lawson, Sharon Erickson Nepstad, and Daniel Ritter – where these ideas were first incubated.

REFERENCES

Abbott, K. W., & Snidal, D. (2002). Values and interests: International legalization in the fight against corruption. *The Journal of Legal Studies, 31*(S1), S141–S177. https://doi.org/10.1086/342006

Alecci, S. (2022). As Sri Lanka's ruling Rajapaksas flee, Pandora Papers reveal ties to UAE properties. *International Consortium of Investigative Journalists.* https://www.icij.org/investigations/pandora-papers/as-sri-lankas-ruling-rajapaksas-flee-pandora-papers-reveal-ties-to-uae-properties/. Accessed on April 5, 2024.

Alianak, S. (2014). *The transition towards revolution and reform: The Arab Spring realised?* Edinburgh University Press.

Aristotle. (1984). *The complete works of Aristotle.* Princeton University Press.

Balán, M. (2014). Surviving corruption in Brazil: Lula's and Dilma's success despite corruption allegations, and its consequences. *Journal of Politics in Latin America, 6*(3), 67–93. https://doi.org/10.1177/1866802X1400600304

Bayat, A. (2017). *Revolution without revolutionaries: Making sense of the Arab Spring.* Stanford University Press.

Beck, C. J. (2014). Reflections on the revolutionary wave in 2011. *Theory and Society, 43*(2), 197–223. https://doi.org/10.1007/s11186-014-9213-8

Beck, C. J. (2015). *Radicals, revolutionaries, and terrorists.* Polity.

Beck, C. J., Bukovansky, M., Chenoweth, E., Lawson, G., Erickson Nepstad, S., & Ritter, D. P. (2022). *On revolutions: Unruly politics in the contemporary world.* Oxford University Press.

Becker, G. S., & Stigler, J. G. (1974). Law enforcement, malfeasance, and compensation of enforcers. *The Journal of Legal Studies, 3*(1), 1–18. https://doi.org/10.1086/467507

Beissinger, M. R. (2013). The semblance of democratic revolution: Coalitions in Ukraine's Orange revolution. *American Political Science Review, 107*(03), 574–592. https://doi.org/10.1017/S0003055413000294

Beissinger, M. R. (2022). *The revolutionary city: Urbanization and the global transformation of rebellion.* Princeton University Press.

Beissinger, M. R., Jamal, A. A., & Kevin, M. (2015). Explaining divergent revolutionary coalitions: Regime strategies and the structuring of participation in the Tunisian and Egyptian revolutions. *Comparative Politics, 48*(1), 1–24. https://doi.org/10.5129/001041515816075132

Biggs, M. (2013). How repertoires evolve: The diffusion of suicide protest in the twentieth century. *Mobilization: International Quarterly, 18*(4), 407–428.

Blau, A. (2009). Hobbes on corruption. *History of Political Thought, 30*(4), 596–616.

Boswell, T., & Dixon, W. J. (1993). Marx's theory of rebellion: A cross-national analysis of class exploitation, economic development, and violent revolt. *American Sociological Review*, *58*(5), 681–702.

Bukovansky, M. (2006). The hollowness of anti-corruption discourse. *Review of International Political Economy*, *13*(2), 181–209. https://doi.org/10.1080/09692290600625413

Bullough, O. (2019). *Moneyland: Why thieves and crooks now rule the world and how to take it back*. Profile Books.

Bunce, V. J., & Wolchik, S. L. (2006). International diffusion and postcommunist electoral revolutions. *Communist and Post-Communist Studies*, *39*(3), 283–304. https://doi.org/10.1016/j.postcomstud.2006.06.001

Carothers, C. (2022). Taking authoritarian anti-corruption reform seriously. *Perspectives on Politics*, *20*(1), 69–85. https://doi.org/10.1017/S1537592720001371

Chenoweth, E., & Stephan, M. J. (2011). *Why civil resistance works: The strategic logic of nonviolent conflict*. Columbia University Press.

Cooley, A., & Snyder, J. (Eds.). (2016), *Ranking the world: Grading states as a tool of global governance* (Reprint ed.). Cambridge University Press.

Cowell, A. (2016, April 14). Revelations from Panama Papers are old news for Africans. *The New York Times*. https://www.nytimes.com/2016/04/15/world/africa/panama-papers-mossack-fonseca-africa.html

D'Anieri, P. (2006). Explaining the success and failure of post-communist revolutions. *Communist and Post-Communist Studies*, *39*(3), 331–350. https://doi.org/10.1016/j.postcomstud.2006.06.002

Davies, J. C. (1962). Toward a theory of revolution. *American Sociological Review*, *27*(1), 5–19.

Dix, R. H. (1984). Why revolutions succeed & fail. *Polity*, *16*(3), 423–446.

Euben, P., J. (1989). Corruption. In T. Ball, J. Farr, & R. L. Hanson (Eds.), *Political innovation and conceptual change*. Cambridge University Press.

Findley, M. G., Nielson, D. L., & Sharman, J. C. (2014). *Global shell games: Experiments in transnational relations, crime, and terrorism*. Cambridge University Press.

Foran, J. (2005). *Taking power: On the origins of third world revolutions*. Cambridge University Press.

Gao, K., & Pearson, M. M. (2022). The role of political networks in anti-corruption investigations. *China Review*, *2*, 81–111.

Gerlach, J. (2014). *Color revolutions in Eurasia*. Springer International Publishing.

Goldstone, J. A. (1991). Ideology, cultural frameworks, and the process of revolution. *Theory and Society*, *20*(4), 405–453.

Goodwin, J. (2001). *No other way out: States and revolutionary movements, 1945-1991*. Cambridge University Press.

Gurr, T. R. (1970). *Why men rebel*. Princeton University Press.

Hale, H. E. (2010). The uses of divided power. *Journal of Democracy*, *21*(3), 84–98. https://doi.org/10.1353/jod.0.0174

Heidenheimer, A. J. (1970). *Political corruption: Readings in comparative analysis*. Transaction Books.

Hess, S. (2013). From the Arab Spring to the Chinese Winter: The institutional sources of authoritarian vulnerability and resilience in Egypt, Tunisia, and China. *International Political Science Review*, *34*(3), 254–272. https://doi.org/10.1177/0192512112460258

Howard, P. N., & Hussain, M. M. (2013). *Democracy's fourth wave? Digital media and the Arab Spring*. Oxford University Press.

Hung, Ho-fung (2015). *The China boom: Why China will not rule the world*. Columbia University Press.

Huntington, S. P. (1968). *Political order in changing societies*. Yale University Press.

Johnson, C. (1966). *Revolutionary change*. Little, Brown and Company.

Johnston, M. (2005). *Syndromes of corruption: Wealth, power, and democracy*. Cambridge University Press.

Johnston, M. (2014). *Corruption, contention and reform: The power of deep democratization*. Cambridge University Press.

Kuran, T. (1995). The inevitability of future revolutionary surprises. *American Journal of Sociology*, *100*(6), 1528–1551.

Kurzman, C. (2004). *The unthinkable revolution in Iran*. Harvard University Press.

Lachmann, R. (2000). *Capitalists in spite of themselves: Elite conflict and economic transitions in early modern Europe*. Oxford University Press.

Lachmann, R. (2020). *First-class passengers on a sinking ship: Elite politics and the decline of great powers*. Verso.

Lawson, G. (2015). Revolutions and the international. *Theory and Society*, *44*(4), 299–319. https://doi.org/10.1007/s11186-015-9251-x

Lee, C. K. (2014). State & social protest. *Dædalus*, *143*(2), 124–134. https://doi.org/10.1162/DAED_a_00277

Lei, Y.-W. (2018). *The contentious public sphere: Law, media, and authoritarian rule in China*. Princeton University Press.

Levey, S. (2011, June 16). Fighting corruption after the Arab Spring. *Foreign Affairs*. https://www.foreignaffairs.com/articles/middle-east/2011-06-16/fighting-corruption-after-arab-spring

Lieberthal, K. (2004). *Governing China: From revolution through reform*. W. W. Norton.

Lorentzen, P. (2017). Designing contentious politics in post-1989 China. *Modern China*, *43*(5), 459–493. https://doi.org/10.1177/0097700416688895

Lorentzen, P. L. & Lu, X. (2018). Personal ties, meritocracy, and China's anti-corruption campaign. *SSRN*. http://dx.doi.org/10.2139/ssrn.2835841

McKenzie, D. (2022, December 13). South African President Ramaphosa will not be impeached over cash-in sofa scandal. *CNN*. https://www.cnn.com/2022/12/13/africa/south-africa-ramaphosa-impeachment-vote-intl/index.html

Messick, R. (2023). UNODC statistical framework to measure corruption: Comments requested. *The Global Anticorruption Blog*. https://globalanticorruptionblog.com/2023/02/08/unodc-statistical-framework-to-measure-corruption-comments-requested/. Accessed on February 13, 2023.

Michelson, E. (2007). Climbing the dispute pagoda: Grievances and appeals to the official justice system in rural China. *American Sociological Review*, *72*(3), 459–485.

Mungiu-Pippidi, A. (2015). *The quest for good governance: How societies develop control of corruption*. Cambridge University Press.

Noonan, J. T. (1984). *Bribes*. University of California Press.

Nye, J. S. (1967). Corruption and political development: A cost-benefit analysis. *American Political Science Review*, *61*(2), 417–427. https://doi.org/10.2307/1953254

Onuch, O. (2015). Comparing the Orange revolution and the EuroMaidan. In D. Marples & F. Mills (Eds.), *Ukraine's Euromaidan: Analyses of a civil revolution* (pp. 27–56). Columbia University Press.

Onuch, O., & Hale, H. E. (2022). *The Zelensky effect*. Oxford University Press.

Paige, J. M. (1975). *Agrarian revolution*. Free Press.

Pearlman, W. (2013). Emotions and the microfoundations of the Arab uprisings. *Perspectives on Politics*, *11*(02), 387–409. https://doi.org/10.1017/S1537592713001072

Pei, M. (2016). *China's crony capitalism: The dynamics of regime decay*. Harvard University Press.

Piven, F. F., & Cloward, R. A. (1977). *Poor people's movements: Why they succeed, how they fail*. Pantheon Books.

Pocock, J. G. A. (2003). *The Machiavellian moment: Florentine political thought and the Atlantic Republican tradition* (Revised ed.). Princeton University Press.

Radnitz, S. (2010). The color of money: Privatization, economic dispersion, and the post-Soviet 'revolutions'. *Comparative Politics*, *42*(2), 127–146. https://doi.org/10.5129/0010415 10X12911363509396

Restrepo, M. L., & Shapiro, A. (2022, July 13). *Sri Lankan protesters party in the president's mansion as he flees the country*. NPR.

Reuters. (2016, March 14). Record Brazil protests put Rousseff's future in doubt. *CNBC*. https://www.cnbc.com/2016/03/14/record-brazil-protests-put-rousseffs-future-in-doubt.html

Reuters. (2022, December 8). Mongolians brave bitter cold to protest 'coal theft' corruption. *Reuters*. https://www.reuters.com/world/asia-pacific/mongolians-brave-bitter-cold-protest-coal-theft-corruption-2022-12-08/

Ritter, D. (2015). *The iron cage of liberalism: International politics and unarmed revolutions in the Middle East and North Africa*. Oxford University Press.

Rose-Ackerman, S. (1999). Political corruption and democracy. *Connecticut Journal of International Law, 14,* 363.

Rose-Ackerman, S., & Palifka, B. J. (2016). *Corruption and government: Causes, consequences, and reform.* Cambridge University Press.

Selbin, E. (1993). *Modern Latin American revolutions.* Westview Press.

Selbin, E. (2010). *Revolution, rebellion, resistance: The power of story.* Zed Books.

Sharman, J. C. (2017). *The despot's guide to wealth management: On the international campaign against grand corruption.* Cornell University Press.

Skocpol, T. (1979). *States and social revolutions.* Cambridge University Press.

Snow, D. A., & Moss, D. M. (2014). Protest on the fly toward a theory of spontaneity in the dynamics of protest and social movements. *American Sociological Review, 79*(6), 1122–1143. https://doi.org/10.1177/0003122414554081

The Australian. (2011). Tunisia revolt sparked by a police slap. *Australian.* https://web.archive.org/web/20110119043055/http://www.theaustralian.com.au/news/world/tunisia-revolt-sparked-by-a-police-slap/story-e6frg6so-1225990556122. Accessed on January 27, 2023.

The Presidency of South Africa. (2021). *Report of the expert panel into the July 2021 civil unrest.* The Presidency of South Africa.

Thorne, J. (2011, January 13). Bouazizi has become a Tunisian protest 'symbol'. *The National.* https://web.archive.org/web/20110116154056/http://www.thenational.ae/news/worldwide/bouazizi-has-become-a-tunisian-protest-symbol

Tilly, C. (1993). *European revolutions, 1492-1992.* Blackwell Publishers.

Transparency International. (2021). The ABCs of the CPI: How the corruption perceptions index is calculated. *Transparency International Org.* https://www.transparency.org/en/news/how-cpi-scores-are-calculated. Accessed on February 13, 2023.

Trotsky, L. (1932). *History of the Russian revolution.* University of Michigan Press.

Tufekci, Z. (2018). *Twitter and tear gas: The power and fragility of networked protest* (Reprint ed.). Yale University Press.

Wedeman, A. (2017). Xi Jinping's tiger hunt: Anti-corruption campaign or factional purge? *Modern China Studies, 24*(2), 35–94.

Zhu, J., Huang, H., & Zhang, D. (2019). Big tigers, big data: Learning social reactions to China's anticorruption campaign through online feedback. *Public Administration Review, 79*(4), 500–513. https://doi.org/10.1111/puar.12866

Zhu, J., & Zhang, D. (2017). Weapons of the powerful: Authoritarian elite competition and politicized anticorruption in China. *Comparative Political Studies, 50*(9), 1186–1220. https://doi.org/10.1177/0010414016672234

CHAPTER 3

ASIAN ART PATRONAGE: RACE, ETHNICITY, AND CULTURAL LEGITIMATION

Patricia A. Banks

Mount Holyoke College, USA

ABSTRACT

Following the tradition of scholarship showing that elites institutionalize their tastes via cultural philanthropy, this chapter investigates patronage of Asian art at the Metropolitan Museum of Art. Drawing on content analysis of museum press releases and other documents, I conceptually elaborate and empirically illustrate different patterns of Asian art patronage among Asian and white patrons as well as among Asian patrons from different ethnic groups. Engaging theory asserting that elites legitimate art tied to their ethnoracial heritage through supporting it at cultural organizations, I elaborate how Asian elites are especially committed to supporting Asian art at the museum. In addition, I illustrate how, compared with each other, Asian elites particularly champion art from their respective ethnic groups – for example, Chinese elites support Chinese art at higher levels than Asian elites who are not Chinese, and Indian elites support Indian art at higher levels than Asian elites who are not Indian. This chapter advances theory about elites and cultural legitimation, elites and organizational contributions, and progressiveness within the elite.

Keywords: Cultural capital; race and ethnicity; art patronage; legitimation; Asian art; collecting

INTRODUCTION

A longstanding view of cultural patronage is that it is organized around class (Bourdieu, 1984; DiMaggio, 1982a, 1982b; Lena, 2019). A growing body of

---

Elites, Nonelites, and Power
Political Power and Social Theory, Volume 41, 71–84
Copyright © 2025 Patricia A. Banks
Published under exclusive licence by Emerald Publishing Limited
ISSN: 0198-8719/doi:10.1108/S0198-871920240000041003

literature, however, shows that it is also structured by race and ethnicity (Banks, 2010a, 2010b, 2017, 2018a, 2019b, 2019c, 2019d; Fleming & Roses, 2007). This research posits that cultural patronage varies across racial and ethnic groups within the elite. Although by some measures the socioeconomic outcomes of Asians are relatively high (U.S. Census Bureau, 2021, 2022a, 2022b), little attention has been paid in sociological scholarship to cultural philanthropy among the Asian elite. This chapter addresses this gap in knowledge by investigating Asian patronage of Asian art.

Following DiMaggio (1982a, 1982b), who showed that elites institutionalize their tastes via cultural philanthropy, here I analyze patronage of Asian art at the Metropolitan Museum of Art. Drawing on content analysis of museum press releases and other documents, I conceptually elaborate and empirically illustrate different patterns of Asian art patronage among Asian and white patrons, as well as among Asian patrons from different ethnic groups. Engaging theory asserting that elites legitimate art tied to their ethnoracial heritage through supporting it at cultural organizations (DiMaggio, 1982b; Fleming & Roses, 2007), I elaborate how Asian elites are especially committed to supporting Asian art at the museum. In addition, I elaborate how Asian elites particularly advocate for art linked to their own ethnic groups. I conclude by discussing how these findings contribute to the scholarship on elites and culture, and in particular how they advance theory regarding elite legitimation of taste, elite contributions to organizations, and progressiveness within the elite.

ELITE ART PATRONAGE AND
CULTURAL LEGITIMATION

The cultural consumption of elites is distinguished by its focus on patronage at cultural institutions (Bourdieu, 1984; DiMaggio, 1982a, 1982b; Lena, 2019). By supporting museums and other cultural organizations, elites not only signal their class status but also reinforce their class position by legitimating the forms of culture they consume. For example, elite Bostonians in the 19th century were "cultural capitalists" who used their wealth to establish cultural institutions (DiMaggio, 1982a, 1982b). Supporting cultural institutions, such as the Museum of Fine Arts in Boston and the Boston Symphony Orchestra, signaled their membership in the elite and helped to institutionalize their tastes. As DiMaggio (1982b) wrote, "It was the vision of the founders of the institutions that have become, in effect, the treasuries of cultural capital upon which their descendants have drawn that defined the nature of cultural capital in American society" (p. 377).

A growing body of literature, however, complicates this view of elite patronage and cultural legitimation by examining how different racial and ethnic groups within the elite engage in distinct forms of cultural philanthropy (Banks, 2010a, 2010b, 2017, 2018a, 2019b, 2019c, 2019d; Fleming & Roses, 2007).[1] For example, elite African Americans act as "Black cultural capitalists" who direct their patronage toward culture linked to the African diaspora (Fleming & Roses, 2007). Describing the cultural activities of the League of Women for Community Service, a group of elite Black women active in early 20th-century Boston, Fleming and Roses (2007), wrote:

> Building upon DiMaggio's description of cultural entrepreneurship in Boston, we suggest that the League members can be regarded as cultural capitalists. While these black women could hardly be considered "capitalists" in the strict economic sense of the term, they were members of a privileged African-American elite who used their status and their modest financial resources to encourage the cultivation and professionalization of black artistic expression. (p. 376)

This tradition of Black cultural patronage by the Black elite has continued into the 21st century. Through activities such as giving money to African American museums and donating art by African American artists to "mainstream" museums, Black elites have contributed to the legitimation of Black culture (Banks, 2010b, 2019c, 2019d).

Building on the scholarship documenting how elites legitimate culture linked to their ethnoracial heritage by patronizing it at cultural organizations, I theorize that support of Asian art at museums is especially common among Asian elites. In addition, I posit that, compared with one another, Asian elites especially champion art from their respective ethnic groups – for example, Chinese elites support Chinese art at higher levels than Asian elites who are not Chinese, and Indian elites support Indian art at higher levels than Asian elites who are not Indian.

METHODS

To cast light on Asian cultural patronage, I use the case of the Metropolitan Museum of Art in New York City. Given that the Metropolitan Museum of Art is the largest art museum in the United States and one of the most important museums for legitimating culture, understanding patronage at this institution is especially important. To study support of Asian art at the museum, I compiled a unique database of press releases downloaded from the museum's website that mention individuals who served on the museum board over the course of 2000–2020. Altogether, the database includes several hundred press releases. The corpus mentions over 100 trustees of whom about 6% are Asian and 82% are non-Hispanic white. I draw on content analysis to inductively identify themes in the text. The final coding scheme, derived from qualitative content analysis, is applied to the full corpus.[2] This chapter specifically focuses on text and images that address Asian art. All data are coded by the author.[3] To further investigate emergent themes in the press release data, additional museum discourse was also collected. This includes texts such as exhibition summaries that include terms like "Korean art" and "Indian art" and other media that mentions trustees such as video transcripts.

ASIAN ART PATRONAGE AT THE METROPOLITAN MUSEUM OF ART

Racial Differences

Compared with white patrons, discourse about Asian patrons more often describes them as champions of Asian art at the museum. Discourse about Ming Chu Hsu, who joined the board in 2018, falls into this category. Hsu was born in Taiwan and immigrated to the United States in her early 20s. She earned her undergraduate degree from New York University (NYU) and her MBA from the business school at Columbia University. Over the course of her professional career, Hsu founded a real estate company and worked as an executive in other firms. In 2022, a press release announced that a curator had been hired to fill a position funded by, and named after, Hsu, as well as Daniel Xu, a founder and the chief information officer of Tencent, an internet services firm based in China. The press statement highlights Hsu and Xu's support of Asian art at the museum, with the name of the curatorship being "Ming Chu Hsu and Daniel Xu Associate Curator of Asian Art in the Department of Modern and Contemporary Art" (Metropolitan Museum of Art, 2022a).

Discourse mentioning Michael ByungJu Kim, a board member born in South Korea in the 1960s, also highlights his contributions to Asian art at the museum. Kim was educated at elite East Coast schools in the United States, earning his undergraduate degree from Haverford College and his MBA from Harvard Business School. In 2005, Kim cofounded MBK Partners, a private equity firm in Seoul, South Korea. Kim's net worth is reported as close to $8 billion. In 2022, a $10 million donation by Kim to the museum was announced. The press release spotlights his commitment to Asian art by noting that he had served on the museum's Asian Art Visiting Committee (Metropolitan Museum of Art, 2022b).

Press releases mentioning Oscar L. Tang, a trustee who first joined the board in 1994, also convey that his patronage has played an important role in supporting Asian art at the museum. Tang was born in Shanghai, China. When he was a child, his family moved to the United States, where he later enrolled in Phillips Academy, an elite prep school. His education at prominent East Coast schools continued when he earned a BS at Yale University and an MBA from Harvard Business School. Professionally, Tang has worked as an investor, even founding an investment firm at one point in his career.

The significant impact of Tang's patronage on the museum's activities related to Asian art is conveyed in press releases that discuss his cash donations to the museum. A 2015 press release reports that Tang made a $15 million donation to support the Department of Asian Art (Metropolitan Museum of Art, 2015a). This donation was part of a larger $70 million capital campaign. The press release describes Tang's donation, along with three other large donations, as "landmark gifts." It also emphasizes the significance of Tang's gift by framing it as part of his long-term commitment to supporting Asian art at the museum. As the press release notes:

> ... Tang ... has been a dedicated major supporter of the Metropolitan Museum's Department of Asian Art since 1984 – has given $15 million to establish an endowment fund in support of new curatorial and conservation staff appointments and programming, as well as the continued growth of the department, on the occasion of its centenary. Metropolitan Museum of Art (2015a)

Compared with Asian patrons, white patrons are less commonly presented as major supporters of Asian art in museum discourse. When white patrons are discussed in museum texts mentioning Asian art, they are more often linked to patronage activities not directly related to championing this art. For example, trustee David Koch, an entrepreneur whose family owns Koch Industries, endowed a staff position in conservation. A press release about the reopening of several galleries, including one featuring South Asian art, notes that the art works had been examined and conserved through the efforts of several staff members, including the "David H. Koch Scientist in Charge" (Metropolitan Museum of Art, 2011). Rather than discussing Koch as directly supporting Asian art, this text describes him as supporting a staff position whose incumbent was involved in preserving Asian art.

In a similar vein, Bonnie J. Sacerdote is mentioned in a press release about Asian art though is not described as directly supporting art falling into this category. Sacerdote graduated with an art history degree from Smith College, one of the Seven Sisters colleges on the East Coast. In 1967, she married Peter M. Sacerdote, who graduated from Harvard Business School three years prior. Peter spent over four decades working in investment banking at Goldman Sachs, while Bonnie's career and community service was focused on education. In keeping with her commitment to education, a lecture hall in the museum's education center was named after her. Her name was also mentioned in a press release highlighting the 100th anniversary of the museum's Department of Asian Art because an event that was part of the celebration was taking place in the "Bonnie Sacerdote Lecture Hall" (Metropolitan Museum of Art, 2015e).

Another white trustee, Daniel Brodsky, is mentioned in a press release about Asian art by virtue of serving as chair of the museum board. Brodsky, a real estate developer who earned an undergraduate degree at the University of Pennsylvania and a master's in public service at NYU, joined his father's real estate firm a year after graduating from NYU. In 2001, he became a trustee at the museum and in 2011 chair of the board. Brodsky is included in a press release about a major gift of Asian art to the museum not because he made the donation, but rather because in his role as board chair he offered acknowledgment of the gift: "Daniel Brodsky, Chairman of the Metropolitan Museum, added: 'We are fortunate to receive these remarkable gifts from such long-time donors and friends of the Department of Asian Art, many of whom are also Trustees'" (Metropolitan Museum of Art, 2015a).

To summarize, it is common for trustees with Asian ancestry to be described as supporters of Asian art in museum texts. A consistent pattern in this discourse is the highlighting of how Asian patrons have been major benefactors around the museum's collection, exhibition, and/or interpretation of Asian art. In contrast,

76 *Asian Art Patronage*

white patrons are less commonly described as major patrons of Asian art in museum discourse.

Ethnic Differences

Not only are Asian and white patrons presented in museum discourse as having different levels of commitment to Asian art, but Asian patrons from different ethnic groups are described as having distinct commitments to Asian art from their own ethnic group. This emphasis on Asian donors as being especially focused on culture produced by their co-ethnics is illustrated, for instance, through press releases and other documents pertaining to Nita Ambani. Ambani, who was born in Mumbai, India, is the founder and director of the Reliance Foundation, which is the philanthropic arm of Reliance Industries Limited, the largest Fortune Global 500 company in India. Ambani's husband, Mukesh Ambani, is the chairman and managing director of the firm, owning a 49.46% stake in the publicly traded company, and the family's net worth is estimated at close to $100 billion (Mukesh Ambani, n.d.).

Although Nita Ambani is mentioned in several press releases, none of them focus on art outside of South Asia, and specifically India. In 2019, Ambani was invited to serve as an honorary trustee at the museum. The press release announcing her naming as honorary trustee emphasizes how she has been a major supporter of the museum's activities around Indian art (Metropolitan Museum of Art, 2019b). For example, the chair of the board commented that "Mrs. Ambani's commitment to The Met and to preserving and promoting India's art and culture is truly exceptional. Her support has an enormous impact on the Museum's ability to study and display art from every corner of the world" (Metropolitan Museum of Art, 2019b). The press release further communicates the significance of Ambani's support of Indian is not only through direct statements about her but also through comments about the cultural significance of exhibitions her donations had supported. For example, it is noted that an exhibition supported by the Reliance Foundation featuring Indian artist Nasreen Mohamedi "was the first museum retrospective of the artist's work in the United States and was also one of The Met Breuer's inaugural exhibitions" (Metropolitan Museum of Art, 2019b).

Press releases announcing exhibitions also highlight Ambani's support of Indian artists. For example, from June to September 2019, the museum held an exhibition featuring the work of Mrinalini Mukherjee, who was born in India and is recognized for her sculpture. The press release emphasizes the significance of the exhibition by noting that it "will mark the first comprehensive display of the artist's work in the United States" (Metropolitan Museum of Art, 2019a); it further highlights the role of Ambani's patronage in this significant cultural event by noting that "the exhibition is made possible by Nita and Mukesh Ambani and the Reliance Foundation" (Metropolitan Museum of Art, 2019a).

Similarly, an earlier 2017 press release announcing a major gift by the Reliance Foundation to the museum emphasizes the donation's significance for programming around Indian art, describing it as "a landmark gift" that "will support a range of exhibitions examining the accomplishments and influence of the arts and artists of India across time and in all media" (Metropolitan Museum of Art, 2017c). The press release also places emphasis on Ambani as specifically committed to supporting Indian art by framing her giving as being linked to her ethnicity. For example, it comments that "with this new gift, Mr. and Mrs. Ambani and the Reliance Foundation will in time have sponsored three important Indian exhibitions at The Met Breuer – along with two at The Met Fifth Avenue – allowing their Indian culture and heritage to be shared with the millions who visit The Met from all over the world" (Metropolitan Museum of Art, 2017c).

A video transcript featuring Ambani receiving an award for her contributions to the museum frames her patronage in a similar manner. She is quoted as saying:

> I must say I am very proud to be an Indian. India has a vast history of art and culture going back to 5,000 years. And I'm in complete awe of The Met; not only are you preserving that art, but you're giving a chance for people from all walks of life to see it. We are the fortunate ones to be blessed, and if we can share our resources and make a better place – that is the biggest karma of all. Metropolitan Museum of Art (2017a)

Korean patrons are also presented in museum discourse as having a particular commitment to supporting art produced by their co-ethnics. This is illustrated in a 2022 press release announcing Michael Kim's multi-million-dollar donation to the museum. The announcement emphasizes his cultural support of contemporary art, noting that a gallery in the modern and contemporary art wing that is being renovated would be named after him and his wife Kyung Ah Park. A comment by the museum's then director also makes specific reference to Korean art in noting how the gift would help the museum demonstrate a global commitment to contemporary art:

> At a moment of ever-increasing interest in the contemporary art world – and especially in the powerful Korean contemporary art scene – Michael Kim's gift is a strong signal of support for a truly global representation of the art of the 20th- and 21st-century at The Met. Metropolitan Museum of Art (2022b)

Press releases mentioning Kun-Hee Lee, a wealthy businessman born in Korea, also highlight Korean cultural patronage. Lee, who was educated at Waseda University in South Korea and George Washington University in the United States, served as chairman of the electronics company Samsung. Several press releases about exhibitions at the museum featuring Korean art include a statement that the exhibition was supported by Lee (Metropolitan Museum of Art, 2018). The significance of Lee's Korean cultural patronage at the museum is made most evident in a 1998 press release announcing the opening of the Arts of Korea Gallery. The press release opens by noting:

> The first permanent gallery dedicated to the display of the arts of Korea at The Metropolitan Museum of Art will open to the public on June 9, signaling the successful completion of an ambitious 30-year plan for the establishment of major new galleries of Asian art and the enrichment of the Museum's Asian collection. Metropolitan Museum of Art (1998)

78   *Asian Art Patronage*

Lee is recognized for his support in the effort through a comment that "The establishment of and program for the Arts of Korea Gallery have been made possible by The Korea Foundation and The Kun-Hee Lee Fund for Korean Art." Lee is not mentioned in any press releases that do not focus on Korean art (Metropolitan Museum of Art, 1998).

Like Lee, Oscar Tang is also described in museum discourse as having an especially strong commitment to supporting art produced by his co-ethnics. One press release with the secondary headline, "Gift Transforms Met Holdings through the Addition of One of World's Earliest Chinese Landscape Masterpieces," illustrates how Tang's donations of art have been described in this manner (Metropolitan Museum of Art, 2017b). In 2016, Tang donated to the museum a painting titled *Riverbank*, attributed to Dong Yuan, who was an artist active in China from the 930s to 960s. *Riverbank* depicts a landscape painted in ink on a silk hanging scroll. The significance of Tang's donation is captured not only by the title of the press release but also by comments from the museum's then-director and CEO, Thomas P. Campbell: "Now, with this gift of *Riverbank*, he [Tang] has added a uniquely important treasure to The Met's holdings and, in the process, further enhanced the Museum's stature as one of the preeminent collections of Chinese painting in the world" (Metropolitan Museum of Art, 2017b). Comments by Maxwell K. Hearn, who was chairman of the Department of Asian art at the time, further emphasize how Tang's donation of this painting had a major impact on the museum's holdings of Chinese art: "This donation, together with earlier gifts and purchases made possible by Mr. Tang, Douglas Dillon, John M. Crawford Jr., and many others, gives The Met the ability to narrate one of the great stories in Chinese art: the rise of a grand tradition of monumental landscape painting in the 10th century and its transformation into a self-expressive art form from the 11th to the 14th century" (Metropolitan Museum of Art, 2017b).

Discourse about Tang's financial contribution to renovate the Chinese galleries in the late 1990s also highlights his specific engagement in Chinese cultural patronage. One press release notes how the Frances Young Tang Gallery, named after Tang's first wife in recognition of the family's gift, "will be the Museum's largest single gallery for the display of Chinese painting" and contribute to almost "doubl[ing] the square footage available for later Chinese art from 7,400 to 13,400 square feet" (Metropolitan Museum of Art, 1997). Press releases also convey how Tang made a significant impact on Chinese art at the museum through mentions of the curatorial position bearing his name and that of his second wife: "Oscar Tang and Agnes Hsu-Tang Associate Curator of Chinese Paintings" (Metropolitan Museum of Art, 2022c).

Like Ambani, discourse about Tang's Chinese cultural patronage frames it as motivated by ethnic and family heritage. The press release announcing his donation of *Riverbank* quoted Tang as saying:

> For a long time, my intention has been to donate *Riverbank* to The Metropolitan Museum of Art. I am making this gift now as an affirmation of my belief that The Met is an ideal platform on which to showcase the richness of the art and history of my family's heritage, and to care for what in China would be considered a "national treasure." Metropolitan Museum of Art (2017b)

Similarly, the 1994 press release about his family's gifts of Chinese art to the museum includes a quote from Tang where he links the gift to his ethnic identity and family history:

> Our family's connection to America goes back three generations. In the 1880s, our mother's father, B. C. Wen, was one of the "First Hundred" students sent by the Imperial Manchu court to study English and Western culture in the United States. Then in the 1920s, our father, P. Y. Tang, was awarded a Boxer Rebellion Indemnity Scholarship, which enabled him to study engineering at Massachusetts Institute of Technology. But it was my generation, displaced by war and revolution, that was taken in by America and it is here that we have made our home. Thus, it is with a profound sense of gratitude for the opportunities that this country has given us, as well as an appreciation for the Metropolitan Museum's important role in expanding public awareness of Chinese culture, that we make this gift. Metropolitan Museum of Art (1994b)

Discourse about Sir Joseph Hotung also highlights his involvement specifically in Chinese cultural patronage. Hotung, born in Shanghai to a wealthy family of Chinese and European ancestry, was a noted collector of Chinese art. The press release announcing his election to the board implicitly accentuates how Chinese art patronage qualified him for trusteeship by noting that he "owns one of the world's foremost private collections of Chinese archaic jade" (Metropolitan Museum of Art, 2000). Press releases about several exhibitions also call attention to Hotung's Chinese cultural patronage by including the statement: "The exhibition is made possible by the Joseph Hotung Fund" (Metropolitan Museum of Art, 2022c). Not only do press releases about exhibitions emphasize Hotung's Chinese cultural patronage, but they also highlight his monetary contributions for publishing catalogs featuring Chinese artists (Metropolitan Museum of Art, 2015b).

Museum discourse discusses not only individual Asian donors as supporting art produced by their co-ethnics but also Asian donors as a whole. This is illustrated by press around the 2015 Costume Institute Ball. The Costume Institute is the arm of the museum focusing on fashion. Each year, it holds a major fundraising ball, the Met Gala, notable in the worlds of art and entertainment, which also accompanies a major fashion exhibition. In 2015, the exhibition involved a collaboration between the Department of Asian Art and The Costume Institute. The exhibition, "China: Through the Looking Glass," explored how Western fashion has been influenced by Chinese aesthetics. A press release about the exhibition highlights Chinese cultural patronage by Chinese patrons by noting that among the sponsors of the exhibition were "several Chinese donors" (Metropolitan Museum of Art, 2015c). This phrase, describing Chinese patrons as a group rather than as individuals, is also used in other communication about the exhibition, such as a promotional video where this statement was flashed across the screen at the video's beginning (Metropolitan Museum of Art, 2015d). The phrase, along with a slight variation using the word "generous" between "several" and "Chinese," appeared three times in the exhibition catalog (Bolton et al., 2015).

Discourse about Japanese donors also highlights how they are especially involved in cultural patronage linked to their ethnicity. This is illustrated by discourse mentioning Dr. Rokuro Ishikawa, who served as an honorary trustee of the museum in the 1990s and 2000s. Ishikawa was born in Tokyo in 1925 to a prominent family, and his father worked as an executive at a large chemical company. Ishikawa was also employed as an executive, serving as the chairman of Kajima Corporation, a major construction firm, in the 1980s and 1990s. The discursive emphasis on Japanese patrons as being especially committed to Japanese cultural patronage is conveyed through how donors are discussed both as individuals and as a group. For example, in 1991, a reinstallation of the galleries featuring arms and armor involved a collection of Japanese arms and armor occupying a separate gallery to the right of the main equestrian court. In a press release about the Japanese gallery, Ishikawa is thanked for his role in helping to secure funding for the project. Collectively, Japanese donors are also recognized for contributing to the effort. Then-chair of the board, Arthur Ochs Sulzberger, commented that "the outstanding display of the Metropolitan's renowned collection of Japanese arms and armor in the new Arms and Armor Galleries would not be a reality were it not for the generosity of the Japanese corporate community," and that the support "has been made possible largely through the leadership of Dr. Rokuro Ishikawa" (Metropolitan Museum of Art, 1991a). Similarly, the museum's then-president said:

> Once again, a dynamic network of Japanese corporations, private organizations, and individuals has been forged to enable visitors to the Metropolitan from all over the world to experience the richness, diversity, and incomparable beauty of masterfully executed and historically important pieces. Metropolitan Museum of Art (1991a)

A press release about the larger renovation also highlights the collective role of Japanese donors in making the reinstallation of the Japanese galleries a reality by noting how "this could not have been possible were it not for the enthusiastic cooperation and generous financial support of Japanese private industry" (Metropolitan Museum of Art, 1991b).

Other museum documents also highlight how Japanese donors as a group are especially involved in Japanese cultural patronage at the museum. For example, a 1987 press release about the opening of the new Japanese galleries at the museum notes how the reinstallation has been made possible in part by funding from "New York's Japanese community" (Metropolitan Museum of Art, 1987). Similarly, a report about a major fundraising campaign at the museum mentions that in 1986–1987, the Arts of Japan Galleries were established in part from financial support from "Japanese corporations and individuals" (Metropolitan Museum of Art, 1994a).

To summarize, museum discourse describes Asian patrons as having different levels of commitment to specific subgenres of Asian art. Asian patrons are presented as having the most significant impact on the museum's activities related to art produced by their co-ethnics.

CONCLUSION

This chapter investigates the institutionalization of elite taste by analyzing Asian art patronage. Using the case of philanthropy at the Metropolitan Museum of Art, I conceptually elaborate and empirically illustrate different patterns of Asian art support by Asians and whites. Compared with white elites, Asian elites have been especially strong champions of Asian art at the museum. In addition, in comparison with one another, Asian elites have supported Asian art linked to their ancestral heritage at higher rates. These patterns highlight how race is a salient boundary distinguishing the museum patronage of Asians and whites, and ethnicity is a salient boundary distinguishing the patronage of Asians. To conclude, I discuss how this chapter advances research on the legitimation of elite taste, elite contributions to organizations and progressiveness within the elite.

As DiMaggio (1982a, 1982b) argued, art patronage is a practice that elites draw on to institutionalize their taste. In the 19th century, white elites legitimated their tastes through establishing fine arts museums and opera houses (Accominotti et al., 2018; DiMaggio, 1982a, 1982b; Lena, 2019). Although this art was not formally categorized by race, it was largely produced by white artists. Black elites have legitimated their own tastes through giving money to Black arts institutions and advocating for Black art at "mainstream" arts organizations (Banks, 2010b, 2019c, 2019d; Fleming & Roses, 2007). Here, I have sought to extend our understanding of elite cultural legitimation by elaborating how Asian elites have championed art linked to their own ethnoracial heritage at a major arts organization.

This chapter also sheds light on racial differences in elite contributions to organizations. A growing body of research documents how Black professionals are more likely than their white counterparts to make organizational contributions related to racial and ethnic diversity (Collins, 1997; Wingfield, 2019). For example, Black executives are more likely than white ones to hold racialized jobs, such as managerial positions related to affirmative action (Collins, 1997). Here, we have seen how the contributions of Asian elites to a major cultural organizations are distinct, thereby shedding further light on race and elite organizational contributions.

Finally, this chapter also sheds light on progressiveness within the elite. In their research, Richard L. Zweigenhaft and G. William Domhoff investigate whether or not members of the elite who are ethnoracial minorities are more likely than their majority counterparts to endorse liberal political positions (Zweigenhaft & Domhoff, 2011, p. 8, 2018). Scholarship on board diversity and corporate social responsibility asks a different but related question: Are firms that have a higher proportion of ethnoracial minorities on the board more socially responsible (Dodd et al., 2022)? These questions share a concern with whether or not ethnoracial minority elites are more progressive than white elites. This study offers unique insight into this question through a cultural lens by suggesting that with respect to the diversification of museums along one line – the integration of Asian art – Asian elites have been especially ardent advocates. At the same time,

Asian elites, like those from other racial and ethnic groups, engage in cultural practices that help to maintain their status.

As scholarship on cultural capital asserts, one mechanism used by elites to maintain their advantage is through institutionalizing their own tastes (Bourdieu et al., 1991; Bourdieu & Passeron, 1990). Given the growing racial and ethnic diversity of the elite (Zweigenhaft & Domhoff, 2011, 2018), a fuller understanding of the legitimation of elite tastes requires attention to the art patronage of Asians and other ethnoracial minorities.

NOTES

1. This is part of a broader turn in sociology that investigates how race and ethnicity organize consumption (Banks, 2018b, 2019a, 2020, 2021, 2022).

2. This chapter draws on data and analysis from a larger project on museum discourse relating to philanthropy. N-gram analysis and other computational methods were used to identify general patterns in the data. Through deep readings of the texts and images, themes emerging from these analyses were refined, and additional themes were identified.

3. Intercoder reliability was checked through comparing how select samples of text were coded by the author and a trained research assistant.

REFERENCES

Accominotti, F., Khan, S. R., & Storer, A. (2018). How cultural capital emerged in Gilded Age America: Musical purification and cross-class inclusion at the New York Philharmonic. *American Journal of Sociology, 123*(6), 1743–1783.

Banks, P. A. (2010a). Black cultural advancement: Racial identity and participation in the arts among the Black middle class. *Ethnic and Racial Studies, 33*(2), 272–289.

Banks, P. A. (2010b). *Represent: Art and identity among the Black upper-middle class.* Routledge.

Banks, P. A. (2017). Ethnicity, class, and trusteeship at African American and mainstream museums. *Cultural Sociology, 11*(1), 97–112.

Banks, P. A. (2018a). Money, museums, and memory: Cultural patronage by Black voluntary associations. *Ethnic and Racial Studies, 42*(15), 2529–2547.

Banks, P. A. (2018b). The rise of Africa in the contemporary auction market: Myth or reality? *Poetics, 71*, 7–17.

Banks, P. A. (2019a). Black artists and elite taste culture. *Contexts, 18*(2), 62–65.

Banks, P. A. (2019b). Cultural justice and collecting: Challenging the underrecognition of African American artists. In G. D. Johnson, S. A. Grier, K. Thomas, & A. K. Harrison (Eds.), *Race in the marketplace: Crossing critical boundaries.* Palgrave.

Banks, P. A. (2019c). *Diversity and philanthropy at African American museums: Black renaissance.* Routledge.

Banks, P. A. (2019d). High culture, Black culture: Strategic assimilation and cultural steering in museum philanthropy. *Journal of Consumer Culture, 21*(3), 660–682. https://doi.org/10.1177/1469540519846200

Banks, P. A. (2020). *Race, ethnicity, and consumption: A sociological view.* Routledge.

Banks, P. A. (2021). Branding indigeneity: Corporate patronage of the arts. *ICOFOM Study Series, 49*(1), 56–66.

Banks, P. A. (2022). *Black Culture, Inc.: How ethnic community support pays for corporate America.* Stanford University Press.

Bolton, A., & Galliano, J., & Metropolitan Museum of Art. (2015). *China: Through the looking glass.* Metropolitan Museum of Art.

Bourdieu, P. (1984). *Distinction: A social critique of the judgement of taste.* Harvard University Press.

PATRICIA A. BANKS

Bourdieu, P., Darbel, A., & Schnapper, D. (1991). *The love of art: European art museums and their public*. Polity Press.

Bourdieu, P., & Passeron, J.-C. (1990). *Reproduction in education, society and culture* (R. Nice, Trans.). Sage Publications.

Collins, S. M. (1997). *Black corporate executives: The making and breaking of a Black middle class*. Temple University Press.

DiMaggio, P. (1982a). Cultural entrepreneurship in nineteenth-century Boston, part II: The classification and framing of American art. *Media, Culture & Society, 4*, 303–322.

DiMaggio, P. (1982b). Cultural entrepreneurship in nineteenth-century Boston: The creation of an organizational base for high culture. *Media, Culture & Society, 4*, 33–50.

Dodd, O., Frijns, B., & Garel, A. (2022). Cultural diversity among directors and corporate social responsibility, *International Review of Financial Analysis, 83*. https://doi.org/10.1016/j.irfa.2022. 102337

Fleming, C. M., & Roses, L. E. (2007). Black cultural capitalists: African-American elites and the organization of the arts in early twentieth century Boston. *Poetics, 35*, 368–387.

Lena, J. C. (2019). *Entitled: Discriminating tastes and the expansion of the arts*. Princeton University Press.

Metropolitan Museum of Art. (1987, March). *New galleries from Japanese art to open at the Metropolitan Museum* [Press release]. https://libmma.contentdm.oclc.org/digital/collection/p16028coll12/id/8478/rec/406

Metropolitan Museum of Art. (1991a, October). *Japanese international business community provides major support for Metropolitan Museum's new arms and armor galleries* [Press kit]. https://libmma.contentdm.oclc.org/digital/collection/p16028coll12/id/10121/rec/2

Metropolitan Museum of Art. (1991b). *Arms and armor galleries re-opening* [Press kit]. https://libmma.contentdm.oclc.org/digital/collection/p16028coll12/id/17007/rec/1

Metropolitan Museum of Art. (1994a). *The fund for the Met*. Metropolitan Museum of Art. https://libmma.contentdm.oclc.org/digital/collection/p15324coll10/id/239050/rec/189

Metropolitan Museum of Art. (1994b, January). *Unprecedented gift of Chinese paintings from Asian-American family on view at Metropolitan through April* [Press release]. https://libmma.contentdm.oclc.org/digital/collection/p16028coll12/id/10671/rec/1

Metropolitan Museum of Art. (1997, April 3). *Metropolitan Museum announces major renovation and reinstallation of galleries for Chinese art opening May 22, 1997* [Press release]. https://libmma.contentdm.oclc.org/digital/collection/p16028coll12/id/5508/rec/1

Metropolitan Museum of Art. (1998, May 20). *Metropolitan Museum to open new gallery for Korean art on June 9* [Press release]. https://libmma.contentdm.oclc.org/digital/collection/p16028coll12/id/5029/rec/11

Metropolitan Museum of Art. (2015a, March 16). *Landmark gifts of art and funding dramatically enhance Met Museum's Asian Art Department as yearlong program of exhibitions and activities begins, celebrating department's centennial* [Press release]. https://www.metmuseum.org/press/news/2015/landmark-gifts-for-asian-art-department

Metropolitan Museum of Art. (2015b, March 16). *Landscapes by revered Chinese painter Wang Hui in fall exhibition at Metropolitan Museum* [Press release]. https://www.metmuseum.org/press/exhibitions/2008/landscapes-by-revered-chinese-painter-wang-hui-in-fall-exhibition-at-metropolitan-museum

Metropolitan Museum of Art. (2015c, May 4). *China: Through the looking glass* [Press release]. https://www.metmuseum.org/press/exhibitions/2015/china-through-the-looking-glass

Metropolitan Museum of Art. (2015d, May 12). *China: Through the looking glass—gallery views* [Video]. YouTube. https://www.youtube.com/watch?v=NUOcySpiX80

Metropolitan Museum of Art. (2015e, May 11). *Asian art 100* [Press release]. https://www.metmuseum.org/press/exhibitions/2015/asian-art-100-release

Metropolitan Museum of Art. (2017a). *The Met Winter Party 2017 honoree: Nita Ambani* [Video transcript]. https://web.archive.org/web/20170221064525/https://www.metmuseum.org/metmedia/video/news/met-winter-party-honoree-nita-ambani

84 Asian Art Patronage

Metropolitan Museum of Art. (2017b, March 3). The Met receives monumental 10th-century Chinese painting *Riverbank* from Oscar L. Tang [Press release]. https://www.metmuseum.org/press/news/2017/riverbank

Metropolitan Museum of Art. (2017c, October 10). *Reliance Foundation provides landmark gift to The Met* [Press release]. https://www.metmuseum.org/press/news/2017/reliance-foundation

Metropolitan Museum of Art. (2018, February 8). *Diamond Mountains: Travel and nostalgia in Korean art* [Press release]. https://www.metmuseum.org/press/exhibitions/2018/diamond-mountains

Metropolitan Museum of Art. (2019a, May 31). *Phenomenal nature: Mrinalini Mukherjee* [Press release]. https://www.metmuseum.org/press/exhibitions/2019/mrinalini-mukherjee

Metropolitan Museum of Art. (2019b, November 12). *Nita Ambani elected to the board of The Metropolitan Museum of Art* [Press release]. https://www.metmuseum.org/press/news/2019/nita-ambani

Metropolitan Museum of Art. (2000, November 9). *Sir Joseph Hotung becomes trustee of the Metropolitan Museum of Art* [Press release]. https://www.metmuseum.org/press/news/2000/sir-joseph-hotung-becomes-trustee-of-the-metropolitan-museum-of-art

Metropolitan Museum of Art. (2022a, March 10). *Lesley Ma named inaugural Ming Chu Hsu and Daniel Xu Associate Curator of Asian Art in the Department of Modern and Contemporary Art at The Met* [Press release]. https://www.metmuseum.org/press/news/2022/lesley-ma

Metropolitan Museum of Art. (2022b, September 6). *The Metropolitan Museum of Art announces $10 million gift from Michael ByungJu Kim* [Press release]. https://www.metmuseum.org/press/news/2022/gift-from-michael-byungju-kim

Metropolitan Museum of Art. (2022c, September 10). *Exhibition at The Met explores themes of the natural world in Chinese Art* [Press release]. https://www.metmuseum.org/press/exhibitions/2022/noble-virtues

Metropolitan Museum of Art. (2011, October 24). *Metropolitan Museum to open renovated galleries for the art of the Arab Lands, Turkey, Iran, Central Asia, and Later South Asia* [Press release]. https://www.metmuseum.org/press/exhibitions/2011/renovated-galleries-for-the-art-of-the-arab-lands-turkey-iran-central-asia-and-later-south-asia

"Mukesh Ambani" (n.d.). *Forbes*. https://www.forbes.com/profile/mukesh-ambani/

U.S. Census Bureau. (2021). *Current population survey, 1968 to 2021 annual social and economic supplements (CPS ASEC)*. https://www.census.gov/content/dam/Census/library/visualizations/2021/demo/p60-273/figure2.pdf

U.S. Census Bureau. (2022a). *2019 Data show baby boomers nearly 9 times wealthier than millennials*. https://www.census.gov/library/stories/2022/08/wealth-inequality-by-household-type.html

U.S. Census Bureau. (2022b). *Table 3. Detailed years of school completed by people 25 years and over by sex, age groups, race and Hispanic origin: 2021*. https://perma.cc/KD54-DRXT. https://www.census.gov/data/tables/2021/demo/educational-attainment/cps-detailed-tables.html

Wingfield, A. H. (2019). *Flatlining: Race, work, and health care in the new economy*. University of California Press.

Zweigenhaft, R. L., & Domhoff, G. W. (2011). *The new CEOs: Women, African American, Latino and Asian American leaders of Fortune 500 companies*. Rowman & Littlefield.

Zweigenhaft, R. L., & Domhoff, G. W. (2018). *Diversity in the power elite: Ironies and unfulfilled promises*. Rowman & Littlefield.

CHAPTER 4

DECOLONIZING PORTO? THINKING ON THE PORTUGUESE "UNFINISHED" DECOLONIZATION PROCESS FROM A COLLABORATIVE ACTION-RESEARCH PROJECT WITH THE CITY'S BLACK COMMUNITIES

Lígia Ferro[a], Beatriz Lacerda[a], Lydia Matthews[b] and Susan Meiselas[c]

[a]University of Porto, Portugal
[b]The New School, USA
[c]Magnum Photos Cooperative, USA

ABSTRACT

The repercussions of Portugal's colonialism are not widely discussed. The marks of colonialism in the public space are still present in the urban landscape of Portuguese cities. Despite the growing activity of the Black movement's in the country, they are still not being systematically considered in the design of public policies. Moreover, the Portuguese census does not include any data collection on ethnic belonging. Therefore, it is difficult to deepen the knowledge of the Black communities. The Black community has been growing in Porto, the second-largest city in Portugal and it remains highly invisible. Starting from a collaborative project between Portuguese and American professionals, acting in the fields of sociology and socially engaged curatorial and contemporary art practices, an experimental approach was developed to map and cocreate with the Black community in Porto. By using digital tools while collecting, analyzing, and sharing data, and by applying an ethnographic

Elites, Nonelites, and Power
Political Power and Social Theory, Volume 41, 85–109
Copyright © 2025 Lígia Ferro, Beatriz Lacerda, Lydia Matthews and Susan Meiselas
Published under exclusive licence by Emerald Publishing Limited
ISSN: 0198-8719/doi:10.1108/S0198-871920240000041004

approach and techniques of exploration from documentary photography, the team developed a collaborative project side by side with the community. An exchange between disciplinary knowledge and "various subject positions," with all participants engaging in an exploration of how to begin decolonizing the city through those tools took place at the project TRAVESSIA. This chapter explores how the Black nonelite is expressing and questioning race and ethnic inequalities in Porto by discussing the results of this collaborative project.

Keywords: Decolonization; Porto; Black communities; White elites; collaborative ethnography

INTRODUCTION

Starting from the second axis of the theoretical approach for this volume, "what is the relative power of elites and nonelites," we will explore how it is possible that almost 50 years after the process of decolonization initiated by Portugal's April 25, 1974 Carnation Revolution, Black communities remain largely invisible and face the lack of access to different fields, services, and resources of society in the country (housing, work, education, culture). Additionally, we will explore how this Black nonelite is expressing and questioning race and ethnic inequalities in the country and namely in Porto, the second-largest Portuguese city. On the one hand, we wish to account for and interrogate how a contemporary White elite in Portugal – including members of academic and cultural communities – have not yet adequately questioned the underprivileged and unequal position and social conditions of local Black people within intellectual and cultural production. What systemic or unconscious forces have contributed to making these disturbing social power relationships remain in place in Portugal – or render their dynamics largely invisible within the critical discourses practiced in research, learning, and cultural programming sites?

On the other hand, we believe it is possible to counter this deeply ingrained tendency by introducing new participatory creative processes that produce alternative narratives in the form of visual data, displayed in a public arena. In this text, we will examine how a Black nonelite critically articulated their experiences of racial and ethnic inequalities by participating in an experimental, interdisciplinary, and internationally generated art project. Entitled *TRAVESSIA*, this 2020–2021 project sought to bring together artists and scholars, specializing in both Visual Culture and Sociology, and Black community members living in the city of Porto. Providing the time and space necessary to share disciplinary expertise and diverse life experiences promoted by the CI.CLO platform and their Biennial '21 Photography of Porto, *TRAVESSIA* generated new forms of visual data that reveal fresh evidence of the complex relationship between elites and nonelites.

As Richard Lachmann pointed out, the relationship between elites and nonelites shapes social inequalities and reinforces the power of elites (in this case, the White elite). As we can see from Lachmann's last works, the global colonial empires maintained and strengthened their powers by using force and violence against colonized populations. Lachman defines an elite as "a group of rulers who inhabit a distinct organizational apparatus with the capacity to appropriate resources from nonelites" (Lachmann, 2020, p. 26). He adds that Portugal's elites were no exception. However, intellectual debate on the means and processes of imposing power on the White elites in former Portuguese colonies hasn't had wide repercussions in Portuguese society so far.

In this chapter, we aim to provide a theoretical framework of Portuguese society and the place of racism within it. In dialogue with Lachmann's contribution to the concept of elites, we wish to root the action-research project *TRAVESSIA* developed in the city of Porto, Portugal.[1]

THEORETICAL FRAMEWORK: WHITE ELITES IN PORTUGAL, A COUNTRY OF RACIST "SOFT MANNERS"

As Lachmann states, "elites differ from ruling classes in two significant ways" (Lachmann, 2020, p. 26). Following Marxist theory, ruling classes aim to reproduce the exploitation of the producing class. Lachmann adds that in the case of elites, besides this first interest, they also invest in "guarding its existing power from, and extending its power at the expense of, rival elites" (Lachmann, 2020, p. 26). The capacity to pursue elites' interests stems from "the structure of relations among various coexisting elites as much as from interclass relations of production" (Lachmann, 2020, p. 26). Consequently, elite conflict constitutes the real threat to elite capacities. Frequently, elites solved conflicts with nonelites through the combination of their "organizational capacities into a single institution" (Lachmann, 2020, p. 27). This was the process of feeding the formation of the states. As the author explains, elites dominate and extract resources from rival elites and nonelites by exercising a set of powers: economic, political, military, and ideological. Imperialism created new elites.

The Portuguese Colonial Empire was the first global empire in history and is considered the oldest of the modern European colonial empires, spanning almost six centuries from the Conquest of Ceuta in 1415 to the devolution of sovereignty over Macau to China in 1999.[2] The Portuguese Colonial Empire in Africa lasted from 1890 to 1975. Several anti-colonial armed movements took action since 1961, first in Angola and then in Mozambique and Guinea-Bissau. A tremendous and bloodthirsty war was fed by the Portuguese dictatorship in the African colonies. Many of the massacres and brutal episodes of this war are now brought to light, especially in the turn of the 21st Century (Afonso & Gomes, 2000).

Trapped by a *lack of memory*, Portugal shares an unfinished decolonization with other former European colonial empires. Debates regarding the colonial empire have only recently emerged in the country. We know that the images of the colonial past present in official discourses "are connected with a certain «amnesic memory» that values the nation from the perspective of the uniqueness of the 'Discoveries,' the specificity of the Portuguese presence in the world and the legacies left in the former colonies" (Cardina, 2016).

Portugal is commonly described as a country of "soft manners," good hosts, and a tolerant spirit. These representations are transmitted from the first school cycle when we learn about the Portuguese's journey through unknown territories and how they relate with other peoples (Araújo & Maeso, 2010, 2013, 2019; Cahen, 2018). There is an idea of *soft colonization*, based on the myth of the Portuguese explorer who was friendly, curious, and an educator, as opposed to the versions of the colonized peoples, who felt invaded and subjugated. Not only do we know that was never a truthful version, but also, this persistent denial contributes to postponing a critical discussion on colonial heritage and ignoring the consequences for the country's African and Afro-descendant communities.

The perpetuation of these "soft manners" narratives is a consequence of the monopoly of White elites with imperialist traits, who continue to argue about the compassion of the Portuguese as good colonialists, supposedly contributing to the development of the colonized countries. Despite the Herculean efforts of many researchers and the Black activist and associative movement (Henriques, 2020; Kilomba, 2020; Roldão et al., 2023), denials of the existence of racial inequalities in Portugal and the consequent invisibility of ethnic minorities remain strong. If on the one hand, there has been a proliferation of social sciences, media, and artistic discourses on the urgency of discussing these issues (Pardue, 2014; Raposo et al., 2021), on the other hand – at almost at the same pace – political forces whitewash these inequalities through an appeal to the native Portuguese, "of first category" (Figueiredo et al., 2021). These ideas and beliefs have been used by far-right forces, such as the emergent party Chega, which lately has been spreading racist and xenophobic ideas and gaining political support from voters (e.g., from 2019 to 2024, the party grew from 1 to 50 representatives).

The Myth of Luso-tropicalism

To understand the power of this narrative, it is important to discuss its ideology, based on the myth of Luso-tropicalism. A benevolent belief system about the Portuguese presence in the colonies, Luso-tropicalism was developed by Gilberto Freyre in his 1933 work Casa-Grande e Sanzala ("The Masters and the Slaves"). As Freyre asserted, "(...) after exhaustive research in national and foreign archives he published his book that revolutionized social studies in Brazil (...)" (Freyre, 1992, p. xi). Throughout his work, the sociologist (White) analyzes the process of Portuguese colonization in Brazil, reconfiguring its dynamics to prove that this was, after all, a good investment in Brazil's economic "awakening." Under the belief of Luso-tropicalism, Freyre (1992) sustains, in long and detailed chapters, the advantages of the "civilizing effort of the Portuguese" (Freyre, 1992, p. 16), whose presence "(...) promoted the mixing of races, latifundium agriculture and slavery, making possible, on such cornerstones, the foundation and development of the great agricultural colony in the tropics" (Freyre, 1992, p. 18). Not surprisingly, the word "invasion" is not mentioned.

Gilberto Freyre's thesis was not always welcomed as it is believed, even during Estado Novo (the name for the dictatorial Portuguese regime, from 1933 to 1974) because "(...) this caused great anxiety to the Portuguese elites since the possibility of biological miscegenation was read as an opening to racial degeneration." (Figueiredo et al., 2021, p. 174). It was only three decades later – and only in response to political pressure from the United Nations to dilute the Portuguese colonial presence in Africa – that Freyre became valued as an assuring resource in the face of the good conditions that held the colonies together. In this period, Freyre was officially invited by the Portuguese state to come and discuss his now highly appreciated observations of the cordial and positive relations that the Portuguese had created with the Indigenous peoples.

Freyre's proposal was that the Portuguese already had natural aptitudes for "(...) biological miscegenation and cultural interpenetration [that] resulted from the mixed nature of the Portuguese themselves, who emerged from long contact with the Moors and Jews in the Iberian Peninsula" (Figueiredo et al., 2021, p. 175). This was very well received, with the exception of biological (which was then replaced by cultural) miscegenation, avoiding the idea of "impure" racial crossing (Figueiredo et al., 2021).

This thesis would justify a few more years of Portuguese exploration in African territory, with the proper legal and linguistic shortcuts to avoid further pressures, and under the pretext that Portugal was a multicultural and multi-continental country that had expanded harmoniously to the "overseas provinces" (Bucaioni, 2016). After serving the strategic purpose of redeeming the country politically in that period, the notion of Luso-tropicalism remained in the collective historical and social representation of the Portuguese way of being.

Even today, it is a redemptive banner used in political and media debates, in schools, and in the wisdom of common sense (Paredes, 2016). Figueiredo et al. (2021) recall how this representation of Portuguese benevolence remains to this day not only in media and everyday discourse but also in institutional arrangements and discourses on immigration – as if the friendly tradition of Luso-tropicalism was maintained.

White Elites' Power over Social Narratives

This ideology helps preserve the White elites' power: the idea of Lusophony becomes understood as an aggregating link between Portugal and the PALOP countries (African Countries of Portuguese-speaking African Countries). During the colonial period, the Portuguese language was forced upon and spread in many countries and territories. However, today, the contexts in which the language was spread are ignored to highlight proudly the wide presence of Portuguese in the world. At the same time, some institutional and educational narratives use the language to remake a closeness between Portugal and the colonized countries, neglecting that "to consider that only one identity category, language, can forge a 'Lusophone' community configures a neo-colonial arrogance because it becomes evident that the supposed Lusophony of the members of the CPLP is not enough to establish this new international identity (...)" (Varela, 2012, p. 13). If, on the one hand, language has the power to connect and can be used as a tool to reinforce new links between these groups, on the other hand, that relationship should not be falsely based on harmonious past traditions, especially because those inequalities continue to the present day (Bucaioni, 2016; Lopes, 2016).

In Portugal today, immigrant communities still face serious disadvantages compared to the White population. These exist in the various spheres of social life – in work, access to housing, education, health and political participation, and civil society representation (Martins & Moura, 2018). In the case of African immigrants and also African descendants, these conditions are compounded by exposure to racist and neocolonial behaviour, which aggravates the well-known cycle of inequalities: their members tend to work in the most precarious and less qualified jobs, which leads to bigger obstacles in full access to housing, education, health care, political participation, and decision-making (Roldão, 2015).

The consequences of these inequalities – and their denial – are present in racist expressions and in what Black people face through exposure to precarious work and health situations, as well as in the urban ghettoization of these groups. But also, such consequences are present through absence: in decision-making positions, in the diversity of professions, in media platforms, in public space. These absences are not invisibilities. People do not choose to hide. Rather, this is a process of social invisibilization by dominant, White elites, who invest in collective efforts to preserve their positions of power (Martins, 2019). They hide behind arguments like Luso-tropicalism, reinforced by long-standing intercultural relations that even today continue to praise Lusophony.

The *TRAVESSIA* project team took aim at the myths and habit patterns that allow racism to perpetuate in the Portuguese context. By envisioning an ethnographical research-intervention approach, following the tendency to look into arts and culture as contexts and tools for identity (re)construction and social mobilization (Poveda et al., 2018), team members began to explore the social conditions, experiences, and practices of the African and African-descendent communities of Porto. Listening carefully to Black residents describe their lived experiences in areas in the city that had personal significance to them, the cocreators of *TRAVESSIA* developed social and artistic strategies to illuminate their counternarratives within the University of Porto's gallery space, thus tackling and undermining the power of White elites in Portugal.

HISTORY, FORM, AND SOCIOLOGICAL AND ARTISTIC METHODOLOGY OF THE *TRAVESSIA* PROJECT

TRAVESSIA began in the Fall of 2020, when curator Lydia Matthews (Director of Parsons Curatorial Design Research Lab/The New School, New York) was invited by Ci.CLO's Artistic Director, Virgílio Ferreira, to generate a socially engaged art project during the COVID-19 pandemic for the Biennial'21 Photography of Porto (Fig. 1). Matthews selected photographer Susan Meiselas (Magnum Photo Foundation, New York), to envision a site-specific work that expanded her 2004 *Cova da Moura* project, made in Lisbon in collaboration with the Cape Verdean community.[3] One of several international photographic projects featured within Ci.CLO's overall thematic "What Happens to the World

Fig. 1. Installation View of *TRAVESSIA*, Biennal'21 Photography of Porto, Reitoria da Universidade of Porto, Gallery One. May 19 – June 27, 2021. *Credits:* © 2021 Susan Meiselas.

Happens to Us," Meiselas' and Matthews' contribution was slotted for display as a formal exhibition in the Rectory of the University of Porto, Portugal. Responding to the passionate uprisings of the Black Lives Matter Movement in the wake of George Floyd's recent murder and the active debates regarding decolonizing university/cultural institutions structures and practices in the United States, both artist and curator sought to understand how these political and discursive issues were being addressed at the time in Portugal, both in the university and in the streets.

At the outset, Virgílio Ferreira from Ci.CLO, the artist and the curator contacted Lígia Ferro (University of Porto, Department of Sociology, Faculty of Arts and Humanities) to learn from her scholarly research addressing immigrant communities, including Black artist residents in the country (Ferro et al., 2016) and her former work on visual sociology (Ferro, 2005). They invited her to participate as a collaborator in exploring themes of the presence and invisibility of African and African descendant communities in Porto. Ferro encouraged Beatriz Lacerda, a Masters' student at that time,[4] to join the project, as well as Dori Nigro, a Black Brazilian-born graduate student and activist performance artist,[5] who was her former student in the course *Urban Ethnography* (Faculty of Arts and Humanities, University of Porto). Together, they formed the University of Porto's interdisciplinary team, working together with Meiselas and Matthews. Because of the logistical complexities brought on by collaborating across international borders during the global pandemic, Matthews invited Cinthia Bodenhorst (University of Vigo, Fine Arts Faculty) to advise the team as the Artistic and Design Coordinator, bringing additional video, exhibition design, and A.R. expertise to the project.

The network of participants grew immediately. Nigro introduced Ferro to Maria Cláudia Henriques, a respected elder who was serving as President and Director of the *Associação Luso-Africana Ponto nos Is* (The Luso-African Association), an institution whose main objective is to support the integration of Immigrant Communities in the Host Community. Lacerda contacted Ismael Calliano, an emerging actor who had immigrated from Mozambique as a child; soon both Henriques and Calliano were connecting the team to people from within their Black social circles, including local barbers, boxers, entrepreneurs, musicians, families living in housing projects, LGBTQAI+ activists, and others (Fig. 2).[6]

Fig. 2. Beatriz Lacerda's Drawing Illuminating the human network formed through the co-creation of *TRAVESSIA*, Featured on One Exhibition Wall. *Credits:* Beatriz Lacerda, Biennal'21 Photography of Porto, Rectory of the University of Porto, Gallery One.

Participants were invited to take walks around Porto to show the team members specific sites and tell their stories in connection with the city – places of inclusion, exclusion, success, and racism. We know how territory is crucial in engaging with urban cultures (Lachmann, 1988), and this dimension remained central to our understanding and work on the Black communities of Porto. Because the global pandemic imposed international travel bans, Meiselas – a documentary photographer famous for her on-the-ground, immersive, community-based techniques – was unable to physically join participants on their walks in Porto. She and Matthews overcame this limitation by accompanying each person using the Zoom platform and deploying the camera in Lacerda's mobile phone (Fig. 3). The walks, therefore, simultaneously took place physically and virtually, with Lacerda and Ferro (due to confinement and childcare, the last sometimes participated online) – and occasionally Bodenhorst – allowing participants to be interviewed across distances.

Fig. 3. Screenshot of Maria Cláudia Henriques' Guided Tour. *Credits:* © 2021 Susan Meiselas.

These exchanges were often videotaped on site and recorded on Zoom; Meiselas would also snap photographic stills from the walks on her computer, capturing visual clues of the stories being shared. After each encounter, team members analyzed and revised their process as needed, often returning to the original participants to glean further information. Even though it was not possible for the artist and curator to gather physically in Porto until the week of the gallery installation in May 2021, the team's core members conferred regularly through digital platforms over a period of 6 months.

Before long, the artist and curator had heard dozens of rich stories about the city of Porto as seen from a Black perspective but had little physical evidence other than hours of unedited camera and video footage. To capture these important Black narratives in ways that could be exhibited publicly, team members took up two strategies: they began editing short videos featuring highlights of the walks (Fig. 4), and they hosted a photographic annotation

Fig. 4. Screenshot of Dori Nigro's Guided Tour. *Credits:* © 2021 Susan Meiselas.

workshop in April 2021, mediated by Meiselas, Ferro, Lacerda, Matthews, and Nigro. In the workshop, participants inscribed their stories onto printed Zoom-derived photographs. They were also invited to offer their own meaningful images from family photo albums or contribute any artifacts that could serve as signifiers of their story. Each annotated photograph revealed how deeply ingrained racist attitudes can be, and how Black community members experience a sense of joy and resilience in the face of such challenges. Their walks and insights served as testimonies to the long way Portugal still has to go in resolving these matters.

TRAVESSIA aimed to embody an inclusive, transformative, and participatory methodological design, including research outcomes and artistic results, as presented in the exhibition that premiered in May 2021. The accumulation of dozens of annotated photographs, artifacts from the community and the artistic process, and QR codes in the form of Angolan sona-inspired drawings that could be triggered through the audience's cellphones to show short videos that further illuminated the annotated photographs. These objects and images were superimposed onto an expansive, neutral diagram of Porto's city's streets, suggesting that the exhibition space itself constituted a "re-mapping" of the city from a Black nonelite perspective – a limitless and deliberately unfinished project.

During the five-week exhibition, *TRAVESSIA* – displayed in the gallery of the University of Porto, in the heart of the city – was an artistic intervention functioning as an initiative of decolonization of the academy and cultural spaces, typically not very diverse in their uses and appropriations. Viewers to the exhibition not only accessed the annotated photographs, videos, and artifacts arising from the walking tours, but also witnessed provocative video performances by the artist Dori Nigro which will be discussed in the following section. Viewers were invited to participate in a public Town Hall-style roundtable discussion to further explore the exhibition's themes, which was well attended by project participants as well as additional audience members. The exhibition enjoyed coverage by the media, helping to disseminate *TRAVESSIA's* layered messages. Additionally, Lacerda offered docent tours of the exhibition to university students and activist groups from the city, allowing the exhibition to serve as an activated platform for ongoing community-building among members of the Black communities in Porto, and prompting discursive interaction across racial lines.

DECOLONIZING PORTO – ANALYZING THE ACTION-RESEARCH PROJECT DATA

For the remainder of this chapter, we will present and discuss five artistic pieces featured in *TRAVESSIA* – two video performances by Dori Nigro and three annotated photographs by Luciane Araújo, Mauricio Igor, and Ismael Calliano – which in the words of these African and Afro-descendant participants, describe the persistent effects of the colonial legacy in Portugal and the consequences of the "historical amnesia" hiding them. They manifest the tension between elites and nonelites, here marked not only by socio-economic conditions but primarily by ethnic-racial belonging.

We also reinforce the importance of the collaborative nature of this project, in the collection, exhibition, and reflection of all the data and materials, which sought to subvert the still common tendencies of White saviorism or even exoticization of the *Other*.

DORI NIGRO: NAVIGATING THE COLONIZED ROADS OF PORTO

Dori produced two video performances exclusively for TRAVESSIA, where he connected the socioemotional and political meanings of his trajectory in Porto with the physicality of streets and crossroads in the city. This has been ongoing research carried out by Dori and his collaborators, that we see here as a living performance, expandable to the streets and in a never-ending dialogue with the city. Through his powerful and metaphorical approach, Dori shares his and others' experiences navigating the colonized roads of Porto in *Porto Nigro* and in *Exú na Álvares Cabral*.

Porto Nigro

The first video performance, *Porto-Nigro* (14′) features Dori standing in front of a blackboard wall, drawing his emotional map of Porto, using chalk to inscribe his position as an Afro-Brazilian immigrant in the city.[7] As the time passes, we see his body moving to draw, we listen to his voice describing the feelings associated with the words, like an intimate guided tour to his subjective trajectory, and consequently, a reflection on Black and African presence in the colonial streets of Porto.

As shown in Fig. 5, starting from upper left to upper right, he writes names of places such as *MARQUÊS*, as one of the most intercultural squares in Porto, where he found African barbers (*SALÃO AFRO*) and felt welcomed. Next to this word, we see the question *DESCOBRIDOR DO BRASIL?* (Discoverer of Brazil?) about the following name ÁLVARES CABRAL, who was the head-sailor and commander of the first Portuguese vessels to arrive in Brazil. Along with street names and statues, Álvares Cabral remains as an icon in the colonial narrative of Portugal's lost empire, being a central figure in history school books as the man who discovered Brazil, with no counternarrative about the social conditions of that invasion and the true meaning of "discovery" of a country with long traditions and native inhabitants. On the right side, we see the acronym *FBAUP* (Fine Arts Faculty of the University of Porto), the institution Dori attended, where he was the only Black student – a place which he associates with feelings of *XENOFOBIA* (Xenophobia).

As we see Dori producing a psycho-geography of Porto, we listen to his speech (inspired by Franz Fanon's arguments on "Black Skin, White Masks" (2008)).

Fig. 5. Screenshot of Dori Nigro's Video Performance *Porto Nigro*. Credits: © 2021 Susan Meiselas.

For example, he addresses Álvares Cabral and the urgency of facing the Portuguese colonial legacy:

> Álvares Cabral, a heritage of public interest, discoverer of Brazil. We must decolonize the Discoveries, the manuals, and the pedagogies that make children identify themselves with the fear of the good colonizers (...) how much is a Black body in the university? Where are Black bodies on maps? How many voices would want to speak if they were not silenced? (...) What did you expect when you took away the gag that closed our mouths? (...) I am imprisoned in an image that I am not: a good image that I am not: good Black man, bad Black man, dumb Black man, intelligent Black man, ugly Black, cute Black (...) it is necessary to decolonize thinking (...) it is necessary to denigrate the universities, the biennials, the arts.

The term denigrate ("denegrir"; to turn Black = turn negro) has been a cause for reflection and reinterpretation (Noguera, 2022). If for years it was a common term to refer to the act of making something worse, less acceptable, less pure, more recently it has been read as a racist expression, which associated Blackness with processes of rottenness. However, when Dori (together with the collective work of Anti-Racist Nucleus of Porto) refers here to the act of denigrating, he does so by subverting the meaning. *Denigrating* public spaces, the arts, and the universities, becomes the next step for decolonization. To decolonize these places is also to achieve independence and Afro-centered epistemological reconfiguration, where the Black subject is no longer in the margin but the center (Kilomba, 2020; Noguera, 2022).

Returning to Dori's questions about the absence of Black bodies in universities and the urgency to decolonize textbooks, these are two self-fueling problems. Not only the link between racial discrimination and academic achievement has been more than proven (Roldão, 2015), but also the colonialist content and the

Euro-centric pedagogy of the classes and textbooks tend to marginalize students who are not White.

Every year in Portugal, racialized and immigrant children are being disproportionately penalized at school, with higher failure rates, leading to greater restrictions in socio-professional choices, thus keeping them out of decision-making positions and higher education degrees (fewer students, fewer teachers). This is not only connected to larger inequalities that these groups face. It's also linked to the pedagogic and social organization of schools and other educational centers which privilege White-culture references, thereby producing discriminating schoolbooks. This can be seen in the work of Araújo and Maeso (2019), where Black enslaved people are described as a product imported by Portuguese explorers, alongside sugar cane and spices.

ÉXU in Álvares Cabral

A second performance video featured in the exhibition was Nigro's *Exú na Álvares Cabral*, also created specifically to complement the annotated photographs and charged objects in the exhibition.[8] Expanding on the re-mapping themes inherent in *Porto Nigro*, the artist takes us to a specific intersection in the city that bears the name of the murderous explorer who "discovered" Brazil. In this performance video (Fig. 6), Nigro and his collaborators Madalena Rodrigues, Luciana Vieira, and Igor Nolasco call upon the trickster spirit of Exú, the Yoruban god of the crossroads, by releasing red and black smoke at the corners of the intersection to evoke the diety's symbolic colors and power. With a Yoruban language voice-over by Caroline Odeyale, African sounds and ephemeral spiritual iconography are superimposed onto the neighborhood where the artist is living in Porto. The relationship with the

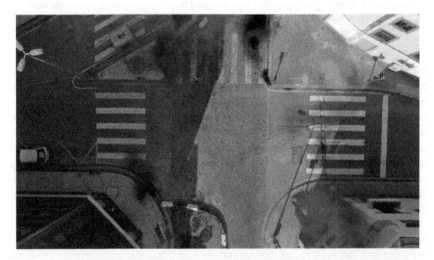

Fig. 6. Screenshot of Dori Nigro's Video Performance *Exú na Álvares Cabral ("Exú in Álvares Cabral")*. *Credits:* © 2021 Susan Meiselas.

Yoruban voice-over is crucial because it comes from the body of a Black woman who has suffered racism, harassment, and xenophobia. Amid all these international layers, Caroline's voice overlaid onto this street (from where her family was evicted twice), evokes an ancestry visible in the fire (black and red) brought by Exú, that is transformative. For a moment, and even if only in this performance, these forces are superimposed on the fiery chaos of coloniality that stifles these streets. In this dialogue, guided by Caroline's evocation, symbolic doors of reparation are opened.

Shot from above by a drone, the video editing shifts inconsistently, with figures moving forward and backward in space, refusing to conform to the dictates of Western linear time. The artist's decolonial lens reveals how Portuguese daily life could be understood in relation to African religions and metaphysics when seen from the position of a nonelite.

LUCIANE DE ARAÚJO SANTOS: THE FEELING OF "STRANGE IMMIGRANT" IN PORTUGUESE ACADEMIA

On the same topic, Luciane, an Afro-Brazilian teacher who came to Portugal to do her master's degree in African Studies, revealed the first time we talked how she felt when she arrived here and realized how maladjusted, inappropriate, and whitewashed the curriculum was. Contrary to her expectations about the prestige of European universities, she became disillusioned with what she experienced at the University of Porto.

The building in Fig. 7 is the Faculty of Arts and Humanities of University of Porto, shot by Luciane on her first day of classes. In her annotated photograph, Luciane starts by placing this information to the reader, admitting her "expectations around a new history, a new place" (translating from the first text on the upper left). Continuing to the right side of the annotated photograph, Luciane reveals she encountered "Watchful eyes, 'well-meaning' phrases, phrases like: 'colonization wasn't that bad'", "Africans themselves don't look up to their thinkers," "if it's so bad why don't you go back to their land?" (translated from the third text). Such comments came not only from students but also from teachers, which shocked her even more, and lead to the "(...) the feeling of 'nonplace,' of not belonging, we are 'strange immigrants'" that seem not to compose the "urban landscape" (translated from the fifth text), leading her to proceed, as has Araújo and Maeso (2019), Figueiredo et al. (2021), Kilomba (2020), Martins (2019) that "'The lords of the land' do not want complaints. We must work, serve, pay and not complain." (translated from the sixth text block).

Hoping to decolonize her educational institution by claiming her right to self-identify (Kilomba, 2020), Luciane concludes by stating:

> Discovering myself Black, becoming a woman, I decided to study history and to choose Africa as a path for my studies which allows me to dream of something promising, different (...) [that] will only be possible with the end of gender, race and class.

Seemingly in dialogue with the video performance *Porto Nigro*, whose work she would have seen only when she attended the opening of the exhibition,

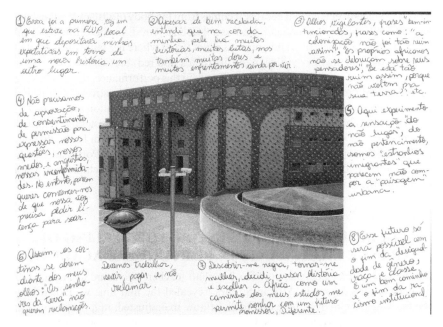

Fig. 7. Annotated photo by Luciane Araújo, Presented in TRAVESSIA Installation at the University of Porto, May 2021. *Credits:* Luciane Araújo.

Luciane also emphasizes the unequal social roles expected for each group of social actors: who can speak and about what? Are the subaltern able to speak (Spivak, 2010)?

Who has dominion over the word, which spreads to the domain of language, of meanings, which impacts the realm of public and political space? The whitewashing, colonist praising, Euro-centric narrative that still dominates public and institutional speech is one of the most violent discriminations against Black people in Portugal (Araújo, 2008). The historical amnesia continues to reproduce domination of White elites over Black nonelites. This domination is exercised through diverse forms of power as Lachmann (2020) stated.

MAURICIO IGOR: "DON'T TOUCH IT [MY HAIR]. IT'S ART!"

Mauricio Igor, an Afro-Brazilian artist who lived in Porto until he was forced to return to Brazil due to economic pressures, was another participant of *TRAVESSIA*. He participated remotely in online meetings and sent us the photo he wanted to see annotated, along with the text that should accompany it (Fig. 8).

During his time in Portugal, the artist was often approached by White people – those whom he had met previously as well as strangers – who, without asking,

Fig. 8. Annotated photo by Mauricio Igor, Presented in TRAVESSIA Installation at the University of Porto, May 2021. *Credits:* Mauricio Igor.

touched his hair and commented with surprise on its softness. Reacting to that invasive act, the artist made several posters with his picture facing the camera and a sign with the warning "Don't touch. It's Art," placing them around the streets of Porto. For his participation in *TRAVESSIA*, Mauricio chooses to reflect upon the urgency of this work.

He starts his annotated picture describing a scene in the elevator where a stranger touched his hair and said "It's soft, isn't it?," like a compliment. These microaggressions occurred often "(…) in the street, in buses, in bars, at parties, even at the hospital."

When confronted with the violence of these actions, it is common to hear justifications that appeal to a convenient ignorance and lack of understanding: "but if it's a compliment, what's the problem?," "I wouldn't mind if they did that

102 *Decolonizing Porto?*

to me or complimented me," "how exaggerated is that reaction?," as if this is not a sign of exoticization and infantilization of others. The compliment itself is another form of veiled racism because it comes in response to the prejudices associated with Black hair (wild, dirty, hard), almost revealing surprise for "even being" soft. Mauricio continues annotating his reflection, stating: "These invasive attitudes reveal the exoticizing gaze to Black phenotypes" and that the sign "Don't touch, it's Art" refers to the "warning signs in museums and cultural spaces that warn not to touch works of art."

The same Afro hair (and bodies) are, in fact, true works of art and should not be touched without proper authorization and care. The artist made a physical impression in the public realm when he wheat-pasted several life-sized posters around the city of Porto, scaled to his actual size: 1,83 cm. He is proud that he caused "(...) strangeness and alteration in the landscape, leaving a warning to Portugal: Don't Touch." This photograph is like an annotated photograph inside another annotated photograph, reflection upon reflection – a portrait embedded in the city, taking up space and looking straight ahead while asserting the objective and direct message to the whole country: "Don't touch. It's Art."

Hair demonstrates expressions of everyday, naturalized racism. Although it is not possible to delve here into the sociology of hair, which, far from being a private matter, has always fulfilled sociocultural functions beyond the most basic ones of protection and warmth (Hallpike, 1969), in the historical context of slavery, hair tells a particularly shameful history of violence. One of the first actions of the colonizers was to shave all the hair of enslaved people. This would eliminate traces of community belonging (Blokland, 2017) in an attempt to homogenize, dehumanize, and "simplify" these people into merchandise (Kilomba, 2020).

Even today, Black hair remains stigmatized, often giving rise to actions of very concrete exclusion, such as being seen as "unfit" for the workplace. The negative representations around Black hair are, like all processes of representation, embedded in the dynamics of value-driven disputes over meanings within social power relations (Hall, 1990). This strategy of "normalizing" Whiteness as a place of neutrality also exists in other forms than just direct, overt racism. Veiled racism manages to be more dangerous because it is neither assumed nor acknowledged. Yet, it causes the same kind of discrimination, where the White body mirrors the non-White (which are all the Others), as if they exist only in reaction, without alterity nor place.

ISMAEL CALLIANO: SANZALA, "A WORD THAT HURTS"

This is one of the stories shared by Ismael Calliano, who arrived in Porto from Mozambique at age eight and was one of the first participants – and a key team member – in the *TRAVESSIA* project. During one of the walking tours produced for the project, led by Ismael and Dori, and followed by Beatriz (in loco) and Lydia and Susan (online), the group stopped in front of a black awning with the word SANZALA. The texts annotated on the photograph (Fig. 9) express the

Fig. 9. Annotated photo by Ismael Calliano and Beatriz Lacerda, Presented in *TRAVESSIA* Installation at the University of Porto, May 2021. *Credits:* Ismael Calliano and Beatriz Lacerda.

dialogue that happened in reaction to this word, between two people who grew up in the same city, but had sometimes opposite experiences based on the color of their skin. Their exchange revealed the stark differences between the word's meaning based on the viewer's racial subject position:

- This word, for example, is a word that hurts.
- Yes, only last year I realized the origin. Since then I have been paying more attention to this word.
- Last year?
- Yes, a Brazilian friend explained that the Senzala was the "house of" the slaves.

- You didn't know?
- No, I don't remember speaking about it.
- But we talked about the term in school.
- We did?
- Yes, you probably didn't notice since you're White.
- Okay, so it's really my lack of knowledge… before my friend mentioned this, I had never looked twice to the meaning behind it.
- Yes, I have always heard that term, especially at times when people said things like "Go back to Senzala!"

Sanzala is the name of a Portuguese coffee brand and the word is dangerously close to the name Senzala which were the "residences" of Black people, enslaved by Portuguese settlers. In the *TRAVESSIA* exhibition, the annotated photograph was accompanied by a branded *Sanzala* coffee cup, filled with beans, some of which were overflowing (coffee being also a very strong symbol of ancient and modern slavery and extraction). Alongside the familiar coffee paraphernalia was another all too familiar item: an illustrated book by Gilberto Freyre, *Casa-Grande e Senzala ("The Masters and the Slaves")* a romanticized version of daily life on a slave plantation which popularized ideas of luso-tropicalism and validated them during the fascist regime in Portugal, still being evoked as a strong historic portrait of that period. The popular and brightly colored book was exhibited on a shelf so that it could be picked up and read by visitors.

These artifacts act as material "ghosts," as small reminders of colonial legacy frequently justified as innocent objects, being "just" a coffee brand, or "just" an old book, while they help naturalize racist and dubious narratives. On the other hand, the dialogue between Calliano and Lacerda asserted an unromanticized counternarrative: that are various versions of colonial legacy that the White elite can just neglect or ignore, while Black nonelites become re-traumatized just by glancing at a street sign or purchasing a morning coffee in a Sanzala branded cup.

Additionally, this photograph, shot looking up a public street, signals the inequalities in the modes of appropriation of public space. The street is not only a place of passage but also a battleground, a producer of meanings and identities, a source of sociability and dynamic with unequal consequences between White elites and Black nonelites (Varela et al., 2018).

CONCLUSION

It has been a long journey of recognizing the various Afro-Portuguese trajectories and places in a Porto that still imagines itself to be White. In a context that includes the denial of colonial violence and the power of White elites to control dominant narratives, it would be difficult to capture the representations of invisibilization without an ethnographic approach that prioritizes the subjectivities of social actors. Through Dori's invitation to closely study his voyage through *Porto Nigro*, we walk, symbolically and in person, through a *bleached Porto*, the excluding Porto (Beard, 2018; Correia, 2022; Martins & Moura, 2018), all the while acknowledging our own personal processes of "unlearning" and relearning that this project demanded.

This journey led us to the institutional landmarks that still exclude and discriminate against Black nonelite groups, as we know from Luciane's experience of the Faculty of Arts and Humanities of University of Porto. From there we walked on some central streets of Porto, such as the one Mauricio posted his activist poster warning the White elites to acknowledge their place in physical and symbolic social interactions. From there we took other roads to reflect upon the words that still hold enormous socio-spatial power today: such as the toponymy glorifying imperialism (street names such as Álvares Cabral) and the coffee brands that paint their awnings with colonial terms like Senzala, as expressed by Ismael.

More than words, these are social and urban communication codes, containing historical, economic, cultural, and political dimensions pointing out to stances, signs of inclusion and signs of exclusion, and above all, denouncing modes of unequal use and appropriation of the public space (Magnani, 2002; Paredes, 2016; Raposo et al., 2019). This process aggravates all the other dynamics of invisibilization already listed, contributing to new modes of exclusion, social inequality, and violence.

Invisibilization is parallel with the essentialization of the Black Other: the only student at the university, the only artist, the activist and antiracist group, "accepted" on special days of occupation and revolt, creating images of resistance domesticated and unidirectional. In several interventions, these pressures were highlighted to correspond to crystallized and stereotyped images in the "central" place of Whiteness, which never recognizes itself in relation, but only unto itself (Anderson, 2015; Kilomba, 2020). The sweet and docile, wild-haired Other; the ugly *Other*; the invincible *Other*; the unknowable *Other*; the exaggerated *Other*; the rejected *Other*; the dangerous *Other*; and the unknown *Other*. At the same time, this experimental sociological and documentary photographic approach revealed that it was possible to not only deepen the knowledge of the city of Porto and its Black communities but also contest the urban configurations and reinforcing links and sociabilities working as community aggregators. By exploring the remaining powers of White elites, Black nonelites expressed and deepened their conscience of White supremacy in a context of an unfinished decolonization process. Lachmann's (2020) approach to the concept of elites and their formation and functioning throughout history of Empires was extremely heuristic to understand how different powers are exercised to build and maintain elites' domination.

Activities on the city streets and those happening in Photography Biennials both provide ammunition for collective thought and action that break the barriers of invisibilization. Above all, these are also combative modes of appropriation to the Whiteness that imposes itself in the city and in its representations, in its maps of absences. These appropriations readjust the territory, even if only by talking about it, occupying it. They epistemologically diversify the means of portraying it, or even taking it hostage to denigrate maps (like in Dori's performance), of talking posters in various streets (like Mauricio's intervention).

In line with former contribution from Hebdige (1979), subverting through art is a form of political and cultural protest capable of launching seeds for challenging White elites' supremacy in a country like Portugal, where colonialism is not discussed in wide segments of society, although social science researchers and artists have been tackling the importance of the topic and instigating such debate. The present text joins those voices demanding an extensive, complex and profound discussion on these matters in Portuguese society, where Black communities should take the lead.

DEDICATION

This chapter is dedicated to the memory of Richard Lachmann, who tragically passed away in 2021. Ferro worked with Lachmann in New York City by the year 2009 and continued in frequent contact with him over the years. Lachmann was a very generous intellectual, passionate about Sociology and society in all its angles and scales. Having him as an interlocutor was a privilege for the ones who were lucky to encounter him. His memory lies in the collective and collegial spirit of the "healthy" spaces of academia.

ACKNOWLEDGMENTS

This paper was first presented at the 2022's Social Science History Association Annual Meeting (November 20, 2022, Chicago, Illinois, USA) on the panel "Between Marx and Mosca: The Critical Legacy of Elite Theory," organized by Rebecca Emigh (UCLA) and chaired by Dylan Riley (University of California at Berkeley), to whom the authors thank for the comments and suggestions.

NOTES

1. For further details visit https://TRAVESSIA462196210.wordpress.com/
2. Macau was the solely Portuguese colony not declaring Independence from Portugal in 1975. Macau's is a singular case in the Portuguese empire which needs to be treated in a special manner and this is not a subject of the present chapter.
3. For more details visit: https://www.susanmeiselas.com/cova-da-moura
4. Beatriz Lacerda completed her Masters' thesis titled "Pela descolonização da cidade Redes e experiências urbanas das comunidades africanas e afrodescendentes do Porto" under the supervision of Lígia Ferro, in 2022, at the University of Porto.
5. For more details on Nigro's work visit https://vimeo.com/dorinigro
6. For more details on Caliano's work visit https://theboard.pt/atores/ismael-calliano/
7. Credits: Porto Nigro (Video performance). Time: 14'23 (loop). Creation: Dori Nigro. Co-creation: Paulo Pinto. Voice-over: Dori Nigro. Production: Dori Nigro and Paulo Pinto. Filming and editing: Dori Nigro and Paulo Pinto. Residence: CRL-Central Elétrica. Support: Porto's Biennial of Photography. Video performance created for the exhibition Travessia, by Susan Meiselas, at Porto Biennial of Photography. Curatorship: Lydia Matthews. Porto, 2021; https://vimeo.com/599470905
8. Credits: Exú na Álvares Cabral (Vídeo performance). Time: 01'08 (Loop). Creation: Dori Nigro. Co-creation: Paulo Pinto. Collaboration: Madalena Rodrigues, Luciana

LÍGIA FERRO ET AL.

Vieira, Igor Nolasco. Voice-over: Caroline Odeyale. Production: Beatriz Lacerda. Filming: José Fangueiro. Editing: Jorge Almeida. Support: Porto's Biennial of Photography. Video performance for the exhibition Travessia, by Susan Meiselas, at Porto Biennial of Photography. Curatorship: Lydia Matthews. Porto, 2021; https://vimeo.com/599476107

REFERENCES

Afonso, A., & Gomes, C. de M. (2000). *Os Anos da Guerra Colonial*. Editorial Notícias.

Anderson, E. (2015). "The white space." Race, space and inclusion? *Sociology of Race and Ethnicity*, *1*(1), 10–21. https://sociology.yale.edu/sites/default/files/pages_from_sre-11_rev5_printer_files.pdf

Araújo, M. (2008). Racismo.pt? In T. Cunha & S. Silvestre (Eds.), *Somos diferentes, somos iguais: diversidade, cidadania e educação* (pp. 5–49). Acção para a Justiça e Paz. https://hdl.handle.net/10316/42649

Araújo, M., & Maeso, S. R. (2010). Explorando o eurocentrismo nos manuais portugueses de História. *Estudos de Sociologia*, *15*(28), 239–270. https://periodicos.fclar.unesp.br/estudos/article/view/2559

Araújo, M., & Maeso, S. R. (2013). A presença ausente do racial: discursos políticos e pedagógicos sobre História, "Portugal" e (pós-) colonialismo. *Educar em Revista*, *47*, 145–171. https://www.scielo.br/j/er/a/fYFNwDhXgxbZq6H6tbNWWfK/?format=pdf&lang=pt

Araújo, M., & Maeso, S. R. (2019). O poder do racismo na academia: produção de conhecimento e disputas políticas. In B. S. Santos & B. S. Martins (Eds.), *O pluriverso dos Direitos Humanos: a diversidade das lutas pela dignidade* (pp. 457–481). Edições 70. https://hdl.handle.net/10316/88865

Beard, J. (2018). *Community formation among recent immigrant groups in Porto, Portugal*. Doctoral dissertation, University of California, Berkeley. eScholarship University of California. https://escholarship.org/uc/item/2zn9n8g8

Blokland, T. (2017). *Community as urban practice*. Polity Press.

Bucaioni, M. (2016). Impossível descolonização: para um novo enquadramento das literaturas da África lusófona: perspectivas críticas. In M. Lupetti & V. Tocco (Eds.), *Giochi di specchi. Modelli, tradizioni, contaminazioni e dinamiche interculturali nei e tra i paesi di lingua portoghese* (pp. 273–286). Edizioni ETS.

Cahen, M. (2018). A mestiçagem colonialista ou a colonialidade de Gilberto Freyre na colonialidade do Brasil. *Portuguese Studies Review*, *26*(1), 299–349. https://shs.hal.science/halshs-02473340/document

Cardina, M. (2016). Memórias amnésicas? Nação, discurso político e representações do passado colonial. *Configurações*, *17*, 31–42. http://configuracoes.revues.org/3281

Correia, N. G. (2022). A influência do passado histórico colonial no racismo contra os africanos e afrodescendentes em Portugal. *Revista Ibero-Americana de Humanidades, Ciências e Educação*, *8*(1), 1320–1331. https://doi.org/10.51891/rease.v8i1.3969

Fanon, F. (2008). *Black skin, white masks*. Groove Press.

Ferro, L. (2005). Ao encontro da Sociologia Visual. *Sociologia, Revista da Faculdade de Letras da Universidade do Porto*, *15*, 373–398. https://ojs.letras.up.pt/index.php/Sociologia/article/view/2398

Ferro, L., Raposo, O., Cordeiro, G., Lopes, J. T., Veloso, L., Nico, M., Abrantes, M., Abrantes, P., Varela, P., Bento, T., & Caeiro, T. (2016). *O trabalho da arte e a arte do trabalho: circuitos criativos de artistas imigrantes em Portugal*. Observatório das Migrações. http://www.om.acm.gov.pt/documents/58428/177157/Estudo_OM58_br.pdf/521e91d4-f875-49cd-ba7a-36a6894c8618

Figueiredo, O. V. A., Arruda, J. S. D., & Araújo, M. (2021). Colonialismo português, luso-tropicalismo, racismo e lutas antirracistas-entrevista com Marta Araújo. *Revista da FAEEBA - Educação e Contemporaneidade*, *30*(62), 168–186. https://doi.org/10.21879/faeeba2358-0194.2021.v30.n62.p168-186

Freyre, G. (1992). *Casa grande e sanzala. Formação da família brasileira sob o regime da economia patriarcal* (3rd ed.). Editora Record.

Hall, S. (1990). Cultural identity and diaspora. In J. Rutherford (Ed.), *Identity: Community, culture, difference* (pp. 222–237). Lawrence and Wishart.

Hallpike, C. R. (1969). Social hair. *Man, 4*(2), 256–264. https://doi.org/10.2307/2799572

Hebdige, D. (1979). *Subculture. The meaning of style.* Routledge. https://doi.org/10.4324/9780203139943

Henriques, J. G. (2020, November 22). Pedro Varela e José Pereira revelam "a primeira geração" de activistas negros em Portugal. Público. https://www.publico.pt/2020/11/22/sociedade/noticia/pedro-varela-jose-pereira-revelam-primeira-geracao-activistas-negros-portugal-1937945

Kilomba, G. (2020). *Memórias da plantação: Episódios de racismo quotidiano* (2nd ed.). Orfeu Negro.

Lacerda, A. B. (2022). *Pela descolonização da cidade: Redes e experiências urbanas das comunidades africanas e afrodescendentes do Porto.* Master's thesis, Faculdade de Letras da Universidade do Porto. Repositório aberto da Universidade do Porto. https://hdl.handle.net/10216/145089

Lachmann, R. (1988). Graffiti as career and ideology. *American Journal of Sociology, 94*(2), 229–250. https://www.jstor.org/stable/2780774

Lachmann, R. (2020). *First class passengers on a sinking ship: Elite politics and the decline of great powers.* Verso.

Lopes, J. S. (2016). *Lugar de brancalo e alo "brancalo fora do lugar": representações sobre branquitude e suas possibilidades de antirracismo entre negralos e brancalos dolno movimento negro em Salvador – BA.* Master's thesis, Instituto de Ciências Humanas, Universidade Federal de Pelotas. UFPEL. http://repositorio.ufpel.edu.br/handle/prefix/3185

Magnani, J. G. C. (2002). De perto e de dentro: notas para uma etnografia urbana. *Revista Brasileira de Ciências Sociais, 17,* 11–29. https://doi.org/10.1590/S0102-69092002000200002

Martins, B. S. (2019, May 25). Os negros em Portugal. *Memoirs Newsletter, 53,* 1–4. https://hdl.handle.net/10316/87191

Martins, B. S., & Moura, A. (2018). Portugal e década internacional de afrodescendentes: a educação e os tempos de violência colonial. *Educação em Revista, 34,* 1–23. https://doi.org/10.1590/0102-4698192750

Noguera, R. (2022). Denegrindo a educação: um ensaio filosófico para uma pedagogia da pluriversalidade. *Revista Sul-americana de Filosofia e Educação, 18,* 62–73. https://doi.org/10.26512/resafe.v0i18.4523

Pardue, D. (2014). Kriolu scenes in Lisbon: Where migration experiences and housing policy meet. *City and Society, 26*(3), 308-330. https://doi.org/10.1111/ciso.12045

Paredes, M. M. (2016). Da desconstrução dos estereótipos às peculiaridades da construção nacional nos Países Africanos de Língua Oficial Portuguesa (PALOP). In P. M. de Paula & S. M. S. Correa (Eds.), *Nossa África: Ensino e Pesquisa* (pp. 57–67). https://repositorio.pucrs.br/dspace/bitstream/10923/14691/2/Da_desconstrucao_dos_estereotipos_as_peculiaridades_da_construcao_nacional_nos_Paises_Africanos_de_Lingua_Oficial.pdf

Poveda, D., Thomson, P., & Ferro, L. (2018). Ethnographic explorations of the arts and education: An introduction. *Ethnography and Education, 13*(3), 268–272. https://doi.org/10.1080/17457823.2018.1462009

Raposo, O., Alves, A. R., Varela, P., & Roldão, C. (2019). Negro drama. Racismo, segregação e violência policial nas periferias de Lisboa. *Revista Crítica de Ciências Sociais, 119,* 5–28. https://doi.org/10.4000/rccs.8937

Raposo, O., Varela, P., Simões, J. A., & Campos, R. (2021). "Nos e fidju la di gueto, nos e fidju di imigranti, fidju di Kabu Verdi": estética, antirracismo e engajamentos no rap criulo em Portugal. *Revista Sociedade e Estado, 36*(1), 269–291. https://doi.org/10.1590/s0102-6992-202136010013

Roldão, C. (2015). *Fatores e perfis de sucesso escolar "inesperado": trajetos de contratendência de jovens das classes populares e de origem africana.* Doctoral dissertation, ISCTE/IUL. Repositório ISCTE. https://repositorio.iscte-iul.pt/bitstream/10071/9342/1/Tese%20Doutoramento_Fatores%20e%20Perfis%20de%20Sucesso%20Escolar%20Inesperado_CRoldao2015.pdf

Roldão, C., Pereira, J. A., & Varela, P. (2023). *Tribuna Negra: Origens do movimento negro em Portugal 1911 – 1933.* Tinta da China.

Spivak, G. C. (2010). Can the subaltern speak? In R. C. Morris (Ed.), *Can the subaltern speak?: Reflections on the history of an idea* (pp. 21–78). Columbia University Press.

Varela, O. B. (2012, September 19). *Manifesto 'Lusofóbico': crítica da identidade cultural 'lusófona' em Cabo Verde*. BUALA. https://www.buala.org/pt/a-ler/manifesto-lusofobico-critica-da-identidade-cultural-lusofona-em-cabo-verde?utm_source=feedburner&utm_medium=email&utm_campaign=Feed%3A+buala-pt+%28BUALA+%7C+Cultura+Contemporânea+Africana%29

Varela, P., Raposo, O., & Ferro, L. (2018). Redes de sociabilidade e trocas geracionais no circuito musical africano da Amadora. *Sociologia – Problemas e Praticas, 86*(1), 109–132. https://journals.openedition.org/spp/4169

SECTION 2

ELITES AND SOCIAL TRANSFORMATIONS

CHAPTER 5

ELITE CONFLICT AND INDUSTRY REGULATION: HOW POLITICAL POLARIZATION AFFECTS LOCAL RESTRICTION AND STATE PREEMPTION OF THE US HYDRAULIC FRACTURING INDUSTRY

Lori Qingyuan Yue[a] and Yuni Wen[b]

[a]*Columbia Business School, USA*
[b]*University of Oxford, UK*

ABSTRACT

We leverage Lachmann's insight on elite conflict to explain the politics surrounding industry regulation in contemporary America and argue that conflicts between political elites create both constraints on industry players and opportunities for them to shape regulation. The widening urban-rural polarization of American society, in particular, has made urban political elites more liberal than those in state politics. The greater the political polarization of a state, the more local restrictions the nascent US hydraulic fracturing (fracking) industry – generally regarded as conservative – face in that state. Players in the industry thus seek interventions by conservative elites at the state government level. The dominance of conservative state legislators and the presence of affiliates of the right-leaning American Legislative Exchange Council (ALEC) are bound to strengthen the industry's lobbying efforts in that state. These, in turn, increase the likelihood of the enactment of state preemption laws that nullify local restrictions. We discuss the implications of

Elites, Nonelites, and Power
Political Power and Social Theory, Volume 41, 113–139
Copyright © 2025 Lori Qingyuan Yue and Yuni Wen
Published under exclusive licence by Emerald Publishing Limited
ISSN: 0198-8719/doi:10.1108/S0198-871920240000041005

this on the study of elite conflict, the politics of industry regulation, and the industry's political strategy.

Keywords: Elite conflict; industry regulation; political polarization; state preemption; corporate political action; lobbying; fracking

INTRODUCTION

Lachmann (2014) defined elites as a group of rulers who are capable of extracting resources from nonelites. While this definition bears some similarity to the ruling class as defined by Marxian theorists and the power elites as discussed by C. Wright Mills and his followers, it differs fundamentally in its emphasis on the *conflict* between elites and the consequences of this conflict. Marxist theory focuses on interclass struggle and perceives the ruling elite as a relatively homogenous group that is basically interested in reproducing its exploitation of the working class. Mills, by contrast, recognizes the difference between regional and national elites, but argues that because regional power cannot compete with national power, it will eventually join the structure and become interlocked in the latter's network. In his mind, therefore, the national power structure is one comprised of people occupying the command posts of a society's economic, political, and military arenas, who are thus unified and cohesive (Mills, 1956; also see Domhoff, 1967). Lachmann, by contrast, does not see the elite as homogenous or cohesive. Rather, in his view, elites are just as interested in "guarding its existing power from, and extending its power at the expense of, rival elites" as they are in the reproduction of the social structure that enables them to exploit nonelites (Lachmann, 2014, p. 12).

A unique contribution of Lachmann's theory is that it not only focuses on elite conflict, but also examines how a conflict of this kind can either enable or inhibit the expansion of economic power and thus have long-term consequences on society. For example, in his classic work on the origins of capitalism in England, Lachmann (1987) argues that the interactions caused by elite conflicts at the national and local level enabled the gentry to privatize common lands and abolish tenant rights, which, in turn, laid the foundation for industrialization. In another book that examines the same question in a broader geographical sense, Lachmann (2000) compares regions and cities within and across England, France, Italy, Spain, and the Netherlands and shows how feudal elites were pushed toward capitalism as they sought to protect their privileges from rival elites. Over time, the dynamics of elite conflict perpetuated manorial economies in certain places while propelling the development of new social relations and political institutions in others. Despite Lachmann's insight that conflict within the political elite can both constrain and enable economic players, empirical work that draws on this insight has been relatively rare.[1] We know particularly little about the modern-day implication of elite conflict, and whether it too can generate risks and opportunities for economic players in the contemporary era, and if so, how. This is an important gap in the literature as the division among elites, especially political ones, is a feature of modern pluralistic societies, in which elites have different political party affiliations or are in charge of different levels or branches of government. As they differ substantially in their beliefs on important policy domains, their conflicts can create challenges for economic players as well as opportunities for them to maneuver attempts at shaping their environments. Thus, given that political elites in many societies have been more polarized in the contemporary era (Desilver, 2022), we should expect Lachmann's insight regarding elite conflicts to shed light on many modern issues pertaining to the political economy.

In this chapter, we apply Lachmann's claim that the conflict between political elites can both constrain and enable economic players to study contemporary industry regulation in the United States. We contend that the urban-rural polarization of American society has widened the ideological divide among political elites and, in turn, created both risks in industries' regulatory environments and opportunities for industry players to reshape the environment. Political polarization refers to a societal condition in which the range of political opinions and attitudes moves away from the center towards more extreme ideological positions, resulting in significant differences and animosity among political parties and/or various factions within the government (DiMaggio et al., 1996). Ideological conflicts between elites can develop along both horizontal and vertical lines, with the former referring to systematic ideological divides and the latter to politics at different levels of government (Lachmann, 1987). Consequently, the two dimensions of division may converge to cause geopolitical polarization among political elites, wherein different levels of government will serve as holdouts of opposing ideological extremes, and, in turn, affect an industry's regulation policy (Emigh et al., 2020).

The ideological orientation of political elites is an important feature of an industry's regulatory environment. As industry operations often have social and environmental impacts, policymakers who embrace different political ideologies can have very different views on how to regulate them (Jenkins et al., 2006). The dominant political ideology in a region has thus been linked to the enactment of pro- or anti-industry policies (Dokshin, 2016; Fremeth et al., 2022; Li & DiSalvo, 2023; Rao et al., 2011). However, political polarization at different levels of government indicates that political elites who dominate the politics of a city or state government may be ideological rivals. In a federalist system where state and local governments share regulatory power over a jurisdiction, industry regulation can turn into a battleground between ideologically divided political elites (Yue & Wang, 2023).

On the one hand, geopolitical polarization increases the possibility that industry players will be challenged by political elites at the level of government who hold an opposing ideology. In a politically polarized environment, industry players are prone to politicization; support and opposition to industries often fall into predefined partisan camps. Industries are thus more likely to face restrictive regulations when working under a political authority that is ideologically opposed to them. On the other hand, urban-rural polarization too creates opportunities for industry players to leverage partisan conflicts among different levels of government to their advantage. They can lobby the level of government that aligns with their political ideologies to fight restrictive regulations enacted by another level with an opposing political ideology. While the ways in which industries influence government regulations have been well studied in the broader literature of political economy and within the specific field of corporate political strategy, the existent research tends to depict the influence exerted by industries on the government as a dyadic exchange between industry players and a single policy supplier or a group of homogenous policy suppliers (Bonardi et al., 2005; Dorobantu et al., 2017; Hillman et al., 2004). Despite the recent focus on the heterogeneity of the policy supply side (Choi et al., 2015; Grandy & Hiatt, 2020; Yue et al., 2019), heterogeneity has been treated as a fixed institutional feature that does not change over time or interact with others. Nonetheless, the geopolitical polarization of elites challenges these assumptions by showing that the power struggles within political elites at the state and local level can create opportunities for corporate political action, and that a city-state conflict can be activated by partisan antagonism.

Worthwhile noting here is that this geographically based division among elites has long been noted by elite theorists. Mills (1956, p. 39), for example, suggests that among elites, "there is the tradition of the town against the hayseed, of the big city against the small-town hick." Mills, however, was formulating his theory against the backdrop of a nation-wide economy that was coming into being, and therefore focusing on how "local society has become part of a national economy" and how "its status and power hierarchies have come to be subordinate parts of the larger hierarchies of the nation" (Mills, 1956, p. 39). He also portrayed the local elites as the backbone of the Republican Party (following the Jeffersonian ethos) and the national elite as being more liberal. We, in turn, argue that the contemporary era's geopolitical polarization has made metropolitan cities more liberal, and state-level political elites, which represent rural communities, more conservative.

We test these arguments by conducting an analysis of ordinances enacted by local governments to prohibit the nascent hydraulic fracturing ("fracking") industry in US states from 2011 to 2020 as well as by studying the oil and gas industry's efforts to lobby the state government in order to nullify them. Fracking refers to the process of drilling down into the earth and using a high-pressure water mixture to release oil and gas from shale. This is an appropriate context, as this industry that has become politicized due to its significant impact on both the economy and the environment. Counties that engage in fracking produce an average of $400 million in oil and natural gas per year; the industry can thus lead to a significant increase in local employment, salaries, and housing prices (Bartik et al., 2019). Yet despite these economic benefits, the practice has also provoked intense opposition due to environmental concerns (Vasi et al., 2015). Between 2011 and 2020, over 500 bans on fracking were enacted by local governments in the United States (Food & Water Watch, 2020). Over the course of this period, the fracking industry became politicized, with liberals being likelier to oppose the technology and conservatives more likely to support it (Boudet et al., 2014; Davis & Fisk, 2014; Jerolmack & Walker, 2018; Li & DiSalvo, 2023). We find that local bans are imposed more frequently on fracking in more polarized states, but also that the industry hires more lobbyists at the state government level to confront the bans, especially in states where political elites are ideologically aligned. This, in turn, increases the likelihood of state preemption over local regulations.

This chapter makes three contributions to the literature on elite conflicts, the regulation of nascent industries, and corporate political strategy. First, it contributes to the elite conflict theory by showing the consequences of geopolitical polarization of political elites on industry regulation in the contemporary era. We show that Lachmann's insight that elite conflicts affect economic players can be widely applied to explain the modern political economy. We also extend the literature by showing how elite conflicts shape the political strategies adopted by industries and the consequent regulatory outcomes relevant to those industries. In doing so, we contribute to a growing body of work that documents the consequences of political polarization (e.g., Chen & Rohla, 2017; Graham & Svolik, 2020; Iyengar et al., 2019; Scala & Johnson, 2017). Second, we contribute to the literature on industry regulation (e.g., Fligstein, 1996; Gao & McDonald, 2022; Ingram & Rao, 2004; Jenkins et al., 2006; Schneiberg & Bartley, 2001) by extending the theorization of political opportunity. We contend that political opportunity is provided not only by partisan control over a level of government, but also by conflicts among its multiple levels. This perspective of political opportunity is especially useful for *nascent industries* that wish to shape regulatory environments when facing jurisdictional uncertainties (Yue & Wang, 2023) Third, we extend the research on the political strategy of industries (e.g., Bonardi et al., 2005; Funk & Hirschman, 2017; Hillman & Hitt, 1999) by showing that heterogeneity on the policy supply side can affect the political strategies of an industry. We demonstrate that such heterogeneity is not a fixed, exogenous feature, but rather a dynamic process that is amplified by elites' conflicts. This chapter also sheds light on state preemption as a new political strategy exercised by industry. While recent research has noted the rise in state governments' preemption of local regulations (e.g., Barber & Dynes, 2023; Riverstone-Newell, 2017; Fowler & Witt, 2019), its focus has fallen on political and institutional factors. This chapter, along with Yue and Wang (2023), examines the role played by various industry players in the process and reveals that lobbying for state preemption is an important political strategy among nascent industries fighting local restrictions.

THEORY

Political Elite Conflicts in Urban-Rural Polarization

Political polarization occurs when the subsets of a society's population assume opposing attitudes toward political parties, ideologies, and policies, thereby giving rise to a bimodal distribution of opinions around conflicting points. According to the Pew Research Center (2021), political polarization is a defining feature of current US politics due to the vast and growing gap between Democrats and Republicans (Pierson & Hacker, 2002). Urban-rural polarization is a type of geopolitical polarization whereby urban areas have grown increasingly liberal and rural areas more conservative (Scala & Johnson, 2017). Journalists and scholars have attributed this urban-rural divide to the "great sorting" of American society in the past three decades (Bishop & Cushing, 2009; Mason, 2018). Since the 1990s, urban areas have come to serve as the hubs of economic and political decision-making, attracted a more diverse and educated population, and grown more liberal and inclined to vote for Democratic political elites. Meanwhile, the lifeblood of rural areas has been diminishing. Left behind by the globalized economy and alienated by the multiculturalism of urban areas, their residents have turned further right to support the Republican political elites. As people flocked to regions where they could find like-minded others, social dynamics carved deep canyons between urban and rural areas of the country.

Urban-rural polarization has significant consequences on conflicts among political elites at the state and local levels. In the United States, most political representatives enter office by winning the most votes in a district rather than through a system of proportional representation (Badger, 2019). As the voting base of Democrats is concentrated in cities, local urban governments have become the party's strongholds. The relatively small number of such districts, however, makes it difficult for Democrats to control a state legislature. By contrast, the Republican voting base is spread across suburban and rural areas, meaning that its representatives get elected in a greater number of districts. As a result, urban-rural polarization manifests itself as "blue cities and red states," with Democratic elites controlling city halls and Republican elites controlling state houses. As the largest cities in any given state are nearly always more liberal than the rest, geopolitical polarization is a pervasive phenomenon that can occur even in Democratic-leaning states, albeit to a lesser degree (Barber & Dynes, 2023).

The sharp divide between the political elites that control city halls and those that control state houses has occurred in the context of the federal structure of the US government. As Morton Grodzins (1966) notes, American federalism is more like a "marble cake," in which the responsibilities of different levels of government are intertwined, than a "layer cake," in which specific functions are clearly assigned to particular levels of government. The geopolitical polarization of urban and rural areas has intensified the conflict between the state and local tiers of political elites. On the one hand, local political elites have increasingly turned to activism to promote policies that the higher tier of government has proven reluctant or unable to generate (Dolan, 2012). In a systematic study of local government activism, for example, Riverstone-Newell (2017) found that localities across the nation have enacted thousands of ordinances, resolutions, and executive orders reserved for state and federal purview. On the other, state political elites have become more active in adopting preemption laws to restrict the assertiveness of local political elites (Briffault, 2018; Fowler & Witt, 2019; Phillips, 2017; Yue & Wang, 2023). Moreover, states have not been punching down local regulation in a politically neutral way; recent preemptions have generally been promoted by conservative state legislatures that wish to thwart progressive local policies (e.g., Fowler & Witt, 2019; Phillips, 2017; Riverstone-Newell, 2017). Consequently, the tension between local and state political elites has been exacerbated by partisan conflicts, which, in turn, are likely to affect both the regulation of industry and its political strategy.

Risks for Industry Regulation

Conflicts between political elites rooted in urban-rural polarization lead to regulatory risks for industry players. In a politically polarized environment, controversial industrial practices tend to be politicized. Party elites may exploit these issues to develop differentiated positions and demonstrate opposition to or support of an industry as an expression of political identity (Baldassarri & Bearman, 2007). Activists, in turn, may frame grievances along partisan lines in order to mobilize broader support (Jerolmack & Walker, 2018; McAdam & Boudet, 2012). As a result, even firms that have not been politically active gradually become politicized (Elinson, 2021; Cutter et al., 2021). As a senior executive at American Airlines remarked, "It really is hard to take a middle ground. One, the world won't let you, and two, it doesn't really serve anyone trying to cater to both sides" (Cutter et al., 2021).

Once industry players are politicized, they are likely to face opposition from political elites with dissimilar ideologies. When urban-rural polarization in a state is high, activists opposed to the development of a conservative-leaning industry may appeal to local political elites in order to promote restrictive policies. Under such conditions, they are likelier to find supportive political allies among local government leaders in liberal areas. Local elites in liberal areas are also readier to support activists as greater geopolitical polarization offers fewer opportunities to promote liberal policies at the state level. Working together, these liberal policy entrepreneurs can turn cities into hubs of progressive policies and enact regulatory constraints on a conservative-leaning industry. Therefore:

> *H1.* The stronger the urban-rural polarization within a state, the greater the number of local restrictive regulations on a conservative-leaning industry in that state.

State Capture and Industrial Lobbying

Lobbying for preferential regulations has been an important political strategy for industries responding to threats in regulatory environments (for overviews, see De Figueiredo & Richter, 2014; Drutman, 2015). Businesses hire lobbyists to do research on the relevant issues and find opportunities to meet with lawmakers and communicate industries' desires. If lobbyists can convince lawmakers that a proposed bill suits their ideological pursuits and/or contributes to their re-election or promotion, lawmakers are likely to promote it.

The polarization of political elites at the city and state level offers industry an opportunity to leverage the state to nullify local restrictions. The effectiveness of an industry's lobbying depends on the preference of policymakers (Hillman & Keim, 1995; Choi et al., 2015). The Republican Party is generally regarded as more pro-business as it favors limited government regulation of the economy.

Moreover, businesses are known to choose their regulators strategically and engage in horizontal regulatory arbitrage by settling in jurisdictions with more favorable laws in order to circumvent less favorable regulation elsewhere (Rao et al., 2011; Sytch & Kim, 2021; Tiebout, 1956). Following the same logic, industry players, especially those facing jurisdictional uncertainties in nascent industries, can likewise engage in vertical venue shifting by choosing a favorable level of regulators (Yue & Wang, 2023). Partisan polarization of local and state political elites creates an opportunity for them to do so.

A conservative-leaning industry can thus lobby the state government to preempt local restrictive regulations. Such preemptions are more likely to succeed in Republican-controlled states, as shown by Fowler and Witt (2019) in their cross-state investigation of preemption legislation in 17 policy areas. Their study reveals that the percentage of Republican state legislators is a stronger predictor of a state's adoption of preemption laws than are certain long-standing institutional features. Goodman (2019) similarly finds that conservative state legislatures are more active in preempting ordinances on local workers' rights. Specific to industry players' lobbying efforts is Yue and Wang (2023)'s recent study of the nascent commercial drone industry's venue-shifting efforts. Although the authors did not take a direct measure of the conservativeness of state legislatures, they did find that the ideological distance between state and local policymakers increased the efforts made by industry players to lobby state government to preempt local restrictions. Attempts to promote state preemption laws are not always successful, however, and, in some cases, policymakers may side with local officials claiming state overreach. In 2016, for example, a preemption bill to rein in local fracking bans was defeated in Colorado after Democrats took over the state legislature (Riccardi, 2019). If local bans are enacted by local liberal holdouts and a state has more political elites affiliated with the Republican Party, then the industry will perceive the state government as more sympathetic to its agenda. When the perceived chance of success is greater, the industry will put more effort into lobbying political elites at the state level to rein in local policies.

> *H2*. The greater the number of local restrictive regulations on a conservative-leaning industry in that state, the more lobbyists the industry will hire to target the state government.
>
> *H3*. The relationship between the prevalence of local opposition and the intensity of industry lobbying at the state level (i.e., *H2*) is strengthened if the state legislature is dominated by the Republican Party.

The perceived chance of success is also likely to increase if elite groups advocating for economic liberalization have greater influence on the state legislature. Among powerful think tanks and membership organizations, the American Legislative Exchange Council (ALEC) has been particularly active in supporting state-level preemption campaigns by supplying "model bills" to affiliated state legislators (Hertel-Fernandez, 2017, 2019). According to its own website, the organization is "comprised of nearly one-quarter of the country's state legislators," its legislative members represent more than 60 million Americans, and its private sector members provide jobs for over 30 million people in the United States (About ALEC, 2020). ALEC targets state legislators who have neither the experience nor resources to formulate concrete policy positions and provides them with its own model bills that are often drafted to favor industrial interests.

At ALEC member meetings, legislators and industries convene to determine what they would like to do at the next state assembly session. As Cara Sullivan, former head of ALEC's Commerce, Insurance, and Economic Development Task Force, noted during an internal meeting in 2014, "One solution (to local opposition) that ALEC has passed is state legislation that preempts the polities from within the state" (quoted by Bottari, 2015). ALEC is known for sponsoring numerous preemption bills, including ones aimed at blocking local policies that raise minimum wage (ALEC, 2013) and banning fracking or other oil and gas operations (Bottari, 2015). If a focal state has a higher percentage of legislators affiliated with ALEC, the industry may perceive a greater chance of preempting local opposition with the help of ALEC legislators and thus put more effort into lobbying.

> *H4.* The relationship between the prevalence of local opposition and the intensity of industry lobbying at the state level (i.e., *H2*) is strengthened if a higher percentage of legislators in a state are affiliated with ALEC.

Impact of Industry Lobbying on State Preemption

The more lobbyists the industry hires, the more likely it will succeed in promoting the enactment of state preemption that nullifies local restrictions. We therefore expect that the intensity of the industry's lobbying of a state government increases the chances of the enactment of state preemption of local restrictions.

> *H5.* A conservative-leaning industry's lobbying efforts at the state government level will lead to the enactment of state preemption of local restrictive regulations.

METHOD

Data

We collected the data from all 29 US states in which fracking activities were registered between 2001 and 2020. Fracking activity is recorded in the National Hydraulic Fracturing Chemical Registry provided by FracFocus, a publicly accessible database that collects information on hydraulic fracturing operations managed by the US Ground Water Protection Council and the Interstate Oil and Gas Compact Commission. We began in 2001, the year in which fracking became widely adopted, and ended in 2020, the most recent year for which data is available. Our unit of analysis is a state-year.

Dependent Variables and Estimation

Table 1 reports the descriptive statistics of all the variables. Our first dependent variable for testing *H1* is *the cumulative number of bans or moratoriums* issued by local governments on fracking in a state in a year. We collected these data from the Food & Water Watch, a nonprofit, environmental, nongovernmental organization (NGO). By 2020, a total of 538 local bans had been imposed on fracking. Fig. 1 shows the occurrence of local bans on fracking in the United States Our second dependent variable for testing *H2–4* is *the number of lobbyists* hired by fracking companies to work on a state government in a year. We began by using FracFocus to identify 1,520 oil companies engaged in fracking activities. We then collected the data on these fracking companies' lobbyists from the National Institute of Money in State Politics (2020), which collects such information from state governments. Although expenditure on lobbying could have served as an alternative measurement, it is incomplete because 33 states do not require lobbyists to report such data (NCSL, 2018). Our third dependent variable for testing *H5* is *state preemption*, which is measured as a dummy variable coded as one if a state government has created legislature or passed orders to preempt local bans on fracking in a year. We identified state preemptions by checking the National Conference of State Legislatures (NCSL) and the Hydraulic Fracking Blog. Altogether, there were eight state preemptions.

We adopted poisson models for the dependent variable, the local ban number. We conducted a dispersion test and found no evidence of overdispersion. In such a situation, the poisson model, which has fewer restrictions than does the negative binomial model, is preferable. One issue in our estimate is the potential endogeneity of urban-rural polarization, which need not be random and can instead be correlated with unobserved variables that also affect the incidence of local bans. To deal with this problem, we adopted a two-stage least-square (2SLS) regression. In the first-stage regression, we used the percentage of agricultural jobs in a state as the instrumental variable for geopolitical polarization. Farming has been a highly Republican occupation; survey results show that 72% of people who work in farming or forestry lean towards the Republican Party (Verdant Lab, 2016). In addition, agricultural work must be conducted in rural areas. As a result, states with a higher percentage of agricultural jobs are more likely to be Republican-leaning and thus have a higher urban-rural polarization score. Meanwhile, policies made by local governments with regard to the fracking industry are independent of the agriculture industry because of the distinct issues, concerns, and stakeholders involved in each sector. We present the first-stage regression with the instrumental variable in Appendix A1. The relatively high F-statistics (beyond the rule of thumb of 10) leads us to reject the possibility of a weak instrument. We collected the agricultural job data from the US Bureau of Labor Statistics. In the second-stage analysis, we used the predicted value from the first-stage regression, which provided us with the exogenous component of urban-rural polarization.

We deployed poisson models for the dependent variable of the number of lobbyists hired by fracking companies and event history models for state

Table 1. Descriptive Statistics for Variables.

Variable	Mean	S.D.	1	2	3	4	5	6	7	8	9	10	11	12	13	14
1. Lobbyist number	5.97	11.96														
2. Local ban number	5.89	24.66	0.04													
3. Conservative dom. in state legis.	0.40	0.49	0.05	−0.05												
4. ALEC legislator ratio	0.19	0.12	0.23	−0.10	0.46											
5. State legislative professionalism	2.00	1.27	0.11	0.33	−0.18	−0.17										
6. State legislative competition	0.26	0.17	−0.09	0.01	0.48	0.12	−0.37									
7. State fiscal capacity (k)	5.57	3.31	0.12	0.14	0.06	0.06	−0.05	0.16								
8. Home rule	0.78	0.41	−0.04	0.03	−0.07	0.10	0.15	0.01	−0.23							
9. Oil industry empl. (per 1,000 ppl)	1.89	3.10	0.20	−0.11	0.14	0.23	−0.42	0.33	0.35	−0.12						
10. Per capita income (10k)	5.03	0.97	0.21	0.39	0.07	0.17	0.24	0.15	0.54	0.07	0.16					
11. Population (1 million)	7.21	8.58	0.26	0.29	−0.08	−0.03	0.67	−0.16	−0.12	0.20	−0.23	0.28				
12. Urban population	0.74	0.14	0.16	0.20	−0.06	0.01	0.52	−0.02	−0.12	0.00	−0.16	0.28	0.53			
13. White population	0.73	0.52	0.20	0.02	0.18	0.02	0.04	0.03	0.03	0.05	−0.07	−0.11	−0.11	−0.13		
14. Diffusion	1.68	3.12	0.09	0.18	0.20	0.15	0.00	0.24	0.26	0.00	0.08	0.59	0.02	0.04	0.14	
15. Urban-rural polarization	0.09	0.07	0.09	0.11	0.03	0.15	0.02	0.16	−0.09	0.02	0.00	0.26	0.08	0.38	0.07	0.25

$N = 560$.

Fig. 1. Distribution of Municipal Bans and Moratoria by 2020.

preemption of local bans. These too are subject to endogeneity problems as unobserved variables may simultaneously influence local bans, lobbyist numbers, and state preemptions. We therefore adopted the control-function method (Wooldridge, 2015) to calculate the residual of both the model that predicts local ban numbers and the model that predicts the number of lobbyists. We then inserted the two residuals into the model for lobbyist number and the model for state preemptions. We adopted state and yearly fixed effects for all the models in order to control for the impact of omitted variables that may have exerted a common effect on the industry in a state at the same point in time.

Independent and Moderating Variables

Our first independent variable, *urban-rural polarization*, captures the partisan difference between urban and rural residents in a state. Overall, we relied on presidential election results to indicate population partisanship and the "metropolitan statistical areas" identified by the US Census to differentiate urban and rural areas. According to the 2010 US Census, "metropolitan statistical areas" are those containing at least one urbanized area with a population of 50,000 or more. We referred to urban counties as those located at the center of "metropolitan statistical areas," and rural counties as those located at the margins of or outside "metropolitan statistical areas." As presidential election results for towns and cities were not available for all the years and states in our samples (Ansolabehere & Rodden, 2012), we used county-level data to ensure longitudinal comparison. In the period of our study, there were 727 urban counties out of a total of 3,143 counties in the entire country.

We measured urban-rural polarization as the difference between the average Democratic voting percentage in the most recent presidential election in a state's urban counties and rural counties. The variable had a higher value if a state's urban countries were more Democratic and rural counties were more Republican. The urban-rural polarization for all states in our observation period ranged from 0.23 to 0.14, and the mean score was 0.09. This confirmed that urban areas are generally more liberal than rural ones.

There are several advantages to using county-level presidential voting results to measure a state's urban-rural polarization. First, county-level voting data are a reliable indicator of an area's dominant political ideology. They also measure the ideological orientation of urban and rural areas with the same indicator and are thus better than other measurements that mix elite and mass partisanship (Kim et al., 2003). Second, county-level presidential election results are more readily available than are data on partisanship within city governments. As Gerber and Hopkins (2011, p. 331) point out, "City elections (and mayoral elections, in particular) occur at different times under different rules, and no comprehensive record of their results currently exists." Third, county-level presidential election data are longitudinal and can thus reflect changes in urban-rural polarization in the 2010s. Tausanovitch and Warshaw (2014) used survey data to measure dominant political ideology in municipalities prior to the 2010s. However, these surveys were discontinued in the 2010s and thus cannot capture the intensification of urban-rural polarization in the period covered by our study. Nonetheless, Tausanovitch and Warshaw (2014) showed that their survey-based measurement closely correlated with the presidential vote share in 2008 ($r = 0.77$), thereby indicating that presidential election results are a reliable measure of the prevalent political ideology in a region.

The cumulative number of bans or moratoriums issued by local governments on fracking in a state in a prior year is the independent variable for *H2–4*. It is measured in the same way as when it serves as the dependent variable for *H1*, except that it is lagged by one year. Similarly, *the number of lobbyists* hired by fracking companies to work on a state government in the prior year is the independent variable for *H5*, and is measured in the same way as when it serves as the dependent variable for *H2–4*, except for being lagged by one year.

We measured the *conservative elites' dominance* within a state legislature by creating a dummy variable (coded 1) to indicate that the Republican Party possesses governorship and constitutes both a majority in the state senate and house in the prior year (Chen, 2007). We obtained the data on the party affiliations of state governors and legislators from the Book of States published by the Council of State Governments.

We measured *the percentage of state legislators affiliated with ALEC* in a prior year. We obtained the list of state legislators involved in ALEC activities from the Center for Media and Democracy (CMD), a nationally recognized watchdog group for corruption and democracy. The CMD has been collecting data on politicians involved in ALEC activities from documents leaked by the ALEC membership directory, rosters of participants at ALEC meetings, published information on ALEC leaders, and politicians' personal announcements of their membership in or departure from the organization. The CMD list also includes politicians who have been featured speakers or have accepted awards at ALEC meetings. In the CMD list, we identified 2,722 unique state legislators involved in ALEC activities in 49 states from 2001 to 2019. We found the time at which each ALEC legislator served by searching state legislatures' webpages and the Ballotpedia database of state legislators. In so doing, we obtained the number of ALEC legislators in a state in a given year and calculated the percentage of ALEC legislators by weighting their number against the total number of legislators in a state.

Control Variables

We included six sets of control variables related to industry regulation and industry lobbying directed at the state. First, we expected local and state governments' decision on fracking to be influenced by the oil industry's contribution to the state's economy. We thus controlled for *the number of people employed by the oil and gas industry* per 1,000 people in the prior year. We collected these data from the US Bureau of Labor Statistics, from which we identified their occupations by code: 47-5011 (Oil and Gas Derrick Operators), 47-5012 (Oil and Gas Rotary Drill Operators), 47-5013 (Oil and Gas Service Unit Operators), and 47-5071 (Oil and Gas Roustabouts).

Second, we controlled for *professionalism of state legislature* for the dependent variable of state preemption. States with more professionalized legislatures have more legislative resources and expertise and are thus less likely to delegate regulative authority over fracking activities to local governments (Flavin & Shufeldt, 2020; Fowler & Witt, 2019). We measured legislative professionalism by using the five categories established by the NCSL for the 50 state legislatures – from full-time professional legislatures to part-time citizen legislatures – based on the amount of time legislators spent on the job, their compensation, and the size of the legislative staff.

Third, we also expected that local and state governments' actions toward fracking were enabled or limited by legal structures defined by state constitutions such as *Home Rule* or Dillon's Rule. In states with Home Rule, local governments have the authority to pass laws on their own; in states with Dillon's Rule, local governments must obtain permission from the state legislature to pass laws or ordinances (Fowler & Witt, 2019). Based on Krane et al. (2001), 10 states operate under Home Rule, and 40 states operate under Dillon's Rule (or modified versions of it). We coded a dummy variable to indicate states operating under Home Rule (indicated as 1).

Fourth, we controlled for the level of *legislative competition*. In an electorally competitive environment, partisan legislators make broader appeals than they would otherwise, thereby improving their chance of innovating policy (Jenkins et al., 2006). We thus measured legislative competition according to the margin of the percentage of seats held by the two parties in state legislatures (Chen, 2007). We obtained the data from the Council of State Governments.

Fifth, we considered the socioeconomic characteristics of a state. We controlled for *population* and per capita *income, the percentage of urban population,* and *the percentage of White population* in the prior year. We collected the data from the US Census Bureau and the Bureau of Economic Analysis.

Finally, we also included the state *fiscal capacity* by measuring the state governments' annual revenue per capita (Jenkins et al., 2006) and collected the data from the Council of State Governments. We also controlled for the *diffusion effect* between states as a state government can pass preemptive laws to follow peer states. We measured the number of states with preemptions in the prior year.

RESULTS

To address the first hypothesis, we first generated a boxplot to compare counties with and without local bans and found those with them were more likely to support Democratic candidates in presidential elections (Fig. 2). Table 2 reports our analysis of the number of local bans on fracking. Model 1 is the baseline model that includes only control variables. It shows that the control variables of legislative competition, high per capita income, and the prevalence of oil industry employment discourage local governments from coming up with restrictive policies on fracking activities, whereas a higher state population and urban population are likely to lead to more local bans. Model 2 indicates that the independent variable — urban-rural polarization — increases the number of fracking bans issued by local governments in a state, thereby supporting *H1*. When the polarization score rises by one standard deviation, the number of local bans increases twofold ($\beta = 1.314$, $p < 0.05$).

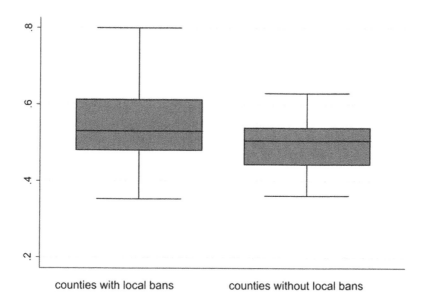

Fig. 2. A Boxplot That Compares Votes to the Democratic Party in Counties With and Without Local Bans Over Fracking.

Table 2. Fixed Effect 2SLS Models on the Impact of Urban-Rural Polarization on Local Bans.

	(1)	(2)
Urban-rural polarization (IV)		1.314**
		(0.541)
State legislative competition	−3.391***	−3.413***
	(0.225)	(0.225)
State fiscal capacity	0.685	0.681
	(0.015)	(0.015)
Oil industry employment (per 1,000 people)	−0.173***	−0.704***
	(0.023)	(0.023)
Per capita income (10k)	−2.292**	−2.212***
	(0.069)	(0.077)
Population (1 million)	0.058**	0.061**
	(0.002)	(0.003)
Urban population	0.628*	0.359*
	(0.302)	(0.320)
White population	−1.023	−0.996
	(0.034)	(0.036)
Diffusion	0.312	0.293
	(0.039)	(0.041)
Log likelihood	−2060.928	−2057.959

$N = 560$; $*p < 0.1$; $**p < 0.05$; $***p < 0.01$; two-sided; State and year-fixed effects are included; Nebraska has a nonpartisan state legislature and was therefore removed from the sample when measuring partisan election pressure for state legislators.

Number of Industry Lobbyists

Table 3 reports the analysis of the number of lobbyists hired by the fracking industry to work on state governments in order to test *H2*, *H3*, and *H4*. Model 1 is the baseline model and shows that the more competitive the two parties in state legislatures are, the more effort the industry will put into lobbying. This is consistent with our expectation that businesses see a greater chance of success from a competitive state legislature that is more open to policy innovation. The addition of oil and gas industry jobs in a state is negatively associated with the intensification of lobbying. The reason may be that when politicians are more reliant on the industry to provide employment, companies see less need to engage in extra lobbying. In addition, the oil and gas industry hires more lobbyists in states with larger urban and White populations, and after a significant number of other states have issued state preemptions.

Model 2 tests the main effect of local bans, showing that this variable has a positive, significant effect on the intensity of lobbying at a state government level. The result confirms that the rise in bans issued by local governments is directly related to more industry lobbying activities on the state government level. When the number of local bans in a state goes from one standard deviation below to one standard deviation above the mean, oil companies hire on average six more lobbyists ($\beta = 0.036$, $p < 0.01$). Hence *H2* is supported.

Table 3. Fixed Effect Poisson Model of the Number of Hired Lobbyists.

	(1)	(2)	(3)	(4)	(5)	(6)
State legislative competition	1.032***	0.934***	0.763***	0.431*	0.901***	0.453**
	(0.221)	(0.221)	(0.237)	(0.244)	(0.219)	(0.227)
State fiscal capacity	0.036	0.025	0.025	0.021	0.011	0.002
	(0.022)	(0.021)	(0.021)	(0.022)	(0.022)	(0.022)
Oil industry employment (per 1,000 people)	−0.080***	−0.049***	−0.048***	−0.052***	−0.054***	−0.065***
	(0.017)	(0.017)	(0.017)	(0.017)	(0.017)	(0.017)
Per capita income (10k)	−0.185	−0.519***	−0.491***	−0.094	−0.420***	0.028
	(0.124)	(0.131)	(0.132)	(0.150)	(0.134)	(0.151)
Population (1 million)	0.026	0.007	0.021	0.038	−0.085**	0.013
	(0.031)	(0.031)	(0.032)	(0.032)	(0.033)	(0.037)
Urban population	12.254**	16.609***	18.056***	15.698***	19.989***	19.711***
	(4.896)	(4.868)	(4.937)	(4.949)	(4.963)	(5.001)
White population	0.300***	0.278***	0.268***	0.206***	0.226***	0.216***
	(0.028)	(0.028)	(0.028)	(0.031)	(0.030)	(0.030)
Diffusion	0.316***	0.333***	0.312***	0.222***	−1.274***	−1.512***
	(0.054)	(0.054)	(0.055)	(0.057)	(0.375)	(0.382)
Local ban number		0.036***	0.036***	−0.0001	0.039***	−0.010
		(0.005)	(0.005)	(0.008)	(0.005)	(0.009)
Conservative dominance in state legislatures			0.160**	0.067		
			(0.078)	(0.081)		
ALEC legislator ratio					−1.632***	−3.899***
					(0.405)	(0.520)
Local ban number × conservative dominance				0.053***		
				(0.009)		
Local ban number × ALEC legislator ratio						0.156***
						(0.022)
Log likelihood	−1,364.538	−1,334.205	−1,332.125	−1,314.696	−1,320.867	−1,295.427

$N = 560$, *$p < 0.1$; **$p < 0.05$; ***$p < 0.01$; two-sided; State-fixed effects, year-fixed effects, and the Inverse Mills Ratio are included. Nebraska has a nonpartisan state legislature and was therefore removed from the sample when measuring partisan election pressure for state legislators.

Models 3–4 test the moderation effect of conservative dominance on state legislatures, showing the effect of interaction between local ban numbers and conservative state legislatures to be positively significant ($\beta = 0.053$, $p < 0.01$). The result indicates that when the state legislature is dominated by conservatives, fracking companies hire more lobbyists to respond to the growth of local bans, thus supporting *H3*. To demonstrate the magnitude of the coefficient, we graph the interaction effect in Fig. 3.

Models 5–6 test the moderation effect of the percentage of ALEC state legislators, showing that the interaction term is positive and significant ($\beta = 0.156$, $p < 0.01$). The result reveals that, despite a negative main effect, a higher percentage of ALEC state legislators amplifies the positive impact of local bans on the intensity of lobbying by fracking companies on the state government level, thus supporting *H4*. To demonstrate the magnitude of the coefficient, we graph the interaction effect in Fig. 4.

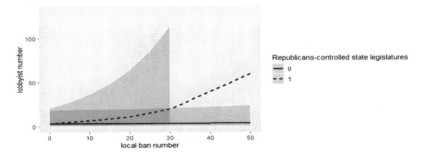

Fig. 3. Moderation Effect Between Local Bans and State Republican Control.

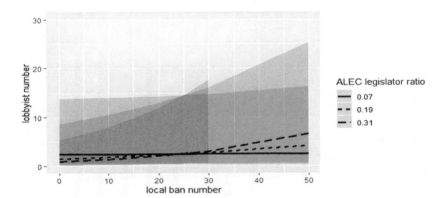

Fig. 4. Moderation Effect Between Local Bans and ALEC Legislators.

State Preemption

Table 4 reports the event history models of state preemption to test *H5*. Model 1 tests the impact of control variables. It reveals that the control variables of ALEC legislator ratio, legislative professionalism, and oil industry employment are associated with a higher chance of state preemption over local bans. There is also evidence for the diffusion effect, namely, that a state is more likely to issue preemption when other states have done so. Model 2 includes the number of lobbyists hired by the fracking industry in a prior year. The coefficient is positive and significant ($\beta = 0.128$, $p < 0.01$), confirming *H5* that more lobbying efforts by the industry lead to a higher likelihood of preemption of local bans on fracking. Specifically, one standard deviation increase in the number of lobbyists

Table 4. Event History Model of State Preemption.

	(1)	(2)
Conservative dom. in state legislatures	−1.838	−1.932
	(1.272)	(1.499)
ALEC state legislator ratio	10.863***	8.475*
	(4.216)	(4.396)
State legislative professionalism	1.215**	2.519**
	(0.582)	(0.992)
State legislative competition	−1.275	4.632
	(3.617)	(4.630)
State fiscal capacity	−0.214	−0.256
	(0.337)	(0.374)
Home rule	−0.595	0.721
	(1.277)	(1.407)
Oil industry employment	0.512***	0.382**
	(0.170)	(0.183)
Per capita income (10k)	−1.143	−1.346
	(1.016)	(1.147)
Population (1 million)	0.077	−0.067
	(0.074)	(0.083)
Urban population	−3.603	−11.518
	(7.292)	(9.391)
White population	−0.601	−5.132**
	(1.200)	(2.191)
Diffusion	0.678***	0.680***
	(0.194)	(0.186)
Local ban number	0.006	0.013
	(0.018)	(0.019)
Lobbyist number		0.128**
		(0.052)
Log likelihood	−26.395	−22.768

$N = 560$; *$p < 0.1$; **$p < 0.05$; ***$p < 0.01$; two-sided; Nebraska has a nonpartisan state legislature and was therefore removed from the sample when measuring partisan election pressure for state legislators.

132   *Elite Conflict and Industry Regulation*

leads to a 13% higher chance of state preemption. In unreported analyses, we also adopted the proportional hazard Cox model and the probit model, and got results similar to those reported here. In addition to *H3*, which focuses on the direct impact of lobbying on state preemption, we conducted an extra test on the moderating impact of Republican dominance and ALEC legislators and found them to be insignificant. Thus, Republican dominance and ALEC legislators enhance the enactment of state preemption primarily through increasing the number of lobbyists that the industry hires.

In sum, our results provide evidence for a causal relationship between urban-rural polarization and state preemption with regard to fracking activities. First, we find that the increased polarization of urban and rural areas is associated with a higher number of local bans on fracking activities within a state (i.e., *H1*). Second, the presence of more local bans within a state motivates fracking companies to increase their lobbying efforts on the state government level (i.e., *H2*), particularly in states where Republican dominate (i.e., *H3*) and where there is a higher percentage of ALEC-affiliated legislators (i.e., *H4*). Third, our results suggest that the increased lobbying efforts of fracking companies on the state government level can be associated with a higher likelihood of state preemption aimed at nullifying local bans on fracking activities (i.e., *H5*).

CONCLUSION

The regulation and politics in the US fracking industry provide an ideal opportunity for testing Lachmann's elite conflict theory (Lachmann, 1987, 2000) in the contemporary era. As the American social sorting process has led to a form of geopolitical polarization in which state governments are controlled by more conservative elites while city governments are controlled by more liberal elites (Mason, 2018), such ideological differences affect both the threat posed to the industry and the opportunity for it to shape regulation. The polarization of elites activates competition between local and state governments, not only by encouraging the local government to impose bans on fracking (Riverstone-Newell, 2017), but also by enabling the industry to lobby the state government to preempt local bans (Yue & Wang, 2023). In particular, the dominance of supportive elites within the upper level of government creates an opportunity for leveraging preemption and thus enhances the industry's lobbying efforts. In this way, our study contributes to the research on the politics of industry regulation, industry political strategy, and elite conflict theory. Below, we elaborate on these contributions and point out the direction for future research.

First, this chapter contributes to the sociological research on the politics of industry regulation. Sociologists have emphasized how industry players, social movement activists, and other stakeholders compete to define the rules of the game, and view political opportunity as a critical factor in the way in which these various groups transform their advocacy into policy outcomes (Fligstein, 1996; Ingram & Rao, 2004; Schneiberg & Bartley, 2001, 2010; Yue et al., 2013).

Partisan control of the government is an important component of political opportunity as it relates to the power of political allies, access to institutional channels, and the cost of political action (Chen, 2007; Jenkins et al., 2006). The existing literature on industry regulation, however, has focused on partisan control over a particular level of government (e.g., Chen, 2007; Dokshin, 2016; Fremeth et al., 2022). We have introduced geopolitical conflicts between political elites to the issue and argue that partisan elites' control of a particular level of government is not alone in affecting industry regulation, but instead interacts with rival elites' control of another level of government. Our study shows that regulations on the fracking industry are the result of interaction between political elites at the local and state governments, and that elites' geopolitical polarization amplifies the policy divide among different levels of government. Therefore, an examination of the impact of elite conflicts that are rooted in urban-rural polarization extends the literature on industry regulation to the theorization of political opportunity.

Second, this chapter contributes to the research on the political strategy of industry by highlighting how heterogeneity on the policy supply side enables industry players to adopt corporate political strategy to shape regulatory environments. While the literature on the political strategy of industry has traditionally focused on the single policy supplier or assumed the homogeneity of policy suppliers (e.g., Bonardi et al., 2005; Gao & McDonald, 2022), a small body of studies has explored the heterogeneity of policy suppliers and power relations among government entities (e.g., Ozcan & Gurses, 2018; Yue et al., 2019; Yue & Wang, 2023). This chapter joins but also departs from this group of studies. Although they assume that preexisting structures, such as decentralization or the constitutional separation of powers (e.g., between different levels or branches of government), indicate cleavages within political authority, this chapter suggests that this need not be the case. Rather, structural differentiation alone may not indicate the existence of a political opportunity. Political polarization is an important condition for creating and escalating conflicts between heterogeneous policy suppliers. In other words, heterogeneity on the policy supply side is not a fixed or exogenous feature, but a dynamic process that can be activated, amplified, and exploited by industry players. This point is also supported by recent research on fracking firms' campaign contributions which shows that they target at Republican candidates in Democratic-leaning districts that are on oil shale (Li & DiSalvo, 2023). Through shaping the supply of policy entrepreneurs, industries might have played an important role in creating their favored political opportunities.

In addition, we shed light on how nascent industries can leverage uncertainties in regulatory jurisdictions to shape their regulatory environments. Nascent industries that develop from new technologies often face jurisdictional uncertainty in regulatory authority (Yue & Wang, 2023). Unlike an established industry in which the government entity with regulatory power is often already set, the government entity with the jurisdictional authority to regulate a nascent industry may be contested. For example, when the federal government recently attempted to regulate the nascent cryptocurrency industry, numerous federal agencies, including the SEC, IRS, CFTC, and Congress, all claimed regulatory authority over it (Ball, 2022). Uncertainties regarding regulatory authority exist not only horizontally between different government branches, but also vertically between different levels of government. This chapter shows that when faced with vertical uncertainties regarding the regulatory authority of state and local governments, state preemption is a political strategy that industry players can adopt to fight unfavorable regulation. This chapter together with Yue and Wang's (2023) study of the US commercial drone industry are among the first studies of the influence of industry lobbying on state preemption of local regulation. In marble-cake Federalism, the powers, goals, and duties of the national, state, and local US elites are interrelated (Grodzins, 1966), and the partisan divisions among them grant industry players new opportunities to exert political influence. As such, this chapter joins an emerging body of work of the political strategies that nascent industries adopt to shape their regulatory environment; while the prior literature has investigated strategies such as framing contest (Ozcan & Gurses, 2018), participation in regulation formation (Gao & McDonald, 2022), and making campaign contributions (Li & DiSalvo, 2023), this chapter add to the list by highlighting the strategy of lobbying for state preemption.

Third, this chapter contributes to studies on the conflict between elites by showing its contemporary application in explaining the formation of industry regulations and the political strategies of industry players to shape them. While Lachmann's early work (1987, 2000) insightfully points out how elite conflicts affect economic players, few empirical studies examine the theory's application in the contemporary era. Lachmann's own recent work focuses on the consequences of elite conflicts on the rise and decline of polities (2020). Studying American elites, he (2020) argues that their division has escalated as the Republican-led governments encourage economic deregulation, which has resulted in waves of corporate mergers that further increase social inequalities. While Lachmann's conclusion draws on how changes in government regulation impoverish *the state*'s capacity to collect revenue and hence lead to *state* decline, this chapter extends his original insight into the domain of industry regulation and suggests that conflicts between American political elites can both challenge and enable industry players. We focus on the ideological rivalries between political elites in contemporary America and show that in politically polarized states, industries find allies in the state house and face challenges in city halls. Our study does not directly assess the sizes of the constrictive versus enabling effects, but does suggest that conflict among elites may lead to a complex set of contentious relationships between political and economic actors and may thus not lead directly to decline in state capacity. Moreover, as modern societies are characterized by political pluralism, we believe that the angle from which we investigated conflicts between political elites can be used to explain a wide range of phenomena in the modern political economy. Our study of industry regulation is likely a mere herald of a vibrant area of research.

This chapter also has implications for elite theory in general. By studying conflict among political elites, it revisits the classic debate on whether elites are homogeneous and unified or heterogeneous and polarized (Mizruchi, 2013; Chu

& Davis, 2016; Benton, 2017; Benton & Adam Cobb, 2019). This debate is central to the conceptualization of a society (like that of the United States) as one governed by either the principle of elitism or that of pluralism. At one end, Marx's social class theory and Mills' power elite theory argue for the existence of relatively homogenous and interconnected elites that dominate the major economic, political, and military decisions of a society; at the other, pluralists argue that organized groups compete for influence when shaping these major decisions (Dahl, 1961). By building on Lachmann's insight and theorizing the conflict between elites and the associated consequences in contemporary America, this chapter provides a middle-ground response to this debate; we show that political elites are unified through think tanks and policy networks such as ALEC but are also divided along partisan and geographical lines. Because political elites adhering to different political ideologies find constituents in different geographies, control different levels of government, and take opposing policy positions towards the same group of industry players, this chapter suggests that they are clearly not as homogeneous or unified as prior elite theories have suggested, and thus calls for a more realistic assessment of modern elites in the United States.

NOTE

1. Lachmann's last book *First-Class Passengers on a Sinking Ship* does examine the consequence of elite conflict in the contemporary context, but focuses on how conflict threatens elite capacities and ultimately leads to the decline of a nation's hegemonic power rather than on the consequence of change in social structure that disadvantages or favors economic forces.

REFERENCES

American Legislative Exchange Council (ALEC). (2013, January 28). Living wage mandate pre-emption act. https://www.alec.org/model-policy/living-wage-mandate-preemption-act/
American Legislative Exchange Council (ALEC). (2020). About ALEC. https://www.alec.org/about/
Ansolabehere, S., & Rodden, J. (2012). Harvard election data archive. http://projects.iq.harvard.edu/eda
Badger, E. (2019). How the rural-urban divide became America's political fault line. https://www.nytimes.com/2019/05/21/upshot/america-political-divide-urban-rural.html
Baldassarri, D., & Bearman, P. (2007). Dynamics of political polarization. *American Sociological Review, 72*(5), 784–811.
Ball, M. (2022). Crypto goes to Washington. *Time*. https://time.com/6215042/crypto-washington-dc-regulation/
Barber, M., & Dynes, A. M. (2023). City-state ideological incongruence and municipal preemption. *American Journal of Political Science, 67*(1), 119–136.
Bartik, A. W., Currie, J., Greenstone, M., & Knittel, C. R. (2019). The local economic and welfare consequences of hydraulic fracturing. *American Economic Journal: Applied Economics, 11*(4), 105–155.
Benton, R. A. (2017). The decline of social entrenchment: Social network cohesion and board responsiveness to shareholder activism. *Organization Science, 28*(2), 262–282.
Benton, R. A., & Adam Cobb, J. (2019). Eyes on the horizon? Fragmented elites and the short-term focus of the American corporation. *American Journal of Sociology, 124*(6), 1631–1684.
Bishop, B., & Cushing, R. G. (2009). *The big sort: Why the clustering of like-minded America is tearing us apart*. Houghton Mifflin Harcourt.

Bonardi, J. P., Hillman, A. J., & Keim, G. D. (2005). The attractiveness of political markets: Implications for firm strategy. *Academy of Management Review, 30*(2), 397–413.

Bottari, M. (2015, March 31). The ALEC-backed war on local democracy. https://www.prwatch.org/news/2015/03/12782/alec-backed-war-local-democracy

Boudet, H., Clarke, C., Bugden, D., Maibach, E., Roser-Renouf, C., & Leiserowitz, A. (2014). "Fracking" controversy and communication: Using national survey data to understand public perceptions of hydraulic fracturing. *Energy Policy, 65*, 57–67.

Briffault, R. (2018). *The challenge of the new preemption*. Columbia Public Law Research Paper, (14-580).

Chen, A. S. (2007). The Party of Lincoln and the politics of state fair employment practices legislation in the North, 1945–1964. *American Journal of Sociology, 112*(6), 1713–1774.

Chen, M. K., & Rohla, R. (2017). The effect of partisanship and political advertising on close family ties. *Science, 360*(6392), 1020–1024.

Choi, S. J., Jia, N., & Lu, J. (2015). The structure of political institutions and effectiveness of corporate political lobbying. *Organization Science, 26*(1), 158–179.

Chu, J. S., & Davis, G. F. (2016). Who killed the inner circle? The decline of the American corporate interlock network. *American Journal of Sociology, 122*(3), 714–754.

Cutter, C., Vranica, S., & Sider, A. (2021, April 10). *With Georgia voting law, the business of business becomes politics*. https://www.wsj.com/articles/with-georgia-voting-law-the-business-of-business-becomes-politics-11618027250

Dahl, R. A. (1961). *Who governs?: Democracy and power in an American city*. Yale University Press.

Davis, C., & Fisk, J. M. (2014). Energy abundance or environmental worries? Analyzing public support for fracking in the United States. *The Review of Policy Research, 31*(1).

De Figueiredo, J. M., & Richter, B. K. (2014). Advancing the empirical research on lobbying. *Annual Review of Political Science, 17*, 163–185.

Desilver, D. (2022, March 10). *The polarization in today's congress has roots that go back decades*. Pew Research Center. https://www.pewresearch.org/short-reads/2022/03/10/the-polarization-in-todays-congress-has-roots-that-go-back-decades/

DiMaggio, P., Evans, J., & Bryson, B. (1996). Have American's social attitudes become more polarized? *American Journal of Sociology, 102*(3), 690–755.

Dokshin, F. A. (2016). Whose backyard and what's at issue? Spatial and ideological dynamics of local opposition to fracking in New York State, 2010 to 2013. *American Sociological Review, 81*(5), 921–948.

Dolan, M. . (2012, February 7). Prop. 8: Gay-marriage ban unconstitutional, court rules. https://www.latimes.com/socal/glendale-news-press/tn-818-0207-prop-8-gaymarriage-ban-unconstitutional-court-rules-story.html

Domhoff, G. W. (1967). *Who rules America?* Prentice-Hall.

Dorobantu, S., Kaul, A., & Zelner, B. (2017). Nonmarket strategy research through the lens of new institutional economics: An integrative review and future directions. *Strategic Management Journal, 38*(1), 114–140.

Drutman, L. (2015). *The business of America is lobbying: How corporations became politicized and politics became more corporate*. Oxford University Press.

Elinson, Z. (2021). Black rifle coffee seeks like-minded Aficionados. *Wall Street Journal*. https://www.wsj.com/articles/black-rifle-coffee-seeks-like-minded-aficionados-11615550401

Emigh, R. J., Riley, D., & Ahmed, P. (2020).The sociology of official information gathering:. In T. Janoski, C. De Leon, J. Misra, & I. W. Martin (Eds.), *The new handbook of political sociology* (pp. 290–320). Cambridge University Press.

Flavin, P., & Shufeldt, G. (2020). Explaining state preemption of local laws: Political, institutional, and demographic factors. *Publius: The Journal of Federalism, 50*(2), 280–309.

Fligstein, N. (1996). Markets as politics: A political-cultural approach to market institutions. *American Sociological Review, 61*, 656–673.

Food & Water Watch. (2020, June 12). Local resolutions against fracking. https://www.foodandwaterwatch.org/insight/local-resolutions-against-fracking

Fowler, L., & Witt, S. L. (2019). State preemption of local authority: Explaining patterns of state adoption of preemption measures. *Publius: The Journal of Federalism, 49*(3), 540–559.

Fremeth, A. R., Holburn, G. L., & Piazza, A. (2022). Activist protest spillovers into the regulatory domain: Theory and evidence from the US nuclear power generation industry. *Organization Science, 33*(3), 1163–1187.

Funk, R. J., & Hirschman, D. (2017). Beyond nonmarket strategy: Market actions as corporate political activity. *Academy of Management Review, 42*(1), 32–52.

Gao, C., & McDonald, R. (2022). Shaping nascent industries: Innovation strategy and regulatory uncertainty in personal genomics. *Administrative Science Quarterly, 67*, 915–967.

Gerber, E. R., & Hopkins, D. J. (2011). When mayors matter: how Estimating the impact of mayoral partisanship on city policy. *American Journal of Political Science, 55*(2), 326–339.

Goodman, C. B. (2019). *State legislative ideology & the preemption of city ordinances: The case of worker rights laws*. Working Paper. Northern Illinois University.

Graham, M. H., & Svolik, M. W. (2020). Democracy in America? Partisanship, polarization, and the robustness of support for democracy in the United States. *American Political Science Review, 114*(2), 392–409.

Grandy, J. B., & Hiatt, S. R. (2020). State agency discretion and entrepreneurship in regulated markets. *Administrative Science Quarterly, 65*(4), 1092–1131.

Grodzins, M. (1966). *The American system: A new view of government in the United States*. Transaction Publishers.

Hertel-Fernandez, A. (2017). American employers as political machines. *The Journal of Politics, 79*(1), 105–117.

Hertel-Fernandez, A. (2019). *State capture: How conservative activists, big businesses, and wealthy donors reshaped the American states – And the nation*. Oxford University Press.

Hillman, A. J., & Hitt, M. A. (1999). Corporate political strategy formulation: A model of approach, participation, and strategy decisions. *Academy of Management Review, 24*(4), 825–842.

Hillman, A. J., & Keim, G. (1995). International variation in the business-government interface: Institutional and organizational considerations. *Academy of Management Review,, 20*(1), 193–214.

Hillman, A. J., Keim, G. D., & Schuler, D. (2004). Corporate political activity: A review and research agenda. *Journal of Management, 30*(6), 837–857.

Ingram, P., & Rao, H. (2004). Store wars: The enactment and repeal of anti-chain legislation in the United States. *American Journal of Sociology, 110*(2), 446–487.

Iyengar, S., Lelkes, Y., Levendusky, M., Malhotra, N., & Westwood, S. J. (2019). The origins and consequences of affective polarization in the United States. *Annual Review of Political Science, 22*, 129–146.

Jenkins, J. C., Leicht, K. T., & Wendt, H. (2006). Class forces, political institutions, and state intervention: Subnational economic development policy in the United States, 1971–1990. *American Journal of Sociology, 111*(4), 1122–1180.

Jerolmack, C., & Walker, E. T. (2018). Please in my backyard: Quiet mobilization in support of fracking in an Appalachian community. *American Journal of Sociology, 124*(2), 479–516.

Kim, J., Elliott, E., & Wang, D. M. (2003). A spatial analysis of county-level outcomes in US Presidential elections: 1988–2000. *Electoral Studies, 22*(4), 741–761.

Krane, D., Rigos, P. N., & Hill, M. (2001). *Home rule in America: A fifty-state handbook*. CQ Press.

Lachmann, R. W. (1987). *From manor to market: Structure change in England, 1536-1640*. University of Wisconsin Press.

Lachmann, R. (2000). *Capitalists in spite of themselves: Elite conflict and economic transitions in early modern Europe*. Oxford University Press.

Lachmann, R. (2014). Hegemons, empires, and their elites. *Sociologia - Problemas e Praticas*, (75), 9–38.

Lachmann, R. (2020). *First class passengers on a sinking ship: Elite politics and the decline of great powers*. Verso Books.

Li, Z., & DiSalvo, R. W. (2023). *Economic geography, regulatory uncertainty, and integrated strategy: Evidence from the fracking boom and state campaign finance*. Working Paper. New York University.

Mason, L. (2018). Ideologues without issues: The polarizing consequences of ideological identities. *Public Opinion Quarterly, 82*(S1), 866–887.

McAdam, D., & Boudet, H. (2012). *Putting social movements in their place: Explaining opposition to energy projects in the United States, 2000–2005*. Cambridge University Press.

Mills, C. W. (1956). *The power elite*. Oxford University Press.

Mizruchi, M. S. (2013). *The fracturing of the American corporate elite*. Harvard University Press.

National Conference of State Legislatures (NCSL). (2018, May 15). 50 state chart: Lobbyist activity report requirements. https://www.ncsl.org/research/ethics/50-state-chart-lobbyist-report-requirements.aspx

National Institute of Money in State Politics. (2020). *FollowTheMoney.org*. https://www.followthemoney.org/

Ozcan, P., & Gurses, K. (2018). Playing cat and mouse: Contests over regulatory categorization of dietary supplements in the United States. *Academy of Management Journal, 61*(5), 1789–1820.

Pew Research Center. (2021, April 22). Republicans and Democrats move further apart from in views of voting access. https://www.pewresearch.org/politics/2021/04/22/republicans-and-democrats-move-further-apart-in-views-of-voting-access/

Phillips, L. E. (2017). Impeding innovation: State preemption of progressive local regulations. *Columbia Law Review, 117*, 2225.

Pierson, P., & Hacker, J. S. (2002). Business power and social policy: Employers and the formation of the American welfare state. *Politics & Society, 30*(2), 277–325.

Rao, H., Yue, L. Q., & Ingram, P. (2011). Laws of attraction: Regulatory arbitrage in the face of activism in right-to-work states. *American Sociological Review, 76*(3), 365–385.

Riccardi, N. (2019, September 11). Democrats step on shaky political ground with fracking bans. https://apnews.com/f5494ec2e11e43a59c5531a787fe3f03

Riverstone-Newell, L. (2017). The rise of state preemption laws in response to local policy innovation. *Publius: The Journal of Federalism, 47*(3), 403–425.

Scala, D. J., & Johnson, K. M. (2017). Political polarization along the rural-urban continuum? The geography of the presidential vote, 2000–2016. *The Annals of the American Academy of Political and Social Science, 672*(1), 162–184.

Schneiberg, M., & Bartley, T. (2001). Regulating American industries: Markets, politics, and the institutional determinants of fire insurance regulation. *American Journal of Sociology, 107*(1), 101–146.

Schneiberg, M., & Bartley, T. (2010). *Regulating or redesigning finance? Market architectures, normal accidents, and dilemmas of regulatory reform*. In M. Lounsbury & P. M. Hirsch (Eds.), Markets on trial: The economic sociology of the US financial crisis: Part A (pp. 281–307). Emerald Group Publishing Limited.

Sytch, M., & Kim, Y. H. (2021). Quo vadis? From the schoolyard to the courtroom. *Administrative Science Quarterly, 66*(1), 177–219.

Tausanovitch, C., & Warshaw, C. (2014). Representation in municipal government. *American Political Science Review, 108*(3), 605–641.

Tiebout, C. M. (1956). A pure theory of local expenditures. *Journal of Political Economy, 64*(5), 416–424.

Vasi, I. B., Walker, E. T., Johnson, J. S., & Tan, H. F. (2015). "No fracking way!" Documentary film, discursive opportunity, and local opposition against hydraulic fracturing in the United States, 2010 to 2013. *American Sociological Review, 80*(5), 934–959.

Verdant Lab. (2016). Democratic vs. Republican occupations. http://verdantlabs.com/politics_of_professions/

Wooldridge, J. M. (2015). Control function methods in applied econometrics. *Journal of Human Resources, 50*(2), 420–445.

Yue, L. Q., Luo, J., & Ingram, P. (2013). The failure of private regulation: Elite control and market crises in the Manhattan banking industry. *Administrative Science Quarterly, 58*(1), 37–68.

Yue, L. Q., & Wang, J. (2023). Policy learning in nascent industries' venue shifting: A study of the US small unmanned aircraft systems (UAS) industry. *Business & Society*. https://doi.org/10.1177/00076503231182666

Yue, L. Q., Wang, J., & Yang, B. (2019). Contesting commercialization: Political influence, responsive authoritarianism, and cultural resistance. *Administrative Science Quarterly, 64*(2), 435–465.

APPENDIX A1. FIRST-STAGE REGRESSION WITH THE INSTRUMENTAL VARIABLE

	OLS Urban-Rural Polarization
Agriculture job	0.234**
	(0.073)
Oil employment	0.002
	(0.001)
Legislature professionalism	−0.004
	(0.004)
State fiscal capacity	−0.007***
	(0.001)
Unemployment rate	−0.005**
	(0.002)
Population	0.001*
	(0.001)
Per capita income	0.020***
	(0.003)
White population	0.013*
	(0.006)
Constant	0.019
	(0.021)
F	12.88
R^2	0.141

$N = 560$; $*p < 0.1$; $**p < 0.05$; $***p < 0.01$; two-sided.

CHAPTER 6

ELITE POLITICS AND ECONOMIC CRISIS: HYPERINFLATION IN ARGENTINA, 1989–1990

Tod S. Van Gunten

University of Edinburgh, UK

ABSTRACT

Hyperinflation is a rare form of macroeconomic crisis that often results from extreme political events, such as revolution or regime change. The 1989–1990 Argentine hyperinflation is puzzling because it occurred in the absence of such an event. Moreover, conventional fiscal mechanisms linking political processes to hyperinflation do not sufficiently explain the Argentine case. Previous theories emphasizing distributional conflict and institutional weakness contain key elements of an explanation of the Argentine hyperinflation but do not capture the range of mechanisms that produced extreme financial instability. This chapter offers an elite theory approach that subsumes elements of these approaches within a broader theory of elite fragmentation, competition, and conflict. Elite fragmentation inhibits collective action in both economic and state elites, resulting in deficits in policymaking capacity. Fragmentation among state policy elites leads to policy volatility and incoherence, while fragmentation among politically mobilized economic elites results in elite stalemates constraining the options of policy elites. These policymaking patterns lead to prolonged delays in the adjustment of unsustainable organizational structures, resulting in explosive forms of crises.

Keywords: Elites; Argentina; crisis; inflation; cohesion

INTRODUCTION

Hyperinflation is an extreme financial event in which the value of money collapses as prices increase rapidly. States create money, and hyperinflation thus ensues from

---

Elites, Nonelites, and Power
Political Power and Social Theory, Volume 41, 141–173
Copyright © 2025 Tod S. Van Gunten
Published under exclusive licence by Emerald Publishing Limited
ISSN: 0198-8719/doi:10.1108/S0198-871920240000041006

underlying political processes. Most historical episodes of hyperinflation occurred due to fiscal crises resulting from state breakdown, revolution and regime change: classic cases include the German Weimar Republic and the French Revolution (Fischer et al., 2002). However, in 1989 and 1990, Argentina experienced hyperinflation in the absence of such an extreme political event. Over two wave-like crises, prices increased at a monthly rate exceeding 50%, and annual inflation reached 3,000% in 1989 and more than 2,000% in 1990. This macroeconomic crisis was also a deep social crisis, leading to widespread shortages, lootings, and civil unrest. Why Argentina experienced such an extreme macroeconomic event in the absence of a deep political crisis is a puzzle.

The Argentine case also defies the conventional fiscal mechanism linking political processes to macroeconomic outcomes as its hyperinflation did not occur primarily due to unconstrained monetary emission ("printing money") to cover conventional fiscal deficits (c.f. Beckerman, 1995). Financial, rather than narrowly fiscal, mechanisms caused hyperinflation in Argentina. Modern fiduciary currency is sovereign debt: most money takes the form of bank deposits ultimately backed by the ability of financial institutions to transact with the state in the form of a national central bank (Ingham, 2005). Hyperinflation resulted in part from financial processes which rendered the Argentine state, and more specifically its Central Bank, effectively insolvent. In parallel, currency runs resulting from collective uncertainty among wealth holders were key causal factors. Hyperinflation resulting from these financial dynamics requires a different account of the political processes generating macroeconomic imbalances.

Plausible existing explanations for macroeconomic instability invoke institutional weakness (Levitsky & Murillo, 2005; Spiller & Tommasi, 2007) and distributional conflict (Alesina & Drazen, 1991). This chapter offers an alternative explanation that subsumes elements of these theories within a broader account of elite politics. Hyperinflation in Argentina resulted from generalized elite fragmentation, which created a deep deficit in elites' capacity to formulate coherent policy. Multiple distinct elite sectors – party, policy and economic elites – were internally fragmented, undermining their capacity for coherent collective action. This elite fragmentation generated volatile, delayed, incoherent, and contradictory economic policies, which in turn fomented macroeconomic instability. Incoherent policies allowed macroeconomic and financial imbalances to accumulate, rendering the Argentine state effectively insolvent.

The paper rests on a narrative account of policymaking episodes drawing on archival and interview evidence, including 27 interviews with elites and other contemporary observers. In addition, I draw on publicly available interviews, published and unpublished documentary evidence, macroeconomic data, and a systematic review of major newspapers.[1]

INSTITUTIONAL WEAKNESS AND DISTRIBUTIONAL CONFLICT THEORIES

Many researchers claim that persistent macroeconomic instability in Argentina results from weak state institutions (Brinks et al., 2020; Dornbusch & de Pablo,

1989; Grimson et al., 2012; Levitsky & Murillo, 2005; Spiller & Tommasi, 2007). This is undoubtedly true but also a truism: institutional weakness has many dimensions and the mechanisms linking these dimensions to macroeconomic instability are poorly specified. The Argentine state bureaucracy – the institutional domain most relevant to macroeconomic policy – ranks low on measures of bureaucratic quality, such as staff turnover and tenure length (Evans & Rauch, 1999; Spiller & Tommasi, 2007). However, the mechanisms linking these general institutional indicators to macroeconomic outcomes have not been carefully specified. The concept of "corporate cohesion" (Evans & Rauch, 1999) is too vague to provide a precise explanation. One suggestion is that rapid turnover among state officials leads to short time horizons and undermines policy continuity (Dornbusch & de Pablo, 1989; Spiller & Tommasi, 2007). The elite politics account presented below incorporates this proposal while also recognizing that this is only one mechanism among several, and that elite turnover is often an endogenous reflection of elite conflict.

Other theories posit that distributional conflict is a key cause of macroeconomic crises and inflation (Hirschman, 1981; Krippner, 2011). One prominent distributional theory is the "war of attrition" model (Alesina & Drazen, 1991), which posits that explosive crises occur because conflict between competing groups leads to delay in the elimination of unsustainable fiscal deficits. In this model, groups with opposing economic interests compete to determine the magnitude of the state's fiscal deficit. Even if these groups agree in principle on eliminating the deficit, they disagree on how this objective is to be achieved (e.g., budget cuts vs. tax increases). Each group attempts to avoid costs by shifting the burden of adjustment onto the other; this conflict delays correction of the fiscal deficit until the crisis reaches a breaking point. Stabilization occurs when one party consolidates political control and forces the other to bear a disproportionate burden of adjustment. Alesina and Drazen (1991, p. 1,173) cite Argentine monetary instability as an exemplary case but do not provide systematic historical evidence.

Like institutionalist accounts, distributional conflict theories contain aspects of an explanation for the Argentine hyperinflation. Hyperinflation resulted in a sense from latent distributional conflict and a political impasse which delayed the elimination of unsustainable policies. However, the model's fiscalist assumptions are not met: as noted, the root causes of hyperinflation were financial (operating through the banking system and exchange rate market) rather than strictly fiscal (operating through the balance of state revenue and spending), requiring a different account of the underlying political processes. More fundamentally, the war of attrition model treats state elites as conduits for the interests of social groups, rather than elite actors pursuing their own objectives. This is an implausible assumption: Argentine political parties did not consistently represent specific economic sectors, and policy elites did not consistently represent party elites. Thus, the account presented here subsumes elements of both institutionalist and distributional conflict theories into a broader elite politics account.

ELITE POLITICS: FRAGMENTATION, STALEMATE, AND THE POLICYMAKING PROCESS

Elite theory posits that relations between heterogeneous sets of powerful actors are crucial causes of economic and political outcomes (Lachmann, 2002, 2020). This contrasts with theories emphasizing such factors as public opinion, electoral competition, and mobilization by nonelite actors. By spanning multiple elites, elite theory can encompass both theories of distributional conflict and weak institutions, which involve economic and state elites, respectively. Further, elite theories seek to anchor analysis in terms of identifiable actors, rather than abstract aggregates such as classes or "the state" (Marcus, 1983). Conflict can arise not because individual elites represent underlying social groups but because of the relations between particular elites pursuing distinct goals and strategies. Elite theories also often invoke the interrelated concepts of elite unity (Mills, 1956), cohesion (Burris, 2005), integration (Higley et al., 1991), fragmentation (Mizruchi, 2013), and stalemate (Lachmann, 2020) developed below.

The core claim of this chapter is that elite fragmentation undermines elite policymaking capacity, leading to economic instability. This is an extension of Lachmann's dictum that "elite conflict is the primary threat to elite capacities" (2020, p. 31). The concept of fragmentation summarizes several dimensions of relations among state and economic elites. The next section defines cohesion and fragmentation in network theoretic terms and identifies three dimensions of cohesion in state elites: relations between party and policy elites, among incumbent policy elites and between groups of policy elites over time. The Cohesion and Fragmentation in State Elites section describes elite fragmentation among economic elites and the concept of elite stalemate. The final theoretical section illustrates the consequences of elite fragmentation, defining five mechanisms through which generalized elite cohesion undermines policymaking capacity and produces instability.

Cohesion and Fragmentation in State Elites

State elites are individuals occupying elected or appointed positions in organizations conferring control over state policies and resources. Party and policy elites are two analytically distinct categories of state elites. Party elites are "politicians": individuals who primarily acquire power through competition for elected office in association with a political party.[2] Policy elites are unelected occupants of state positions conferring direct policy authority. In many states, party elites substantially delegate direct decision-making authority over economic policy to policy elites, giving them considerable autonomy (Huber & Shipan, 2002). For example, heads of state delegate substantial control over economic policy to finance ministers, central bankers, and occupants of other key state offices.

Elite cohesion shapes state actors' capacity for collective action and coherent policymaking (Centeno, 1997; Evans, 1995; Van Gunten, 2015). Cohesion is a multidimensional concept (Moody & White, 2003); here, I define elite cohesion in terms of the structure of informal elite networks. Elites participate in sustained relationships that facilitate trust and cooperation (or "social capital") in state careers and policymaking processes. Network ties help coordinate the action of heterogeneous elites by building informal coalitions within and beyond the state. These networks constitute an informal social structure underlying the formal organizational structure of the state.

In network theory, cohesion is a feature of patterns of relationships. Specifically, a cohesive network is held together by multiple independent paths, while a fragmented elite lacks such paths (Moody & White, 2003; Van Gunten, 2015). Network cohesion depends on the level and organization of clustering; clusters are subgroups of a network with many connections within latent group boundaries but few connections across clusters. In a cohesive network, clustering patterns congeal into a single, densely connected network community. In a fragmented network, there are many different clusters which may (or may not) be internally cohesive but which lack dense connections to other clusters.

Three key dimensions of cohesion and fragmentation among state elites are most relevant here. The first dimension concerns relations between party and policy elites. In some regimes, policy elites are embedded within party organizations, creating cohesive networks binding party and policy elites. For example, parties with well-developed economic advisory roles in electoral campaigns and other subunits foster ties between policy and party elites.[3] In other regimes, party elites recruit policy elites outside of party organizations, and relations between party and policy elites are at arm's length and instrumental. The former reflects a situation of elite cohesion among party and policy elites, while the latter can result in fragmentation among these two elite segments.

The second dimension concerns cohesion among incumbent policy elites that are active at the same time (synchronic cohesion). Interorganizational cohesion, or the structure of relations between state organizations, is one aspect of this dimension (Van Gunten, 2015). States consist of multiple organizations with inter-related policy jurisdictions (for example, finance ministries and central banks). These organizations themselves have complex internal structures with multiple internal subunits, and operational organizations coexist with high-level advisory bodies. Elites within these multiple organizational hierarchies may inhabit a well-connected, cohesive elite network, or may fragment into disjointed organizational silos. Cohesive networks across these entities facilitate communication, joint formulation of priorities and plans, and prevent conflict. In contrast, fragmentation fosters internal competition and even outright factional conflict among informal elite networks.

Third, elite cohesion has a temporal dimension. Electoral calendars and other political cycles generate high-level elite turnover in modern states. Most obviously, alternation between political parties usually leads to changes in state personnel, but changes in governing party are not the only cause of elite turnover. For example, even in relatively stable elites, within-period cabinet-level changes are common. In a cohesive elite, changes of elite personnel are relatively fluid and decoupled from policy change; turnover is often a vacancy chain process (White, 1970) in which deputies move into their former superiors' positions.[4] In a fragmented elite, elite turnover often involves shifts in control between competing networks. New appointees bring their own networks of loyal subordinates and high-level change thus cascades through administrative levels, making turnover events large-scale changes with new elites imported into the state displacing incumbents. Moreover, fragmented elites generate higher rates of turnover because elite conflict is a frequent cause of high-level resignations.

As noted above, institutional theories invoke elite turnover as a determinant of state incapacity (Evans & Rauch, 1999; Spiller & Tommasi, 2007), but the mechanisms linking these are poorly defined. Sociological institutionalists argue that career stability is a proxy for competence and "corporate coherence," which instills shared norms and discourages malfeasance. However, normative anomie and corruption have limited explanatory purchase on policy outcomes. Mechanisms specified below posit a role for elite turnover that does not rely on the poorly defined notion of "corporate coherence." Thus, elite theory subsumes this aspect of institutional theory by providing a better specification of the relationship between elite turnover and policy incapacity.

To summarize so far, in network theoretic terms elite fragmentation is equivalent to a low level of cohesion. Three dimensions of cohesion and fragmentation are relations between party and policy elites, among incumbent policy elites, and between elites active at different moments of time. The latter dimension encompasses elite turnover (emphasized in institutional accounts) by noting that high turnover rates are often a reflection of underlying fragmentation generating elite conflict and high-level resignations.

Relations Between Economic and State Elites

While relations among state elites have the most direct impact on policymaking capacity, state elites do not operate in isolation. State elites face pressure from other groups motivated to shape economic policies, especially economic elites. The relative power of economic and state elites is a longstanding debate in elite theory; classic perspectives include business power theories emphasizing the ability of capitalists to discipline the state (e.g. Block, 1977) and state autonomy theories (Skocpol, 1985). A full discussion is beyond the scope of this chapter; here, I emphasize that the ability of economic elites to pressure or constrain state elites does not imply that state elites act coherently in the interests of economic elites. Instead, constraints and pressure in the absence of coherent collective action by economic elites erodes policymaking capacity without achieving economic elites' goals.

Whether or not economic elites effectively control state policies depends in part on their capacity for collective action. From the perspective of economic elites, macroeconomic stability is a public good; distinct elite sectors have diverging interests with respect to relevant policies (such as state spending, taxation, and interest rates), creating coordination problems. Unresolved collective action problems impede economic elites' ability to pressure state elites to act coherently in their interests. Collective action capacity depends on a range of factors including the structure of relations among economic elites. Cohesive formal and informal networks create capacity for collective action, and in the absence of such networks, elites may pursue individualistic rather than collective benefits (Chu & Davis, 2016; Mizruchi, 2013). Further, encompassing associations bringing together diverse economic sectors provides a venue for the formation of collective goals and strategies, while the absence of such organizations fragments business (Schneider, 2004).

Collective action failure among economic elites does not imply greater state elite capacity. Capacity for coherent action is not zero-sum, and disorganized action by economic elites can constrain state elites without giving economic elites effective leverage over state policies. For example, economic elites may have de facto veto power over some policies but still lack the ability to proactively design and implement coherent alternatives. Thus, a politically mobilized but poorly coordinated economic elite may remove policy options from the table without placing a coherent policy strategy back on the table.

A fragmented and poorly organized economic elite paired with a cohesive and cooperative state elite might cede all power and initiative to the latter. But simultaneous fragmentation of both state and economic elites can create an elite stalemate in which these competing elites mutually constrain one another such that neither can achieve their objectives. Elite stalemates often have destabilizing consequences (Higley & Burton, 2006, p. 229; Lachmann, 2002). The war of attrition model is essentially a theory of stalemate, though this model assumes that stalemates occur only between economic elites (or between elites and non-elites). However, stalemate between state and economic elites can also produce the delays predicted by this model. When economic elites can constrain the options of state elites but lack the ability to proactively set policy agendas, the outcome can be a prolonged irresolution of underlying economic problems. This situation of stalemate results from the simultaneous fragmentation of both economic and state elites.

Thus, generalized fragmentation among both state and economic elites produces a situation of elite stalemate. This stalemate compounds and interacts with processes generated within the state elite, undermining policymaking capacity in ways described in the Policymaking in Fragmented Elites section. Elite theory therefore subsumes distributional conflict theories as one component of constraint on state elites' policy options within a broader pattern of elite competition and conflict.

Policymaking in Fragmented Elites

Elite fragmentation undermines policymaking capacity through five distinct mechanisms. First, elite fragmentation results in policy volatility: frequent, erratic, unpredictable, and poorly planned policy changes. This is in part because competing elite network clusters pursuing independent goals and objectives do not share policy preferences and are therefore likely to often change course. Successive elites may be motivated to quickly unwind the policy legacies of their predecessors. Further, elite turnover often results in improvisation and poor

148 *Elite Politics and Economic Crisis*

planning, especially when difficult economic circumstances drive turnover in the first place. Internal factionalism can also produce volatility when multiple groups of policy elites simultaneously influence policy outcomes. Policy volatility increases macroeconomic instability by causing market uncertainty.

Second, elite fragmentation creates incentives for short-termism and delay – the key element of the war of attrition model. Fragmentation tends to reduce policy elite tenures, and elites expecting short tenures have incentives to pursue short-run patches rather than more difficult long-term solutions. Because incumbent elites have few connections beyond their immediate circle of allies, they do not expect their successors to continue current policies (and may expect the opposite); therefore, there is limited motivation to attempt policies whose implementation timeline stretches out over years. Fragmented policy elites are not irredeemably locked into short-termism, as implied by some accounts of weak institutions, but the window of opportunity for ambitious policymaking tends to be short and concentrated early in policy elites' tenures. Elites approaching the end of their tenures are often embattled and lack "political capital" to pursue ambitious policies. In this context, time horizons shrink and short-termism predominates.

Third, fragmentation focuses elite reputation formation on individuals and informal network clusters rather than organizations or the policy elite as a collective. The form in which external actors assess elite reputation matters for policy credibility, a factor stressed by many institutionalist theories (Bernhard et al., 2002; Leblang & Satyanath, 2006; Spiller & Tommasi, 2007). Credibility refers to market actors' expectations regarding whether elites will implement announced policies in practice, including whether policy will change over relevant time horizons. Individualization (as opposed to collectivization) of reputation focuses market expectations on particular policy elites' political position within the state. When elite turnover is a probabilistic signal of impending policy change, market actors monitor factional politics for signs of personnel changes. This creates the potential for self-fulfilling feedback effects (Merton, 1948): market actors adopt destabilizing economic strategies (e.g., capital flight) in anticipation of elite turnover and policy change, which then bring about turnover and the expected policy change. Reputational individualism is also vulnerable to credibility traps in which market actors do not trust incumbent elites, but the replacement of incumbents itself creates expectations of policy change. Because credibility is important in economic policy and particularly in high-inflation situations, this makes economic outcomes sensitive to turnover and conflict among policy elites.

Fourth, elite fragmentation foments contradictory and incoherent policies due to turnover and low interorganizational cohesion. Macroeconomic and financial policies involve complex interactions between policies under the jurisdiction of multiple organizations (for example, fiscal and monetary policy). Low interorganizational cohesion increases the potential for poor coordination and self-defeating or mutually canceling policies. Elites in different organizations pursuing different goals and priorities who are unwilling to defer to one another may adopt policies at cross-purposes. Outright factionalism is an extreme version of this phenomenon. Elite turnover produces similar effects: large-scale rotation in elite networks results in improvisational and poorly planned policy changes. Sequential and iterative policymaking episodes by distinct groups of policy elites with differing goals and priorities lead to incremental adjustments of prior policies that accumulate incoherence. Factionalism also undermines policy coherence when competition between factions leads to elite turnover resulting in improvised and iterative policy shifts.

Fifth, stalemate between economic and state elites also foments contradictory and incoherent policies. When economic elites fail to act collectively, policy elites are subject to multiple and contradictory pressures. Pressure from economic elites removes policy options from the table, leaving policy elites with few good choices. These constraints compound the effects of short-termism, incremental adjustment, and competition among policy elites. Policy elites working with a limited toolkit under severe external pressures are more likely to adopt suboptimal and incoherent policies. These policies may themselves amplify distributional conflict, creating new sources of pressure from economic elites.

In summary, generalized elite fragmentation is a situation in which divisions among competing elite individuals and groups affect both economic and state elites. An elite stalemate between economic and state elites results from fragmentation within both key elite sectors. Elite fragmentation undermines policymaking capacity through four distinct mechanisms: policy volatility, short-termism, reputational and credibility problems, and contradictory and incoherent policies. Volatile, poorly designed, and incoherent policies in turn foment instability, including the extreme instability of hyperinflation.

ELITE RELATIONS IN ARGENTINA
Fragmentation of State Elites

Argentine state elites are fragmented along the three dimensions discussed above. First, policy elites are not embedded in cohesive networks connecting them to party elites. Neither major political party active in the 1980s had a substantial internal corps of policy elites. Reasons for this fragmentation included limited governing experience due to frequent interruptions of democratic governance under military regimes and party factionalism. For example, the Radical Civic Union (UCR or Radical) party in power at the outset of hyperinflation had last governed between 1958 and 1966, during which it also experienced a factional split. By the 1980s, the few remaining policy elites associated with the party were ill-equipped for governance. After achieving poor economic outcomes during his first year in office, President Raúl Alfonsín (1983–1989) delegated policy authority to a network of independent economists with few ties to Radical party elites.[5] Similarly, the Justicialist (Peronist) party was largely proscribed after 1955 and governed for only three years in the 1970s, ending in a military coup. Following Carlos Menem's 1989 electoral victory, the party had an electoral machine but effectively no governing apparatus (Levitsky, 2003). As a result, Menem primarily recruited elites from outside the party, many of whom had openly not even voted for him (see de Pablo, 2011, p. 53).

Second, synchronic cohesion (relations between incumbent elites) and especially interorganizational cohesion was low. Van Gunten (2015) compared the network structure of Argentine and Mexican policy elites, showing that elite cohesion is higher in Mexico than in Argentina; as defined above, fragmentation is equivalent to low cohesion. The Argentine policy elite consists of many discrete elite clusters of varying size and degrees of internal cohesion but persistently few connections between clusters. The vernacular term "economic team" describes these informal clusters and generally refers to a cluster of officials loyal to the Economy Minister. In practice, "teams" were relatively isolated entities often disconnected from other elites. At times, the Economy Minister's network of allies was limited to a few officials, with other state organizations controlled by competing networks. In other words, interorganizational cohesion was variable and often low. Factionalism was acute during the early Menem administration; in this period, a variety of elite clusters competed for influence. Senior elites leading these organizations lacked prior connections and understood themselves as competitors, leading to elite conflict.[6] At this time, the "economic team" was a small network competing with other elite factions within the state. As the Minister later wryly observed, "With time I realized that you can't be Minister of Economy without the support of 50 or 60 people you can trust...and unfortunately there were only three or four of us" (Rapanelli in de Pablo, 2011).

Third, policy elites fragmented over time. This fragmented structure partly reflects the lack of network connections between successive elite clusters active over time. Economic policy during hyperinflation was under the control of a rapid succession of elite network clusters; between January 1989 and January 1991, there were six Economy Ministers and six Central Bank presidents (see Table 1). This brief period substantially accounts for the high turnover and short tenures of economic policy elites observed by institutionalists (Dornbusch & de Pablo, 1989). Crucially, the turnover involved not just replacement of senior elites but entire swathes of the policy elite as subordinates departed along with their superiors. In the absence of a robust bureaucratic or party corps, turnover entailed replacing large numbers of senior officials with entirely new networks of officials with no established relations to their predecessors. High turnover was also a reflection of elite fragmentation, and, as shown in Table 1, conflict with other elites often resulted in high-level resignations.

Stalemate: Economic and State Elites

Like state elites, Argentine economic elites were fragmented, undermining their capacity for collective action. Two important elite economic sectors during hyperinflation were landholding agrarian exporters and wealth holders.[7] Agrarian exporters were historically "the" Argentine elite, dominating the state in the early 20th century and continuing to hold substantial political weight. The association of large agrarian landholders, the Argentine Rural Society, was the most consistently organized and vocal representative of economic elites (Heredia, 2003; Schneider, 2004). In contrast, wealth holders were a heterogeneous and diffuse sector consisting of individuals and organizations holding liquid assets.[8] Wealth holders lacked

Table 1. Tenure and Reason for Departure of Senior Elites, 1989–1990.

Position	Elite	Dates	Tenure	Reason for Departure
Economy Minister	Sourrouille	February 1985–March 1989	4 years	Resignation under pressure from dissenting party elites and economic instability
Economy Minister	Pugliese	April–May 1989	6 weeks	Resignation due to outcome of Presidential election and economic instability
Economy Minister	Rodriguez	May–July 1989	6 weeks	End of presidential mandate
Economy Minister	Roig	July 1989	1 week	Deceased
Economy Minister	Rapanelli	July–December 1989	5 months	Resignation in the context of conflict within policy elites and economic instability
Economy Minister	Gonzalez	December 1989–February 1991	14 months	Change of position in cabinet reshuffle
Central Bank President	Machinea	July 1986–March 1989	3 years	Collective resignation under pressure from dissenting party elites and economic instability
Central Bank President	Garcia Vazquez	April–July 1989	3 months	End of presidential mandate
Central Bank President	Gonzalez Fraga	July–November 1989	5 months	Resignation in the context of conflict within policy elites and economic instability
Central Bank President	Ianella	December 1989	3 weeks	Resignation in the context of conflict within policy elites and economic instability
Central Bank President	Rossi	December 1989–January 1990	1 month	Resignation in the context of conflict within policy elites and economic instability
Central Bank President	Folcini	January–March 1990	2 months	Resignation in the context of conflict within policy elites and economic instability
Central Bank President	Gonzalez Fraga	April 1990–January 1991	10 months	Resigned

effective political representation; however, they held a potent but blunt instrument of structural power: capital flight. Agrarian elites, wealth holders, and other economic sectors (e.g. industrialists) pursued competing, and often incompatible, goals during the crisis.

Collective action failure among elites reflected in part the structure of relations among economic elites. Corporate board interlock networks are highly fragmented (Lluch & Salvaj, 2014), similar to the late-20th century corporate networks in the United States (Chu & Davis, 2016). Unlike other Latin American countries, Argentina did not have a high-level association in which economic elites could discuss policy goals and strategies (Schneider, 2004). Agriculture, industry, and finance each had separate associations pursuing particularistic sectoral demands, but there was no organizational structure in which economic elites could coordinate an approach to macroeconomic stability. Sectors were often internally fragmented: for example, conflict between domestically owned and international banks resulted in an organizational rift in the financial sector in the 1990s, presaged by conflicts discussed below.

Given this fragmentation, the constraints imposed by economic elites were disorganized rather than coherent. Agrarian elites pressured the state through lobbying and (limited) direct access to state positions, giving these elites an effective veto over certain policies, but as shown below, they had limited ability to proactively design coherent policy. The limited capacity of economic elites to govern directly is exemplified by an exceptional period of direct access discussed below: at the beginning of his government President Menem directly delegated control over economic policy to economic elites, but this period lasted only a few months and ended in the return of hyperinflation. Economic elites did exercise substantial structural power; however, structural power was a blunt instrument that constrained the options of state elites without providing a proactive policy agenda. Economic and state elites were locked in a stalemate in which the former could constrain the options of policy elites but lacked capacity for collective action; state elites could impose substantial costs on economic elites but could not control economic elites' destabilizing investment strategies. This stalemate was part of the broader pattern of generalized elite fragmentation.

THE MACROECONOMICS OF INFLATION IN ARGENTINA

Argentine hyperinflation was the culmination of chronic high inflation spanning decades: annual inflation averaged above 20% from 1950 to 1970 and over 100% during the 1970s, reaching near-hyperinflationary levels in 1976.[9] The 1983–1989 government of UCR President Raul Alfonsín struggled to control inflation and achieved only moderate success mid-decade. However, by late 1988, the macroeconomic situation was extremely fragile. This fragile situation exploded into hyperinflation in the first half of 1989.

Argentina experienced two distinct waves of hyperinflation during 1989–1990, and this pattern is critical to understanding the elite politics of the crisis. Fig. 1 shows the monthly rate of inflation and exchange rate depreciation from 1989 to 1991. The first wave of hyperinflation began with accelerating currency depreciation in February 1989 and passed the 50% threshold – a conventional definition of hyperinflation (Cagan, 1956) – in May. Following the victory of Peronist Carlos Menem in the May 1989 elections, Alfonsin brought forward the transfer of presidential power originally scheduled for December. The political transition was followed by a "honeymoon" period of comparatively moderate inflation lasting several months. However, currency depreciation beginning in the final months of 1989 developed into a second wave in early 1990. Inflation fell to comparatively moderate (though still double digit) levels by mid-1990, before finally stabilizing in 1991.

The two-wave pattern establishes key facts about the crisis and its resolution. First, because hyperinflation occurred during governments of the two main political

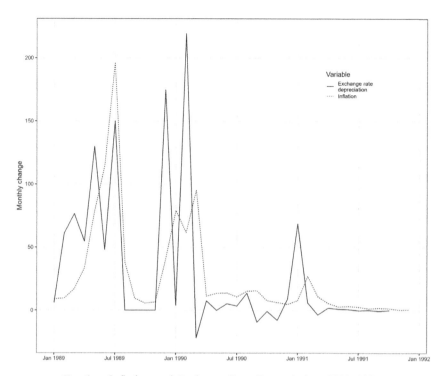

Fig. 1. Inflation and Exchange Rate Depreciation, 1989–1991.

parties, any explanation must apply equally to both parties. Second, contemporary observers attributed hyperinflation to pre-electoral political uncertainty and fear of Menem's "populist" rhetoric during the elections (Machinea, 1990). The main problems with this explanation are that inflation stabilized when Menem took office and then returned when there was no equivalent source of political uncertainty. Third, subsequent accounts attribute the end of the crisis to the adoption of the 1991 Convertibility Law, which fixed the Argentine currency to the dollar at a one-to-one rate (Levitsky & Murillo, 2005; Weyland, 2004). However, while inflation remained high by international standards through early 1991, hyperinflation per se ended a year before the law's passage.

As noted in the introduction, a standard explanation for hyperinflation is that extreme political events such as revolution and regime change disrupt normal mechanisms of state finance; states unable to control spending or raise tax revenue resort to unrestrained printing of paper money (Fischer et al., 2002). This account provides both a macroeconomic mechanism and an underlying political cause. The macroeconomic mechanism is uncontrolled money creation to pay for large fiscal deficits driven by exceptional demands on expenditure or the failure of revenue collection. The underlying cause of these deficits is an extreme political event.

However, no extreme political event equivalent to revolution or regime change occurred in Argentina in 1989.[10] Similarly, there were two main problems with the conventional fiscal mechanism. First, the central government deficit prior to hyperinflation was substantial but not large enough to account for hyperinflation as opposed to merely high inflation (Beckerman, 1995).[11] Fiscal deficits were necessary but not sufficient to explain hyperinflation. Second, the conventional account ignores the modern macroeconomic literature on hyperinflation, which emphasizes the causal role of exchange rate markets (Fischer et al., 2002, pp. 850–852; Dornbusch, 1985). According to these accounts, a rapidly depreciating exchange rate – that is, a currency run – is the proximate cause of hyperinflation.[12] This is consistent with the evidence in Fig. 1 that shows currency depreciation preceding rising inflation in both waves.[13]

These stylized facts are inconsistent with the fiscalist assumptions of the war of attrition model. An additional problem is that the war of attrition model postulates crises end when one side of a distributional conflict concedes and bears the costs of eliminating the fiscal deficit. However, the Argentine hyperinflation did not end with a qualitative change in spending, revenue, or both. As shown in Fig. 2, the Argentine state did achieve a sustained fiscal surplus beginning in 1991, but it did so because both revenue and spending increased in real terms as the economy recovered

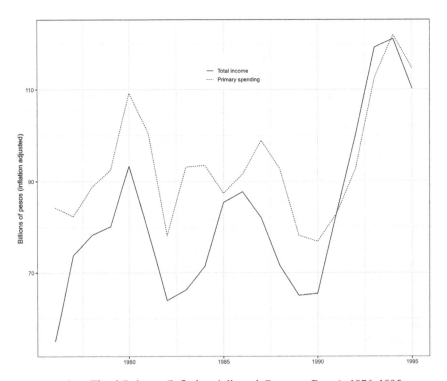

Fig. 2. Fiscal Balance (Inflation-Adjusted Constant Pesos), 1976–1995.

following the prolonged crisis. This is consistent with modern macroeconomists' recognition of the endogeneity of fiscal deficits in high inflation situations; in other words, causality runs from inflation to the deficit as well as vice versa (Fischer et al., 2002, p. 839).[14] Because spending increased in real terms following the crisis, the war of attrition model requires a substantial increase in revenue from new sources. Revenue did increase as a percentage of GDP from 1990 but resulted from the recovery of existing revenue sources rather than a major change in the structure of taxation (Fig. 3).[15] Thus, there is little evidence that a qualitative change in fiscal policy preceded the end of the crisis.

In general terms, the macroeconomic mechanisms that produced hyperinflation were financial rather than narrowly fiscal. The Argentine state was indebted

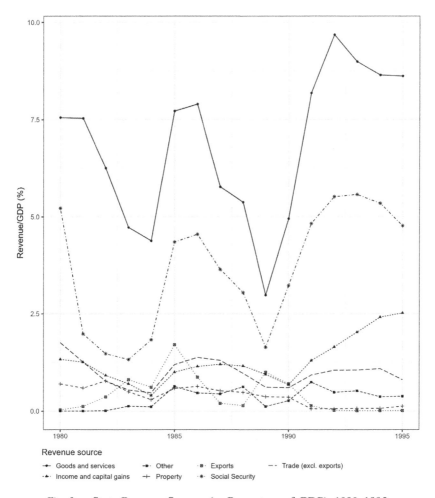

Fig. 3. State Revenue Sources (as Percentage of GDP), 1980–1995.

156

to the point of insolvency; external sovereign debt was a crushing burden but not the crucial factor underlying hyperinflation. Rather, most contemporary and informed macroeconomic accounts of the Argentine hyperinflation focus on the so-called quasi-fiscal deficit (Almansi & Rodriguez, 1989; Beckerman, 1995; Graziano, 1990). The Argentine state – more specifically, the Argentine Central Bank – was heavily indebted at high interest rates to the domestic banking system. The flow of interest payments on this debt constituted money creation, a source of inflation. The existence of this deficit had self-defeating effects: high Central Bank interest rates intended to control inflation but instead paradoxically resulted in automatic expansion of the money supply. The Central Bank tried to absorb this liquidity to prevent inflation, but available means of doing so inevitably increased its own debt.

Wealth holders' bank deposits were a counterpart of this Central Bank debt. In other words, wealth holders "lent" funds to banks (in balance sheet terms, deposits are bank liabilities or debt), which in turn lent these to the Central Bank. Following decades of high inflation, most wealth holders' assets were short-term time deposits (similar to certificates of deposit in the United States) earning high interest rates. Bearing in mind that most modern money is bank money (Ingham, 2005), this meant that most Argentine money paid interest. Banks could only pay these high interest rates by receiving the corresponding flow of interest payments from the Central Bank. This is the financial context that rendered the Argentine Central Bank insolvent.

To clarify this macroeconomic mechanism, it is helpful to anticipate a key turning point in the conclusion of the crisis. The solution to state insolvency is generally default and rescheduling of debt. Hyperinflation ended – though not immediately – when the Argentine Central Bank effectively defaulted on its debt in January 1990. With the so-called Plan Bonex, the Argentine state repudiated the Central Bank's debt to the banking system and forcibly converted savings deposits into long-term, dollar-denominated bonds known as Bonex (Beckerman, 1995; Reinhart & Rogoff, 2009). Taken together, these two measures eliminated the Central Bank deficit by effectively partially expropriating the assets of wealth holders. In a sense, this amounted to default on money itself. While the state nominally recognized its liabilities at face value in the form of Bonex bonds, rescheduling short-term savings deposits to a ten-year horizon imposed substantial losses on wealth holders in the short run. Depositors needing immediate access to their funds had to sell bonds at a discount as high as 70% (Beckerman, 1995, p. 678). This policy played a key role in bringing the hyperinflation crisis to an end by effectively eliminating the Central Bank deficit – though, as shown below, in the short run, an incoherent roll-out of the policy contributed to the second wave of hyperinflation.

Wealth holders' assets were also linked to the second macroeconomic mechanism driving hyperinflation, the linkage between the US dollar market and the inflation rate. Prices were closely related to the dollar market because the daily dollar exchange rate was the main indicator available to producers and commercial firms setting prices within a context of extreme uncertainty. Depreciation of the dollar exchange rate drove prices upwards, and currency depreciation was driven by capital flight as panicked wealth holders sought to protect the value of their assets. Currency runs involve complex self-fulfilling dynamics: regardless of wealth holders' own beliefs, if they believe that other wealth holders expect the currency to fall, they have an incentive to convert their assets immediately (Morris & Shin, 1998). These currency runs were the proximate cause of hyperinflation, while the expansion of liquidity through extremely high interest rates (ultimately paid by the Central Bank deficit) provided necessary fuel for the fire.

This macroeconomic context clarifies the distributional conflict at the heart of hyperinflation. In a context of chronic inflation, wealth holders tried to maintain the real value of their assets either by holding high interest rate time deposits or by converting assets to dollars. When wealth holders feared immanent currency depreciation, their incentive to exchange local currency for dollars magnified. Agrarian exporters sat on the other side of the foreign exchange market because export revenues were the main source of dollars. Both sides sought to minimize losses; while wealth holders benefited from a lower exchange rate (that is, a cheaper dollar), agrarian exporters benefited from a higher exchange rate because of their dollar revenues. In this sense, hyperinflation was the result of these competing economic strategies; as shown below, however, the state itself was an active participant in this distributional conflict.

ORIGINS AND CONTINUITY OF THE CENTRAL BANK DEFICIT

As the previous section shows, insolvency of the Argentine Central Bank was a primary financial cause of hyperinflation. The first question is therefore: why was Argentine state indebted to the banking system, creating the "quasi-fiscal" deficit? The deficit resulted from an incoherent and contradictory organizational structure that accumulated over the course of a decade. In the fragmented Argentine policy elite, a succession of officials pursuing incompatible goals tinkered with policies left in place by their predecessors, creating a contradictory structure. These iterative policymaking cycles allowed contradictions to accumulate, becoming increasingly difficult to unwind. The short time horizons characteristic of a fragmented policy elite generated strong incentives to postpone difficult decisions. By the late 1980s, the situation was intractable; it took two waves of hyperinflation to finally force a solution.

Beginning in the 1970s, the Argentine Central Bank paid interest on bank reserves (financial system deposits in the Central Bank required for regulatory and monetary policy purposes). In balance sheet terms, these reserves are liabilities (debts) of the Central Bank. This unusual policy originated in conflict over the financial system. The 1973–1976 Peronist government partially nationalized the banking system by instituting a policy of 100% reserve requirements – that is, banks had to forward all deposits to the Central Bank. After seizing power in 1976, military rulers delegated authority to market-oriented policy elites who rapidly reversed nationalization and liberalized the financial system. Reversing nationalization was difficult because uniform reduction of reserve requirements (which is what the measures technically required) had unequal consequences across segments of the banking system.[16] This constrained the options of policy elites, who adopted an incremental reform intended as a temporary, transitional measure: an organizational structure known as the "monetary regulation account" into which banks paid in fees and earned interest and was designed to net out across the financial sector (Beckerman, 1995).

This attempt to liberalize the financialization system resulted in a major banking crisis within a few years (Baliño, 1987). Combined with factional conflict in the military junta, this economic instability led to disruptive policy elite turnover: in the chaotic final years of the military regime, multiple informal groups cycled rapidly through the main economic policy organizations. In 1982, Domingo Cavallo (later a key elite during hyperinflation) took over the Central Bank and pursued policy goals that differed substantially from the liberalizing objective of previous elites.[17] Cavallo seized the window of opportunity early in his tenure and rapidly adopted a battery of reforms; he then resigned after only 53 days in office due to further factional conflict in the military. Replacement elites started another incremental cycle, disrupting measures left in place by Cavallo. These iterative policymaking processes in a fragmented elite pursuing disparate goals rendered Central Bank policy incoherent; one outcome was the "temporary" suspension of fee payments into the monetary regulation account while continuing to pay out interest, generating a deficit (Beckerman, 1992, p. 15). This was a major origin of the Central Bank's "quasi-fiscal" deficit.

As a result of these episodes, the Alfonsín government inherited unsustainable organizational structures in 1983. Factional struggles between the Central Bank and the Economy Ministry during the early years of the democratic government delayed an effective response.[18] In 1986, a single cohesive "economic team" led by Economy Minister Juan Sourrouille centralized control over economic policy, ending internal factional conflicts; however, by this time, the window of opportunity for ambitious policymaking had closed. Early relative success gave way to rising inflation and prolonged economic malaise. Given the reputational individualism characteristics of a fragmented elite, poor performance undermined the Sourrouille team's reputation among economic and party elites. Senior policy elites became convinced that they personally lacked credibility and offered their resignations in favor of others with less tarnished reputations.[19] However, facing the limited supply of competent and politically acceptable elites, the President refused.[20] Elites were locked in a credibility trap.

In this context, policy elites' time horizons shortened, and they postponed major reforms and instead resorted to incremental muddling through. Policy elites recognized the Central Bank deficit as a problem but adopted only incremental reforms which did not address the fundamental problem.[21] The dilemma was genuinely challenging (Beckerman, 1995). Accumulation of Central Bank debt made these contradictory structures difficult to unwind: the debt had to be paid, but paying the debt balance with banks entailed money creation and therefore further inflation. Postponing resolution of the debt issue allowed elites to moderate inflation in the present at the cost of allowing incoherent organizational structures to persist. Addressing the deficit required a complex financial reform which would inevitably impose large but uneven costs on economic elites. The difficulty is evident from the solution eventually adopted in 1990 (the plan Bonex), which entailed a deeply unpopular default and expropriation of wealth holders. This policy was only adopted out of desperation once a second wave of hyperinflation was underway. Addressing this problem earlier would have been challenging even in a cohesive elite; in a fragmented policy elite, the incentive to postpone difficult policy decisions was overwhelming.

To summarize, the organizational structures creating the Central Bank deficit emerged from iterative and sequential policymaking cycles in a fragmented policy elite. These episodes clarify the relationship between elite turnover and policy capacity that has been emphasized in institutionalist accounts. Elite turnover was one manifestation of patterns of elite competition in a fragmented elite; frequent changes in state personnel undermined capacity to deliver coherent policies because repeated tinkering by successive elites generated accumulating incoherence, while short-termism inhibited genuine reforms needed to address deep structural problems. An institutionalist explanation based on the notion of "corporate coherence" either treats elites as more passive (lacking in shared norms to motivate action) or as pursuing strictly individualistic motives through corruption. But these assumptions are a poor fit for the repeated active policymaking cycles generating contradictory policies. Elite fragmentation, rather than weak institutions, provides a better explanation for the persistence of policy incoherence.

THE FIRST WAVE: JANUARY–JULY 1989

Policy Incoherence in the Plan Primavera

In late 1988, policy elites launched a final attempt to slow inflation in advance of the upcoming Presidential elections. This set of policies, known as the "Plan Primavera" or spring plan, was a contradictory and incoherent mix that created catastrophic downside risks in the event of failure. Alongside a price agreement with industrial and commercial elites and a battery of other measures, the plan featured an unconventional mechanism for extracting revenue from agrarian exporters. For reasons explained below, this amplified the risk of an explosive currency run. These risks were later realized when the plan collapsed in early 1989, setting in motion the first wave of hyperinflation.

The contradictions of the Plan Primavera partly reflected a deepening stalemate between the state and economic elites. The Radical party faced opposition from organized labor (a key Peronist constituency) and thus sought support from economic elites. However, the latter were increasingly irritated by poor economic performance, and agrarian elites were increasingly vocal in the late 1980s (Machinea, 1990). In an attempt to shore up political support following electoral losses, Alfonsín made concessions to economic elites, including agrarian exporters. Most significantly, he agreed to agrarian elites' longstanding demand for elimination of export taxes on most agricultural commodities. The removal of export taxes constrained the options of policy elites attempting to balance the state budget.

These stylized facts appear consistent with the war of attrition model: on this interpretation, agrarian elites' power to resist taxation delayed elimination of the fiscal deficit. However, the importance of this distributional conflict was not primarily its direct effect on the state budget because, as shown in Fig. 3, export taxes were a relatively minor revenue source.[22] Furthermore, policy elites did not capitulate to economic elites' demands; instead, they worked around them by introducing a mechanism to capture agricultural export revenue through the foreign exchange market. The Plan Primavera required agrarian exporters to sell dollars to the Central Bank at a lower exchange rate than that paid by dollar buyers – notably, wealth holders. In other words, the Central Bank bought cheap dollars from agricultural exporters and sold them at a higher cost to wealth holders, retaining the difference as state revenue. This was in effect an implicit tax on exports expected to generate a significant share of the projected deficit due to foregone taxes (Machinea, 1990, pp. 77–78).

In the war of attrition model, distributional conflict is exogenous to state action. In this case, however, state elites created a new axis of latent distributional conflict between agrarian elites and wealth holders by segmenting the exchange rate market. The main axis of overt conflict was not between political elites representing distinct economic elites, but rather between agrarian elites and the state. Policy elites' attempt to work around the constraints imposed by economic elites had the unintended consequence of increasing, rather than reducing, conflict with economic elites.[23] Agrarian elites complained bitterly about the "discriminatory" treatment and jeered President Alfonsín at the annual fair of the Argentine Rural Society, a symbolic event representing agrarian exporters. Thus, while distributional conflicts were undoubtedly central to elite conflict, conflicts between state and economic elites (rather than between different economic sectors, as posited by the war of attrition model) were at the core of this conflict. Moreover, state policies shaped distributional conflict rather than merely reflecting it.

The primary impact of this elite stalemate was to undermine policy coherence by removing state elites' policy options in an already difficult situation (rather than any direct fiscal impact, as discussed above). These constraints interacted with the incentives resulting from the fragmented character of the policy elite. As noted in the previous section, by late 1988, policy elites were locked into a credibility trap and focused on very short time horizons. Policy elites correctly believed that their own credibility was severely limited due to the reputational damage they had suffered from earlier perceived policy failures, and they were now self-consciously "muddling through" on the assumption that their window of opportunity for major policy initiatives had closed.[24] Policy elites' only goal was to reach the scheduled elections with a modicum of stability. Given the constraints imposed by economic elites and their own short time horizons, policy elites felt they had few options and adopted policies they themselves recognized as risky and suboptimal.

This combination of external constraint and short-termism resulted in a set of economic policies which was an incoherent and risky gamble. Maintaining the tiered exchange rate system to extract revenue from agrarian elites required extremely high interest rates to incentivize wealth holders to keep assets in domestic currency, rather than seek safety in the dollar. But, because the Argentine Central Bank ultimately paid high interest rates by creating currency (through the Central Bank deficit), this defeated the policy's goal of controlling inflation. Policy elites sought to absorb this liquidity, but the available tools meant increasing the Central Banks' own debt – and therefore further future interest payments. Reliance on the foreign exchange rate market to collect revenue was thus contradictory and amplified risks in the case of failure.

The incoherent design of the "Plan Primavera" illustrates the interaction of stalemate between state and economic elites and the fragmentation of the policy elite. Economic elites had sufficient power to obtain important policy concessions, but policy elites still retained sufficient autonomy to impose a functionally equivalent means of revenue extraction. Combined with the short time horizons characteristic of a fragmented elite, the result was an incoherent set of policies that ultimately failed.

Toward Hyperinflation: February–April 1989

As noted above, the proximate cause of hyperinflation was a currency run resulting from wealth holders' collective conversion of local currency assets to dollars. The currency run resulted from wealth holders' lack of confidence that policies announced in the Plan Primavera would continue. This credibility deficit reflected wealth holders' understanding of policymaking processes in the fragmented policy elite, exacerbated by volatile and incoherent policymaking.

Up until February 1989, wealth holders maintained substantial local currency balances because the Central Bank's extremely high real interest rates made these balances profitable (Beckerman, 1995). Wealth holders' strategies depended on their expectations about the relative returns on high-interest local currency holdings and dollar assets; these expectations rested in turn on the likelihood that current policies would continue.[25] In early February, these expectations changed when the Central Bank abruptly announced its withdrawal from the dollar market, leading to a sharp currency devaluation; more than any other moment, this decision marks the beginning of the hyperinflation crisis. Fig. 4 reports the US dollar exchange rate paid by wealth holders during the first wave and identifies breakpoints marking the acceleration of currency depreciation.[26] The first breakpoint coincides with the February devaluation. Nevertheless, the crisis did not immediately spiral out of control and the exchange rate stabilized during February. The currency run accelerated again following the collapse of the Plan Primavera price agreement in early March (the second breakpoint labeled in Fig. 4). By mid-March, a sustained currency run was underway.

The policy elite's credibility deficit helps account for the exchange rate market's extreme vulnerability to a currency run. As argued above, a credibility trap is a

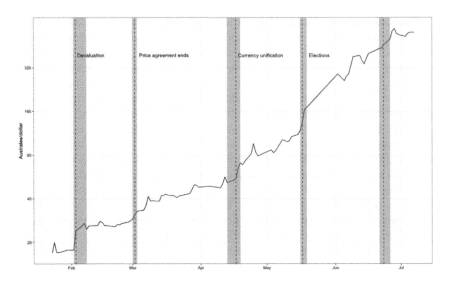

Fig. 4. US Dollar Exchange Rate During the First Hyperinflation.

situation in which incumbent elites are reputationally damaged, undermining market confidence, but the replacement of incumbents itself creates uncertainty. This uncertainty gave wealth holders an overwhelming incentive to seek safety in the dollar. The February devaluation and later collapse of the price agreement were an additional blow to the reputations and credibility of incumbent policy elites. Informed observers had good reasons to expect elite turnover, and new elites in turn implied new policies with unknown implications. Consistent with this, rumors of impending elite resignations emerged following the devaluation and grew after the collapse of the price agreement.[27] Both policy elites and wealth holders explicitly understood the Plan Primavera as incumbent elites' "final attempt" to provide stability in advance of the elections (Machinea, 1990, p. 75). The collapse of this plan created radical uncertainty because wealth holders understood that incumbent elites had no further cards to play, but elite turnover entailed new uncertainties about future policy. Observers in March 1989 did not yet know the outcome of elections and could not know that the transfer of presidential authority would be accelerated, so the horizon of uncertainty stretched out for nine months. Given this extended uncertainty, wealth holders collectively decided to convert local currency assets to dollars.

This credibility trap acquired a self-fulfilling dimension due to elite fragmentation, vis-a-vis party elites. Incumbent policy elites were relative outsiders not embedded in cohesive networks linking them to party elites, and their relationship to party elites was almost entirely based on their connection to an increasingly unpopular president. This rendered policy elites vulnerable to challenges by party elites. A vocal minority of dissenting party elites was strongly critical of Economy Minister Juan Sourrouille and his allies, and the Radical party's presidential candidate turned on Sourrouille, ultimately openly calling for his resignation. Facing this internal conflict, Sourrouille finally resigned. This high-level turnover ricocheted down the state apparatus as subordinates followed suit. The result was that during an accelerating financial crisis, the upper echelons of state organizations were suddenly empty, with new and untested elites taking their places. As noted above, the UCR had a limited internal corps of policy elites, and Alfonsín had few options to replace senior leaders. Seeking to quell party conflict, he appointed a party elite whose previous economic policy experience in the 1960s left him unprepared to govern and overwhelmed by the ballooning crisis.[28]

Through a feedback process, poor economic performance increased elite conflict and elite turnover; the turnover resulted in improvisation and volatility, which in turn exacerbated instability. New elites struggled to identify policies with a plausible chance of success and made a series of abrupt policy changes which amplified uncertainty in the exchange rate market. The capstone of this improvisational decision-making was a major policy change: "unification and liberation" of the exchange rate, that is, the abandonment of the exchange rate to market forces and the elimination of the tiered exchange rate regime introduced in the Plan Primavera. Freeing the exchange rate during a currency run was incoherent: there was no plausible way in which this would contribute to policy elites' stated goal of lowering inflation. By eliminating the tiered exchange rate, policy elites hoped to reduce conflict with agrarian exporters.[29] However, they simultaneously reinstated export taxes on agricultural commodities, making the policies functionally equivalent. The attempt to reduce conflict with economic elites backfired again: agrarian elites continued to militate against the new regime.[30]

While failing to resolve distributional conflict with agrarian elites, these volatile policy changes amplified wealth holders' uncertainty, adding fuel to the currency run. Because the policy change made further currency depreciation more likely, wealth holders had a strong incentive to convert funds to dollars immediately. Rumors about the policy change circulated at least a week before formal announcements, creating uncertainty that amplified the incentive toward capital flight.[31] Policy elites and President Alfonsín repeatedly denied further forthcoming policy changes, an indication of widespread uncertainty and speculation[32]; these high-level denials only reinforced the rumors. As shown in the breakpoint analysis reported in Fig. 4, the mid-April policy was a significant turning point in the crisis. Whereas the exchange rate doubled approximately every 30 days in the six weeks before this decision, the doubling time fell to eight days following the decision to "free" the exchange rate. Within weeks, the rate of inflation passed the 50% threshold: hyperinflation had begun.

THE SECOND WAVE: NOVEMBER 1989–MARCH 1990

On May 14, 1989, Peronist Carlos Menem won the presidential elections in the midst of hyperinflation. The crisis deepened and, amid daily price increases and widespread scarcity of basic goods, looting spread around the country. Following failed negotiations to accelerate the transfer of presidential authority, Alfonsín unilaterally resigned. Hyperinflation reached a crescendo as Menem took office – prices tripled in two days surrounding the presidential transition in July – and then subsided, falling below 10% monthly by September (González Fraga in de Pablo, 2011, p. 56). After

164 *Elite Politics and Economic Crisis*

three months of accelerating hyperinflation, the currency run ended suddenly and unexpectedly, permitting a moderation of inflation.

The Limited Capacity of Economic Elites

President Menem's initial strategy after taking office was to delegate control over economic policy to economic elites associated with Bunge y Born, a corporation epitomizing the historic agrarian elite.[33] This was an exceptional moment as Argentine economic elites rarely enjoyed direct high-level control over economic policy. The war of attrition model predicts that such a shift should consolidate political power, ending distributional conflict by forcing the opposing party to capitulate. However, this did not occur: the experiment in delegation to economic elites lasted only five months and ended in a second wave of hyperinflation.

In reality, economic elites were no more capable of implementing consistent and coherent economic policies than other policy elites. Direct delegation to economic elites did not fundamentally change the dynamics of policymaking within the fragmented elite; economic elites were simply the latest informal elite network competing for control over the state. Despite rhetoric of an alliance with economic elites, in reality the Bunge y Born "economic team" was a handful of former managers who did not represent agrarian elites more broadly.[34] This network competed for influence with a heterogeneous set of other elites occupying positions in the early Menem administration, giving them only partial control over economic policy. Most significantly, the Bunge y Born network did not control the Central Bank, which had been delegated to prominent financial adviser Javier González Fraga, who was determined to assert his independence from the Economy Ministry and pursue his own policy agenda.[35] As a result, the early Menem administration was factionalized, and interorganizational cohesion was minimal.

After a few months, Menem's "honeymoon" period ended when the dollar began to drift upwards, stimulating fears of a new currency run. Deteriorating macroeconomic conditions aggravated the underlying factional competition among policy elites, especially between the Economy Ministry and Central Bank. Senior officials resigned over policy disputes between the organizations, heightening the visibility of elite conflict.[36] Latent tension degenerated into outright conflict, culminating in the Central Bank's president resignation in response to open pressure from the Economy Minister.[37] Open factional conflict focused wealth holders' attention on the political fortunes of individual policy elites, encouraging widespread speculation about elite resignations and consequent policy changes.[38] Elite conflict thus fueled uncertainty and amplified wealth holders' incentive to convert assets to dollars.

In December, self-fulfilling dynamics resembling the first hyperinflationary wave developed. Uncertainty about impending policy changes intensified the currency run, and bad economic news exacerbated elite conflict, eventually leading to elite turnover and producing policy change. As the crisis intensified, the Bunge y Born "team" resigned in response to bad economic news and internal factional conflict. As in April, replacing elites in the middle of an accelerating crisis led to improvised and incoherent policies. Given the limited supply of competent policy elites, Menem appointed an inexperienced political ally as Economy Minister. The newly formed economic team aggravated uncertainty by announcing a rapid and contradictory series of policy changes.[39] Elite turnover gave intermittent influence on a diverse range of elite factions pursuing incompatible goals. For example, an influential adviser to Menem promoted "liberation" of the exchange rate, a repetition of the April decision. This incoherent policy – as before, there was no plausible means through which renouncing control over the exchange rate during a currency run would further the goal of low inflation – opened the door to a second wave of hyperinflation.[40]

Factional competition reached a fever pitch in the final days of 1989 as policy elites realized they were again on the verge of hyperinflation. Competing factions promoted a wide range of policy proposals to the new Economy Minister and President, who were "desperate" for ideas to prevent a new crisis (Cavallo & de Pablo, 2001, p. 148). One of these was a small network of policy elites promoting a plan they sometimes called "dollarization" (Curia, 1991). This faction initially achieved Menem's approval, but leaks – likely an effort by another faction to sabotage the plan from within – triggered dramatic headlines in the final days of the year.[41] On December 30, the large-circulation daily newspaper *Clarin* breathlessly proclaimed "[Authorities] develop plan to dollarize the economy,"[42] a sensational and confusing rumor that amplified uncertainty and contributed to the ongoing currency run.[43] On New Year's Day, an emergency cabinet meeting rejected this plan and agreed instead to adopt the Plan Bonex, the default and expropriation measures described above.

Toward the End: The Plan Bonex

The Plan Bonex was a critical step in ending hyperinflation in Argentina (Beckerman, 1995). Without elimination of the unsustainable organizational structures generating the Central Bank deficit, definitive stabilization was impossible. It took elites almost a year to devise and implement a solution to this problem; consistent with the war of attrition model, this delay was a crucial part of the explanation for the crisis. But contrary to this model, distributional conflict between economic sectors was not the main reason for the delay. Also contrary to the model, there was no fundamental consolidation of political power enabling one group to impose costs on another. The main change was that the political cost of a deeply unpopular policy now appeared smaller than the return of hyperinflation.

To be sure, distributional issues were at stake: by effectively expropriating a significant share of wealth holders' assets, the Plan Bonex imposed substantial costs on a diffuse set of economic elites to end the prolonged crisis. But these costs were imposed by the state rather than economic elites: the Plan Bonex was adopted only after the Bunge y Born managers had resigned. Rather, short-termism and competition in a fragmented elite were the primary cause of delay. Elites working in the Central Bank drew up the proposal in the first months of the Menem administration, but internal opposition from Central Bank president González Fraga delayed its adoption.[44] Elites adopted the plan only when they were on the verge of a second hyperinflation.

Further, conflict in the factionalized policy elite of the early Menem government made implementation of the plan incoherent. The Plan's authors had already resigned due to elite conflicts, leaving the complicated reform without overall oversight.[45] In their absence, the Plan's primary advocate was Domingo Cavallo, the former central banker president mentioned above. Now Foreign Minister, Cavallo, had no direct economic policy authority, creating friction with the Economy Minister. Soon after the plan was announced, these elites became enmeshed in multi-way conflicts over complex details with substantial distributional implications. Policy elite factions aligned themselves with different positions, forcing the inexperienced Economy Minister to intervene and resulting in more resignations in the Central Bank.[46] Rather than resolving these issues, the government postponed key decisions for over a month, prolonging the climate of uncertainty.

Conflict between elite factions in different policy organizations, especially the Economy Ministry and the Central Bank, contributed to this chaotic policy-making process. As shown in Table 1 above, three different individuals served as president of the Argentine Central Bank in as many months. Policy conflict with the Economy Minister and other elites was the main reason for this high turnover rate. Policy debates provoked a series of high-level resignations the Central Bank, which ricocheted down the organizational ranks as allied subordinates resigned along with senior officials. This intense conflict rendered the Central Bank functionally inoperative; elites became paralyzed and incapable of major decisions, allowing unresolved issues to fester.[47] In the midst of hyperinflation, Argentina effectively did not have an operative Central Bank.

The incoherent implementation of the Plan Bonex was a major incentive for capital flight. After announcing the expropriation, elites granted a series of exemptions for specific categories of deposit holders in a chaotic and incremental manner drawn out over several months. Depositors exempted from the expropriation had a strong incentive to immediately exchange these funds for dollars, contributing to the currency run and thereby the rapid increase in prices. All told, these exemptions amounted to more than half the outstanding deposit base at the end of December.[48] The staggered way elites granted these exceptions extended the duration of the crisis.[49] After initially stabilizing in January, the exchange rate exploded toward the end of the month, fueling hyperinflation in February and March. Counterfactually, given that the currency run had essentially come to a halt, a consistent and coherent financial policy implemented at this stage could have avoided further hyperinflation. However, having first announced mass expropriation of savings and then partially reversing that decision, policymakers created an enormous incentive to wealth holders to convert funds to dollars. Thus, even a policy which finally addressed one of the root causes of the crisis – the Central Bank deficit – was implemented in an incoherent and contradictory manner, generating the second wave of hyperinflation.[50]

CONCLUSION

As noted in the introduction, the Argentine hyperinflation resulted in large part from the effective insolvency of the Argentine state, and more specifically its Central Bank. Over more than a decade, a series of policy elites developed an incoherent and self-defeating monetary system; by early 1989, this problem required an urgent solution. However, Argentine elites postponed the eventual solution – effective default on the state's monetary obligations – by over a year. When policy elites finally addressed the Central Bank deficit with the Plan Bonex, the policy was so poorly executed that it fueled a second wave of hyperinflation. Nevertheless, by mid-1990, the financial mechanisms generating hyperinflation had been disarmed, though definitive stabilization would take another year. This delay is one of the key features of the influential war of attrition model (Alesina & Drazen, 1991): accumulation of financial imbalances resulted in a much deeper crisis than would have occurred had state elites been capable of earlier action. But as has been argued, the political process driving this delay was not primarily a distributional conflict between economic sectors but a broader pattern of elite fragmentation involving both economic and state elites.

Distributional conflict played a role not anticipated in the war of attrition model or in social conflict accounts of inflation (Hirschman, 1981) more generally. At the heart of hyperinflation lay a latent distributional conflict between wealth holders and agrarian exporters. The former sought dollars to protect the real value of their assets, while the latter were the main suppliers of dollars on the foreign exchange market. However, this latent conflict was not exogenous to state action but dramatically amplified by the 1988 Plan Primavera, the collapse of which was among the proximate causes of hyperinflation. This incoherent policy reflected political constraints imposed by agrarian elites, but the main impact was to render economic policy contradictory and risky (rather than any direct impact on the state budget). Similarly, the 1990 Plan Bonex imposed severe distributional consequences by effectively expropriating wealth holders. From the perspective of the war of attrition model, the delay in adopting this policy must reflect the resistance of the losing side in the distributional struggle – in this case, wealth holders. However, there is no evidence that other economic elites lobbied for this solution. Indeed, when economic elites (the Bunge y Born group) briefly controlled economic policy, they failed to introduce measures capable of ending the crisis. Rather than an exogenous factor driving the crisis, distributional conflict was substantially endogenous to the actions of state elites.

Rather than the main driver of hyperinflation, distributional conflict was one reflection of a broader pattern of generalized elite fragmentation in Argentina. The main explanation for hyperinflation is that elite fragmentation resulted in a chaotic and conflictive policymaking process that created contradictory and incoherent policies with perverse effects. The five mechanisms introduced above were on display to varying degrees at different moments of the crisis. First, frequent abrupt policy swings such as those of April and November 1989 created deep uncertainty, incentivizing capital flight. Second, short-termism and delay were key factors in the period immediately preceding hyperinflation: elites with short time horizons allowed the Central Bank deficit to fester, and the Plan Primavera was crucially shaped by the incentives of policy elites explicitly trying to hold on for just a few more months. Third, wealth holders had little confidence in elites' policy announcements (in standard language, policies lacked credibility) at least in part because of the reputational individualism of the Argentine policy elite and because informed observers knew that incumbents' hold on state positions was weak. These reputation effects fueled the currency runs driving hyperinflation. Fourth, policies were often contradictory and incoherent to conflicts within the state; the clearest example is the outright factionalism prevailing in the first few months of the Menem administration. Fifth, conflict with economic elites – the distributional conflicts fueled by state action – imposed constraints on policy elites' options that also contributed to policy contradiction and incoherence.

This elite politics account subsumes aspects of both distributional conflict theories, as just noted, and institutional theories (Evans & Rauch, 1999; Spiller & Tommasi, 2007). The latter often cite high rates of elite turnover as a symptom of institutional weakness and point to short-termism and credibility problems as reflections of weak policymaking capacity. However, summarizing these dimensions as "institutional" effects ignores the elite competition and conflict that drives such processes. For example, Evans and Rauch (1999) cite the absence of shared norms, or malfeasance (corruption), among state officials. It is hard to see how normative anomie per se could result in the policies and pathologies that produced hyperinflation, and there is little evidence of outright corruption in this domain. Rather, policy elites operated in situations of constraint due to competition and conflict with economic elites, party elites, and other policy elites. It is these processes arising from elite fragmentation, rather than anomie or malfeasance, which provide an explanation for a crisis as extreme as the Argentine hyperinflation.

Elite fragmentation is a longstanding, structural characteristic of Argentine politics and not merely a conjunctural feature of the 1980s. In this sense, the hyperinflation crisis is one manifestation of structures of elite competition and conflict that have generated macroeconomic instability over decades. Fragmentation and conflict also characterized elite politics during the late-2001 financial crisis (Van Gunten, 2015), and at time of writing, Argentina is one of the few countries in the world with a rate of inflation above 100%. The failure to stabilize inflation under the 2015–2019 conservative government of Mauricio Macri is an episode that could be used to further test the elite fragmentation theory developed here. Elite theory might also help account for other Latin American hyperinflation episodes in the 1980s, including in Brazil and Bolivia. Nevertheless, macroeconomic instability is also common in countries with relatively cohesive elites, such as Mexico; elite fragmentation primarily explains patterns of policymaking that promote macroeconomic instability, rather than directly account for crises as such. Further developments in elite theory should address these scope conditions.

ACKNOWLEDGMENTS

The author thanks Rebecca Jean Emigh and Dylan Riley for generous, insightful, and patient feedback on numerous drafts of this paper and Guadalupe Moreno and Fernán Gaillardou for informative discussions. All remaining inadequacies are the author's sole responsibility. This research was supported by the Social Science Research Council, the National Science Foundation (SES-0957298), and the Robert F. and Jean E. Holtz Center at the University of Wisconsin-Madison.

NOTES

1. Public interview sources include the Oral History Archive of Contemporary Argentina at the Instituto de Investigaciones Gino Germani, University of Buenos Aires (referred to as IIGG archive below).

2. For purposes of analytical clarity, I disregard military rule in this exposition.

3. This describes relations between party and policy elites in Mexico and Chile during some periods, for example.

4. This describes the process of elite turnover in the Mexican policy elite, for example.

5. As Economy Minister Juan Sourrouille put it, "I was never a Radical, at least not until [joining government]...I was more of an independent" (IIGG archive). An ally described their appointment as "a hard pill to swallow" for party elites (Mario Brodersohn, IIGG archive).

6. The lack of prior ties between these elites is summed up in their first conversation: "I didn't choose you and you didn't choose me" (González Fraga in de Pablo, 2011, p. 57).

7. Other economic elites, including industrial and commercial elite sectors also appear in the narrative below, but for analytical tractability I focus on agrarian elites and wealth holders.

8. This category overlaps with many other social groups since practically *all* elite sectors (and some non-elites) held some liquid assets. Nevertheless for analytical purposes this is a meaningful elite bloc.

9. Inflation data are taken from the International Monetary Fund, International Financial Statistics in 2008. These data are no longer available from the IMF at time of writing.

10. The latest transition from military rule to democracy occurred six years earlier. The 1989 transfer of presidential power from Alfonsín to Menem was the first transition between democratically elected parties to occur in decades. While this certainly created uncertainty, as noted above invocations of electoral uncertainty must contend with the fact that a distinct second wave of hyperinflation occurred after the elections.

11. This was particularly true of the second wave: in the second half of 1989 the government deficit was small or even in surplus.

12. In hyperinflationary settings "everyone watches the exchange rate as the signal for setting wages and prices" (Dornbusch, 1985, p. 16).

13. Consistent with this, Fischer et al. (2002, p. 850) show that exchange rate changes preceeded inflation in Argentina from 1967 to 1991.

14. A contemporary analysis of budget deficit found that in January–May 1989 (the period of accelerating hyperinflation) the deficit increased by 95% primarily due to falling revenue, particularly in value–added and capital gains taxes. Declining revenue was due to recession rather than tax policy changes. Spending declined but could not offset lost revenue. *Source:* FIEL reported by Clarín, July 2, 1989.

15. Revenue increased from 17% to 22% of GDP from 1989 to 1992, but such levels of revenue were not unprecedented; a similar level had been achieved in the mid-1980s.

16. Piekarz (1984) describes these challenges.

17. Cavallo's main goal was to reduce private sector debt, and he was not ideologically committed to free markets at this time (Cavallo & de Pablo, 2001).

18. Machinea (1990, pp. 36, 58) and José Luis Machinea IIGG archive.

19. José Luis Machinea and Juan Sourrouille, IIGG archive.

20. José Luis Machinea IIGG archive. The President's reaction was "what do you want, for me to nominate [two conservative former officials]? No, I don't have anyone but you and I'll have to resign myself to that" (Torre, 2021, p. 358).

21. In 1986, the central bank eliminated the monetary regulation account but replaced it with a functionally equivalent structure (Beckerman, 1992, p. 13).

22. At their peak, export taxes accounted for only about 10% of revenues, and the lost income from export taxes was eclipsed by collapse of other revenue sources.

23. Policy elites hoped that this mechanisms would "produce a less negative reaction" than export taxes (Machinea, 1990, p. 77), but the result was the opposite.

24. Juan Sourrouille, IIGG Oral history interview; Machinea (1990, pp. 66, 73).

25. As one contemporary observed noted, "the big question that the financial market asks is whether the Central Bank can continue its exchange rate policy until the elections" (Graziano, 1990, p. 28).

26. As shown in Fig. 4, the growth in the Austral/Dollar exchange rate was approximately exponential (note the logged vertical axis; each tick represents a doubling of the exchange rate). The breakpoint analysis (Bai & Perron, 2003) identifies deviations from this exponential trend, that is, moments when the rate of depreciation accelerated or decelerated.

27. La Nación, February 9, 1989.

28. Pablo Gerchunoff, IIGG archive.

29. Pablo Gerchunoff, IIGG archive.

30. La Nación, 4/15/89 and 4/21/89.

31. For example, La Nación, April 8, 1989.

32. La Nación, April 20 and 26, 1989.

33. Bunge y Born held a near monopoly on grain exports in the early 20th century. By the late 1980s the firm had diversified into numerous industrial sectors, but still retained substantial agrarian interests.

34. As noted above, the team amounted to "three or four" officials. These elites' capacity was further undermined by the death of Economy Minister Miguel Roig barely a week into the Menem presidency.

35. For example, González Fraga unilaterally suspended policies which benefited agrarian exporters and discretely inserted a clause increasing the central bank's autonomy into proposed legislation (Javier González Fraga interview).

36. *Clarín*, November 11, 1989.

37. Javier González Fraga interview.

38. For example, in mid-November Menem denounced "bad faith" rumors about the Economy Minster's impending resignation. *Clarín*, November 17, 1989. The rumors were confirmed days later.

39. For example, the incoming Central Bank President declared that the bank would not devalue the currency – and then promptly devalued.

40. In the words of a prominent contemporary financial analyst, these measures were "totally inconsistent measures as a result of the intervention of various hands." Miguel Angel Broda, Carta Economica No. 79, December 1989–January 1990.

41. Eduardo Curia interview and *Clarín*, December 31, 1989.

42. Clarin, December 30, 1989.

43. Beckerman (1995, p. 678) cites "dollarization" rumors as a main cause of the second hyperinflation. While downplaying the importance of the rumors, influential financial analyst Broda conceded that rumors "gave [hyperinflation] an additional push" Estudio Broda, Carta Económica, No. 80, February 1990.

44. González Fraga interview.

45. One of the plan's authors, Roque Fernández, resigned due to fear of leaks; González Fraga prohibited the other from entering the Bank because the proposal was so incendiary. González Fraga interview.

TOD S. VAN GUNTEN   171

46. E.g. *Clarín*, 1/14/90.
47. Anonymous interviews.
48. International Monetary Fund, "Argentina – Recent Economic Developments," 26 November 1990, p. 37.
49. Some exceptions were announced in late February, six weeks after expropriation (de Pablo, 2005).
50. This interpretation of the second hyperinflation was advanced by Javier González Fraga, among others. González Fraga interview.

REFERENCES

Alesina, A., & Drazen, A. (1991). Why are stabilizations delayed? *The American Economic Review, 81*(5), 1170–1188. https://doi.org/10.3386/w3053

Almansi, A. A., & Rodriguez, C. A. (1989). *Reforma monetaria y financiera en hiperinflación*. Documentos de Trabajo 67. Centro de Estudios Macroeconomicos.

Bai, J., & Perron, P. (2003). Computation and analysis of multiple structural change models. *Journal of Applied Econometrics, 18*(1), 1–22. https://doi.org/10.1002/jae.659

Baliño, T. (1987). *The Argentine banking crisis of 1980*. IMF Working Paper WP/87/77. International Monetary Fund.

Beckerman, P. (1992). *Public sector "debt distress" in Argentina, 1988-89*. Policy Research Working Papers 902. The World Bank.

Beckerman, P. (1995). Central-Bank 'distress' and hyperinflation in Argentina, 1989-90. *Journal of Latin American Studies, 27*(3), 663–682. https://doi.org/10.1017/S0022216X00011640

Bernhard, W., Broz, J. L., & Clark, W. R. (2002). The political economy of monetary institutions. *International Organization, 56*(4), 693–723. https://doi.org/10.1162/002081802760403748

Block, F. (1977). The ruling class does not rule: Notes on the Marxist theory of the state. *Socialist Revolution, 33*, 6–28.

Brinks, D. M., Levitsky, S., & Murillo, M. V. (2020). The political origins of institutional weakness. In D. M. Brinks, S. Levitsky, & M. V. Murillo (Eds.), *The politics of institutional weakness in Latin America* (pp. 1–40). Cambridge University Press. https://doi.org/10.1017/9781108776608.001

Burris, V. (2005). Interlocking directorates and political cohesion among corporate elites. *American Journal of Sociology, 111*(1), 249–283. https://doi.org/10.1086/428817

Cagan, P. (1956). The monetary dynamics of hyperinflation. In M. Friedman (Ed.), *Studies in the quantity theory of money* (pp. 25–117). University of Chicago Press.

Cavallo, D., & de Pablo, J. C. (2001). *Pasión por crear*. Planeta.

Centeno, M. A. (1997). *Democracy within reason: Technocratic revolution in Mexico*. The Pennsylvania State University Press.

Chu, J. S. G., & Davis, G. F. (2016). Who killed the inner circle? The decline of the American corporate interlock network. *American Journal of Sociology, 122*(3), 714–754. https://doi.org/10.1086/688650

Curia, E. L. (1991). *Dos años de economía de Menem*. El Cronista Ediciones.

de Pablo, J. C. (2005). *La economía argentina en la segunda mitad del siglo XX* (Vol. 2). Editorial La Ley.

de Pablo, J. C. (2011). *Política económica en condiciones extremas: entrevistas a Javier González Fraga, Néstor Rapanelli, Jorge Remes Lenicov, Jesús Rodríguez*. EDUCA.

Dornbusch, R. (1985). *Stopping hyperinflation: Lessons from the German inflation experience of the 1920s*. NBER Working Paper 1675. National Bureau of Economic Research.

Dornbusch, R., & de Pablo, J. C. (1989). Debt and macroeconomic instability in Argentina. In J. Sachs (Ed.), *Developing country debt and the world economy*. University of Chicago Press.

Evans, P. (1995). *Embedded autonomy: States and industrial transformation*. Princeton University Press.

Evans, P., & Rauch, J. E. (1999). Bureaucracy and growth: A cross-national analysis of the effects of "Weberian" state structures on economic growth. *American Sociological Review, 64*(5), 748. https://doi.org/10.2307/2657374

Fischer, S., Sahay, R., & Végh, C. A. (2002). Modern hyper- and high inflations. *Journal of Economic Literature*, *40*(3), 837–880. https://doi.org/10.1257/002205102760273805

Graziano, W. (1990). *Historia de dos hiperinflaciones: De Sourrouille a Erman González*. Fundación Gabriel y Darío Ramos.

Grimson, A., Castellani, A., & Roig, A. (2012). Institutional change and development in Argentina. In A. Portes & L. Smith (Eds.), *Institutions count: Their role and significance in Latin American development* (pp. 39–59). University of California Press.

Heredia, M. (2003). Reformas estructurales y renovación de las élites económicas en Argentina: Estudio de los portavoces de la tierra y del capital [Structural reforms and renewal of economic elites in Argentine: Studies on the spokesmen for land and capital]. *Revista Mexicana de Sociología*, *65*(1), 77. https://doi.org/10.2307/3541516

Higley, J., & Burton, M. G. (2006). *Elite foundations of liberal democracy*. Rowman & Littlefield.

Higley, J., Hoffman-Lange, U., Kadushin, C., & Moore, G. (1991). Elite integration in stable democracies: A reconsideration. *European Sociological Review*, *7*(1), 35–53.

Hirschman, A. O. (1981). On the social and political matrix of inflation: Elaborations on the Latin American experience. In *Essays in trespassing: Economics to politics and beyond* (pp. 177–207). Cambridge University Press.

Huber, J. D., & Shipan, C. R. (2002). *Deliberate discretion: The institutional foundations of bureaucratic autonomy*. Cambridge University Press.

Ingham, G. (2005). *The nature of money*. Polity Press.

Krippner, G. R. (2011). *Capitalizing on crisis: The political origins of the rise of finance*. Harvard University Press.

Lachmann, R. (2002). *Capitalists in spite of themselves: Elite conflict and European transitions in early modern Europe*. Oxford University Press.

Lachmann, R. (2020). *First-class passengers on a sinking ship: Elite politics and the decline of great powers*. Verso.

Leblang, D., & Satyanath, S. (2006). Institutions, expectations, and currency rises. *International Organization*, *60*(01). https://doi.org/10.1017/S0020818306060073

Levitsky, S. (2003). *Transforming labor-based parties in Latin America: Argentine Peronism in comparative perspective*. Cambridge University Press.

Levitsky, S., & Murillo, M. V. (2005). Building castles in the sand? The politics of institutional weakness in Argentina. In S. Levitsky & M. V. Murillo (Eds.), *Argentine democracy: The politics of institutional weakness* (pp. 21–44). The Pennsylvania State University Press.

Lluch, A., & Salvaj, E. (2014). Longitudinal study of interlocking directorates in Argentina. In D. Thomas & G. Westerhuis (Eds.), *The power of corporate networks. A comparative and historical perspective* (pp. 257–275). Routledge.

Machinea, J. L. (1990). *Stabilization under Alfonsin's government: A frustrated attempt*. Documento CEDES 42. Centro de Estudios de Estado y Sociedad.

Marcus, G. E. (1983). 'Elite' as a concept, theory and research tradition. In G. E. Marcus (Ed.), *Elites, ethnographic issues* (pp. 7–28). University of New Mexico Press.

Merton, R. K. (1948). The self-fulfilling prophecy. *Antioch Review*, *8*(2), 193. https://doi.org/10.2307/4609267

Mills, C. W. (1956). *The power elite*. Oxford University Press.

Mizruchi, M. (2013). *The fracturing of the American corporate elite*. Harvard University Press.

Moody, J., & White, D. R. (2003). Structural cohesion and embeddedness: A hierarchical concept of social groups. *American Sociological Review*, *68*(1), 103. https://doi.org/10.2307/3088904

Morris, S., & Shin, H. S. (1998). Unique equilibrium in a model of self-fulfilling currency attacks. *The American Economic Review*, *88*(3), 587–597.

Piekarz, J. (1984). Compensacion de reservas de efectivo minimo – La cuenta de regulacion monetaria, el resultado cuasi fiscal del banco central y la transformacion del sistema financiero argentino. *Ensayos Economicos*, *31*, 29–137.

Reinhart, C. M., & Rogoff, K. S. (2009). *This time is different: Eight centuries of financial folly*. Princeton University Press.

Schneider, B. R. (2004). *Business politics and the state in twentieth-century Latin America*. Cambridge University Press.

Skocpol, T. (1985). Bringing the state back in: Strategies of analysis in current research. In P. B. Evans, D. Rueschmeyer, & T. Skocpol (Eds.), *Bringing the state back in* (pp. 3–37). Cambridge University Press.

Spiller, P. T., & Tommasi, M. (2007). *The institutional foundations of public policy in Argentina: A transactions cost approach*. Cambridge University Press. https://doi.org/10.1017/CBO9780511818219

Torre, J. C. (2021). *Diario de una temporada en el quinto piso: Episodios de política económica en los años de Alfonsín*. EDHASA Argentina.

Van Gunten, T. S. (2015). Cohesion, consensus, and conflict: Technocratic elites and financial crisis in Mexico and Argentina. *International Journal of Comparative Sociology*, *56*(5), 366–390. https://doi.org/10.1177/0020715215626238

Weyland, K. (2004). *The politics of market reform in fragile democracies: Argentina, Brazil, Peru and Venezuela*. Princeton University Press.

White, H. (1970). *Chains of opportunity: System models of mobility in organizations*. Harvard University Press.

CHAPTER 7

ELITES, COLONIALISM, AND PROPERTY RIGHTS IN HISTORICAL PERSPECTIVE

Abhishek Chatterjee

University of Montana, USA

ABSTRACT

This chapter proposes a framework explaining the evolution of property rights in land, assuming two unequal groups of actors: elites possessing means of violence and nonelite land cultivators. It then shows that all intermediary groups – those acting between the chief violence holders (i.e., rulers) and cultivators – are in effect (greater or lesser rulers and cultivators). Using this framework, this chapter explains most of the developments in the evolution of land rights in 19th century colonial Bengal. The proposed theoretical framework explains how different, hierarchically arrayed claims over land and the resulting allocation of rights was a function of asymmetries in power and information between three groups: rulers, direct cultivators, and intermediaries without their own coercive means. It explains inter alia why private property in land was not likely to emerge in this configuration, and that the (non-private) property rights of the other two groups wouldn't attain stability as long as rulers perceived an information asymmetry. In such a situation, land rights would attain neither "private," nor "public" character.

Keywords: Political economy; state formation; colonialism; property rights; land; market; India; East India Company

Adam Smith (2003, Book V, Chapter 1, Part II) argued that property "necessarily requires the establishment of civil government." This reiteration of the earlier positions of Locke and Montesquieu (Van Creveld, 1999, p. 207) was a principle that was practiced in most of Europe by the mid-19th century, land being one of

---

Elites, Nonelites, and Power
Political Power and Social Theory, Volume 41, 175–210
Copyright © 2025 Abhishek Chatterjee
Published under exclusive licence by Emerald Publishing Limited
ISSN: 0198-8719/doi:10.1108/S0198-871920240000041007

176 *Elites, Colonialism, and Property Rights*

the more protected properties. Privatization of land was not, however, as widespread in the non-European world (i.e., excepting European settlements). But as with regions of Europe before the existence of private property the absence of property in land did not necessarily mean that land was either "public" or "common." For example, Blaufarb (2019, p. 1) describes prerevolutionary French land as being "rarely owned independently and completely by a single person" but having "multiple, partial owners who stood in legally enforced relations of superiority and dependence toward one another." Similarly, in parts of India at various times, different groups – cultivators (*raiyats*) and "landlords" (or *zamindars*) among them – shared unequal rights over land. While some cultivators had permanent rights to cultivate and retain part of the land's products, landlords were entitled to a fixed share, and the state reserved the right to set its demand on zamindars and to regulate the relationship between the other two. These rights were not static. Different combinations would obtain at various points in time: Cultivators' rights could become temporary, and zamindars' rights to collect from cultivators could become more, or less permanent. Further, either of these rights could be more, or less, saleable.

What explains these different combinations and the changes therein? The question is important because private property in land, as recognized today, is one specific combination such that the same individual or group has permanent rights of use/appropriation, regulation, and alienation, while the state only retains the right to a payment in some cases (as "tax"). This chapter proposes a theoretical framework, part of which explains changes in property rights in land between the late 18th and late 19th century in the British Indian Presidency (i.e., governing unit) of Bengal (present day Bangladesh, and the Indian states of West Bengal, Bihar, and Orissa). Bengal is theoretically interesting because some policy makers then supported private property and could have allocated such rights to their favored groups. Yet private (or for that matter, "public") land never emerged in British India, and the framework suggests why this was unlikely in any (nonsettler) colonial context.[1] Thus this chapter's purpose is twofold: Accounting for the lack of absolute private property in land, and explaining the variation in the kinds of (non-absolute private) property over time, involving three principal groups: rulers, cultivators, and intermediaries (or subcontractors) without their own independent means of violence.

EXTANT THEORETICAL APPROACHES AND EXPLANATIONS

The Efficiency Framework

Explanations for the historical emergence of private property rights can be roughly divided into two broad categories.[2] The "efficiency" approach (North, 1990, p. 7) following Coase's work (1937, 1959, 1960), explained property rights outcomes as efficient adaptations to transaction costs (Alchian & Demsetz, 1973; Demsetz, 1967; North & Thomas, 1976).[3] Private property rights in land emerged when the expected costs of coordinating activities and apportioning such rights among various – rationally egoistic – individuals and groups fell below the expected benefits accruing from the establishment of such rights (Demsetz, 1967). Accordingly, private property emerged when relative prices changed, due to the expansion of trade, or changing land-to-labor ratios (Demsetz, 1967, p. 352; North & Thomas, 1976, p. 23). Similarly, expected efficiency gains led to removing the hurdles to the commodification of land (De Soto, 2003, Chapter 5; Priest, 2021, Chapters 7 and 9).

An implication of the above is that private property rights emerge because (egoistically) rational humans find them collectively efficient. Often the converse is also implied, namely, that all collectively efficient property arrangements are private (e.g., Alchian & Demsetz, 1973). Not all approaches under the efficiency framework concur with either proposition. Privatization may be socially inefficient in the long term if owners discount the future too much (Schlager & Ostrom, 1992, p. 256). More importantly, socially efficient property arrangements may not be either private, or indeed "common" or public (Ostrom, 1990, 2000, 2010). Private property itself is comprised of a set of further rights such as usage, exclusion, and alienation; socially efficient property rights have been shown to contain some elements of the set, but not others (Ostrom, 2000, pp. 335–340; Schlager & Ostrom, 1992, pp. 255–257). This insight, that property rights outcomes – efficient or not – may amount neither to "private," nor "public," but contain elements of both is one that this chapter incorporates, even as it abandons one implicit assumption of the efficiency framework, namely, the absence of power asymmetries or hierarchies.

The Power/Conflict Approach

Power/Conflict and Ideology

Power, or involuntary societal hierarchies *as a starting point of analysis,* appears to be absent from the efficiency framework. Indeed, in this approach even hierarchical feudal relationships are seen as outcomes of voluntary contracts between parties (e.g., North & Thomas, 1971, pp. 778–779). Marx (1906), Veblen (1898, p. 358), and Polanyi (2001) argued that the emergence of private property in land involved force. For Marx, force was employed in the pursuit of economic interests, while ideology and culture were equally important for the other two. For Polanyi (2001, pp. 178–181), markets in land were created in England under the influence of Benthamite policymakers, and in France by liberal revolutionaries who saw markets – and their corollary, absolute private property rights – as the most efficient way of organizing society. More recently, Blaufarb (2019, pp. 8–14) favors an ideational explanation for the rise of private property in land in the aftermath of the French Revolution.

Power and (Bourgeois and/or Non-bourgeois) Economic Interests

Marx's (1906, pp. 784–848) discussion of the so-called primitive accumulation could be seen as one of the early critiques of one version of the efficiency

178   *Elites, Colonialism, and Property Rights*

approach, and its emphasis on demographic change, leading to change in relative prices, as the crucial explanatory factor. He pointed to the roles of both the social power of "industrial capitalists" (vis-à-vis feudal lords) in ending feudal privileges (pp. 786–787), and of feudal lords in the "forcible driving of the peasantry from the land" (pp. 789–790, pp. 794–795) as factors that created private property in land. This view implies that there is no determinate effect of demographic changes on property rights in land without taking into consideration power relationships, more specifically, class relations.[4]

While Sweezy and Lefebvre (1978, p. 40), and even Max Weber ([1927] 2003, pp. 93–94) attributed the privatization of land to the power and interests of the bourgeoisie, Brenner (1985, especially pp. 284–299) argued that it was the landed "capitalist" aristocracy that was the chief agent of privatization. The strength of this aristocracy in England, and the fact that it had taken over the state led to the early emergence of private property in land, relative to France and indeed, much of the rest of the Continent. The French monarchical state, although also fundamentally allied with the aristocracy, prevented the latter from expropriating the peasantry (Brenner, 1985, pp. 289–290).

Why could the aristocracy expropriate the peasantry in England with state facilitation, but not in France (where the state blocked it), especially since both states were allies to this class?[5] Lachmann's (2002) "elite conflict" theory provides an answer. But, as I shall argue below, this answer raises an additional set of conceptual questions that are best addressed within a bargaining framework like those underpinning the efficiency approach, modified, however, to account for power asymmetries.

Elite Conflict and Private Property
Lachmann (2002, p. 9) defines elites as rulers who can appropriate resources from others through distinctive organizational apparatuses that they inhabit. Further, they can do so because they might possess the means of coercion, means of production, or the means of salvation (p. 241). Elites' capacity to pursue their interests depends on the existence of other elites; where no others exist, they are just like classes. Social changes are outcomes of elite conflicts, where elites try to subordinate "part or all of a rival elite's organizational apparatus within its own," (Lachmann, 2002, p. 9) by undermining its rival's "capacity to extract resources from non-elites" (p. 11). Using this model of elite interaction, Lachmann (2002) explains changes in property rights – among many other things – in Europe. His argument is that high levels of elite conflict generally led to more security and protection for the nonelite producing groups, while the dominance of single elites led to the opposite outcome (pp. 31–38, for example). Private property in land arose in England when the gentry or landlord was able to successfully fend off rivals, including the crown and the clergy, in the process of capturing "a significant share of agrarian income to themselves from their tenants in the century after Reformation" (p. 180). Privatization was the way in which they managed to seize most of the gains in productivity that the yeomen farmers produced (pp. 190–194). This did not happen in prerevolutionary France owing to the high levels of elite conflict and the inability of any single elite group to displace its rivals (p. 195, for example).

It's not clear if Lachmann (2002) extends the elite conflict argument to the French Revolution, which produced private property in land, including those lands that peasants came to possess. In places it appears that he does, for instance, when he points to peasants taking advantage of conflicts between elements of the Third Estate – especially the bourgeoisie – and the aristocracy to attack seigneurial privileges (2002, pp. 187–188). In other places, the Revolution seems to be depicted as exogenous, with the peasantry and the bourgeoisie overthrowing the state, and with it the structure of elite relations (2002, p. 231). The endogenous interpretation of the Revolution would not be able to explain why private property should emerge because of elite conflict (since elite conflict presumably prevents the emergence of such property). The exogenous interpretation would, of course, eschew the application of the elite framework to the Revolution. In both cases, the role of the bourgeoisie or factions thereof would seem to be important. In the endogenous case, it is probably related to the anomalous outcome of private property (from the perspective of the elite conflict framework). For theoretical parsimony in the discussion that follows, I take the elite framework to apply to property rights in the ancien régime, with the Revolution (and the role of the bourgeoisie in it) being exogenous to it.

Thus, the structure of relations among *non-bourgeois* elites provides a partial answer to the question raised above about contrasting outcomes in England and pre-Revolutionary France; partial, because it still doesn't reconcile Brenner's proposition of the alliance between the state and the landed elite (in France) with conflict (over land tenures) between these putatively allied groups. This is because the crucial mechanism of "elite conflict" is underspecified and requires further elaboration. The potential for conflict – unless it is defined narrowly as physical, armed conflict – is inherent in the very definition of elites insofar as different such groups seek to extract resources from the same or overlapping groups of direct producers. Such interactions contain elements of both conflict and cooperation. This means that, prior to observing outcomes, it is very difficult to epistemically distinguish conflict from cooperation, or low levels of conflict from high levels of conflict. To avoid tautology, it's best to see the latent conflict between elites as leading to a process of negotiation or bargaining, the outcomes of which have consequences for property rights. Since bargaining would not necessarily be between equals, outcomes should reflect power asymmetries.

For an explanation of this kind, power needs first to be defined, and then integrated into a theoretical framework of bargaining between elites leading to institutional outcomes, thus also providing the micro-foundations for an "elite theory" of the historical development of property rights (Lachmann, 2002, p. 12). I now turn to this task. I first discuss the literature – growing out of an "internal" critique of the efficiency approach – that provides the foundations for such an explanation, highlighting crucial concepts that I then use to propose my explanatory framework.

Power and Economic Interests in a Bargaining Framework

North (1981, 1990, pp. 58–59), abandoning the "pure" efficiency approach, incorporated some of Marx's insights to demonstrate that institutions should not be expected to be optimal solutions to scarcity (or otherwise) because they often result from groups attempting to gain (distributional) advantages over others (also see Fligstein, 2018; Knight, 1992, p. 40; Moe, 2005). This framework does not completely dispense with the bargaining and transaction costs component of the efficiency model but adds background power considerations.[6]

A second, closely related reason why the "pure" efficiency approach fails (in its own terms) is that, in situations akin to a two (or more) person "prisoners' dilemma," it is difficult to explain how collectively efficient institutions could arise, even in the absence of power considerations. For instance, rational egoists would prefer violating others' property claims when this was advantageous to them but would prefer others to respect their own claims. Neither is this problem solved by postulating a contract enforcing state, since the latter must also be a rational egoist.

Thus, North (1981, pp. 24–29, 1990, pp. 58–59) also demonstrated that wealth maximizing rulers – especially without positing very long horizons – have no incentive to design socially efficient institutions, including allocating property rights. An egoistically rational ruler has incentives to favor powerful groups in society, and to reduce the costs of measurement, monitoring, and revenue collection, which are all components of transaction costs (1981, pp. 24–29). While this could still lead to the emergence of private property rights – if the powerful are interested in such rights – this outcome would have produced both winners and losers, and thus would not have been socially efficient (also see Lane, 1958, 1975, pp. 13–14, 1979, p. 10).

A second problem, that of credibility, follows directly from the discussion above of rational egoists in a prisoners' dilemma situation. Even if rulers promised to uphold property rights of powerful groups in return for a payment or other resource assistance, these groups were unlikely to believe this promise, knowing that rulers, as rational egoists, would likely violate commitments when it was in their advantage to do so (North, 1990, p. 59; also see Acemoglu et al., 2005, p. 394). To make such commitments credible and solve this collective action problem, rulers would have to somehow restrict their own freedom of action in such ways that unilaterally reneging on pacts would be extremely difficult, if not impossible. Credible commitments are thus costly for those making them (which also make them credible).

Both North and Weingast (1989) and Acemoglu et al. (2005, pp. 393–394, pp. 435–436) point to institutional changes that weakened the autonomous ability of England's monarchy to make policy unilaterally as exemplifying such a credible commitment to the state's chief creditors. These changes must have been very costly to rulers, especially because they weakened their political power considerably; rulers now had to share power with the Parliament, and creditors were directly incorporated into the state as the Bank of England. Why would rulers agree to such institutional concessions? One answer is that the relative power of the groups affected the very structure of the situation, compelling actors into costly (mutual) cooperation to preempt worse (mutual) outcomes (see Chatterjee, 2016, pp. 802–806; 2017, pp. 17–22).

Integrating power into a bargaining framework would entail two recognitions: That, unlike in usual bargaining setups, actors may not have symmetric choice sets (hence expected costs), and that the more powerful actor may be able to influence the alternatives available to the relatively less powerful (Gruber, 2000, p. 7; Knight, 1992, p. 41, pp. 131–136). Such asymmetric choices and the ability of one group or actor to control the options available to others can, in turn, be explained once power is defined as the extent of reciprocal dependence of one group of actors on another (Emerson, 1962). Therefore, given two groups each of which controls resources that the other values, the group that, uniquely had alternatives to the resources that the other possesses would be less dependent on the other and, ergo, would have more bargaining power. Further, groups' relative capacity for collective action, and hence coherence (among other factors), would affect dependence – hence bargaining power – since coherence is directly relevant to groups' ability to prevent others from accessing resources they control.

This view of power is implicit throughout the framework I present in the following section. I highlight how specific resources, including coercive ones, factor into groups' bargaining abilities, and how power asymmetries, which also tend to cumulate over time (e.g., Gaventa, 1982, pp. 3–15), allow one group to dictate the alternatives available to others. In this way of seeing, the "pure" efficiency or "private ordering" (Hodgson, 2009) approach becomes a special case where similarly situated individuals or groups adjust their behaviors to higher order institutional changes that result from power relationships.[7] Such adjustments often complement the higher level changes in ways that further reinforce those higher level institutions (Aoki, 2001). For example, the nature of property rights tends to have effects on other practices, such as sub-leasing, that in turn further buttress those property rights institutions (for a similar approach, see Firmin-Sellers, 1995, p. 879).

THE FRAMEWORK

Consistent with the limited (to the ancien régime) interpretation of the elite conflict approach, the framework I propose initially posits only one type of elite and thus only two groups (rather than merchants or capitalists as a third). Every other elite group is shown to emerge from the two initial types. The framework partially confirms Lachmann's (2002, pp. 31–38) proposition that non-bourgeois inter-elite conflict was historically not propitious for the emergence of private property in land. Partially, because once concepts such as "conflict," "cooperation," or "dominance" are defined within the bargaining framework, Lachman's corollary, that low levels of conflict due to the dominance of a single elite-led private property to emerge, as in England, does not necessarily follow. Rather, the framework implies that the superior bargaining power of certain *intermediate* elites – those situated between the state and cultivators – should lead private property to emerge.

"Defining Rights," "Abilities," and Types of Property Rights in Land

I distinguish between "rights," on the one hand, and "abilities," or "capacities" on the other. Rights emerge when individuals' and groups' capacities vis-à-vis certain objects (in this case, land) are acknowledged, and recognized by others in society, especially those in a position to forcibly prevent the exercise of such capacities. A person might, for instance, have the capacity to cultivate a piece of land but would not have that right until others, and especially those in a position to forcibly prevent it, regularly allow that person to cultivate (see Hodgson, 2015). The following discrete kinds of rights over land could emerge historically (Schlager & Ostrom, 1992).[8]

(1) The right to access/cultivate land.
(2) The right to appropriate some or all of the product of land (withdrawal rights).
(3) The right to exclude others from using land and to regulate the land's use.
(4) The right to alienate/transfer any and all of the rights defined above for any reason (payment or otherwise) to others by consent, permanently and temporarily.
(5) The right to pledge any and all of the rights enumerated above for debts.

Absolute private property rights in land obtain only when all these rights are vested in one agent, or group. Short of absolute property in land, any (proper) subset of the first three rights could be more, or less, commodified; that is, they could vary in the extent to which (4), and sometimes (5), applied to them. In cases where especially (4) applied, one could also refer to "property" existing in the rights to which they applied; there could be vendible "property" in the right to collect from cultivators, for instance. Historical variation could be considerable in the extent to which each of these rights was shared among different individuals or groups, or over different parcels of land.

Sketching the Framework

Background Assumptions (or Why Rulers Always Have an Advantage Against Cultivators)

I first assume, in any society, a population of cultivators who would prefer at least to have the ability to access and use land and appropriate its products. Second, there are organized groups or agents specializing in violence that can deprive cultivators of the products of their cultivation. This entails the existence of a second group of agents, initially undifferentiated, who prefer and possess the ability to appropriate some of the cultivators' product. It does not matter for this framework if they appropriate this product by demanding a "payment" as protection from their own violence, or that of other coercion specialists. Thus, they can be entrepreneurs (Lane, 1958), or racketeers (Lane, 1958, pp. 402–404; Tilly, 1985) and "stationary bandits" (Olson, 1993).[9] The relationship between the two groups, nonetheless, is coercive, and not of an exchange between equals, inasmuch as generally better organized specialists in violence can credibly threaten the very physical security/existence of others. Thus, violence specialists have an advantage in bargaining situations; although using coercive means also entails a cost to the user, the possible costs to those on whom it is used is much higher, especially if the latter do not possess coercive means.

The protective "service" that violence specialists offer tends to a natural monopoly because of the economies of scale involved (Lane, 1958, p. 402). Since the capacity for violence would also give them the ability to set rules that might attain legitimacy with the passage of time (Lane, 1958, p. 403), I refer to them interchangeably as rulers, or prospective rulers.

Again, the efficiency approach would portray the relationship between violence specialists and cultivators as that between equals involving the exchange of protection for a payment. From this perspective, the violence specialist cannot change property arrangements; it merely protects or enforces preexisting arrangements – which, recall, are solely a function of transaction costs among nominal (here, cultivating) equals (Demsetz, 1967) – for a payment.[10] There would of course be bargaining between the two parties about the exact amount. And assuming that the following costs were common knowledge, the bargaining range would be between cultivators' costs of providing for their own protection (including organizing themselves, something that violence specialists couldn't affect), which is the most that cultivators would be willing to pay – and violence specialists' "production costs," the least that the latter would be willing to accept. This approach further implies that the outcome (i.e., the payment amount) would be determined solely by the bargaining skills of the two parties; cultivators always have the option to decline to pay if inter alia the payment demanded were higher than the expected costs of setting up their own protection.

Yet power asymmetries greatly diminish the probability of an outcome that would be equally satisfactory to cultivators. Indeed, cultivators would always be better off without the very existence of violence specialists than with.

Beginning from a point where property "rights" do not yet exist there is no conflict between rulers' *ability* to demand a portion of the proceeds from land as a payment, and cultivators' *ability* to access, use, and appropriate some of the products of land. Indeed, this ability of cultivators is a necessary condition of the ability of violence specialists to garner some part of the proceeds from land. Even though there is no conflict between the abilities to, respectively, demand a payment and use land and appropriate its products, conflict over the amount each group appropriates is always possible; those who hold coercive means have a decided advantage. While a rational violence specialist would not demand an amount that interfered with cultivators' ability to subsist on cultivation, there is sufficient room for conflict over what this amount would be. Cultivators would prefer to keep much more than the subsistence amount or, alternatively, live at higher levels of subsistence.[11] But violence specialists would prefer to extract all the possible surplus above the minimum subsistence level, and, under many conditions, they would be able to do so. The best outcome for cultivators would be the "right" to cultivate subject to being able to meet payment demands that would be set at a level that would extract all the possible surplus (given the labor input) while leaving them with basic subsistence. To show this, it would first be useful to define cultivators' maximum ability to pay (MAP) as the difference between their maximum output and the minimum levels of subsistence that would allow them to continue cultivating, including their costs of production. This definition is similar to the broader concept of "surplus" that Marx (1906, especially pp. 239–241) developed from the classical economists and the physiocrats. Simplifying this exposition further, I assume that the MAP is an average over a certain area, and that it exhibits potentially knowable variance that is conditional on factors such as weather. I also assume that, although the distribution of MAP can change over time, it displays some stability over the medium term, approximately 15–25 years. I now consider two possible situations involving the distribution of the knowledge of MAP: Cultivators had better knowledge of MAP (and rulers knew this), and – the scenario I consider first – this amount was common knowledge.

Property Rights With Two Undifferentiated Groups (or a Single Elite)

MAP as Common Knowledge. The basic asymmetry between rulers and cultivators is that while the former possess the coercive means of enforcing any contract, the latter do not. Therefore, while rulers can enforce any contract that is in their own interest, cultivators must rely on *rulers' interests* to ensure adherence to any contract. In the language of the concept introduced earlier, any rights, beyond the one to cultivate, would not be credible if these rights were, for any reason, incompatible with rulers' ability to collect up to cultivators' MAP.[12] Rulers' own "right" to collect up to the MAP amount, however, is credible since cultivators could not restrict this ability without risking considerable harm to themselves (for example, by stopping cultivation altogether in a coordinated way, a "cultivation strike" which would involve both loss of income and additional organizational costs, which rulers could affect).[13]

Cultivators could attempt to create their own permanent violence specializing organization. But such an organization would have to at least rival the existing ruler in coercive capacity.[14] Unless this new organization were to be vastly more efficient than the incumbent one in terms of its ability to create at least an equal amount of coercive capacity for a fraction of the cost, the costs of creating such an organization would likely be at least as high as having to pay the incumbent violence specialist all but the subsistence amount.[15] Consequently, cultivators would be better off not challenging the rights of all but the most inefficient violence specialists to collect an amount up to the one that left just enough for subsistence. Further, if violence specialists knew this, they would concede to cultivators the right to subsist from land as long as they met their payments. The property rights emerging in this situation are likely to include cultivators' rights to access and cultivate, and to appropriate enough product for subsistence. Violence specialists were also likely to allow alienation of these rights if it did not interfere with their ability to collect regularly. Following from their ability, turned right, to revoke the cultivation and appropriation rights of those who failed to pay the mutually known MAP, violence specialists would retain the right to exclude and otherwise regulate use of land.[16]

Cultivators Know MAP Better. It is arguably more realistic to assume that MAP would not be common knowledge, at least initially: While individual cultivators would have an accurate estimate of these amounts, violence specialists were unlikely to know them with any accuracy. Further, they would know that cultivators had an incentive to understate these amounts. Cultivators, in turn, would not expect violence specialists to give much credence to their claims about their MAP. Their rights over land were likely to be even more precarious than in the scenario where the MAP was common knowledge. Whatever the specific ways that violence specialists used to estimate the MAP, the ability to reallocate rights would be crucial to both estimating and enforcing payment. Rights were thus likely to fluctuate during this process and stabilize only when something approximating true MAP levels became common knowledge and attained the status of custom (this follows from the first scenario). Since none of the strategies of eliciting more information was likely to be perfect, some cultivators would probably be able to retain some of the MAP over some periods of time to the extent that they could successfully hide the MAP amount.

The upshot is that violence specialists would credibly grant cultivators the stable right to cultivate, appropriate, and perhaps pass on these rights hereditarily under the condition that they be able to meet payment demands up to their *commonly known* MAP.[17] Cultivators' cultivation and appropriation rights would continue to be precarious as long as violence specialists perceived an informational disadvantage which prevented them from realizing the MAP (Table 1).

Neither situation – with just one coercion-wielding elite – would be propitious for the emergence of anything approximating property. In both cases, rulers would tend to extract up to the MAP, and retain exclusion and regulation rights to that end, leaving cultivators with, at best, the stable right to cultivate and appropriate up to their minimum subsistence levels. Property in *collection rights* begin to emerge only with the appearance of intermediate elites.

Table 1. Property Rights Outcome Without Intermediaries Between Rulers and Cultivators.

	Knowledge of MAP	
	Time (assuming information improves)	
	Rulers Perceive an asymmetry ⟶	**Rulers no longer perceive asymmetry**
Cultivators' Rights	Cultivation and appropriation rights insecure.	Stable and heritable cultivation and appropriation rights subject to MAP payment.
Rulers' Rights	Right to MAP. Right to unconditionally exclude cultivators from land.	Right to MAP. Right to exclude cultivators upon non-recovery of MAP. Right to change cultivators' marginal rights (hence regulate the relationship between itself and the cultivator by reallocating marginal rights. *Rulers are unlikely to be neutral in doing so*).

Property Rights With Intermediaries

Admittedly, explaining these outcomes when assuming just two undifferentiated groups is insufficient. The framework so far did not consider the relationship between different groups of violence specialists, or between violence specialists and their "subcontractors" (Lane, 1958, p. 407). Similarly, cultivators cannot be assumed to be an undifferentiated group either, not least because violence specialists' actions would lead to inequalities within this group, for instance, in selectively rewarding some cultivators over others. I first define and then theoretically justify the disaggregation of the respective groups. I use the terms "subcontractors" and "intermediaries" interchangeably but note when "intermediaries" are not the primary "subcontractors."

Thus, I distinguish subcontractors with their own independent means of coercion although not enough to directly challenge rulers – I call them "sub-rulers" – from those without such means. Those possessing independent coercive means would be in a better bargaining position vis-à-vis rulers relative to those without. However, the categories are not mutually exclusive. Subcontractors without coercive means could become sub-rulers in the absence of sufficient control and supervision; conversely, sub-rulers could be transformed into "employees" – or, at least, subcontractors without independent coercive means – by dispossessing them of their means of administration (including coercion) as was the case in the development of the "modern state" (Weber, [1919] 2004, p. 37).

Subcontractors emerge when rulers who lack knowledge of MAP and face unacceptably high costs of determining and then collecting it designate a subgroup of cultivators with presumably better knowledge of MAP levels to collect on their behalf in return for a share in this amount. This in effect would allow said cultivators to keep some of the surplus by paying less than *their* MAP. Rulers would prefer to pay – which amounts to letting agents keep – anything less than their expected costs of collecting and gathering information; subcontractors, by contrast would accept anything more than their costs of collection (which, again, would leave them with a share of others' MAP). Rulers could have identical arrangements with preexisting noncultivators with their own means of violence – sub-rulers – who in turn collect from direct cultivators. The precise historical details of how actors came to occupy this intermediary role – and thus become co-claimants of a portion of the MAP – do not immediately matter for this framework. The two relationships relevant to property rights are those between rulers and noncoercion-wielding intermediaries on one hand, and between rulers and sub-rulers, on the other. For the purposes of this chapter, I focus on the implications of the first, and make only brief comments on the second.

Property Rights With Intermediaries Without the Means of Violence

The relationship between rulers and subcontractors seems to be an instance of a principal-agent relationship, an idealization used to explain a variety of phenomena including historical ones like relationships between chartered companies and their agents (Adams, 1996), agrarian labor contracts (such as sharecropping), and the linkage between such contracts and credit markets (inter alia Bell, 1989;

Braverman & Stiglitz, 1982; Emigh, 1999, especially p. 465, pp. 479–481). Yet principal-agent models don't explain property rights, but rather contracting arrangements and distributional outcomes, given predefined property rights; indeed, preexisting property rights explain contracts to the extent that any alteration of rights will change the outcomes of these models (e.g., Bardhan, 1989, p. 238; Newbery, 1989, p. 288).

In the long run, the appearance of subcontractors is likely to lead to the creation of property in collection rights and, as compared to the situation without subcontractors, to more secure cultivation and appropriation – although not *unrestricted* alienation – rights for cultivators. The latter would tend to preclude the emergence of absolute private property in land. I now explain each, in order, and Table 2 summarizes the outcomes.

Subcontractors' collection rights would be temporary as long as rulers perceived an informational disadvantage in MAP knowledge vis-à-vis the former.[18] Rulers, expecting subcontractors to understate this amount, would, if possible, retain the ability to allocate collection rights competitively (assuming that other potential candidates were available). Collection rights would stabilize once rulers no longer perceived an informational disadvantage; at this stage, rulers were unlikely to oppose the heritability and alienability (including salability) of such rights. Once these rights attained the status of property

Table 2. Property Rights Outcome With Intermediaries Without the Means of Violence.

	Knowledge of MAP Time (assuming improved information)	
Rulers Perceive an asymmetry ⟶		Rulers no longer perceive asymmetry
Cultivators' Rights	Cultivation and appropriation rights oscillate between more and less security.	Stable and heritable cultivation and appropriation rights subject to a predictable payment. No unrestricted right to alienate (including to sell) their cultivation and appropriation rights. Cultivators have strong incentives to further lease (some part of) these rights and become part claimants of the societal MAP.
Subcontractors' Rights	Right to collect from cultivators will be temporary. Temporary powers to exclude or otherwise coercively extract from cultivators.	Stable heritable, and alienable (including saleable) collection rights. No right to exclude cultivators unilaterally. Subcontractors have incentives to further lease some part of their collection rights (which might lead to further sub-leasing arrangements).
Rulers' Rights	Right to a portion of the MAP. Right to unconditionally exclude subcontractors (from collecting). Right to temporarily reallocate the right to exclude cultivators between itself and subcontractors.	Right to a portion of the MAP. Right to exclude subcontractors upon nonpayment or under payment. Right to regulate the relationship between cultivators and subcontractors, including the right to reallocate marginal rights between them (*rulers are likely to be neutral between the two*).

(especially if saleable), subcontractors themselves could further lease their collection rights, perhaps in part, to others. Intermediaries with collection rights would also prefer to have the right to exclude cultivators from land – leading to absolute private property in land – but rulers would retain this right for themselves. Subcontractors would therefore be dependent on rulers for an important part of their ability to recover MAP amounts from cultivators.

While cultivators' rights would likely be precarious so long as rulers perceived an informational asymmetry, inserting subcontractors between the two would likely result in a fluctuation of cultivators' rights, with periods of stability and security interspersed with those of precarity.[19] Although rulers would prefer to facilitate subcontractors' recovery of the entire MAP amount, they would also have the countervailing incentive to ensure that subcontractors did not increase their share of this amount (for instance, by concealing it or colluding with cultivators), or otherwise impair its regular realization. Facilitating subcontractors' recovery (and determination, if applicable) of the MAP may entail giving the latter more powers, in the form of rights, against cultivators, at least temporarily. But given that subcontractors could use these same powers to either over-extract (motivated by an imminent expiration of their collection rights) or garner a greater share of the MAP while concealing this from rulers, the latter would also have strong incentives to curtail those rights. This, in turn, would be tantamount to giving rights to cultivators.

Heritable cultivation and appropriation rights of cultivators, and heritable (and alienable) collection rights of subcontractors would only emerge over time as rulers no longer perceived a disadvantage in their MAP knowledge. Rulers were also likely to be increasingly neutral in allocating marginal rights – beyond the ones already noted – between the other two. When rulers no longer perceived a relative information deficit, the status quo property rights would lead to a direct distributional struggle between the other two groups: Subcontractors would continue to have an incentive to press for the right to exclude cultivators, which the latter would resist. Rulers, however, would have no incentive to change property rights; they would tend to believe that additional changes would not affect their own revenue. This is what would make them neutral. Explained differently, once rulers perceived that they received their portion of the societal MAP, they would have no further incentive to enable subcontractors to extract more. The latter, however, would still be locked in a distributional struggle with direct cultivators over the remainder of the MAP; cultivators would prefer to retain some of the (remainder of the) MAP, while subcontractors, knowing this, would seek to prevent it. One very effective means to the latter end would be the right to exclude cultivators from pieces of land. But this is precisely the right that rulers would have no incentive to concede. For this reason, rulers would also not allow the salability of cultivators' stable (cultivation and withdrawal) rights in a way that allowed subcontractors to buy these – thus gaining de facto exclusion rights – and turn cultivators into at-will tenants.

In contrast, with no subcontractors between rulers and cultivators, rulers would never be "neutral" when it came to distributing rights between themselves and cultivators. Thus, again, even regarding marginal rights beyond the ones discussed, cultivators would be better off when subcontractors stood between them and rulers.

Two implications are crucial. First, incentives and thus the pattern of cooperation and conflict between groups were likely to change as a function of differential knowledge of the MAP. Nonetheless, rulers would always have a crucial (relative) advantage: Owing to their sole possession of coercive means and the fact that the others would face a collective action problem (North, 1981, p. 32), they could create a zero-sum situation between the other two groups and thus become the ultimate arbitrators between them. A second implication is the pervasive incentive among all groups to ape violence specialists in trying to capture some amount of the collective MAP, and hence insert themselves into the collection apparatus in some capacity, either in addition to, or instead of their usual occupations. Individual cultivators facing the prospect of parting with their MAP would prefer to gain a portion of the collective MAP by leasing collection rights from chief subcontractors or exchanging some of their use and appropriation rights (if any) for the ability to collect from others. Several layers of "informal" – that is, not explicitly authorized by the ruler – but not necessarily "illegal" collection arrangements could emerge, right down to those bereft of stable rights who cultivated exclusively. This second implication can be seen as instances of individual adaptations to higher order property rights (see Table 2).[20]

Finally, in this chapter I do not discuss property rights outcomes with rulers, and intermediate sub-rulers (or subcontractors with their independent means of violence), except to note that this scenario would be relevant to the precolonial Indian subcontinent under the Mughal Empire, as well as some of the European cases referred to earlier. An examination of that scenario will have to await a more expansive study.[21]

EXPLAINING THE EVOLUTION OF PROPERTY RIGHTS IN COLONIAL BENGAL

Preconditions and Empirical Implications of the Theoretical Framework: Mechanisms and Outcomes

The conditions of a single ruling elite, and intermediaries without their own means of violence were approximated in the Presidency – a governing unit first under the East India Company (EIC), and then the Crown – of Bengal, which, as noted earlier, encompassed present day Bangladesh, and the Indian states of West Bengal, Bihar, and Orissa. The EIC first bought, from the local rulers, the right to collect revenue in the province of Bengal (comprising current Bangladesh, and West Bengal); after two battles, the EIC displaced the incumbents and became the ruler of the entire province. I now describe, but do not explain, the initial conditions, especially the various groups – the rulers, subcontractors and cultivators – and their respective property rights when the EIC took power. Given these conditions, I then adumbrate the expectations of the theoretical framework (per Table 2) before summarizing how well the framework explains historical outcomes.

190

The Status Quo Ante: Precolonial Property Rights

Bengal had close to a tributary relationship with the Mughal Empire (Habib, 1999, p. 217; 1982, p. 245; Ray, 1979, p. 18). Hindu and Afghan chieftains reigned over various parts of the province, while the emperor placed there some of his putative agents – selected from the court nobility, the *nawabs* – who were charged with supervising revenue collection (the office of the *Diwan*) and maintaining law and order (the office of the *subahdar*). Such officers were normally subject to frequent transfers and were paid in *jagirs*, or revenue assignments, in lieu of salary (hence they were also referred to as *jagirdars*). With the gradual dissolution of the Mughal Empire by the early 18th century after the death of Emperor *Aurangzeb*, both offices had become substantially independent of the empire when Murshid Quli Khan, one such officer, combined both offices and became the ruler (*nawab*) of Bengal.

Several layers intervened between Bengal's ruler and the direct cultivators. As Habib (1999, especially Chapter 5) established, the term "zamindar" as used in official Mughal circles was a very general one, applying to a vast category of lesser and greater political-economic agents, with varying levels of independent coercive capacities which they used not only to collect revenue, but also to levy additional taxes and maintain law and order. Generally, zamindars had collection rights over villages or groups thereof rather than any specific piece of land (Habib, 1999, pp. 173–174); such rights were saleable and inheritable. Formally, zamindars could be removed, but not without compensation (Ray, 1979, p. 15). Murshid Quli consolidated several zamindaris and made such rights permanent and hereditary, subject to payment of the amount demanded (Sinha, 1961, p. 3). The rights were also made alienable. Below the zamindars were a host of other collectors and sub-collectors. Even a medium-sized zamindar would farm out collection for fixed periods of time to different sub-collectors – under different names like *taluqdars* and *ijradars* – who in turn would collect from larger, village-level cultivators (sometimes called *jotedars*). These cultivators were larger, because they held their land at superior terms – more land at lower or fixed rates than other cultivators, and more stably, directly from the zamindar – and cultivated these lands through under-tenants (Ray, 1979, pp. 53–56). Officially, the Mughal Empire recognized the right of cultivators (*raiyats*) to use the land as long as they made regular payments that were fixed and prohibited zamindars from removing cultivators from lands that had been cultivated historically. As noted, some *raiyats*, referred to as *khudkasht* (later as "resident" *raiyats* under the EIC), had more secure rights – stable cultivation rights, and sometimes at lower levels of payment – than others (Chandra, 1982, pp. 458–59; Habib, 1999, p. 137).[22] These rights however were not alienable.

Mechanisms and Outcomes

As a relative newcomer to Bengal, the EIC should have initially perceived an informational asymmetry relative to other groups. As a firm interested in maximizing short-term profit, it should have sought to reduce its costs of acquiring information and collecting revenue. The theoretical framework would therefore predict, or rather retrodict, that the EIC should have had to depend on local intermediaries for revenue collection; it would also retrodict that, since the new rulers perceived an informational deficiency, revenue collectors' rights would be temporary. The situation in Bengal preceding EIC rule is a good test of this expectation because intermediaries (zamindars) under the local rulers had attained stable, heritable, and alienable collection rights.[23] The framework would predict a diminution of these rights under the new rulers. Cultivators too had attained fixed rights under the local rulers, as enumerated above; the framework would expect their rights to remain unchanged so long as rulers believed that these rights did not hinder subcontractors' MAP collection. However, cultivators would lose some of their rights if rulers (temporarily) granted subcontractors more powers under the perception that these were necessary for MAP recovery.

The case of Bengal also allows for examining an important implication of the framework: Even as respective groups' rights stabilize over time because of rulers' (perceived) improved informational situation, cultivators would have more marginal property rights (beyond the ones noted) when subcontractors intermediated between them and rulers, relative to the situation without intermediation. This case especially enables this empirical examination: Although most of Bengal's revenue was collected through zamindars – the principal intermediaries – the state directly collected from cultivators of some lands in the same province, and sometimes the two kinds of lands shared considerable proximity. This makes it possible to detect any variation in state allocation of collection rights over these two varieties of land. A "default" expectation from a perspective that sees rulers as neutral contract enforcers might be that cultivators' rights should have been uniform over both kinds of lands. However, the theoretical framework would predict fewer rights for cultivators in the absence of subcontracting intermediaries.

How well does the theoretical framework explain outcomes in Bengal? The evidence presented below shows that the Company knew that it was basing its demands on very little reliable information, that the costs of acquiring such information were prohibitive, and that it therefore had to depend on subcontractors, the most suitable of whom were zamindars (a conclusion determined by trial and error). The framework accounts for the contraction of the zamindars' property rights following the EIC's accession, in accordance with the postulated mechanism. However, it doesn't completely explain the timing of the stabilization of subcontractors' (i.e., zamindars') collection rights. At the time that the EIC state accorded zamindars the permanent – and thus heritable, and alienable – right to collect from cultivators in return for a fixed annual payment to the state (as a part of the so-called Permanent Settlement), there was still some debate about the maximum possible revenue yield. Even though by that time the Company had almost 30 years' experience to rely on, at least one influential policymaker estimated that the land could yield far more than it hitherto had, and yet another counseled temporary – ten years, rather than permanent – collection rights until the rulers had better information than they had. Indeed, the framework would retrodict the acceptance of this suggestion, given rulers' levels of confidence in their own estimates. I argue that, instead of waiting for better information, rulers opted to trade possibly higher, but uncertain revenues in the future for high enough (based on preceding years' collections), predictable revenue in the long run. Thus, although their perceived level of knowledge influenced their behavior – which is consistent with an important aspect of the theoretical framework's mechanism – the specific way in which it did deviates from theoretical expectations.

One way of interpreting the Permanent Settlement's deviation from what the framework would have retrodicted is this: Instead of waiting to acquire better knowledge of the MAP, rulers selected an amount that they determined would be the MAP, knowing, at the same time, that it was probably a bad approximation of the "true" amount, even if on the higher side. It thus meets two conditions of the theoretical framework simultaneously: Rulers set a MAP, while at the same time knowing they had an informational disadvantage relative to subcontractors (the relatively higher demand was to compensate for this disadvantage) (see row 1, column 1 of Table 2). Rulers in effect were committed to recovering an amount without knowing if it could be recovered, given the current distribution of property rights; had they a good approximation of the "real" MAP they wouldn't have had this dilemma. The theoretical framework would therefore predict reallocations of cultivators' rights (and reciprocally, subcontractors' rights beyond those of collection) until the rulers perceived that marginal changes in property rights would no longer have any effect on their own revenue, corresponding to the situation in the framework where rulers no longer perceived a disadvantage in MAP knowledge. At this point, the rights of cultivators would stabilize, and rulers would become neutral in allocating additional rights between cultivators and subcontractors. Importantly, exclusion rights – an important aspect of "private" property – would remain with rulers.

The framework accurately retrodicts and explains both the fluctuation of cultivators' rights, and the rulers' subsequent actions in protecting cultivators once rulers determined that more security for cultivators would have no effect on their own revenue. The evidence also bears out the expectation that cultivators would have more rights when subcontractors intermediated, than when they did not.

The theoretical framework rules out absolute private property. Indeed, part of the explanation offered here is about the non-emergence of such property in land; absolute private property, in other words, appears as a contrast in the framework. Yet, besides absolute private property, many other kinds of property as *theoretical* possibilities did not emerge. The *empirical* task would be to demonstrate that absolute private property – rather than all the other kinds of (theoretical) property that also did not emerge – was a plausible *historical* counterfactual, or an alternative (*historical*) possibility that did not come to pass. In this case of Bengal, since the chief rulers were well aware both of absolute private property and the moral and efficiency-based justifications for it, it is possible to examine whether this was one of the alternatives. I demonstrate the plausibility of this contrast (or counterfactual) by examining an early instance where some state elites advocated for absolute private property in land on ideological grounds. Again, the framework explains why their preference for absolute private property did not prevail.

The Evolution of Land Rights Under Early EIC Rule to the Permanent Settlement

Property Rights Changes Under Early EIC Rule: Zamindars as Subcontractors, and the Weakening of Zamindari Rights

The EIC government insinuated itself as a zamindar in the configuration described above by the early 1700s; when it took over the *Diwani* (revenue offices) of Bengal, Bihar, and Orissa (subsequently governed under the Presidency of Bengal) in 1765, it became the de facto ruler of these provinces by replacing the *nawabs*.

Unsurprisingly, the new government was aware of its coercive advantage in Bengal. Its officials, from the first Governor General Warren Hastings to his foe Philip Francis, a prominent member of the Governor General's Council in Calcutta, justified their status as the new sovereign by their superiority of force (Guha, 1963, pp. 31–32, p. 190). In 1776, Francis disapprovingly claimed that Hastings, in his pursuit of revenue extraction, was intent on reducing all major ranks of locals to "a competent subsistence" (Francis, 1776, p. 192). The new rulers, however, knew that they sorely lacked the information that they would need to do this effectively. They also were keenly aware of their informational disadvantages vis-à-vis the zamindars and the various officials that handled collections under the Bengal *nawabs*, chief among them the *Amils* and the *qanungoes* (village-level record keepers), who were accused of colluding with zamindars (*Amini Report* in Ramsbotham, 1926, p. 136). Finally, they also generally accepted that a detailed measurement and assessment of the land was costly enough to make it impracticable.

Consequently, they were forced at first to depend on the collection mechanism of their predecessors (Fifth Report, Vol. 1, pp. 3–4). Simultaneously the new government sought to procure better information by placing supervisors alongside native officials (Ramsbotham, 1926, pp. 7–10). As Ramsbotham (1926, pp. 9–10) would later point out, this system failed because "their instructions were impossible to carry out: they had been ordered to prepare a rent-roll and to obtain by enquiry the facts on which a just and satisfactory settlement could be made. From the commencement of their task, they were confronted by this powerful opposition of the zamindars and kanungos [*qanungoes*] who successfully prevented any knowledge of the actual revenue paid by the cultivators from coming to the knowledge of the Company" (for examples of similar phenomena from other parts of the world, see Emigh et al., 2016, especially pp. 83–84).

The Company then decided to abolish this system altogether, and, in 1772, proclaimed its intention to "stand forth as dewan... to take upon themselves the entire care and management of the revenues" (*Fifth Report,* Vol. 1, pp. 5–6). Having dispensed with the old system, the Company had also dispensed with people who had the knowledge and experience – even though they couldn't be forced to share the former – to ensure regular payments. Next the Company decided to farm out the collection for a period of five years (Fifth Report from the Committee of Secrecy, 1773, pp. 11–12). This meant that any older rights that zamindars might have had were abrogated, and they were forced to bid for five-year collection rights. The rationale was that competition among locals, who

194   *Elites, Colonialism, and Property Rights*

presumably knew better what the land yielded, would reveal something approximating the "real" revenue amount (Ascoli, 1917, p. 33; *Fifth Report*, Vol. I, p. ccxix; *Fifth Report,* Vol. II, p. 24). But to ensure that farmers – who could be both zamindars, and moneyed non-zamindars – would have some interest in improving their collectorates, and not extracting from cultivators (or other middlemen) more than the latter could afford, they would be given farms for a period of five years (Fifth Report from the Committee of Secrecy, 1773, p. 12). "Supervisors" were revived under the new name of "Collector," (to be distinguished from the various collectors, from direct cultivators in the sense used earlier to refer to subcontractors) and one Collector was to be tasked with maintaining independent accounts of the farms, along with a native assistant (called *Dewan*). All extra taxes/imposts or *abwabs* on cultivators – that zamindars hitherto retained or at least claimed the right to impose – were prohibited (Fifth Report from the Committee of Secrecy, 1773, pp. 1,315). As salaried employees of the state, collectors were prohibited from becoming farmers (p. 16).

Other administrative changes included creation of a Board of Revenue, located in Calcutta, tasked with checking district accounts and translating and transmitting the Board's decisions to the various districts (Ramsbotham, 1926, p. 23). It also included an office of Accountant General (to be manned by a senior European Company servant), which would prepare monthly statements for the Board of Revenue, and the introduction of civil (or revenue) and criminal courts, with the Collector presiding over the former (Ramsbotham, 1926, p. 22, p. 24). Zamindars were made subject to these Company courts. These changes represented a diminution of zamindars' rights relative to what they had before, since their tenures became temporary – five-year terms without any expectation of renewal, relative to permanent and hereditary until 1772 – and they lost the right to impose additional taxes.

Events so far comport with the expectations of the theoretical framework. The introduction of new rulers with superior bargaining power – and poor knowledge of the MAP – led to a drastic weakening of subcontractors' collection rights.

However, the shorter tenures, without any necessary expectation of renewal, created incentives that jeopardized rulers' original objective of maximizing extraction. One effect of the new policy was that non-zamindars – often urban moneyed interest presumably without sufficient knowledge – would "overbid" and then abandon their farms after extracting what they could. Also, zamindars would prevent others from bidding, or hold farms under relatives' names. The result was that arrears began accumulating; by 1774, barely two years after going into effect, the scheme was acknowledged a failure among official circles (Ascoli, 1917, p. 33; Ramsbotham, 1926, pp. 26–31; Guha, 1963, pp. 66–70).

After this, officials closer to the ground started advocating for one logical solution, namely, longer leases exclusively for existing zamindars (and not for non-zamindars, including urban speculators) (Ascoli, 1917, p. 34; Ramsbotham, 1926, pp. 43–45, pp. 65–71). The length of the term, however, was in dispute. Although Hastings and Richard Barwell, another member of the Council, advocated for leases for life, and even transference over a generation, the EIC's directors in London postponed a decision, but advised favoring renewal for zamindars who fulfilled their engagements (*Fifth Report*, Vol. I, p. cccii, p. cccxvii).

The Parliament passed Pitt's India Act in 1784 requiring the EIC inter alia to make revenue collection rules and procedures permanent. Based on their interpretation of this act, the Company's Court of Directors in London announced their intention, in 1786, to fix revenue demands from subcontractors in perpetuity. To that end, they instructed the new governor general, Cornwallis, to first conclude a ten-year contract with the zamindars, and then make it perpetual (Ascoli, 1917, p. 41). Thus, in 1793, the Permanent Settlement made zamindari tenures permanent, subject to a fixed annual payment. The framework would expect this only when rulers no longer perceived a relative information deficit. Yet the evidence does not support this interpretation since there was still considerable variance in government estimates of the MAP; indeed, large enough for John Shore, the principal adviser to the governor general, to suggest waiting another 10 years for more precise information before making zamindars' tenures permanent. Shore's recommendation is precisely what the theoretical framework would have retrodicted as the outcome. Yet Cornwallis overruled Shore in making zamindari tenures permanent even as the government perceived an information deficit. From the perspective of the theoretical framework, what accounts for this "premature" stabilization of zamindars' rights?

Before advancing my explanation for this deviation from theoretical expectations, and to maintain chronological consistency, I consider the historical possibility of the establishment of absolute private land; it would certainly be relevant to the part of the explanatory framework that implies the non-emergence of such property. Absolute private property would be a less plausible contrast if relevant actors were either unaware, or never contemplated, establishing such property. Therefore, the following interlude has two objectives: First, to establish absolute private property as a valid contrast and thus support the explanation for why such property did not emerge; and second, to supply some chronological context that will facilitate the subsequent explanation for the Permanent Settlement.[24]

The Possibility of Absolute Private Property

In 1776, Philip Francis – introduced above – advocated that zamindars be accorded absolute private property rights in land, similar to land held in "fee simple" in England. In addition, Thomas Law, one of the EIC's Collectors (i.e., civil servant in charge of revenue collection), whom Cornwallis acknowledged as one of his chief influences, also supported it (Guha, 1963, pp. 228–246).

I now consider Francis's plan and reactions to it a little more closely to examine the implication that rulers wouldn't have any incentive to concede rights amounting to absolute private property.

Francis based his argument partly on private property's long-term superiority in terms of efficiency, and, relatedly, on his view of the proper role of the new government, which he acknowledged was ruling over a "conquered people" (Parkes & Merivale, 1867, p. 28). Although his argument was not necessarily in favor of zamindars – he had earlier advocated for private property for both zamindars' subcontractors and direct cultivators (Parkes & Merivale, 1867, p. 28)

196

– but for private property as such, he thought that zamindars would be the ideal group on whom to bestow this (Guha, 1963, p. 155, p. 157).[25]

Francis argued that government should base its demands on what delivering minimum services, including contingencies, cost it, and not on any estimates of the maximum the land could yield (Francis, 1776, p. 53). This, in turn, was based on his view, expressed some years earlier in a letter to the Prime Minister Lord North that the government should only demand "a fixed tribute," enough to maintain a "sufficient army...for the purposes of internal tranquility and foreign defense" to guard against "the country from being ruined in detail by Europeans" (Parkes & Merivale, 1867, pp. 28–29).

He argued that his proposal would obviate surveys, or investigations of rent rolls. The overall tax on land would be low enough that any errors and inequality in assessment – due to lack of sufficient knowledge – would be inconsequential (Francis, 1776, pp. 126–129). Quoting Montesquieu, he argued that only very approximate knowledge, which the government already had, would suffice (p. 129).

Given this view of the role of the new government, Francis thought that Bengal was highly over-assessed, and he disdained all efforts by the government to determine the maximum amount that the land in Bengal could yield (Francis, 1776, p. 122).[26] What the Company extracted from Bengal was more of a rent, of which he disapproved since it implied that the EIC was the ultimate owner of all lands (that position was held by other members of the Governing Council, James Grant being the most notable among them). He further argued that granting absolute private property rights would remove incentives for zamindars or others in their position to hide their wealth, and instead incentivize them to use it to improve the land (Francis, 1776, p. 53).

The revenue assessment principle that Francis was suggesting goes squarely against the crucial assumption of this framework, that rulers seek to extract all of the societal MAP. Relatedly, rulers with much greater bargaining power could never credibly grant zamindars the right to exclude others from land. For this reason, reactions to Francis's suggestion constitute at least a partial check of this assumption, especially because the ideology underlying Francis's recommendations did not match the power relationships in India. It probably would have, had there been a well-organized group of zamindars with their own coercive capabilities capable of challenging the EIC.

Francis's views, unsurprisingly, were in a minority among Bengal's ruling elites. The most frequent retort to arguments like his was that zamindars historically never had rights equivalent to the English freeholder. (Since assessments on Bengal zamindars were much lower under Mughal rule, Francis had argued that they must have paid something akin to "quit rent," again trying to make the case that zamindars were just like the English freeholder; Francis, 1776, pp. 30–36). While justifying efforts to gather more and better information about revenue through local accounts, which Francis opposed, Hastings argued that Francis's general principles might apply in England where the government took only about a fifth of the land rent but did not apply in Bengal where the state traditionally claimed as much as nine-tenths of the rent (Francis, 1776, p. 144).[27] Hastings was thus justifying the inapplicability of English standards of rights based on the purported fact that rulers in India traditionally captured most of what the land produced. What went unremarked was the source of this differential ability and why rulers could, and indeed, should continue to have it. Francis believed rulers *should* not. Not for the first time, those like Hastings and Grant who sought to justify the EIC extraction efforts appealed to tradition, including Mughal despotism, without commenting on why such traditions should continue, or indeed, what allowed them to continue. Francis, of course argued that these were just excuses to justify the Company's arbitrary powers (*Fifth Report*, Vol. I, p. ccxv).

Francis's views, predictably, did not win the day, and he returned to England in 1780, where his ideas received some publicity due especially to Edmund Burke (see for instance, Marshall, 1987, pp. 121–122).

Stabilization of Zamindars' Rights: Explaining the Permanent Settlement
The quality of information about the maximum amount Bengal could yield had largely been limited to what scattered past records indicated was demanded (but not necessarily recovered) since the late 1760s, or what proportion of the gross produce of land this represented. Beyond this, the quality of information was still quite poor. As late as the late 1780s, the difference in estimate between John Shore, who had served in revenue offices since 1769, and Grant was substantial. John Shore argued that, in 1765, Bengal could yield at most around 22 million in sicca rupees, while Grant thought that the maximum figure was closer to 50 million (even though past revenues had not come anywhere close to Grant's amount). The EIC Directors, anxious to minimize any charges in India, prohibited any "scrutiny into the value of the lands by measurement" (*Fifth Report*, Vol. I, p. 31).[28] Moreover, the very nature of the officialdom – temporary, and often concerned with their private businesses – made the establishment of institutional knowledge difficult (*Fifth Report*, Vol. II, p. 2).

Ruling elites realized both that zamindars needed to be incentivized to not impair rulers' ability to realize a certain amount of stable revenue, and that their quality of information was not sufficiently high to ensure that subcontractors (the zamindars) weren't obscuring the true value of their own extraction. Rulers therefore should have implemented longer collection leases permitting renewal until they gathered better information of the societal MAP. In fact, this was the very solution that Shore proposed in the late 1780s. Cornwallis overruled him and declared the settlement permanent in 1793.

Francis's views and his campaign on behalf of the zamindars may have influenced the Court and thus the tenure length alone. Conclusive evidence, beyond Francis's own, for this proposition, is difficult to find; other contemporaries claim that his ideas influenced the Settlement (Parkes & Merivale, 1867, p. 70). The *Fifth Report* (Vol. I, p. 29, p. 35) and some other official documents suggested a second possibility: The Court, intent on immediately minimizing expenditures in India, traded possible higher revenues in the future – although fluctuating in the interim – for predictable and stable revenues in the long run. A fixed demand would obviate regular (and, from the EIC's perspective, expensive) land surveys. The proposition also implies that rulers had some basis for estimating the maximum amount that zamindars could be induced to deliver with the promise of no future rises in demand (in effect, trading off probable current losses for future gains). Rulers could base this on past demands. Importantly, the permanent demand was likely to be higher than past ones because rulers would want to partially make up for no future enhancements, thus exchanging some part of the latter for a higher demand in the present.

This explanation finds support, first from the actual revenue demand, which was set around Rs. 28 million, the highest level recorded in recent years, and then from the debate between Shore and Cornwallis over the wisdom of a perpetual, rather than ten-year, term. Responding to Cornwallis's argument that a perpetual settlement would encourage thrifty zamindars while the incompetent ones would lose their rights, Shore avers that zamindars would not offer more for a perpetual, rather than a ten-year, term. This means that the government wouldn't gain anything by a perpetual lease (*Fifth Report,* Vol. II, p. 518). Of course, it wasn't quite voluntary for the zamindars to accept or reject the government's demand, but the reply nonetheless presumes the policy rationale described above.

An additional factor that was expected to hedge against future government losses was this: Since about a third of Bengal's cultivable land was lying waste, zamindars would be induced to bring those under cultivation to meet their demands; To the extent that some of these lands were outside the designated Settlement, the government would "resume" them by assessing them anew. New revenue assessments would also come from lands formerly held revenue free – including land for police stations and other offices formerly under the zamindar – that the government would resume.

Insofar as collection rights of zamindars became permanent, alienable, transferable, and collateralizable, the Permanent Settlement created private property in these (collection) rights. It bears repeating that it did not create any private property rights in land, and neither was it intended to by its formulators, including the EIC's Board of Control (*Fifth Report* Vol. I, p. 33), and Cornwallis (*Fifth Report,* Vol. II, pp. 513–514). Thus, rulers retained the right to intervene between zamindars and the eventual cultivators to determine the rights of all intermediaries and, ostensibly, to maintain customary rights.

In summary, the theoretical framework cannot explain the timing of the stabilization of zamindars' rights given rulers' (perceived) quality of information. It would have expected something akin to Shore's recommendation to prevail. Yet, evidence suggests that the EIC directors (and Cornwallis) favored immediate predictability over more accuracy of revenue yields. Thus, they sought to maximize a *stable and predictable* revenue based on information that they knew was quite approximate; simple maximization based on better information, as the framework would have expected, would have sacrificed short-term predictability and stability. On the other hand, as I discuss below, the framework can explain much of the dynamics of 19th century property rights – changes in the relative rights of cultivators, and zamindars – following the Settlement. The framework confirms, in the process, the expectation that cultivators would have better property rights when subcontractors (here, zamindars) intruded between them and rulers.

Post Settlement Dynamics in Property Rights

Fluctuation of Cultivators' Rights: Diminution

Recall that the framework retrodicts that cultivators' rights would fluctuate – in addition to subcontractors' collection rights being temporary – so long as rulers perceived an information asymmetry (column 1, Table 2). The Permanent Settlement belied one of these theoretical expectations since subcontractors' collection rights stabilized even as rulers perceived an information deficit. Historical developments, on the other hand, conformed to expectations that rulers – lacking adequate knowledge of MAP – would have incentives to periodically both strengthen and weaken cultivators' rights (also see section "Property Rights With Intermediaries Without the Means of Violence," and section "Mechanisms and Outcomes").

The EIC had set a rigid revenue demand, allowing no remissions, without having enough information about whether this was a good approximation of the MAP, specifically, if it was too high. At the same time, the government had made it more difficult for zamindars to realize that amount. The Settlement had decisively confirmed the loss of any quasi-sovereignty that some zamindars (especially as erstwhile sub-rulers) might have pretended to. As noted earlier, these zamindars were placed under the jurisdiction of revenue courts to be run by government revenue officers, the Collectors. In addition to collecting the state's share of the revenue, Collectors had the authority to inspect zamindars' books, and intervene in any dispute between them and the cultivators.[29] *Raiyats'* cultivation and appropriation rights, unlike zamindars' own collection rights, could not be summarily sold for arrears of revenue (zamindars had to go through courts to force a sale). Prominent zamindars therefore protested the Settlement not only because of the heavy demand, but also because they had fewer tools to recover this amount and were prevented from levying additional taxes. More privileged *raiyats* and lower level sub-contractors knew this and would withhold their payments, knowing that zamindars only recourse now was the judicial process, which was soon overwhelmed and hence became glacial (Ray, 1979, pp. 85–86; *Fifth Report,* Vol. I, p. 99). The result was that quite a few zamindaris were sold for arrears. During each of the years 1796–1797, and 1797–1798, land assessed at around 10% of the total assessment was sold for arrears (*Fifth Report*, Vol. I, p. 101); in 1798–1799 it rose to 20% of Bengal's total land revenue assessment (Islam, 1979, p. 61).

It wasn't until the developments above started affecting the government's revenues that zamindars secured some of what they had been agitating for. The government's revenue was affected partly because of the strategies that zamindars adopted to counteract the part of the Permanent Settlement that allowed for summary sale of zamindaris (or any portion thereof) for arrears. Zamindaris advertised for sale often fetched less than their values in terms for their total revenue assessments. For example, in 1796–1797 land assessed for a total of Rs. 2,870,061 was put up for sale, and the land that finally sold bore an assessment of Rs. 1,418,756, and fetched Rs. 1,790,416 (*Fifth Report*, Vol. I, p. 101). The government thus suffered a loss of Rs. 1,079,645 for that year relative to the original assessment. These losses could, at least partially, be attributed to

200   *Elites, Colonialism, and Property Rights*

strategies that zamindars employed. Since they often had superior knowledge of the value of the land's produce, they would often represent the lands that were up for sale for more than they could yield. This would lead the rest of their lands to be underassessed (*Fifth Report,* Vol. I, pp. 110–111). Lands thus sold, after not yielding as much as expected, would be put up for sale again, but they would then sell for much less than the first time; zamindars would buy them back at a much lower price and lower assessment under the names of their employees or family members. The other related strategy was to prevent others from bidding, thus lowering the selling price; if it sold, they would prevent the new owners from collecting (Islam, 1979, pp. 59–61).

In 1799, the government passed Regulation VII, notorious as *Haftam* or "the seventh," which allowed zamindars to distrain crops and sell land for arrears without going through the civil courts. The respondents could appeal, but the process put the burden on the appellant which made it very difficult for them to succeed. Then in 1812, the government passed Regulation V, which sought to putatively correct the excesses arising out of the *Haftam* by giving *raiyats* the rights to appeal to the Collector. It also prohibited distraint of the cultivators' bullocks or plough, and summary sale of the cultivators' land without going through the courts. On the other hand, it also allowed zamindars to contract freely with all non-*khudkasht* cultivators, instead of requiring them to give ten-year leases (e.g., Ray, 1979, pp. 85–88).[30] This allowed them to dictate leases, and hence rents, for all but the most privileged *raiyats,* namely, the ones that could substantiate their *khudkasht* status.

Thus, again, the framework accurately explains changes in cultivators' rights as a function of rulers' relative lack of knowledge of the MAP: Rulers would not have had to periodically reallocate cultivators' rights had they a good approximation of the MAP (row 1, column 1 of Table 2).

Diminishing Information Asymmetry and the Stabilization (and Enhancement) of Cultivators' Rights
The two regulations enabled zamindars' efforts at cornering the right to exclude (by giving them the right to freely contract with most direct cultivators) with the state's apparent backing. Had they been able to hold on to this right, they would have been able to acquire something close to private property in all lands unoccupied by *khudkasht* cultivators. Many of them would subsequently claim that they had this right prior to Act X of 1859, which I discuss next (e.g., IOR/L/PJ/5/412, *Report of the Rent Law Commission,* p. 96). But since the government's revenue demand did not vary (having been fixed nominally), it got lighter over time This attenuated the relationship between zamindars' property rights and the state's ability to recover the amount demanded, and the government now knew this. This situation corresponds to the second column of Table 2. The framework, recall, predicts that at this stage, rulers would become neutral in allocating rights between the other two groups, but the latter would be locked in a continuous distributional struggle.

It was therefore not surprising when, in the aftermath of the Revolt of 1857, the new government of the Crown (not the EIC) acted to strengthen *raiyats'* rights. Policymakers believed that the zamindars had misused their rights which had led to agricultural disturbances, necessitating additional protections for cultivators (e.g., IOR/L/PJ/5/413, Justice Cunningham's minute on the Rent Bill 1881, especially pp. 4–7). Act X of 1859 gave all cultivators who had cultivated a land for 12 years (irrespective of whether they had prior customary *khudkasht* status) an "occupancy" status, which meant that they could not be ejected if they paid a rent. And – here the law created many problems – it stipulated that the rent should be "fair and equitable" without clarifying what it meant, other than observing that, in case of dispute, the rate previously paid will be deemed as such. Zamindars tried to evade this law by moving their tenants around to ensure that they did not hold at the same rate for 12 years.

The number of disputes, and lawsuits increased. Partially to clarify matters, and because of peasant riots in Pabna in the mid-70s, the government convened a rent commission, which developed a draft bill which was revised as the Bengal Tenancy Act of 1885. This act defined a "settled *raiyat*," with rights of occupancy according to the earlier twelve-year rule, with the addition that land could be held anywhere in a particular village or inherited from a settled *raiyat*. It clearly specified conditions under which rents of such cultivators could be raised and established a ceiling. It also distinguished between a *raiyat* and a "tenure holder" based on the amount of land held (in turn, related to whether the land was being directly cultivated or being collected from) and stipulated that only the former could enjoy occupancy rights.[31] Further, tenure holders – that is, noncultivators with collection rights – could not also hold (even part) occupancy rights, but cultivators with occupancy rights could acquire part (though not complete) tenurial interests. In the case where a tenure holder acquired any part of an occupancy right, it would automatically pass to the under-*raiyat* (i.e., the *raiyat* who temporarily leased from the occupancy *raiyat*) (*Bengal Tenancy Act* 1885, Chapter V, Section 22). Further, *raiyats* with occupancy rights could not contract themselves out of this right.[32] The last two stipulations obviously would have prevented tenure holders, zamindars being the largest of this kind, from buying up these rights and converting them into quasi-private property in land by turning cultivators into at-will tenants. The right to exclude, as a result, remained with rulers.

Again, once rulers perceived that they knew enough to be able to extract their share of the MAP, the rights of the other two groups stabilized (as in the second column of Table 2), and rulers became increasingly neutral in allocating further rights between cultivators and subcontractors. This, in turn, translated to relatively more rights for cultivators. An additional implication of this is that cultivators would be better off in terms of their rights when subcontractors intruded than when they didn't: While rulers would be neutral between subcontractors and cultivators, they wouldn't be so between themselves and cultivators.[33] To show this, I now discuss cultivators' rights in situations where zamindars did not stand over them.

Coda: A Brief Comparison With Lands Where the Government Was the Zamindar
Lands that the EIC held in Bengal directly (including Bihar and Orissa) were subsequently excluded from the Permanent Settlement. These included lands the

government repossessed from zamindars for a variety of reasons, and conquered lands (e.g., Baden-Powell, 1892, pp. 445–447). To the extent that these lands were under cultivation, laws protecting tenants should have applied there too. The framework would suggest that they would not (compare the second row and second column of Table 1 to the corresponding cell of Table 2).

As a zamindar member of the Bengal Rent Commission, who was dissenting from the draft bill, pointed out, Act X of 1859 placed the burden on the zamindar of proving that a *raiyat* did not hold land at a uniform rate since the Permanent Settlement (rents could not be raised otherwise) (IOR/L/PJ/5/412, *Report of the Rent Law Commission*, pp. 98–99, para 11). This allowed *raiyats* to successfully challenge attempts at raising their rents in civil courts. However, the government exempted itself from this rule in the draft bill. The sequence of events was as follows. Even after passing Act X of 1859, the government – unlike zamindars – could raise rents without having to demonstrate that a set of conditions had been met. But Act VIII of 1869 transferred all cases having to do with rent enhancements to civil courts run by independent judges, rather than revenue courts where the Deputy Collector was the deciding officer, in order to lessen the growing burden on the latter (IOR/L/PJ/6/107, File 1780, *Report of the Govt of Bengal*, Appendix I, para. 17). One unintended consequence was that the civil courts also applied Act X to the state, which impeded the state's ability to raise rents on its tenants. The Bengal government then passed Act III in 1878, which put the burden of proof on the *raiyat* (for government-held lands only). However, even this did not completely solve the problem since the act did not comment on the grounds of enhancement and required the government to serve notices on each *raiyat* individually. This necessitated Act VIII of 1879, which held that the rents demanded by the settlement officer could be announced generally though a local publication and were binding unless the occupancy *raiyat* instituted a civil suit within four months to challenge the assessment. As a result, the government subsequently won almost all such suits (IOR/L/PJ/6/107, File 1780, *Report of the Govt of Bengal*, Appendix III, L.P., no. 3571/2A). Unsurprisingly, therefore, the government excepted itself from some stipulations of the Act of 1885 that protected *raiyats* (that is, the Act of 1885 did not nullify Act VIII of 1879) (IOR/L/PJ/5/412, *Report of the Rent Law Commission*, 1 para. 3).

Put simply, the government excepted itself from laws that were designed to secure the rights of cultivators vis-à-vis zamindars in situations where it was in the role of the zamindar, thus confirming another implication of the theoretical framework.

CONCLUSION

This chapter has proposed a theoretical framework of property rights involving rulers, cultivators, and subcontractors without their own independent means of coercion, and applied it to explain the evolution of property rights in land in colonial Bengal. The framework explains why rulers would always tend to have an advantage vis-à-vis cultivators, and thus depicts bargaining between unequals over the products of land to show how property rights emerge from this process.

It explains how information and collection costs led rulers to engage subcontractors to collect from direct cultivators. Taking a "disaggregated" approach to the concept of land rights, it also explains why rulers – who alone possessed coercive means of enforcement – would not accord their subcontractors any permanent *collection* rights as long as the rulers perceived an information asymmetry vis-à-vis the subcontractors as to the maximum payment that cultivators could be charged. On the other hand, cultivators' rights would tend to fluctuate, since rulers would have incentives both to enable subcontractors to collect the maximum possible amount *and* ensure that subcontractors did not use these abilities to either over-extract or claim a larger portion of the amount extracted. The first incentive would lead cultivators' rights to dwindle, while the second would lead cultivators to gain more protections against subcontractors. Finally, rights – including subcontractors' *collection* rights, and cultivators' cultivation and appropriation rights – would stabilize once rulers no longer perceived an information asymmetry (Table 2). Further, rulers would become increasingly neutral in allocating additional, marginal rights between the other two groups as they perceived that additional measures would not affect their own revenue. Two corollaries follow from this framework: First, absolute private property in land would be unlikely to emerge, since rulers would always retain the right of exclusion; and second, cultivators would tend to be better off – in terms of their marginal rights – when subcontractors intermediated between them and rulers than with no such intermediation.

The framework explains why zamindars – the traditional intermediaries between rulers and cultivators – initially lost their formerly heritable and alienable rights to collect from cultivators upon the EIC's accession as Bengal's new rulers. The evidence shows that – consistent with the framework – this was due to rulers' self-perceived informational disadvantage (vis-à-vis zamindars), for which rulers tried to compensate by making zamindari tenures temporary. The framework however fails to adequately explain the Permanent Settlement that stabilized and privatized zamindars' *collection* rights, since the EIC government still perceived an information deficiency at the time of the Settlement. This chapter presents an alternative explanation for this "premature" (from the framework's perspective) stabilization. On the other hand, consistent with the framework, cultivators' rights fluctuated so long as rulers perceived an informational deficit. Also consistent with theoretical expectations, the colonial state began protecting cultivators once it perceived that changes in rights to favor cultivators' (and, reciprocally, to disadvantage zamindars) would have no effect on the fixed land revenue. Finally, this chapter also demonstrates the second corollary noted in the previous paragraph. The EIC government excepted itself from the laws that were designed to protect cultivators from intermediate zamindars when the state itself assumed the role of the zamindar. The argument thus accounts for all the outcomes listed in cells of Table 2, excepting the first outcome listed in row 2, column 1.

The theory, of course, rules out the emergence of absolute private property as long as subcontractors did not possess their own means of coercion. This chapter does not address in any detail how the framework would change with the inclusion of sub-rulers (or subcontractors with their own means of coercion). The framework is also applicable only to situations where land was the predominant resource for rulers; thus, it would have to be modified in cases where, for instance, mercantile wealth became an equally important resource. Bengal conformed to the framework's assumption of land as rulers' predominant source because the EIC as a ruling power had earlier marginalized the indigenous mercantile class, never depending on them as a significant revenue source (see Chatterjee, 2016). Neither did the EIC, nor the Crown following them, develop throughout the 19th century any alternative sources of revenue that the state itself did not directly control.

These limits of the framework notwithstanding, it confirms Lachmann's (2002, p. 39) contention that "if elite structure can explain the persistence of European feudalism before the sixteenth century, then a similar model can address the persistence of non-capitalist modes of production in Asia." Yet "elite conflict" (or interaction) is more of an approach than a fully articulated theoretical framework: As argued earlier, it lacks well-formulated concepts ("conflict" being an example) and clearly specified parameters, as evidenced in the lack of clarity over the exogeneity or endogeneity of the French Revolution. By incorporating power into the bargaining framework associated with efficiency explanations of property rights, this chapter overcomes some of the deficiencies in Lachmann's elite approach. It shows that "conflict" is not a very useful explanatory concept since elite relationships are mixtures of conflict and cooperation, and thus much better conceptualized within a bargaining framework.

One implication of the argument not pursued in this chapter is, nonetheless, worth exploring, at least as a hypothesis: Some scholars have argued that property rights in Bengal reflected the weakness of the colonial state (Robb, 2016, p. 66; Roy & Swamy, 2016, p. 31). The preceding discussion is not inconsistent with this. The EIC's overwhelming imperative to reduce expenses in the very short term, and thus maximize profit, led it to rely on subcontractors instead of creating its own mechanisms. Further, that it had more bargaining power than the other groups meant that no other groups (especially zamindars) could convert their extant privileges into absolute private property rights This closed off a possible path to the kind of development that could have led to demands from these groups for state investments in capacity. Therefore, the rulers' superior bargaining power led to an infrastructurally weak state. Thus, both outcomes – the nature of property rights, and a weak state – are at least partially endogenous to the explanation proposed here.

Lachmann's quote above points to another implication, related but broader. Ever since Marx (1853a, 1853b, 1853c) speculated about the possible emergence of "the material foundations of Western society in Asia" following "the annihilation of old Asiatic society" under British rule, scholars have debated the contribution of colonialism to the underdevelopment of India (e.g., Habib, 1975, 1985; Morris, 1963). Morris (1963) prominently represented the view that underdevelopment could not be attributed to colonialism because other factors predating British rule – among them, political instability; low levels of technology in both agriculture and manufacturing; and geography and climate that impeded efficient transportation – predominated, producing an economy that had been stagnating for centuries. Thus, the introduction of railways, or the telegram, and better administration of the country were not enough to overcome its preexisting defects. Yet even Morris (1963, pp. 615–616), who otherwise maintained that the colonial government aimed to promote the "welfare of the society," conceded that the state was quite inadequate when it came to actively stimulating economic development. It was an authoritarian, yet economically laissez faire state that did little beyond fulfilling the typical "night-watchman" functions and was quite unwilling to commit to expenses that could not pay for themselves in short order. Morris attributed this to policymakers' ideology. However, again, ideology would seem to be an inadequate explanation, as this chapter has demonstrated for at least one economic institution, namely, property rights in land as a factor of production (for a similar argument about the institutions of capital, see Chatterjee, 2017). The outcome – authoritarian yet night-watchman tendencies – was more plausibly a reflection of an infrastructurally weak, although despotically strong, state, both unwilling to, and incapable of, promoting capitalist development.

ACKNOWLEDGMENTS

Profuse thanks to Rebecca Emigh and Dylan Riley for reading multiple drafts of this chapter and offering their comments. They have immensely improved this chapter. Thanks also to Jason Brownlee for his discipling suggestions.

NOTES

1. It should be noted here that something approximating "private" land could also be found in India. These were zamindars' "personal" lands for which they hired laborers. Such holdings however were relatively minor.

2. I exclude here the early normative philosophical literature on private property.

3. Coase (1960) showed that assuming zero transaction costs and rational agents, the price mechanism is efficient. This, of course, obviates any other institution. The implication of the argument, however, is that since transaction costs are almost invariably positive, there is almost always a role for non-market institutions (Coase, 1937). Thus, the substitutions between markets and non-market institutions are determined by the marginal (transaction) costs of each.

4. A more direct causal hypothesis for change in property rights is evidenced in Marx (1970[1859], p. 21) where he argues that technological change creates a tension between productivity and existing property rights, and this tension is resolved through bourgeois revolution that alters property relations (see Cohen, 2000, especially Chapter VI). Also see the "Manifesto," in Tucker (1989, pp. 477–478). Ironically this view comes close to the efficiency framework because it's quite simple to translate change in "productive forces" to changes in relative prices that classes then react to.

5. I bypass the extensive – Marxist and non-Marxist – debate on state autonomy in political science and sociology in favor of the brief observation that, even though the older transition debate does not accord the state any autonomy (it's always controlled by one or in the case of Sweezy briefly by more classes), Brenner's argument depends on the monarchy being potentially autonomous.

6. Power is implied because, unlike in the efficiency framework, this view posits "winners" and "losers" due to institutional rules. Further, winners not only have no incentive to compensate the losers, they also have every incentive to further capitalize on their advantages in an effort to make these permanent.

7. Since higher order changes dictate their relative costs.

8. This is not the only way to classify different rights over land. This classification, however, suffices in identifying the most salient features of relationships with land during the period of interest to this chapter.

9. Although, arguably "stationary bandits" offer some protection against "roving bandits" (Olson, 1993). These distinctions don't matter very much for this framework because as Lane (1958, p. 403) observed, it is in practice difficult to distinguish between a predatory "plunderer," and one providing protection.

10. Except in the sense that this payment itself emerges as a limited "right" subject to services rendered.

11. Again, the efficiency framework implies that cultivators would be better off (and live at higher levels of subsistence) with the "protective services" of violence specialists than without.

12. Why wouldn't cultivators use the strategy of producing just enough for subsistence in this case? It is because they will be compelled to produce enough – in their own interests – to cover the costs of protection. More generally, violence specialists would set a rate, and cultivators would seek to produce enough – above subsistence – to meet that demand.

13. There's also the option of escaping the reach of all violence specialists (see, for instance, Scott, 2009). Coercion wielders could then try to prevent this by force, or by enticement. Yet another possibility is of cultivators themselves becoming "roving bandits."

14. Taking up arms temporarily would also be an option; but any concessions gained would not be credible since rulers could retract them as soon as cultivators relinquished their arms. Over a period, a permanent organization would always have more coercive capacity than a temporary one.

15. Creating such an organization would include some cultivators turning themselves (within a certain period) into violence specialists (and relinquishing cultivation). These "new" violence specialists would then have to depend on extraction from the remaining cultivators, which could recreate the same situation for cultivators.

16. In case of relative abundance of land, this same ability (to exclude) would become the ability to raise or lower demands while holding cultivators to specific pieces of land.

17. Limited payment free land was also likely to make appearances in instances where violence specialists used enticement to bring new lands into cultivation (in case of relative abundance of land).

18. Rulers would be expected to have better estimates of their intermediaries' collection costs, since they would be better able to extrapolate from their own expected costs of collection. Another implied assumption is that rulers' quality of information would improve over time (through better record collection, observation, etc.).

19. Thus, there wouldn't be an optimal distribution of rights that would also be stable.

20. If the collection of (any portion of the societal) MAP can be described as "exploitation" then this situation can also be described as one where there is a pervasive incentive for those with even meager rights to exploit those without any.

21. One crucial difference between the two scenarios is that many sub-rulers – if they overcame their collective action problem – could unite to replace rulers, while subcontractors without their own means of violence could not. Rulers in their bargaining relationship with sub-rulers would face an additional cost which they wouldn't have faced with subcontractors without their own means of coercion. This would be the cost of removing sub-rulers forcibly, which would be inversely proportional to the gap between their respective coercive capacities. Combined with relative knowledge of MAP, this cost would explain variation in the nature of the property rights.

22. Although this seemed to have varied over time. *Raiyats* without resident rights, called *paikasht raiyats,* seemed to have paid less than *khudkasht raiyats* during relative scarcities of labor, as in the aftermath of the great famine of 1770 (Ray, 1979, pp. 57–58). But this was reversed by mid-19th century.

23. The EIC upon displacing the local rulers deprived zamindars of the limited means of coercion they possessed under the *nawabs.*

24. The non-emergence of private property in land is also related to an (ideological) explanation for the Permanent Settlement due principally to Guha (1963, especially pp. 222–228) which contended that the Settlement was an ideologically motivated effort at creating a property-owning landlord class to improve agriculture. I do not pursue that argument here for lack of space except to point out below that neither the EIC's Board of Control, nor Cornwallis (who was ultimately responsible for it) envisaged the Settlement to create absolute private property in land. Cornwallis may have relied on the ideology underpinning Francis and Law's recommendations to justify just the length of the zamindari tenures (discussed further below), but the ideology could not have been the *reason* for his decision.

25. He however also thought that all zamindaris should be broken up and reduced to smaller sizes. Francis argued that the evocation of cultivators' plights by those like Hastings was disingenuous (*Fifth Report*, Vol. I, p. cccxiii). He thought that cultivators should be protected, but this could happen naturally since zamindars would need them, and since the famine of 1770 (which killed about a third of the Bengal population), their services were scarce; cultivators would obtain favorable leases as a result.

26. The famine of 1770, during which the EIC maintained revenue collections at the same level, probably also influenced his views. Such demands may have exacerbated the effects of crop failure. See Sinha (1961, pp. 48–60).

27. "Rent" in these discussions is equated and used interchangeably with "net produce of land" (Francis, 1776, pp. 190–191).

28. In this, they shared Francis's disapproval of attempts to determine the MAP with more precision, but for different reasons.

29. Thus, in the context of the theoretical framework, they were part of "rulers," or the state.

30. Recall from above that *khudkasht* cultivators traditionally – that is, under the preceding regimes – had the hereditary right to cultivate as long as they met customary payments.

31. Leasing and sub-leasing arrangements (right up to those who cultivated exclusively and had no other occupancy rights) had created a host of greater and lesser tenure holders.

32. *Raiyats* were however not allowed to make certain improvements in land (like building small factories or digging wells).

33. Also see section "Property Rights With Intermediaries Without the Means of Violence."

REFERENCES

INDIA OFFICE RECORDS

IOR/L/PJ/5/412 Volume containing Report of the Rent Law Commission, Report of the Rent Law Commission.
IOR/L/PJ/5/413 Volume containing papers on Rent Law Commission, with draft bills (1863–1883).
IOR/L/PJ/6/107, File 1780 Amendments to the Bengal Tenancy Bill (1883, 14 September), Report of the Govt. of Bengal.

OTHER OFFICIAL DOCUMENTS

Fifth Report from the Committee of Secrecy Appointed by the House of Commons Assembled at Westminster in the Sixth Session of the Thirteenth Parliament of Great Britain to Enquire into the State of the East India Company. London, 1773.
Firminger, W. K. (Ed.). (1917). Great Britain Parliament House of Commons Select Committee on the East India. In *The Fifth Report from the Select Committee of the House of Commons on the Affairs of the East India Company: Dated 28th July, 1812 (Volumes 1 and 2)*. R. Cambray & Company.

Francis, P. (1776). *Original Minutes of the Governor General and Council of Fort William on the Settlement and Collection of the Revenue of Bengal with a Plan of Settlement Recommended to the Court of Directors in January 1776.*

BOOKS AND ARTICLES

Acemoglu, D., Johnson, S., & Robinson, J. A. (2005). Institutions as a fundamental cause of long- run growth. In P. Aghion & S. N. Durlauf (Eds.), *Handbook of economic growth* (Vol. IA). North Holland.

Adams, J. (1996). Principals and agents, colonialists and company men: The decay of colonial control in the Dutch East Indies. *American Sociological Review, 61*(1), 12–28. https://doi.org/10.2307/2096404

Alchian, A. A., & Demsetz, H. (1973). The property right paradigm. *The Journal of Economic History, 33*(1), 16–27.

Aoki, M. (2001). *Toward a comparative institutional analysis.* MIT Press.

Ascoli, F. D. (1917). *Early revenue history of Bengal: And the Fifth Report, 1812.* Clarendon Press.

Baden-Powell, B. H. (1892). *The land systems of British India: Book 1. General. Book 2. Bengal.* Clarendon Press.

Bardhan, P. (1989). A note on interlinked rural economic arrangements. In P. Bardhan (Ed.), *The economic theory of agrarian institutions.* Clarendon Press.

Bell, C. (1989). A comparison of principal-agent and bargaining solutions: The case of tenancy contracts. In P. Bardhan (Ed.), *The economic theory of agrarian institutions.* Clarendon Press.

Blaufarb, R. (2019). *The great demarcation: The French Revolution and the invention of modern property.* Oxford University Press.

Braverman, A., & Stiglitz, J. E. (1982). Sharecropping and the interlinking of agrarian markets. *The American Economic Review, 72*(4), 695–715.

Brenner, R. (1985). The agrarian roots of European Ccpitalism. In T. H. Aston & C. H. E. Philpin (Eds.), *The Brenner debate: Agrarian class structure and economic development in pre-industrial Europe.* Cambridge University Press.

Chandra, S. (1982). Standard of living: Mughal India. In T. Raychaudhuri, I. Habib, & D. Kumar (Eds.), *The Cambridge economic history of India* (Vol. 1, pp. c.1200–c.1750). CUP.

Chatterjee, A. (2016). Financial property rights under colonialism: Some counterfactual possibilities. *Journal of Institutional Economics, 12*(4), 797–824. https://doi.org/10.1017/S1744137416000023

Chatterjee, A. (2017). *Rulers and capital in historical perspective: State formation and financial development in India and the United States.* Temple University Press.

Coase, R. H. (1937). The Nature of the firm. *Economica, 4*(16), 386–405. https://doi.org/10.2307/2626876

Coase, R. H. (1959). The Federal Communications Commission. *The Journal of Law and Economics, 2*, 1–40.

Coase, R. H. (1960). The problem of social cost. *The Journal of Law and Economics, 3*, 1–44.

Cohen, G. A. (2000). *Karl Marx's theory of history: A defense.* Clarendon Press.

De Soto, H. (2003). *The mystery of capital: Why capitalism triumphs in the West and fails everywhere else* (Reprint ed.). Basic Books.

Demsetz, H. (1967). Toward a theory of property rights. *The American Economic Review, 57*(2), 347–359.

Emerson, R. M. (1962). Power-dependence relations. *American Sociological Review, 27*, 31–41. https://doi.org/10.2307/2089716

Emigh, R. J. (1999). Means and measures: Property rights, political economy, and productivity in fifteenth-century Tuscany. *Social Forces, 78*(2), 461–490. https://doi.org/10.2307/3005564

Emigh, R. J., Riley, D., & Ahmed, P. (2016). *Antecedents of censuses from medieval to nation states.* Palgrave Macmillan US. https://doi.org/10.1057/9781137485038

Firmin-Sellers, K. (1995). The politics of property rights. *American Political Science Review, 89*(4), 867–881. https://doi.org/10.2307/2082514

Fligstein, N. (2018). *The architecture of markets: An economic sociology of twenty-first-century capitalist societies.* Princeton University Press.

Gaventa, J. (1982). *Power and powerlessness: Quiescence and rebellion in an Appalachian valley*. University of Illinois Press.

Gruber, L. (2000). *Ruling the world: Power politics and the rise of supranational institutions*. Princeton University Press.

Guha, R. (1963). *A rule of property for Bengal: An essay on the idea of permanent settlement*. Mouton.

Habib, I. (1975). Colonialization of the Indian economy, 1757–1900. *Social Scientist, 3*(8), 23. https://doi.org/10.2307/3516224

Habib, I. (1982). Agrarian relations and land revenue: North India. In T. Raychaudhuri, I. Habib, & D. Kumar (Eds.), *The Cambridge economic history of India* (Vol. 1, pp. c.1200–c.1750). CUP.

Habib, I. (1985). Studying a colonial economy – Without perceiving colonialism. *Modern Asian Studies, 19*(3), 355–381.

Habib, I. (1999). *The agrarian system of Mughal India* (pp. 1556–1707). Oxford University Press.

Hodgson, G. M. (2009). On the institutional foundations of law: The insufficiency of custom and private ordering. *Journal of Economic Issues, 43*(1), 143–166. https://doi.org/10.2753/JEI0021-3624430107

Hodgson, G. M. (2015). Much of the 'economics of property rights' devalues property and legal rights. *Journal of Institutional Economics, 11*(4), 683–709. https://doi.org/10.1017/S1744137414000630

Islam, S. (1979). *The permanent settlement in Bengal: A study of its operation 1790–1819*. Bangla Academy.

Knight, J. (1992). *Institutions and social conflict* (1st ed.). Cambridge University Press. https://doi.org/10.1017/CBO9780511528170

Lachmann, R. (2002). *Capitalists in spite of themselves: Elite conflict and European transitions in early modern Europe*. Oxford University Press.

Lane, F. C. (1958). Economic consequences of organized violence. *The Journal of Economic History, 18*(4), 401–417. https://doi.org/10.1017/S0022050700107612

Lane, F. C. (1975). The role of governments in economic growth in early modern times. *The Journal of Economic History, 35*(1), 8–17. https://doi.org/10.1017/S0022050700094274

Lane, F. C. (1979). *Profits from power: Readings in protection rent and violence-controlling enterprises*. State University of New York Press.

Marshall, P. J. (1987). *Bengal: The British bridgehead, Eastern India 1740–1828. The New Cambridge history of India* (Vol. II, Part 2). Cambridge University Press.

Marx, K. (1853a, June 25). *The British rule in India*. The New York Daily Tribune.

Marx, K. (1853b, August 5). *India*. New York Daily Tribune.

Marx, K. (1853c, August 8). *The future results of British rule in India*. The New York Daily Tribune.

Marx, K. (1906). *Capital, Volume I: A critique of political economy*. Charles Kerr & Company.

Marx, K. (1970). *A Contribution to the critique of political economy*. International Publishers.

Moe, T. M. (2005). Power and political institutions. *Perspectives on Politics, 3*(2), 215–233. JSTOR.

Morris, M. D. (1963). Towards a reinterpretation of nineteenth-century Indian economic history. *The Journal of Economic History, 23*(4), 606–618.

Newbery, D. M. (1989). Agricultural institutions for insurance and stabilization. In P. Bardhan (Ed.), *The economic theory of agrarian institutions*. Clarendon Press.

North, D. C. (1981). *Structure and change in economic history*. Norton.

North, D. C. (1990). *Institutions, institutional change and economic performance*. Cambridge University Press.

North, D. C., & Thomas, R. P. (1971). The rise and fall of the manorial system: A theoretical model. *The Journal of Economic History, 31*(4), 777–803. https://doi.org/10.1017/S0022050700074623

North, D. C., & Thomas, R. P. (1976). *The rise of the Western world: A new economic history*. Cambridge University Press.

North, D. C., & Weingast, B. R. (1989). Constitutions and commitment: The evolution of institutions governing public choice in seventeenth-century England. *The Journal of Economic History, 49*(4), 803–832.

Olson, M. (1993). Dictatorship, democracy, and development. *American Political Science Review, 87*(3), 567–576. https://doi.org/10.2307/2938736

Ostrom, E. (1990). *Governing the commons: The evolution of institutions for collective action* (1st ed.). Cambridge University Press.

Ostrom, E. (2000). Private and common property rights. In *Encyclopedia of law and economics, Vol. II: Civil law and economics*. Edward Elgar.

Ostrom, E. (2010). Beyond markets and states: Polycentric governance of complex economic systems. *The American Economic Review, 100*(3), 641–672. https://doi.org/10.1257/aer.100.3.641

Parkes, J., & Merivale, H. (1867). *Memoirs of Sir Philip Francis, with correspondence and journals. Commenced by the late Joseph Parkes, completed and edited by Herman Merivale.*

Polanyi, K. (2001). *The great transformation: The political and economic origins of our time*. Beacon Press.

Priest, C. (2021). *Credit nation: Property laws and institutions in early America*. Princeton University Press.

Ramsbotham, R. B. (1926). *Studies in the land revenue history of Bengal, 1769–1787*. H. Milford, Oxford University Press.

Ray, R. (1979). *Change in Bengal agrarian society, c1760–1850*. Manohar.

Robb, P. (2016). *Ancient rights and future comfort: Bihar, the Bengal Tenancy Act of 1885, and British rule in India* (1st ed.). Routledge.

Roy, T., & Swamy, A. V. (2016). *Law and the economy in colonial India*. University of Chicago Press.

Schlager, E., & Ostrom, E. (1992). Property-rights regimes and natural resources: A conceptual analysis. *Land Economics, 68*(3), 249–262. https://doi.org/10.2307/3146375

Scott, J. C. (2009). *The art of not being governed: An anarchist history of upland Southeast Asia*. Yale University Press.

Sinha, N. K. (1961). *The economic history of Bengal from Plassey to the Permanent Settlement*. Firma K.L. Mukhopadhyay.

Smith, A. (2003). *The wealth of nations*. Random House Publishing Group.

Sweezy, P. M., & Lefebvre, G. (1978). *The transition from feudalism to capitalism*. Verso Books.

Tilly, C. (1985). War making and state making as organized crime. In D. Rueschemeyer, P. B. Evans, & T. Skocpol (Eds.), *Bringing the state back in* (pp. 169–191). Cambridge University Press. https://doi.org/10.1017/CBO9780511628283.008

Tucker, R. C. (1989). *The Marx-Engels reader*. W W Norton & Company.

Van Creveld, M. (1999). *The rise and decline of the state*. Cambridge University Press.

Veblen, T. (1898). The beginnings of ownership. *American Journal of Sociology, 4*(3), 352–365.

Weber, M. ([1919] 2004). *The vocation lectures*. Hackett Pub.

Weber, M. ([1927] 2003). *General economic history*. Dover.

CHAPTER 8

DO EVENTS SHAPE RACE? A COMPARATIVE-HISTORICAL EXAMINATION OF THE CATHOLIC IRISH IN 17TH-CENTURY BARBADOS AND MONTSERRAT

Caroline Virginia Reilly

University of California, Los Angeles, USA

ABSTRACT

Ethnoracial categories and classifications can change over time, sometimes leading to increased social mobility for marginalized groups or nonelites. These ethnoracial changes are often attributed to emulation, where nonelites adopt the elite's social, cultural, and political characteristics and values. In some cases, however, nonelites experience ethnoracial shifts and upward mobility without emulating elites, which events can help explain. I argue that the type of event, whether endogenous or exogenous, affects the ability of elites to enforce their preferred ethnoracial hierarchy because it will determine the strategy – either insulation or absorption – they can pursue to maintain their power. I examine this phenomenon by comparing the cases of Irish social mobility in 17th-century Barbados and Montserrat. Findings suggest that endogenous events allow elites to reinforce their preferred ethnoracial hierarchy through insulation, whereas exogenous events constrain elites to employ absorption, which maintains their power but results in hierarchical shifts. Events are thus critical factors in ethnoracial shifts.

Keywords: Elites; nonelites; race; ethnicity; racialization; power; events

---

Elites, Nonelites, and Power
Political Power and Social Theory, Volume 41, 211–238
Copyright © 2025 Caroline Virginia Reilly
Published under exclusive licence by Emerald Publishing Limited
ISSN: 0198-8719/doi:10.1108/S0198-871920240000041008

INTRODUCTION: HOW ETHNORACIAL HIERARCHIES CHANGE

There are two dominant approaches to explaining changes in social categories and categorization that can transform ethnoracial hierarchies. The first stems from nonelite transformations of categorization, where people's everyday interactions and experiences can result in informal changes in how they identify themselves and others (cf. Feliciano, 2016; Nobles, 2004; Roth, 2016) and even classificatory changes (cf. Alba & Nee, 1997; Fox & Guglielmo, 2012; Ortiz, 2017). The second arises from elite transformation of classification, which occurs when people with substantial sociopolitical power change official classifications of race and ethnicity, such as through legislation and official surveys meant to capture a nation's demographic composition, like a census (cf. Nobles, 2004). While categorization and classification often inform one another (cf. Emigh et al., 2015; Ortiz, 2017; Porter & Snipp, 2018; Snipp, 2003), changes in either one occur by different means and produce distinct outcomes that affect informal interactions, (in)formal protections and privileges, or both. Here, I propose another way in which categorization and classification may change, namely, through events. In particular, I examine how events, whether endogenous or exogenous, might affect ethnoracial hierarchies.

Nonelite Transformation of Categorization

Nonelites primarily transform social categorization by emulating the dominant group; this in turn can change their location within the relevant sociocultural hierarchy or their sociolocation. Ethnoracially marginalized groups, which comprise the nonelite, attempt to mirror salient racialized indicators of the dominant group – high educational attainment, occupational prestige, and religion – to achieve social mobility (Alba & Nee, 1997; Gordon, 1964; Ignatiev, 1995; Penner & Saperstein, 2008; Roediger, 2007; Saperstein & Penner, 2012). Individually, ethnoracially marginalized people may change aspects of their physical appearance and behavior, such as wearing White hairstyles (Dickens et al., 2019) and performing racially coded forms of professionality (Pitcan et al., 2018), to abate microaggressions and secure acceptance from others and society more broadly.[1]

Nonelites mirror the ethnoracial indicators of elites to establish both individual and group proximity to Whiteness, especially in the Euro-American context.[2] Whiteness is synonymous with success in Euro-America, resulting in redefining high-status, successful, ethnoracially marginalized people – that is, well-educated and wealthy – as culturally White (Ortiz & Telles, 2012; Saperstein et al., 2014; Saperstein & Penner, 2012). Over time, nonelites adopt various characteristics of the dominant group, leading to shared cultural and socioeconomic experiences between the two groups (Barth, 1969; Bèlanger & Pinard, 1991; Lake & Rothchild, 1996; Olzak, 1989). Increased cultural, social, and economic similarities between marginalized and dominant groups thus often result in recategorizing ethnoracially marginalized as members of the elite to varying degrees (Gans, 1973; Gordon, 1961, 1964; Penner & Saperstein, 2008).

Ethnoracial classifications often shift as racialized sociocultural indicators do (Emigh et al., 2015; Porter & Snipp, 2018; Snipp, 2003), reflecting legal statuses like free or unfree (Emigh et al., 2015) or groups' racialized experiences (cf. Alba & Nee, 1997; Fox & Guglielmo, 2012; Ortiz, 2017). Consequently, ethnoracial classification can result from reclassifying either a marginalized group as members of the dominant group (cf. Alba & Nee, 1997; Roediger, 2007) or legal members of the dominant group as a distinct, marginalized ethnoracial group (cf. Porter & Snipp, 2018; Snipp, 2003). European–American immigrants represent the former, as they went from ethnoracially marginalized groups to being White (Alba & Nee, 1997; Gans, 1973; Gordon, 1961, 1964; Roediger, 2007). Latino Americans, however, exemplify the latter, going from legally White to Hispanic as a result of their collective action to have their classification represent their racialized experiences (Ortiz, 2017; Porter & Snipp, 2018; Snipp, 2003).

Elite Transformation of Classification

In contrast to nonelites, elites hold significant social, political, and economic power, giving them a pivotal role in shaping classifications. Elites' "vastly disproportionate control over and access to valuable resources" (Khan, 2012, p. 362) grants them sociopolitical power and wealth (Cousin et al., 2018, p. 230; Khan, 2012). Because elites occupy positions of power and authority that allow them to preserve their wealth, status, and resources (Khan, 2012), they are pivotal in shaping sociocultural norms, values, and hierarchies (Cousin et al., 2018; Khan, 2012). The ethnoracial classifications elites implement reinforce the privileging or penalization of dominant and marginalized groups, respectively (cf. Chung, 2020), which in turn reinforce the same in informal interactions (cf. Dickens et al., 2019; Gaddis, 2015; Pager et al., 2009; Pitcan et al., 2018).

Elites also transform classifications to protect their social, political, and economic power and interests when threatened. Typically, elites change classifications when conflict among them or between them and nonelites threatens their power and status (Lachmann, 1990). Elites primarily protect their interests either by galvanizing nonelites around those interests (Bro, 2023) or, less commonly, by incorporating nonelites into the elite (Bro, 2023; Lachmann, 1990). In rare cases, elites fully incorporate nonelites, granting them access to the elite's privileges and resources (cf. Bro, 2023). In other cases, elites turn nonelites into a "servile elite" – a group chosen by elites to increase their own power while maintaining the group's subordinate status (Lachmann, 1990, p. 403; White, 2008, p. 321). Recruiting a servile elite includes bringing nonelites under the same ethnoracial classification as the elite, thereby giving them various sociocultural privileges but generally keeping them from the elites' status, political power, and resources.

Elites and the Racial State

The racial state is a hierarchized state where race and ethnicity are deeply intertwined with governing and social institutions, and these institutions and their actors are themselves racialized (Omi & Winant, 1994). Race is the "ideological 'glue'" that organizes and establishes who is proper or criminal, civilized or savage, or free or enslaved (Gramsci, 1971, p. 328, as cited in Omi & Winant, 2015, p. 76). Ethnoracial classifications name and position actors within an ethnoracial hierarchy, affecting people's sociolocation and interactions with other people, formal structures, and policies (Omi & Winant, 1994). Classifications also aid state institutions in passing racially motivated policies (e.g., racial segregation in the United States) that protect elite interests and shape people's experiences (cf., Barth, 1969; Cousin et al., 2018). Consequently, ethnoracial classifications help maintain the elite's status, authority, and resources, while ethnoracial reclassification can effectively protect elite power when threatened.

Because of the centrality of ethnoracial classification in people's sociolocation and lived experiences, racialized actors have competing interests that can lead to conflict. Elites want to maintain their power and resources, whereas nonelites, especially those who do not share ethnoracial similarities with elites, want to disrupt the existing hierarchy in order to access the elites' privileges (Omi & Winant, 1994, pp. 84–85). The racial state manages this conflict through racial domination – the active oppression of marginalized groups – and racial hegemony – the normalization of racial differences and consequent development of a "racial 'common sense'" – in an unstable equilibrium (Gramsci, 1971, as cited in Omi & Winant, 2015, pp. 146–147). Racial domination is critical in establishing and consolidating elites' power, whereas racial hegemony maintains their power by justifying political, cultural, and socioeconomic differences between ethnoracial groups through "racial common sense" narratives perpetuated by formal and informal institutions (Gramsci, 1971; Omi & Winant, 1994, 2015).

Events, Categorization, and Classification

I propose a third way that ethnoracial categorization and classification can change, namely, through events. Events can transform structures, including ethnoracial categorization, classification, and hierarchies; they must also be defined in relation to those structures (Riley, 2008; Sahlins, 1985; Sewell, 2005). However, dissensus exists over whether events necessitate structural transformation. Sewell (2005, p. 100) posits that events are a rare subclass of happenings that transform social structures. Conversely, Sahlins (1985) maintains that events are the relation between happenings and a given cultural system that can be structurally transformative or readily accepted as part of a social structure's order given their similarity to previous events, like protests or slave revolts. Subsequently, events culminate from the "structure of the conjuncture" – a sociohistorically contingent system of relations established and constituted by the relevant cultural categories and actors' interests – and occur regularly (Sahlins, 1985, pp. xiv, 125). Although events have objective qualities that stem from their context, actors' varied interpretations of them give events significance and effect. Consequently, events should be understood through the values that actors attribute to them and their effect on social structures (Sahlins, 1985).

I categorize events as endogenous or exogenous and argue that the type of event affects how socially transformative it is. Endogenous events arise from a society's internal factors, which elites are familiar with and prepared to handle (Koning, 2016). Endogenous events often occur through established structural processes of change, either formal or informal (e.g., a court appeal or protest), and subsequently are predictable (Koning, 2016; Noble, 2000), thereby granting elites considerable control over social transformations. Conversely, exogenous events result from external factors that challenge social structures, systems, and institutions (e.g., invasion, war, or a collapsing global economy; Noble, 2000). These events are inherently unpredictable, making it difficult for elites to prepare for them, and they can profoundly destabilize existing systems, resulting in significant social changes (Koning, 2016; Noble, 2000).

This articulation of event type aligns with that of Sahlins (1985). Endogenous and exogenous events are either relatively nontransformative or significantly transformative, respectively, according to the "structure of the conjuncture" from which they culminate (Sahlins, 1985, pp. xiv, 125). Endogenous events are familiar to actors in a given society, allowing them to understand these events as part of the social order. Additionally, elites can prepare for endogenous events and dampen their effects, preserving elites' preferred social order. But unfamiliar events (i.e., exogenous) result in more significant social change, transforming structures by hamstringing the ability of elites to enforce their preferred hierarchy.

The presence and acceptance of endogenous events also align with the racial state's unstable equilibrium, the incessant conflict the state manages via racial hegemony and domination (Gramsci, 1971, p. 182, as cited in Omi & Winant, 2015, pp. 146–147). Racialized actors are in constant conflict, culminating from the structure of the conjuncture with regularity, like endogenous events (Omi & Winant, 1994). The racial state manages the conflict through formal and informal processes (Omi & Winant, 2015), allowing elites to mitigate changes to the social structure.

That said, endogenous events occasionally transform structures (e.g., the modern civil rights movement) as exogenous events tend to do, forcing elites to actively protect or restore their preferred ethnoracial hierarchy through either insulation or absorption. Elites employ insulation when the conflict challenging their preferred social order does not threaten to alter the ethnoracial hierarchy significantly (Omi & Winant, 1994, pp. 86, 106). The event's relatively low threat allows to implement relatively unimportant, symbolic changes to the hierarchy that maintain its present function, namely, the augmentation and protection of elites' power (Omi & Winant, 1994). Examples of insulation include granting a marginalized group social privileges that cause no substantial changes to the ethnoracial hierarchy (e.g., participating in discriminating against other marginalized groups but with little opportunity for socioeconomic mobility; Omi & Winant, 1994). As a result, ethnoracially marginalized groups may experience various ethnoracial categorical shifts, like positive changes in their everyday interactions, but not reclassification.

Conversely, elites employ absorption when conflict significantly destabilizes a society and is a greater threat to the ethnoracial hierarchy when elites ignore rather than deal with it (Omi & Winant, 1994, pp. 86, 106). When an event poses a threat dangerous to the ethnoracial hierarchy if left unaddressed, elites must significantly change the hierarchy to maintain their power in society (Omi & Winant, 1994, p. 86). Absorption strategies include implementing formal changes – such as ethnoracial reclassification or eliminating discriminatory laws – that incorporate nonelites into a salient, socially valued symbolic category of elites, like Whiteness. Incorporating nonelites into categories of status and privilege creates similarity between them and elites while keeping them separate from elites' resources and power, similar to the "servile elite" (White, 2008, p. 321). Subsequently, elites may ethnoracially reclassify nonelites as members of the dominant group to maintain their power in and control over society and its valuable resources.

While Omi and Winant (1994) do not clarify how elites choose absorption or insulation beyond a threat assessment, I argue that the type of event affects which strategy elites employ. Insulation is the elite's preferred restoration strategy since it entails only minor changes to their preferred hierarchy. But they will also implement absorption and significantly alter the ethnoracial hierarchy when necessary, granting nonelites privileges, reclassifying them, and incorporating them into the elite. Given that endogenous events are predictable and elites are prepared to handle them, elites can employ insulation in these cases because the type of event allows them to implement their preferred strategy. Conversely, the unpredictable and destabilizing nature of exogenous events constrains elites' ability to implement their preferred restoration strategy, forcing them to employ absorption and alter the ethnoracial hierarchy. The type of event, then, determines the strategy elites pursue and how well they enforce their preferred ethnoracial hierarchy. It also helps explain under which circumstances elites recategorize and reclassify ethnoracially marginalized groups, as well as how they do so without the latter needing to emulate the dominant group.

THE CATHOLIC IRISH UNDER ENGLISH IMPERIAL RULE

Irish Americans are an oft-studied exemplar of how an ethnoracially marginalized group was ethnoracially recategorized and reclassified by adopting various sociocultural characteristics of the dominant group, White Americans (cf. Ignatiev, 1995; Roediger, 2007). Here, I examine how events affected Irish people's categorization and classification in the colonial Caribbean, regardless of their efforts to emulate elites. Specifically, I look at the relationship between endogenous and exogenous events and ethnoracial hierarchical changes for Irish people in 17th-century Barbados and Montserrat.

The English empire's ethnoracial hierarchy during the 1600s reflected England's colonization efforts both close to home and abroad, including their colonization of Wales, Scotland, and Ireland – the last proving the most difficult to "civilize" (cf. Leyburn, 1989/1997, pp. 83–95). England justified its colonizing efforts as a mission to civilize barbarous pagans, paganism having served as a pretext for invading Ireland since the 12th century (Lebow, 1976, pp. 74–75).

Subsequently, religion became a primary ethnoracial organizing principle during the 17th century. The related ethnoracial hierarchy across England's empire placed the Catholic Irish well below the English elite, comfortably below White nonelites, consisting mainly of English, Welsh, and Scots, and just above enslaved Black people. The Catholic Irish's liminal status – belonging neither among the other nonelites nor among the enslaved – in turn posed a severe threat to the power and authority of the Barbadian and Montserratian elites, whether they were conspiring with enslaved Black people or with competing European empires to overthrow their colonizers.

Yet, by the end of the 17th century, the Irish of Barbados and Montserrat displayed different levels of ethnoracial recategorization and reclassification following specific events, as signified by social and economic mobility in each island's racial state (cf. Alba & Nee, 1997; Ignatiev, 1995; Roediger, 2007). This, together with Barbados and Montserrat's shared ethnoracial hierarchies, makes comparing the islands methodologically advantageous for examining how events can destabilize a society and affect the categorization, classification, and subsequent social mobility of nonelites. The Irish's liminal status, combined with their European ancestry, made them a strategic group for elites to mobilize in order to protect their own power and resources; this is because recategorizing and reclassifying them maintained European dominance over non-Europeans – in other words, the ethnoracial hierarchy that preserved elites' resources, authority, and power provided by slave labor.

Racialization of the Catholic Irish

During their colonization of Ireland, the English racialized the Irish by identifying them as biologically inferior to the English and British more broadly. Describing the Irish as a "people *bred* to be dominated" (Painter, 2011, p. 135, emphasis added) and referring to them as the "wild Irish" (Lebow, 1976, p. 75), English officials instilled widespread belief in Irish racial inferiority and fear of Irish people throughout the empire, portraying them as "eaters of human flesh, murderers and thieves who reveled in sodomy and incest" (Lebow, 1976, p. 75; Leyburn, 1989/1997, p. 83). The English further identified the biological inferiority of Irish people not only through their behaviors but also through their culture, their religion in particular. At this time, Catholicism was racially salient, since prior to the introduction of chattel slavery, "race" referred primarily to groups with kinship ties and cultural practices (Pritchett & Vasquez, 2023). Catholicism, its rituals, and its imagery differentiated the Irish from the English empire's Anglicans (cf. Beckles, 1990; Block & Shaw, 2011; Shaw, 2013). Thus, Catholicism was blamed as another source of Irish inferiority and so served as the primary means of discriminating against them (Block & Shaw, 2011; Painter, 2011; Shaw, 2013).

Subsequently, English officials across the empire discriminated against Catholic Irish and Irish people more broadly. During the colonization of Ireland, tens of thousands of Catholic Irish were forcibly transported to the colonial Caribbean for indentured servitude (Beckles, 1990; Doan, 2006; Fergus, 1994; Shaw, 2013). In colonial Barbados and Montserrat, the Irish had difficulty gaining freedom and wealth, and the few who did were barred from holding political office because of laws requiring a disavowal of Catholicism and adherence to Anglicanism to hold office (Beckles, 1990; Shaw, 2013). The Barbadian Catholic Irish endured regular arrest, public whippings, and deportation for practicing Catholicism or slandering English customs, religion, and nationality (Beckles, 1990; Block & Shaw, 2011; Shaw, 2013). The Montserratian Catholic Irish, meanwhile, were segregated to a small sector of the island with nonarable land (Akenson, 1997; Fergus, 1994), leaving little possibility for socioeconomic mobility and making them much easier for Montserratian elites to surveil (Cawley, 2015; Hobson, 2007; Pulpisher & Goodwin, 2001; Ryzewski & Cherry, 2015; Zacek, 2010).

Stagnation Versus Success

Despite experiencing religious discrimination and oppression on both islands, the Barbadian and Montserratian Catholic Irish displayed stark differences in social mobility. Barbados's Catholic Irish largely remained a liminal group in the social order, their sociolocation primarily changing from indentured servants to paid laborers, with Irish men entering "skilled" positions (e.g., overseer) and Irish women shifting from field to house labor on the sugar plantations (Beckles, 2013; Block & Shaw, 2011; Menard, 2006; Shaw, 2013). But while some Irish gained considerable wealth by owning sugar plantations, indentured servants, and enslaved people (Block & Shaw, 2011; Menard, 2006; Shaw, 2013), most struggled to find land after becoming paid laborers (Engerman, 1986; Gemery, 1986; Menard, 2006; Zacek, 2010). The elites also prevented wealthy Irish from participating in government and exercising the same social power as their English counterparts via anti-Catholic discrimination (Beckles, 1990; Engerman, 1986; Gemery, 1986; Shaw, 2013). General social mobility for the Irish was thus fairly nominal, maintaining a sociolocation comfortably below the island's other nonelites though above enslaved persons.

The mobility of the Montserratian Irish, however, was more substantial and complex. Unlike Barbados, Montserrat's Irish were either Catholic or Anglican, with Protestant Irish enjoying the wealth, resources, power, and status of the English elite (Hobson, 2007; Ryzewski & Cherry, 2015; Zacek, 2010). Emulating the dominant group thus granted these Irish membership in the elite. Most, however, remained Catholic (Griffin, 1911; Jacoberger, 2015; Messenger, 1967; Pulpisher & Goodwin, 2001) and experienced discrimination, segregated from the island's other nonelites to nonarable land (Akenson, 1997; Fergus, 1994). Nonetheless, a small contingent of wealthy Catholic Irish emerged despite discrimination, amassing wealth from their sugar plantations and enslaved people (Akenson, 1997; Doan, 2006; Pulpisher & Goodwin, 2001; Ryzewski & Cherry, 2015; Shaw, 2013). By the end of the 17th century, Catholic Irish enjoyed relative economic prosperity and religious freedom, privileges typically reserved for the elite and the other nonelites. Moreover, the elites tolerated the public practice of Catholicism despite its illegality across England's empire (Akenson, 1997; Block & Shaw, 2011; Fergus, 1978, 1994; Shaw, 2013; Zacek, 2010).

Different Majorities, Different Vulnerabilities

The different levels of social mobility experienced by the Irish on Barbados and Montserrat resulted largely from different vulnerabilities, identifiable by the islands' majority populations. Enslaved Black people comprised the majority of Barbados's population (Handler, 1969), and the threat of a revolt was ever present for Barbados's elites (Shaw, 2013). Fearing slave rebellions (Beckles, 2013), they enacted severe sanctions against enslaved persons suspected or convicted of rebellion (Shaw, 2013). Because the Catholic Irish were close in size to the enslaved population (Handler, 1969), they also presented a promising solution to the elites' problem since they could be used to surveil and control the movements of enslaved people (Rugemer, 2013). For Barbados's elites, the Catholic Irish were thus a promising tool that could be enticed to maintain social order with little change to the ethnoracial hierarchy.

Conversely, the Catholic Irish made up the majority of Montserrat population, with enslaved people close behind (Fergus, 1978, 1994; Griffin, 1911; Pulpisher & Goodwin, 2001). Because Montserrat faced threats of invasion from the Catholic empires of France and Spain, which the island's Catholic Irish majority were gladly prone to assist in order to gain religious freedom (Hobson, 2007), the elites perceived them as a constant threat needing to be controlled. Unlike Barbados's elites, however, Montserrat's could not turn to their second largest population, enslaved people, to control the Catholic Irish threat (Akenson, 1997; Fergus, 1978, 1994). Instead, they focused on controlling the Catholic Irish through segregation and surveillance (Akenson, 1997; Fergus, 1994; Shaw, 2013). Interference from exogenous factors, combined with their population majorities, thus left Montserrat's elites with little leverage in maintaining the social order, giving the Catholic Irish greater opportunity for upward mobility following an invasion.

The Racial State in Context: Barbados and Montserrat

Barbados and Montserrat were also highly stratified slave societies with strict ethnoracial hierarchies. Despite the prevalence of indentured labor on these islands in the 17th century, the economies of both relied on African chattel slavery, meaning that slavery and anti-Black racism were critical components of the culture, politics, and social identification of their inhabitants (Amussen, 2007; Griffin, 1911; Handler, 1969; Handler & Reilly, 2015; Libby, 1991; Maudlin & Herman, 2016; Messenger, 1967; Pulpisher & Goodwin, 1982). Consequently, maintaining the ethnoracial hierarchy was imperative to both economies; the elites of both islands could not allow enslaved persons to surpass the bottom stratum of the hierarchy without undermining their economies, sociocultural order, personal wealth, and dominance. Any hierarchical shifts, then, had to occur among their ethnically stratified European population. While the Catholic Irish were heavily racialized and marginalized, they were also officially included in the broader category of "White" because of their European ancestry. The Protestant English, however, did not consider them "Christian" (Shaw, 2013), which was necessary to be classified and categorized among the other White nonelites. Because of their European ancestry, their marginalization, and the demographic constraints discussed above, the Catholic Irish were the most promising group for targeting any efforts to maintain the ethnoracial hierarchy following a destabilizing event.

METHOD

I used comparative process tracing (CPT) to analyze and compare elite strategies of maintaining power in 17th-century Barbados and Montserrat. CPT tracks processes of change in two societies to identify variations between them in two steps (Bengtsson & Ruonavaara, 2017). The first requires a theoretical model to identify pathways of change, determine the most desirable or likely pathway given that model, and establish pathways for both cases. Establishing pathways entails pinpointing the critical juncture, or destabilizing event, and identifying the social conditions preceding and following the event for each case. The second is to compare the two processes with the desirable pathway, identifying variations between the cases and establishing how those variations are connected to each case's outcome (Bengtsson & Ruonavaara, 2017).

Establishing Pathways: Social Conditions Before and After an Event

Barbados's Pathway
I used primary data, accessed via microform, to construct and analyze the CPT pathway for Barbados's elites. "The Covenant to be Taken by the Whole Kingdom" (1643) and the Acts and Statutes of Barbadoes [sic] (1654) outline the social conditions and related ethnoracial hierarchy prior to the destabilizing event. "The Covenant," which was an oath to be taken by all the kingdom's inhabitants to assist Protestant authorities in suppressing a "Popish" uprising, reflected England's discriminatory policies toward Catholicism within the empire, while the Acts and Statutes of Barbadoes reflected the elite's concerns over a large influx of Irish indentured servants due to Cromwell's forcible transportation of Irish to the island following his invasion of Ireland (Doan, 2006; Shaw, 2013). The Laws of Barbadoes [sic] (LoB) (1699), on the other hand, describe social conditions following the destabilizing event and reflect an overwhelming concern with a growing riotous, enslaved Black population.

This destabilizing event, which followed the Acts and Statutes of Barbadoes (1654) and preceded the LoB (1699), was the planned slave revolt of 1692. Although not the only rebellion to be planned or carried out in 17th-century Barbados, the slave revolt of 1692 has been regularly cited as a moment of crisis for the island's elites that exposed the precarity of their power and fear of losing it (cf. Beckles, 1985, 1990; Block & Shaw, 2011; Doan, 2006; Handler, 1982; Menard, 2006; Rodgers, 2007; Sharples, 2015; Shaw, 2013). Moreover, the conspiracy represents the most extensively planned plot to usurp elite power (Beckles, 1990; Block & Shaw, 2011; Shaw, 2013). Specifically, I analyzed a letter written by a wealthy Englishman to an acquaintance after the conspiracy was thwarted (Bohun, 1692). Given that the significance of an event arises from the relevant actors' interpretation thereof (Sahlins, 1985), this correspondence explains why the failed rebellion was socially destabilizing despite being one of many in 17th-century Barbados history.

Montserrat's Pathway

Unlike Barbados, Montserrat has few archives from the 17th century that survive or remain undamaged owing to various natural disasters. Places holding Montserratian documents originating in the 1600s or copies also greatly restrict access to them because of their rarity. Thus, it was necessary to rely on secondary sources to construct and analyze the CPT pathway for Montserrat's elites. Much of the literature on 17th-century Montserrat provides quotations from primary data, most often legislation and correspondence between the Montserratian elite and the English Crown, that have often been repeated across secondary sources. Consequently, their repetition allowed me to cross-compare them, enabling me to construct a holistic picture of each quotation and its meaning. These secondary sources reiterated the social construction of Montserrat, primarily analyzing the fashioning of legislation in a slave society and the heavy Catholic Irish influence on the island.

Cross-referencing the information found in the secondary sources and the primary sources they quoted allowed me to locate 17th-century Montserrat's destabilizing event and the social conditions prior to and following it. The most commonly referenced and analyzed crisis was France's invasion of the island in 1667 (cf. Cawley, 2015; Fergus, 1978; Higham, 1923; Hobson, 2007; Jacoberger, 2015; Ryzewski & McAtackney, 2015; Zacek, 2010). Although the French invaded Montserrat multiple times between 1664 and 1782, their 1667 invasion marked their longest occupation of the island, lasting six months (Fergus, 1978). After England regained control, Montserratian elites and the Crown had to strategize on how to maintain the territory, which centered on how to manage their Catholic Irish "problem" (cf. Fergus, 1978; Jacoberger, 2015; Messenger, 1967).

To determine Montserrat's social conditions before and after the 1667 French occupation, I focused on discriminatory practices levied against Catholics, analyzing instances and results of being Catholic. When addressing Montserrat's Irish elite, I focused primarily on the sociolocation and social mobility of those who were Catholic. I established social mobility by analyzing changes in discrimination against and subsequent social acceptance of Catholicism from before the 1667 French invasion until after England regained control by specifically examining protections implemented both for them and for Irish inhabitants more broadly.

ANALYSIS

To identify key differences leading to the varied outcomes for the Catholic Irish on Barbados and Monserrat, I examined the established pathways of change for the elites on both islands and then compared them. Juxtaposing social conditions on the two islands before and after the destabilizing event, I identified and analyzed changes in the sociolocation and the formal protections or privileges of the Catholic Irish to establish their social mobility on each island. Lastly, I compared the CPT pathways of Barbados and Montserrat to determine the extent of variation in social mobility for the Catholic Irish in each colony and the reason for those differences.

Barbados

Before the 1692 Conspiracy

England's policies marked the Irish as dangerous because of their religion and policed them accordingly. Written in 1643 during England's conquest of Ireland, "The Covenant to be Taken by the Whole Kingdom" described the Anglican Church as the "True Protestant Religion" while simultaneously designating Catholics as enemies of the kingdom (Firth & Rait, 1911). English elites described "Papists" as seeking "to bring to utter Ruin and Destruction the Parliament and Kingdom, and, that which is dearest, the True Protestant Religion." Protection "from the Justice thereof" (i.e., of Parliament) meant that the Crown forbade Catholics from practicing their religion or participating in government (Firth & Rait, 1911). Catholicism, according to English elites, thus was dangerous to Protestantism and English government, and Catholics lay beyond the protections afforded the rest of the kingdom.

In the 1654 Acts and Statutes of Barbadoes (ASB), Barbadian elites explicitly mirrored the culture and laws of England: "We being of one Nation should be governed by the same Law, which our brethren in *England* are" (ASB, Preamble; emphasis in original). Just like their "brethren in *England*," Barbadian elites targeted the Catholic Irish. The first written act of the 1654 legislation granted that:

> a Liberty of Conscience in matters of Religion be allowed to all, excepting such Tenets as are Inconsistent to a Civil Government, and that Laws be put in execution against Blasphemy, Atheism and open Scandalous living, Seditious preaching, or unfound Doctrine sufficiently proved against him. ASB (Act 1)

The descriptors "Tenets ... Inconsistent to a Civil Government," "Blasphemy," "open Scandalous living," and so on echo the English Parliament's belief that the Catholic Irish were a formidable, uncivil, and treacherous threat (Lebow, 1976; Leyburn, 1989/1997). English elites considered Catholicism as antithetical to their customs and culture (Handler & Reilly, 2015), and including such descriptors as these, as well as "unfound Doctrine," specifically excluded Catholic Irish from the protections the Commonwealth enjoyed (ASB, Act 1). Merely practicing Catholicism was punishable as rebellious action and sedition simply because it went against English civility, customs, and religion (Beckles, 1990; Block & Shaw, 2011; Shaw, 2013), whereas non-Irish indentured servants were punished for explicitly speaking against English rule, rebelling against elites, and committing treason (Block & Shaw, 2011; Rugemer, 2013; Shaw, 2013).

Although not explicitly stated in Barbados's 1654 legislation, Catholicism and its adherents were thus a primary target for discrimination for the Barbadian elites.

These elites continued to target the Catholic Irish, using negative Catholic stereotypes to establish the Irish as the root cause of societal issues and a group to be feared and regulated:

> And whereas it hath been taken into serious consideration, that the main and chief cause of our late troubles and miseries hath grown by loose, base, and uncivil languages tending to sedition and division, too commonly used among many people here: It is therefore agreed, that at the next general Assembly a strict Law be made against all such persons, with an heavy penalty to be inflicted upon them that shall be guilty of any reviling speeches of what nature soever. ASB (Act 20)

"[L]oose, base, and uncivil languages" parallel English perceptions of Catholic Irish backwardness. Irish people often spoke their native tongue in Barbados, communicating in Irish Gaelic while laboring on plantations despite threats from overseers to speak only English (Beckles, 1990; Gerbner, 2010; Shaw, 2013). Barbados's elites considered Gaelic an uncivil language spoken by uncivilized people, and they feared revolts from indentured Irish and enslaved Black people as the Irish taught their fellow field laborers Gaelic (Gerbner, 2010; Shaw, 2013). The elite's concern over collaboration between Catholic Irish and enslaved Black people is clear through their claim that "uncivil languages," or all non-English languages, were "too commonly used among many people here" and exacerbated issues of "sedition and division," especially among the Catholic Irish and enslaved Black people.

To mediate the threat posed by the combined Irish and enslaved majority, English elites undermined the "uncivil" collective's comradery by designating either group under separate phenotypic racial categories, namely, "White" and "Black"/"Negroe(s)," respectively (cf. ASB, Act 12). The Barbados Assembly declared that no person should "entertain any man, or woman, White or Black, above one night, if he doth not know him to be a Free-man," targeting all unfree people, who were predominantly Catholic Irish and enslaved Black people (ASB, Act 12). The elites further maintained distinct privileges for White people, even if unfree and non-Christian, by providing and detailing formal guidance in multiple statutes over how to regulate and (negatively) treat enslaved people (cf. ASB, Acts 12, 23, 48), far more than any other marginalized group. The elites thus effectively distinguished the Irish from the enslaved by highlighting their phenotypic differences, rather than the religious differences that distinguished them from the island's other nonelites. Consequently, in the ethnoracial hierarchy where the Catholic Irish remained a distinct group from the other nonelites, they occupied a liminal space of White but not Christian, or fully White, in a society where Christianity ensured basic rights and civil liberties. This also left them isolated from possible alliances with other marginalized groups. The Irish thus had little opportunity for upward social mobility.

The Conspiracy of 1692

On October 21, 1692, a member of the Barbadian elite wrote to an acquaintance about a thwarted slave rebellion, detailing how "the *Negro's* in this Island had made a PLOT to have destroyed all the Christians therein" and how the English prevented the implementation of this "wicked Design." In this wicked plot, enslaved Black people intended to take "up the Surname and Offices of the Principal Planters and men in the Island, to have Enslaved all the Black men and Women to them, and to have taken the White Women for their Wives" (Bohun, 1692). The writer displays a specific fear over enslaved Black men taking up the positions of the elites, the elite's slaves for themselves, and White women for wives. In other words, the elite feared enslaved Black men flipping the racial hierarchy upside down, entirely disrupting the social order of the racial state.

The Barbadian elites' response was to arrest between 200 and 300 enslaved persons and try and condemn many of them. Of those tried and condemned, "many were Hanged, and a great many Burned. And, (for a Terror to others) there are now seven Hanging in Chains, alive, and Starving to Death" (Bohun, 1692). Although execution and mutilation were not uncommon punishments for enslaved individuals (Beckles, 1990; Rugemer, 2013), the type of execution – namely, being set on fire – and the level of torture were far rarer and meant to terrorize other enslaved people, displaying their fear of the potential societal upheaval where enslaved Black men could become the Barbadian elite. More-over, the public display of such defiling and brutal punishments told Barbadians how serious the planned revolt was and that the elites would do anything to protect chattel slavery and the existing racial hierarchy. The attempted rebellion of 1692 thus represented a major endogenous, destabilizing event for the Bar-badian elite. The enslaved rebels' plan to overtake the positions of the White elite would have entirely disrupted the latter's racialized organization of their slave society, affecting their wealth, property, labor, social status, and understanding of racial dominance.

After the Conspiracy

The Barbadian elites' concerns over insurrection by enslaved people were clear in the LoB passed seven years later in 1699, which included several laws restricting the "wandering" of indentured and enslaved persons (LoB, Acts 21, 198, 329, para. 1). They believed that indentured servants made "use of all advantages and occasions to disturb the public Peace" (LoB, Act 21), and that enslaved people needed "good regulating and ordering" to restrain them from "the Disorders, Rapines and Inhu-manities to which they are naturally prone and inclined" (LoB, Act 329, para. 1).

The Barbados assemblymen made their racialized concerns over another rebellion apparent not only by sanctioning punishments specific to Black and enslaved people but also by referencing the earlier revolt:

> If any Negroes or other Slaves, shall make Mutiny or Insurrection, or rise in Rebellion against this Place or People, or make preparation of Arms, Powder, Bullets, or Offensive Weapons, or hold any Council or Conspiracy of, or raising Mutiny or Rebellion against this Island, *as hath been formerly attempted* [emphasis added] ... [officers of the peace should] proceed by Marshal

Law against the Actors, Contrivers, Raisers, Fomenters and Concealers of such Mutiny or Rebellion, and them punish by Death or other Pains as their Crimes shall deserve. LoB (Act 329, para. 20)

Although the Catholic Irish also planned and carried out various rebellions throughout Barbados's colonial history (Beckles, 1990; Block & Shaw, 2011; Handler, 1982; Sharples, 2015; Shaw, 2013), sometimes even conspiring with enslaved people (Beckles, 1990), the elites now targeted Black people as their primary concern. The specification of "Death or other Pains" as punishment for any enslaved person planning and executing a revolt also mirrored the elites' brutal and severe response to the 1692 plot.

Elites even included compensation for "the Loss of the Negroes and other Slaves that shall suffer Death by this Act" to encourage all people, including plantocrats and the Catholic Irish, to report all possible insurrectionists: "[Such a loss] would prove heavy for the Owner of them to only bear" (LoB, Act 329, para. 20). Moreover, "the Loss may be borne by the Publick, whose safety by such Punishments is hereby proved for and intended" so that "the Owners of Negroes may not be discouraged to detect and discover the Offences of their Negroes" (LoB, Act 329, para. 20). Although slave insurrection posed a threat to Barbadian elites' preferred social order, elites justified compensating slave owners as being in the interest of *public* safety.

In addition to hyper-surveillance of enslaved people, Barbados's elites now offered a moderate degree of social acceptance to the Catholic Irish. Despite passing multiple acts embargoing the import of Catholic Irish indentured servants, the elites allowed laws requesting the acquisition of Christian servants to expire, marking them as "obsolete" or "expired" (LoB, Acts 229, 337, 346, 419). Moreover, the assemblymen now referred to "all Servants" rather than specifically "Christian Servants" when passing acts governing servants and servant labor, signifying the inclusion of Catholic Irish in laws protecting servants: "All Servants whose time shall expire at any time hereafter having had no Indenture or Contract, shall receive for their Wages Four Hundred Pounds of good Muscovado sugar" (LoB, Act 21, para. 7). These regulations now signified formal acceptance of the Irish, granting them protections previously reserved for Christian servants.

Barbados's elites also sought to further distinguish enslaved Black persons from the Catholic Irish, specifically designating the latter as White and as in opposition to Black people. When seeking to prevent "excessive drinking," the perceived cause of "many Enormities [that] have been committed" in Barbados (LoB, para. 3), they would fine "any white Person whatsoever" who bought alcohol from or drank it with Black people (LoB, Act 382, para. 3). Subsequently, Irish people, who were known to collaborate with the enslaved, were now formally policed from spending time with Black people and only allowed to interact with White people socially.

Nonetheless, Barbados's elites continued to pass laws discriminating against the Catholic Irish for their religion. An act "for preventing Danger which may happen from Popish Recusants" (LoB, Act 254) both perpetuated fears of the

Irish threat voiced in the 1654 legislation and reinforced the 1654 ethnoracial hierarchy by continuing to distinguish the Catholic Irish from the other White nonelites. Barbados's elites used this fear of Catholic insurrection to exclude Catholic Irish from participating in government, despite considering them White when seeking to regulate the enslaved:

> All and every Person or Persons that shall bear any Office or Offices, Civil or Military, or shall receive any Pay, Salary, Fee or Wages by reason of any Patent or Grant ... shall take the Oaths of Supremacy and Allegiance; and likewise make and subscribe a Declaration in the said Act expressed. LoB (Act 254, para. 1)

The mandatory oath read: "I [name] do declare, that I do believe, that there is not any Transubstantiation in the Sacrament of the Lord's Supper, or in the Elements of Bread and Wine, at or after the Consecration thereof by any person whatsoever" (LoB, Act 254, para. 3). Since the doctrine of transubstantiation was a key marker of difference between Catholics and Anglicans, the elites' requirement of this oath effectively disenfranchised Catholics, regardless of wealth, by preventing them from participating in elections, holding public office, or serving in the military. This left Catholics situated below all other White nonelites in the ethnoracial hierarchy, reinforcing the Barbadian elites' preferred, preconspiracy hierarchy.

In sum, Catholic Irish continued to occupy the same sociolocation, below the other nonelites but above the enslaved, as they had before the conspiracy of 1692. Notably, they experienced some semblance of social mobility in social status, as the Barbadian elites classified them as "White," referred to "White" rather than "Christian" in the 1699 law code, and pitted them against the elites' primary population of concern – enslaved people. But any changes in social status were rather insignificant because the Catholic Irish were still prevented from accessing positions of sociopolitical power as well as elite resources. The absence of considerable social changes for the Catholic Irish thus showed how the Barbadian elite used insulation to maintain control of society and its socioeconomic and sociopolitical order following an endogenous destabilizing event. As elites are generally prepared for endogenous events because of their recurrence, the Barbadian elite proactively managed threats of insurrection, particularly slave rebellions, by utilizing the Catholic Irish, a manipulable group incentivized by social acceptance in a society that regularly discriminated against them, to help maintain social stability, the racial state, and elite power.

Montserrat

Before the 1667 French Occupation

Similar to Barbados, the Montserratian elite perceived their island's Catholic Irish majority as a threat to their power (Griffin, 1911; Hobson, 2007; Jacoberger, 2015; Rodgers, 2007; Ryzewski & Cherry, 2012; Shaw, 2013). On January 1, 1634, Father Andrew White, a Jesuit, captured the widespread discrimination against Catholicism and the large number of Catholic Irish when he wrote in his journal: "By noon we came to Monserat, where is a noble plantation of Irish

Catholiques whome the Virginians would not suffer to live with them because of their religion" (Griffin, 1911, p. 84; see also Cawley, 2015).

Many English colonies in the Atlantic, most notably Virginia and St. Kitts, expelled Catholic Irish for practicing their religion and for insubordination more broadly, many of whom then moved to Montserrat (Griffin, 1911; Hobson, 2007; Jacoberger, 2015; Ryzewski & Cherry, 2012). The immense Catholic Irish population this created made Catholicism a prominent feature of Montserrat and the colony something of a haven for the Catholic Irish (Akenson, 1997), who comprised nearly 70% of the population (Fergus, 1981; Hobson, 2007; Shaw, 2013); this earned Montserrat the moniker of "the Irish colony" from Lord Willoughby, Barbados's governor from 1650 to 1652 (Higham, 1923; Jacoberger, 2015, p. 45; Shaw, 2013, p. 182). Given the Catholic Irish's clear majority, the Montserratian elite were concerned they would undermine their own power given the chance, especially in favor of a Catholic-friendly empire, such as France, that might invade the island (Hobson, 2007).

Because they were the majority, the Catholic Irish did enjoy some benefits, such as tolerance of private worship (Cawley, 2015; Jacoberger, 2015; Messenger, 1967; Shaw, 2013), but they were also heavily policed because of their "uncivil" religion. Montserratian elites required all inhabitants to swear loyalty to the Anglican Church and Crown in order to receive large plots of land suitable for sugar plantations (Fergus, 1994), thus effectively barring Catholic Irish from amassing wealth and power that would rival that of the elites. Moreover, the elites segregated the Catholic Irish to St. Patrick's Parish (Zacek, 2010), an overcrowded region on the outskirts of society inhospitable to sugar cultivation and processing (Fergus, 1994; Hobson, 2007; Jacoberger, 2015; Pulpisher & Goodwin, 2001; Ryzewski & Cherry, 2012; Zacek, 2010). In placing the overwhelming Catholic Irish majority on the edge of society and on land limiting their socioeconomic prosperity, the Montserratian elite thereby effectively limited their social involvement in the colony and cemented their position below that of the island's other White nonelites (Cawley, 2015; Jacoberger, 2015; Pulpisher & Goodwin, 2001; Zacek, 2010).

Montserrat's elites further regulated the Catholic Irish's sociolocation by preventing the transference of intergenerational wealth among them. Since the elites considered any marriage officiated and consecrated outside the Anglican Church to be void (Akenson, 1997; Zacek, 2010) and since property and wealth in 17th-century Montserrat passed intergenerationally through legitimate heirs, the consequent annulment of Catholic marriages left Catholic Irish children as bastards unable to lay claim to their parents' wealth (Akenson, 1997; Zacek, 2010).

The few Irish wealthy enough to occupy positions of power in Montserrat – including the governor, military officers, and prominent plantocrats – and be counted among the elite had to convert to Anglicanism (Fergus, 1978; Hobson, 2007; Jacoberger, 2015; Messenger, 1967). Because every government official was required to swear an oath of fealty to the Church of England and consequently to the Crown, this prevented all Catholics from accessing elite power (Akenson, 1997; Fergus, 1978; Hobson, 2007; Jacoberger, 2015; Pulpisher & Goodwin, 1982). While some Catholic Irish hid their religious ties to occupy positions

228   *Do Events Shape Race?*

among the elite (Akenson, 1997; Fergus, 1978), most elite Irish who participated in assemblies and held public office were Protestants who had been educated among the English elite (Hobson, 2007; Jacoberger, 2015; Shaw, 2013; Zacek, 2010). Socialized in the English elite's customs, the Irish elite were practically indistinguishable from the other island elites (Shaw, 2013; Zacek, 2010). Moreover, they proved themselves highly beneficial to the elite more broadly, greatly bolstering Montserrat's economy and faithfully serving the state that amassed them great wealth (Hobson, 2007; Jacoberger, 2015; Shaw, 2013). The Montserratian elite thus effectively maintained an ethnoracial hierarchy by marginalizing Catholics, allowing only wealthy Irish socialized in English elite culture and practicing Anglicanism to access any modicum of power and privilege.

The Montserratian Irish thus generally occupied a complex and liminal position as an ethnoracial group. Regardless of religion, all Irish faced scrutiny and suspicion from the Montserratian elite. But the Irish elite, Protestant and English by custom, displayed considerable power and privilege as a servile elite for the English elite, owning large, prosperous plantations and serving as members of the state, whereas the Catholic Irish were segregated from society, excluded from government, and so experienced socioeconomic immobility. Subsequently, Montserrat's ethnoracial hierarchy was similar to that of Barbados, with only wealthy Protestant Irish among the elite, nonelites below the elite, and the Catholic Irish comfortably below the other nonelites and above only the enslaved.

The French Occupation of 1667

In 1667, the French invaded and took control of Montserrat for six months, an exogenous event for which Montserrat's elites were unprepared (Cawley, 2015; Fergus, 1978; Higham, 1923). Although much of this lack of preparation was the fault of Lord Willougby, Governor of the Leeward Islands, who neglected and disregarded Montserrat's military (Cawley, 2015), Willoughby blamed the entire French occupation on the "restless" and "treacherous" Catholic Irish (Cawley, 2015; Fergus, 1978; Higham, 1923; Hobson, 2007; Jacoberger, 2015; Ryzewski & McAtackney, 2015). Given the Montserratian elite's previous fears of the Catholic Irish and their collusion with Catholic empires, Willoughby had no trouble convincing the Crown that the Catholic Irish were the sole reason for France's victory (Cawley, 2015; Fergus, 1978, 1981) and not his failure to fortify the island.

The Catholic Irish's actions during previous French invasions did nothing to convince the Crown otherwise. When the French invaded Montserrat, the Catholic Irish aided the invaders and participated in widespread insurrection (Block & Shaw, 2011; Cawley, 2015; Fergus, 1978, 1981; Higham, 1923; Hobson, 2007; Jacoberger, 2015). Unique to the 1667 invasion, however, was the Protestant Irish elite's participation in the revolt (Block & Shaw, 2011; Fergus, 1981). Anthony Briskett, a "Protestant" plantocrat and Montserrat's presiding governor, joined his fellow Irishmen and aided the French invaders, in return for which the French captains endorsed him for the position of governor (Fergus,

1981). By placing an Irishman in charge, they hoped to regulate the Catholic Irish more easily (Block & Shaw, 2011, p. 51).

By the end of the year, however, France had returned Montserrat to England (Cawley, 2015; Fergus, 1981). Although England may have regained control, the abrupt upheaval of English Montserratian society entirely destabilized the colony's social order and elite control of power. The French had sought to form a Franco-Irish colony where Catholic Irish would be relocated to more profitable tracts of land and enjoy the same benefits as other French inhabitants, an unimaginable reality under English rule (Fergus, 1981). Such actions had threatened the re-establishment of the elite's power and caused already poor relations between the Catholic Irish and the other nonelites to deteriorate even further (Fergus, 1981). England and its Montserratian elite thus had to restore their control of the island, their power, and the former ethnoracial hierarchy among a contentious population and disgruntled Catholic Irish majority who posed a significant threat of future social destabilization.

After the French Occupation

After regaining control of Montserrat, the Crown sent authorities to re-establish English rule on the island. First, the elites punished those among them who had aided the French, most notably stripping former Governor Briskett of his 1,000-acre plantation lands (Fergus, 1981; Hobson, 2007; Pestana, 2005). Second, the elites rewarded all former elites, English and Irish, who had remained loyal to England during the invasion, returning to them their appropriated plantations and dividing Briskett's confiscated land among them (Fergus, 1981; Jacoberger, 2015).

The elites even instated the Irishman William Stapleton as Deputy Governor of Montserrat because of his loyalty to the English during the invasion (Block & Shaw, 2011; Fergus, 1981; Jacoberger, 2015; Shaw, 2013). Governor Willoughby noted that not only was Stapleton loyal to the crown – "a Gentleman of known valour, good conduct, and great integrity" (Block & Shaw, 2011, p. 53; Fergus, 1981, p. 328; Jacoberger, 2015, p. 46) – but he was also an Irishman who could effectively contain the rebellious Catholic Irish – "borne in Ireland, and therefore understands the better to govern his Countrymen" (Block & Shaw, 2011, p. 53; Fergus, 1981, p. 328; Jacoberger, 2015, p. 46). Although his religious affiliation is unclear,[3] Stapleton showed the Crown that an Irishman could be trusted and help England maintain control of Montserrat (Block & Shaw, 2011), thus granting an Irishman access to the elite and its power.

Despite wanting to reward only those who were loyal to the Crown during France's invasion, the Crown and Montserratian elite had to make some concessions to the Catholic Irish in order to earn their favor and avoid future insurrections. In particular, Stapleton sought to earn favor by formally enforcing cordiality between the Irish and English. In 1668, an act was passed which is characterized as follows:

> Sect. 2 sets forth several odious distinctions used by the English, Scotch, and Irish reflecting on each other (English Dog, Scots Dog, Tory, Irish Dog, Cavalier, Roundhead, and many other

230 *Do Events Shape Race?*

opprobrious, scandalous, and disgraceful terms), and therefore ordains that if any such or the like reflections are used in the island by any person, stranger, or foreigner, the offenders shall be prosecuted as breakers of the public peace, and shall abide such fines or punishments as shall be imposed on them by the Governor and Council; and if any murders, riots, or unlawful assemblies should arise upon such words, the offender shall suffer as a mutineer and disturber of the public peace. Messenger (1967, p. 15); see also Fergus (1981, p. 332)

Montserrat's elite, and an elite Irishman in particular, thus outlawed language typically used by English, Scots, and Irish people to offend one another. Although the legislation protected every Montserratian from explicit ethnic slurs, it also marked a formal protection for the Catholic Irish against slander and hateful speech, an unprecedented gain in English territories for Catholics (Fergus, 1981; Messenger, 1967; Shaw, 2013). Consequently, the Catholic Irish received privileges typically afforded the island's other nonelites as well as the elites, thereby significantly altering Montserrat's former ethnoracial hierarchy and its associated privileges.

Given Briskett's treachery and Stapleton's unprecedented protections for Catholics, many elites and nonelites still feared Catholic Irish insurrection and the possibility of future treason by Stapleton. Even an English cavalry officer who trusted Stapleton's loyalty wrote to the Crown in 1671 that "his majesty would take special Care, yet after Colonel Stapleton's time (whose fidelity he is sure of) that not only an English Governor be always instituted, but that there be some Citadel and small Garrison of English in pay" (Ryzewski & McAtackney, 2015, p. 126; Shaw, 2013, p. 47).

Similarly, in 1668, Lord Willoughby wrote to the Crown about his apprehension of the Catholic Irish despite his staunch endorsement of Stapleton's governorship:

That We with all other of his Majesty's Loyal subjects of this Island have so much above any other of our neighbors been devastated, wasted and destroyed in the late unhappy War, not only by our Enemies in the time of their short stay with us, but have likewise than as many times since in a most barbarous manner been Robbed, Plundered Stripped & almost utterly Consumed of all that we had in the world by a Party of Rebellious & wicked people of the Irish nation our neighbors & Inhabitants in such sort, as it is almost Impossible either for man or pen to utter or describe. Messenger (1967, p. 14)

Because of this widespread fear of the Catholic Irish, the Crown required frequent status reports from Montserrat's elites. Stapleton's reports, however, painted the Catholic Irish as a law-abiding and peaceful people (Jacoberger, 2015; Messenger, 1967) despite their large numbers. In 1676, he wrote to the Lords of Trade that Montserrat was for "the most part Roman Catholics" (Jacoberger, 2015, p. 47; Messenger, 1967, p. 17), outnumbering Protestants six to one, but that they posed "no scandal to the Protestant Church" (Jacoberger, 2015, p. 47; Messenger, 1967, p. 17). He further explained that the Protestant Church was "the prevalent persuasion" in Montserrat, juxtaposing this with his observation that the "Protestant Tenet or persuasion [was] not prevalent and professed in all the [English Caribbean] islands" that did not have a Catholic Irish majority (Jacoberger, 2015, p. 47; Messenger, 1967, p. 17). The contrast between Montserrat's loyalty to Protestantism, and consequently the Crown, and the lack of said loyalty in other largely non-Catholic colonies emphasized that the Catholic Irish were loyal to the Crown and capable of being loyal subjects, regardless of their religion.

Some 14 years later, in 1690, the Governor of the Leewards, Christopher Codrington, continued to emphasize the loyalty of the Catholic Irish to the Crown. Despite previously calling the Catholic Irish a "threatening horde of nameless traitors" (Block & Shaw, 2011, p. 57), Codrington now described them as follows:

> The Irish on Montserrat do there enjoy their estates and Livelihoods as quietly and happily as the English subjects do ... there are but few men so desperately wicked that will gratify their Revenge at the Expense of their own Ruin and I believe fewer so very generously virtuous and pious, at least wise on this side of the Tropic, that will either hang or starve for their Country or Religion. Block and Shaw (2011, p. 57), Shaw (2013, p. 181)

Codrington's description of the Montserratian Irish as enjoying "their estates and Livelihoods as quietly and happily as the English subjects do" marked the Irish as now compatible with the island's other White nonelites. Experiencing a similar sociolocation, they now accessed social acceptance from the elites and relative wealth unavailable to them prior to the 1667 invasion. Indeed, they enjoyed enough privilege that Codrington believed any insurrection on their part would merely be "at the Expense of their own Ruin." Just as Stapleton contended, Codrington further described the Catholic Irish as coexisting with and not entirely opposed to Protestantism. To safeguard control of Montserrat, the Governor further believed that the Crown and its elite needed to ensure "sufficient security of the fidelity of the Irish in case [Montserrat] be attacked," rather than police and punish them (Block & Shaw, 2011, p. 71).

To this end, Codrington highlighted to the Irish what they would lose should they rebel and gain should they be loyal:

> At Montserrat I at large laid before the Irish the ruin in all respects they would certainly bring upon themselves should they prove treacherous to the Government, and on the other hand the advantage of behaving themselves like good subjects ... they then with great appearance of joy promised faithful obedience to their majesties Government. Block and Shaw (2011, p. 58), Shaw (2013, p. 181)

Rather than discriminating against the Catholic Irish, Codrington further offered them the "advantage" of religious freedom, a heretofore unconscionable act for English elites:

> By cordially uniting with us, they [the Catholic Irish] may rationally promise to themselves to secure the island and for the future to live happily and with esteem among us, and even as to their Religion may have some toleration and allowance. Block and Shaw (2011, pp. 57–58), Shaw (2013, p. 181)

Formal toleration of Catholicism in English territories was unprecedented and granted the Catholic Irish on Monserrat a privilege allowed only to Protestants across the English empire – the freedom to practice religion publicly. Montserrat's elites now allowed the Catholic Irish to erect churches so they could worship openly and communally (Akenson, 1997; Messenger, 1967; Zacek, 2010)

232 *Do Events Shape Race?*

and permitted Roman Catholic priests to "minister to their community openly" (Fergus, 1994, p. 20; Messenger, 1967). The protection of Catholic religious practice signifies how desperately the elites needed the Irish's loyalty, effectively reclassifying them with the island's other nonelites with no concessions other than promises not to rebel.

In sum, Montserrat's elites experienced an exogenous event that entirely destabilized their social order when the French invaded in 1667 and altered their ethnoracial hierarchy by establishing a state that allowed Catholicism and granted wealth to Catholic Irish individuals. Knowing the Catholic Irish would again aid invaders promising prosperity and religious freedom, the Crown and its elites appointed to govern Montserrat decided to gain their loyalty rather than attempt to punish and control them as before the invasion. Subsequently, the Catholic Irish enjoyed economic prosperity and religious freedom, living as part of the island's other nonelites. This represented a marked shift in sociolocation for them, from having sat below the other nonelites in terms of wealth and privileges prior to France's invasion. Effectively, the Catholic Irish now joined the other nonelites without needing to emulate the English, while the Protestant Irish elite maintained their position among the powerful. Thus, the Montserratian elite had to employ absorption because the French invasion had constrained their ability to influence the Catholic Irish by any other means than incentivization and the ensuring of their loyalty. In doing so, they altered Montserrat's ethnoracial hierarchy, erasing the marginalized "subclass" of Catholic Irish.

CONCLUSION: COMPARING BARBADOS AND MONTSERRAT

Barbados's elites were able to maintain their preferred ethnoracial hierarchy – Catholic Irish above the enslaved but below the island's other nonelites – following the 1692 conspiracy through insulation, whereas Montserrat's elites altered their ethnoracial hierarchy using absorption, granting the Catholic Irish unprecedented privileges following France's 1667 invasion and occupation of the colony. Before and after the rebellion, the Barbadian elites prevented Catholic Irish from occupying positions of power and treated them as a potential threat. Although the Catholic Irish experienced changes in their everyday racialized experiences, working alongside Protestant White nonelites, they continued to suffer religious discrimination, thus in effect undergoing recategorization. Conversely, Montserrat's elites went from discriminating against the Catholic Irish (i.e., not allowing them to occupy government office, hold positions of power, or worship publicly) prior to the French occupation to granting them legal protection against ethnoracial slurs and tolerance of worship following the exogenous event. The Montserratian Catholic Irish thus experienced privileges typically reserved for the island's other nonelites without emulating the elites. While they remained Catholic, they were effectively reclassified among the other nonelites.

Although each island's elite class faced unique vulnerabilities, largely due to demographic differences, that affected the events and their outcomes, the primary difference between Barbados's and Montserrat's pathways was the type of destabilizing event that occurred in each case. Barbadian elites faced an endogenous event for which they were prepared because of its relatively regular occurrence – rebellion, which allowed them to employ insulation, thereby managing the endogenous event and preserving their ethnoracial hierarchy. Montserratian elites, however, experienced an exogenous event, which is naturally unpredictable (i.e., they did not know when an invasion would occur) and for which they were unprepared (i.e., did not fortify Montserrat), forcing them to alter their ethnoracial hierarchy. The French, aided by Montserrat's Catholic Irish, usurped the elite's power and control over the island, leaving them in fear of losing control again. Fearing the Catholic Irish would aid future invaders as well, the elite were forced to gain their loyalty, and so they employed absorption, granting the Catholic Irish formal protections and freedoms typically reserved for themselves and the island's other White nonelites without needing to emulate the dominant group.

Barbados's pathway thus largely confirms theories of emulation and elites. Although Barbados's Catholic Irish began operating alongside the Protestant White nonelites, resulting in minor social changes, they also maintained their ethnoracial distinction of Catholicism, which left them below the other nonelites in the ethnoracial hierarchy. In accordance with elite theory, Barbadian elites then mobilized the Catholic Irish against the primary threat to their ethnoracial hierarchy, namely, enslaved people, by offering them privileges inconsequential to social mobility. The Catholic Irish, who once collaborated in rebellions and shared their language with enslaved people, now actively policed them when offered some privileges. But because they largely resisted emulating the English elite, they continued to be excluded from positions of power, consequently preserving the elites' preferred ethnoracial hierarchy.

Montserrat, however, challenges present theories of how ethnoracial hierarchies change. Although the Protestant Irish of Montserrat exemplified ethnoracial recategorization and reclassification via emulation, becoming members of the dominant group by adopting English aristocratic norms and customs, the Catholic Irish refused to emulate the English elite, proudly maintaining their Catholicism. Nonetheless, they gained formal protections from slanderous and hateful speech and the ability to practice their religion freely and openly, both unprecedented privileges for non-Anglicans. English elites thus effectively reclassified the Catholic Irish among the island's other nonelites, substantially changing the ethnoracial hierarchy and conceding more power than typically preferred by elites (Bro, 2023, p. 381; Lachmann, 1990, p. 403).

Events thus explain why Barbados affirms and Montserrat refutes present theories of emulation and elite preservation of power. Events can significantly transform structures, typical of exogenous events, or be accepted as part of the existing structure if familiar to elites, typical of endogenous events. Barbados reflects the latter. Since rebellions were a regular, endogenous event, Barbadian elites were prepared to deal with the threat and able to implement insulation, maintaining their preferred ethnoracial hierarchy. Montserrat, however, reflects the former, experiencing an exogenous event that significantly destabilized society and forced the elites to resort to absorption, thereby transforming the ethnoracial hierarchy. As such, these findings add nuance to understanding how ethnoracial hierarchies can shift even when to the detriment of elites.

Despite these insights, this research has limitations. For the analysis of Montserrat, I relied on secondary data because of the limited availability of archives. Most of these data contained information analyzed primarily by historians (cf. Beckles, 1985, 1990, 2013; Shaw, 2013), who often examined topics related to racialization shifts in the colonial Caribbean but not those shifts explicitly. I also focused on the racialization and social mobility of Irish people as related to elite strategies of insulation and absorption following endogenous and exogenous events and did not attempt to analyze in depth how other ethnoracially marginalized people may have experienced increased oppression as a result. Analyzing this other dimension of structural transformation, however, is critical to understanding how privilege and oppression are related, constructed, and used by various actors to gain social mobility.

Future research should examine how the social mobility and ethnoracial reclassification of one group are achieved through the oppression of other marginalized groups. In Barbados, for example, the Catholic Irish gained social mobility through increased policing of enslaved Black people, indicated by elites' encouragement of White, rather than Christian, hyper-surveillance of the enslaved. While I did not analyze the mechanism of gaining privileges at the expense of other marginalized groups, it is a narrative apparent in my analysis of Barbados. I thus urge other researchers to examine how elites identify strategic groups in relation to ethnoracial hierarchies, and how those strategic nonelites may oppress other marginalized groups to establish proximity to the elites.

ACKNOWLEDGMENTS

I wish to thank Dr Noelle Chaddock for encouraging me to investigate the racialization of the Irish and Dr Clayton Fordahl for guiding me through the first iterations of this research. I owe a special thanks to Dr Rebecca Jean Emigh and my fellow Emights for reading and providing constructive feedback on multiple versions of this work. I would also like to thank Dr Dylan Riley for providing invaluable feedback on this chapter. Finally, I thank Sarah Collins, M.A., who was my sounding board throughout my project.

NOTES

1. All racial identifiers are capitalized to underscore the sociocultural nature of race, acknowledging racialized experiences of oppression and privilege in society. The capitalization of racial identifiers is in accordance with the National Association of Black Journalists' guidelines.

2. In the United States, higher educational attainment and higher socioeconomic status are associated with Whiteness, and non-White individuals are sometimes considered "culturally" or "partially" White when they display these characteristics, exemplified in

greater social acceptance when following expectations of Whiteness (Ortiz, 2017; Ortiz & Telles, 2012).

3. Fergus (1981, p. 331) states that Stapleton was a Protestant, but Block and Shaw (2011, p. 53) suggest he was a Catholic.

REFERENCES

Acts and statutes of Barbados. (1654). William Bentley.

Akenson, D. H. (1997). *If the Irish ran the world: Montserrat, 1630–1730.* McGill-Queen's University Press.

Alba, R., & Nee, V. (1997). Rethinking assimilation theory for a new era of immigration. *International Migration Review, 31*(4), 826–874.

Amussen, S. D. (2007). *Caribbean exchanges: Slavery and the transformation of English society, 1640–1700.* University of North Carolina Press.

Barth, F. (1969). Introduction. In F. Barth (Ed.), *Ethnic groups and boundaries: The social organization of cultural difference* (pp. 9–37). Waveland Press.

Beckles, H. M. (1985). Plantation production and white "proto-slavery": White indentured servants and the colonisation of the English West Indies, 1624–1645. *The Americas, 41*(3), 21–45. https://doi.org/10.2307/1007098

Beckles, H. M. (1990). A "riotous and unruly lot": Irish indentured servants and freemen in the English West Indies, 1644–1713. *William and Mary Quarterly, 47*(4), 503–522. https://doi.org/10.2307/2937974

Beckles, H. M. (2013). Servants and slaves during the 17th-century sugar revolution. In S. Palmié & F. A. Scarano (Eds.), *The Caribbean: A history of the region and its people.* University of Chicago Press.

Bèlanger, S., & Pinard, M. (1991). Ethnic movements and the competition model: Some missing links. *American Sociological Review, 56*(4), 446–457.

Bengtsson, B., & Ruonavaara, H. (2017). Comparative process tracing: Making historical comparison structured and focused. *Philosophy of the Social Sciences, 47*(1), 44–46.

Block, K., & Shaw, J. (2011). Subjects without an empire: The Irish in the early modern Caribbean. *Past & Present, 210*(1), 33–60. https://doi.org/10.1093/pastj/gtq059

Bohun, E. (1692). *A brief, but most true relation of the late barbarous and bloody plot of the negro's in the island of Barbado's [sic] on Friday the 21. of October, 1692.* https://quod.lib.umich.edu/e/eebo2/A77407.0001.001/1:1

Bro, N. (2023). The structure of political conflict: The oligarchs and the bourgeoisie in the Chilean congress, 1834–1894. *Theory and Society, 52*(3), 353–386. https://doi.org/10.1007/s11186-022-09491-3

Cawley, C. (2015). *Colonies in conflict: The history of the British overseas territories.* Cambridge Scholars Publishing.

Chung, E. A. (2020). *Immigrant incorporation in East Asian democracies.* Cambridge University Press. https://doi.org/10.1017/9781107337077

Cousin, B., Khan, S., & Mears, A. (2018). Theoretical and methodological pathways for research on elites. *Socio-Economic Review, 16*(2), 225–249. https://doi.org/10.1093/ser/mwy019

Dickens, D. D., Womack, V. Y., & Dimes, T. (2019). Managing hypervisibility: An exploration of theory and research on identity shifting strategies in the workplace among Black women. *Journal of Vocational Behavior, 113*, 153–163. https://doi.org/10.1016/j.jvb.2018.10.008

Doan, J. E. (2006). The Irish in the Caribbean. *ABEI Journal, 8*, 105–116. https://www.revistas.usp.br/abei/article/view/179391/166012

Emigh, R. J., Riley, D., & Ahmed, P. (2015). The racialization of legal categories in the first U.S. census. *Social Science History, 39*, 485–519.

Engerman, S. L. (1986). Servants to slaves to servants: Contract labour and European expansion. In P. C. Emmer (Ed.), *Colonialism and migration: Indentured labour before and after slavery* (pp. 263–294). Springer.

Feliciano, C. (2016). Shades of race: How phenotype and observer characteristics shape racial classification. *American Behavioral Scientist, 60*(4), 390–419. https://doi.org/10.1177/0002764215613401

Fergus, H. A. (1978). The early laws of Montserrat (1668–1680): The legal schema of a slave society. *Caribbean Quarterly, 24*(1/2), 34–43.

Fergus, H. A. (1981). Montserrat 'colony of Ireland': The myth and the reality. *An Irish Quarterly Review, 70*(280), 325–340.

Fergus, H. A. (1994). *Montserrat: History of a Caribbean colony*. Macmillan Caribbean.

Firth, C. H., & Rait, R. S. (Eds.). (1911). June 1643: The covenant to be taken by the whole kingdom. In *Acts and ordinances of the interregnum, 1642–1660* (pp. 175–176). His Majesty's Stationery Office and British History Online.

Fox, C., & Guglielmo, T. A. (2012). Defining America's racial boundaries: Blacks, Mexicans, and European immigrants, 1890–1945. *American Journal of Sociology, 118*(2), 327–379.

Gaddis, S. M. (2015). Discrimination in the credential society: An audit study of race and college selectivity in the labor market. *Social Forces, 93*(4), 1451–1479. https://doi.org/10.1093/sf/sou111

Gans, H. (1973). Introduction. In N. Sandberg (Ed.), *Ethnic identity and assimilation: The Polish community*. Praeger.

Gemery, H. A. (1986). Markets for migrants: English indentured servitude and emigration in the seventeenth and eighteenth centuries. In P. C. Emmer (Ed.), *Colonialism and migration: Indentured labour before and after slavery* (pp. 33–54). Springer.

Gerbner, K. (2010). The ultimate sin: Christianising slaves in Barbados in the seventeenth century. *Slavery & Abolition, 31*(1), 57–73. https://doi.org/10.1080/01440390903481654

Gordon, M. M. (1961). Assimilation in America: Theory and reality. *Dædalus, 90*(2), 263–285.

Gordon, M. M. (1964). *Assimilation in American life: The role of race, religion, and national origins*. Oxford University Press.

Gramsci, A. (1971). *Selections from the prison notebooks* (Q. Hoare & G. N. Smith, Eds. & Trans.). International Publishers.

Griffin, M. I. J. (1911). Catholics in colonial Virginia. *Records of the American Catholic Historical Society of Philadelphia, 22*(2), 84–100.

Handler, J. S. (1969). The Amerindian slave population of Barbados in the seventeenth and early eighteenth centuries. *Caribbean Studies, 8*(4), 38–64.

Handler, J. S. (1982). Slave revolts and conspiracies in seventeenth-century Barbados. *New West Indian Guide, 56*(1/2), 5–42.

Handler, J. S., & Reilly, M. C. (2015). Father Antoine Biet's account revisited. In A. Donnell, M. McGarrity, & E. O'Callaghan (Eds.), *Caribbean Irish connections: Interdisciplinary perspectives* (pp. 33–46). University of the West Indies Press.

Higham, C. S. S. (1923). The accounts of a colonial governor's agent in the seventeenth century. *The American Historical Review, 28*(2), 263–285.

Hobson, D. L. (2007). *The domestic architecture of the earliest British colonies in the American tropics: A study of the houses of the Caribbean Leeward islands of St. Christopher, Nevis, Antigua and Montserrat. 1624–1726*. Unpublished doctoral dissertation. Georgia Institute of Technology.

Ignatiev, N. (1995). *How the Irish became white*. Routledge.

Jacoberger, N. A. (2015). *"Lowly laborers": Race, class, and identity in Montserrat, 17th–19th centuries*. Unpublished doctoral dissertation. St. John's University.

Khan, S. R. (2012). The sociology of elites. *Annual Review of Sociology, 38*(1), 361–377. https://doi.org/10.1146/annurev-soc-071811-145542

Koning, E. A. (2016). The three institutionalisms and institutional dynamics: Understanding endogenous and exogenous change. *Journal of Public Policy, 36*(4), 639–664. https://doi.org/10.1017/S0143814X15000240

Lachmann, R. (1990). Class formation without class struggle: An elite conflict theory of the transition to capitalism. *American Sociological Review, 55*(3), 398–414. https://doi.org/10.2307/2095764

Lake, D. A., & Rothchild, D. (1996). Containing fear: The origins and management of ethnic conflict. *International Security, 21*(2), 41–75.

The Laws of Barbados collected in one volume by William Rawlin. (1699).

Lebow, R. N. (1976). *White Britain and Black Ireland: The influence of stereotypes on colonial policy.* Institute for the Study of Human Issues.

Leyburn, J. G. (1989/1997). *Scotch-Irish: A social history.* University of North Carolina Press.

Libby, D. (1991). Proto-industrialization in a slave society: The case of Minas Gerais. *Journal of Latin American Studies, 23*(1), 1–35.

Maudlin, D., & Herman, B. L. (Eds.). (2016). *Building the British Atlantic world: Space, places, and material culture, 1600–1850.* University of North Carolina Press.

Menard, R. R. (2006). *Sweet negotiations: Sugar, slavery, and plantation agriculture in early Barbados.* University of Virginia Press.

Messenger, J. C. (1967). The influence of the Irish in Montserrat. *Caribbean Quarterly, 13*(2), 3–26.

Noble, T. (2000). *Social theory and social change.* St. Martin's Press.

Nobles, M. (2004). Racial/colour categorization in US and Brazilian censuses. In S. Szreter, H. Sholkamy, A. Dharmalingam, & International Union for the Scientific Study of Population (Eds.), *Categories and Contexts: Anthropological and historical studies in critical demography* (pp. 107–125). Oxford University Press.

Olzak, S. (1989). Labor, unrest, immigration, and ethnic conflict in urban America, 1880-1914. *American Journal of Sociology, 94*(6), 1303–1333.

Omi, M., & Winant, H. (1994). *Racial formation in the United States: From the 1960s to the 1990s* (2nd ed.). Routledge.

Omi, M., & Winant, H. (2015). *Racial formation in the United States* (3rd ed.). Routledge, Taylor & Francis Group.

Ortiz, V. (2017). Towards unifying racial and ethnic paradigms. *Ethnic and Racial Studies, 40*(13), 2240–2248.

Ortiz, V., & Telles, E. (2012). Racial identity and racial treatment of Mexican Americans. *Race and Social Problems, 4*(1), 41–56. https://doi.org/10.1007/s12552-012-9064-8

Pager, D., Western, B., & Sugie, N. (2009). Sequencing disadvantage: Barriers to employment facing young black and white men with criminal records. *The Annals of the American Academy of Political and Social Science, 623*(1), 195–213. https://doi.org/10.1177/0002716208330793

Painter, N. I. (2011). *The history of white people.* W. W. Norton & Company.

Penner, A. M., & Saperstein, A. (2008). How social status shapes race. *Proceedings of the National Academy of Sciences, 105*(50), 19628–19630. https://doi.org/10.1073/pnas.0805762105

Pestana, C. G. (2005). The problem of land, status, and authority: How early English governors negotiated the Atlantic world. *The New England Quarterly, 78*(4), 515–546.

Pitcan, M., Marwick, A. E., & Boyd, D. (2018). Performing a vanilla self: Respectability politics, social class, and the digital world. *Journal of Computer-Mediated Communication, 23*(3), 163–179. https://doi.org/10.1093/jcmc/zmy008

Porter, S. R., & Snipp, C. M. (2018). Measuring Hispanic origin: Reflections on Hispanic race reporting. *The Annals of the American Academy of Political and Social Science, 677*(1), 140–152.

Pritchett, E. N., & Vasquez, R. (2023). History of race in America. *Dermatologic Clinics, 41*(2), 335–343. https://doi.org/10.1016/j.det.2022.08.004

Pulpisher, L. M., & Goodwin, C. M. (1982). A sugar-boiling house at Galways: An Irish sugar plantation in Montserrat, West Indies. *Post-Medieval Archeology, 16*, 21–27.

Pulpisher, L. M., & Goodwin, C. M. (2001). Getting the essence of it: Galways plantation, Montserrat, West Indies. In P. Farnsworth (Ed.), *Island lives: Historical archaeologies of the Caribbean* (pp. 165–203). University of Alabama Press.

Riley, D. (2008). The historical logic of *Logics of History*: Language and labor in William H. Sewell Jr. *Social Science History, 32*(4), 555–565. https://doi.org/10.1017/S014555320001083X

Rodgers, N. (2007). The Irish in the Caribbean 1641–1837: An overview. *Irish Migration Studies in Latin America: Society for Irish Latin American Studies, 5*(3), 145–156.

Roediger, D. R. (2007). *The wages of whiteness: Race and the making of the American working class.* Verso Books.

Roth, W. D. (2016). The multiple dimensions of race. *Ethnic and Racial Studies, 39*(8), 1310–1338. https://doi.org/10.1080/01419870.2016.1140793

Rugemer, E. (2013). The development of mastery and race in the comprehensive slave codes of the greater Caribbean during the seventeenth century. *William and Mary Quarterly, 70*(3), 429–458.

Ryzewski, K., & Cherry, J. F. (2012). Communities and archaeology under the Soufrière Hills volcano on Montserrat, West Indies. *Journal of Field Archaeology, 37*(4), 316–327.

Ryzewski, K., & Cherry, J. F. (2015). Struggles of a sugar society: Surveying plantation-era Montserrat, 1650–1850. *International Journal of Historical Archaeology, 19*(2), 356–383.

Ryzewski, K., & McAtackney, L. (2015). Historic and contemporary Irish identity on Montserrat: The "emerald isle of the Caribbean." In A. Donnell, M. McGarrity, & E. O'Callaghan (Eds.), *Caribbean Irish connections: Interdisciplinary perspectives* (pp. 119–139). University of the West Indies Press.

Sahlins, M. (1985). *Islands of history*. University of Chicago Press.

Saperstein, A., & Penner, A. M. (2012). Racial fluidity and inequality in the United States. *American Journal of Sociology, 118*(3), 676–727. https://doi.org/10.1086/667722

Saperstein, A., Penner, A. M., & Kizer, J. M. (2014). The criminal justice system and the racialization of perceptions. *The Annals of the American Academy of Political and Social Science, 651*(1), 104–121. https://doi.org/10.1177/0002716213503097

Sewell, W. H. (2005). *Logics of history: Social theory and social transformation*. University of Chicago Press.

Sharples, J. T. (2015). Discovering slave conspiracies: New fears of rebellion and old paradigms of plotting in seventeenth-century Barbados. *The American Historical Review, 120*(3), 811–843. https://doi.org/10.1093/ahr/120.3.811

Shaw, J. (2013). *Everyday life in the early English Caribbean: Irish, Africans, and the construction of difference*. University of Georgia Press.

Snipp, C. M. (2003). Racial measurement in the American census: Past practices and implications for the future. *Annual Review of Sociology, 29*(1), 563–588. https://doi.org/10.1146/annurev.soc.29.010202.100006

White, H. C. (2008). *Identity and control: How social formations emerge* (2nd ed.). Princeton University Press.

Zacek, N. A. (2010). *Settler society in the English Leeward islands, 1670–1776*. Cambridge University Press.

CHAPTER 9

HISTORICAL TRAJECTORIES OF OFFICIAL INFORMATION GATHERING IN INDIA

Patricia Ahmed[a], Rebecca Jean Emigh[b] and Dylan Riley[c]

[a]*South Dakota State University, USA*
[b]*University of California, Los Angeles, USA*
[c]*University of California, Berkeley, USA*

ABSTRACT

A "state-driven" approach suggests that colonists use census categories to rule. However, a "society-driven" approach suggests that this state-driven perspective confers too much power upon states. A third approach views census-taking and official categorization as a product of state–society interaction that depends upon: (a) the population's lay categories, (b) information intellectuals' ability to take up and transform these lay categories, and (c) the balance of power between social and state actors. We evaluate the above positions by analyzing official records, key texts, travelogues, and statistical memoirs from three key periods in India: Indus Valley civilization through classical Gupta rule (ca. 3300 BCE–700 CE), the "medieval" period (ca. 700–1700 CE), and East India Company (EIC) rule (1757–1857 CE), using historical narrative. We show that information gathering early in the first period was society driven; however, over time, a strong interactive pattern emerged. Scribes (information intellectuals) increased their social status and power (thus, shifting the balance of power) by drawing on caste categories (lay categories) and incorporating them into official information gathering. This intensification of interactive information gathering allowed the Mughals, the EIC, and finally British direct rule officials to collect large quantities of information. Our evidence thus suggests that the intensification of state–

Elites, Nonelites, and Power
Political Power and Social Theory, Volume 41, 239–283
Copyright © 2025 Patricia Ahmed, Rebecca Jean Emigh and Dylan Riley
Published under exclusive licence by Emerald Publishing Limited
ISSN: 0198-8719/doi:10.1108/S0198-871920240000041009

society interactions over time laid the groundwork for the success of the direct rule British censuses. It also suggests that any transformative effect of these censuses lay in this interactive pattern, not in the strength of the British colonial state.

Keywords: States; societies; information gathering; colonialism; historical trajectories; censuses

INTRODUCTION

Official information gathering is considered to be synonymous with state power, so much so that the capacity to conduct a census is often considered to be a definition of state strength (Centeno, 2002, p. 110; Soifer & vom Hau, 2008, p. 220). This "state-driven" perspective, developed by Foucault (1978/1991, pp. 96, 98–99, 102) and Bourdieu (1994, p. 7), suggests that information gathering is primarily accomplished by strong states, which monopolize political power in their territories (review in Emigh et al., 2016a, pp. 6, 8–10; Emigh et al., 2021, p. 11; Monten, 2014, p. 176). Information, once collected, can transform social systems of categorization. Sometimes this transformation is accomplished because the information collection system itself transforms actors' consciousness, sometimes it occurs because social actors take up the official categories, and sometimes this happens because states change their bureaucracies to reflect the information that they collected (review in Emigh et al., 2020, pp. 293–299). This state-driven perspective of information gathering is strongly associated with colonialism per se (Anderson, 1983/2006, pp. 163–164; reviews in Appadurai, 1993, p. 314, and Willmott, 2023, pp. 18–19).[1]

Our work, however, suggests a different scenario: Outcomes associated with official information gathering, such as censuses and land surveys, are determined not by state strength but by the intensity of the interaction between states and societies (Emigh et al., 2016a, p. 15; 2016b, pp. 214–216; 2019, p. 406). In cases as diverse as the United States, the United Kingdom, Italy, and Puerto Rico, outcomes such as the successful redaction of a census (or a land survey) and its transformative power depended on whether, and to what extent, state and social actors interacted with respect to interests, actions, and input in the information collection (Emigh et al., 2016a, pp. 208–209; 2019, p. 406; Emigh et al., 2021, pp. 8–10). Where there was intense interaction and conflict that had to be negotiated, official information gathering was more successful and more transformative.

To understand these interactive processes, long-term historical trajectories of information gathering must be considered (Emigh et al., 2016a, pp. 45–46). If a short time period is considered, especially one that begins with the collection of a particular census, state actors appear to have considerable agency to design, collect, and deploy information (Emigh et al., 2020, p. 304). Obviously, state strength is important; however, not all strong states are able to gather needed information or classify populations (Emigh et al., 2016a, pp. 198–203, 220; 2016b, pp. 212–216; Emigh et al., 2021, p. 62). However, our approach also suggests that social influences (i.e., the "society-centered" approach), not only state strength, must be considered to examine the long-run patterns of state and social interaction. In particular, we point to three sets of social relationships. First, information gathering depends on lay categories (Emigh et al., 2016a, p. 23). Second, social actors, whom we call information intellectuals (Emigh et al., 2016a, pp. 25–26), must be able to transform these lay categories into official ones. Finally, the power between state and social actors influences where and when social and state actors can take up and deploy these transformed information categories (Emigh et al., 2016a, pp. 44–45). These relationships change over time, and, in particular, previous rounds of information gathering set the stage for subsequent ones, leading to historical trajectories of information gathering (Emigh et al., 2016a, pp. 44–46).

Here, we examine these social relationships and the long-term historical trajectories of official information gathering in India, focusing on the period before British direct rule in 1858. We do so because the British censuses of India during direct rule are often used as examples of the state-driven perspective, that is, as prima facie examples of the power and strength of states to create and implement transformative censuses (Bhagat, 2001, pp. 4,352–4,353; Cohn, 1996, p. 8). However, when analyses begin with British direct rule, it is difficult to understand the influence of the long-run historical trajectories, which, we argue above, are crucial to understanding outcomes. We focus on three periods – the early pre-Vedic (starting ca. 3300 BCE) through the Gupta period (ca. 300 BCE–700 CE), the medieval period (ca. 700–1700 CE), and the East India Company (EIC) period (ca. 1757–1857 CE) – as a backdrop for the later censuses conducted during direct British rule. We analyze, whenever possible, original reports and data, as well as secondary sources. The former include religious (Vedas, etc.) and legal texts (*Smritis, Dharmashastras*, etc.) and official reports authored by key functionaries. We examine these time periods for two purposes. First, we try to understand each time period in terms of lay categories, information intellectuals, the relative power of state versus social actors, and whether the historical trajectory of information gathering was based on a state-centered process, a society-centered process, or an interactive process. We also try to understand whether information gathering in any period had any transformative effect. Second, we use these three time periods together as a backdrop to the censuses during British direct rule to better understand how these later direct rule censuses emerged out of this long-term historical trajectory.

DIRECT RULE CENSUSES IN INDIA

The censuses conducted under British direct rule (1858–1947) form the backdrop to our study. The all-India British colonial censuses, starting in 1871, were challenging yet relatively successful, endeavors deployed by the British Crown following the collapse of the EIC. Three central questions remain, however, about these censuses. First, to what extent did the British devise and exploit them as part of a larger divide-and-conquer strategy (i.e., they were state driven) (Appadurai, 1993, pp. 319–320; Bhagat, 2006, p. 121; Cohn, 1987, pp. 230, 250)? Second, to what extent did local actors promote them to maintain and elevate their social status (i.e., they were society driven) (U. Chakravarti, 1998, p. 48; Viswanathan, 2003, p. 37)? Third, to what extent did pre-existing information-gathering techniques and social categories adapted by the British facilitate their administrative rule (i.e., they were driven by an interactive state and society process) (S. Guha, 2003, p. 155; Peabody, 2001, p. 819)? Because these questions are unresolved, it is difficult to interpret the effects of direct rule British colonial information gathering. We examine these three positions before turning to our examination of the long durée historical trajectory of information gathering.

State-Driven Enumeration

Colonial enumeration and census classification can be a state-driven, top-down project, as the governmentality and orientalism variants of this argument suggest. Applied to British direct rule of India, Foucault's (1975/1977, p. 19–21; 1991, pp. 101–102; 1978/2007, pp. 364–366; reviews in Rose et al., 2006, pp. 83, 86–87, and Scott, 1995, p. 193) work on governmentality and surveillance suggested that historically constituted complexes of knowledge and power shaped colonial projects of political sovereignty (Raman, 2012b, p. 230). Cohn (1987, p. 230; 1996, p. 3) argued that the direct rule British colonial censuses objectified caste and other categories used to order and govern the Indian population. Indians, in turn, viewed themselves and Indian society through the prism of official categories, politicizing caste divisions (Cohn, 1987, pp. 230, 250; Dirks, 1992, p. 76; 1997, p. 209; Kaviraj, 1997, p. 328). Official knowledge, once acquired, was deployed to dismantle old forms of life, replacing them with British colonial institutions, procedures, and calculations, giving rise to new power and knowledge regimes (Foucault, 1991, p. 92; Scott, 1995, p. 193; review in Kalpagam, 2000, pp. 39–40). These new forms of power and knowledge shaped the colonial ambitions of political sovereignty (cf. Scott, 1995, p. 193).

Thus, a governmentality framework links the classification and enumeration of subject populations with the administrative interests of direct Crown rule of India (Bhagat, 2006, p. 121; Kumar, 2004, p. 1,087; Pant, 1987, p. 148; R. S. Smith, 2000, p. 1; Walby & Haan, 2012, p. 302). A classified, enumerated, and territorially defined population was subject to interventions through laws and regulations (Kalpagam, 2000, p. 49; R. S. Smith, 1985, p. 155). In post-EIC India, laws limited which castes could serve in the army while identifying other castes and tribes as criminal (Kumar, 2004, p. 1,087). Official recognition and legal regulation of caste and other categories could create and widen social cleavages (Bhagat, 2001, pp. 4,353–4,355; 2003, p. 687). Divided populations, pitted against one another, were vulnerable to colonial subjugation (Bhagat, 2001, p. 4,353; review in Gill, 2007, p. 242). For P. Chatterjee (1993, pp. 15, 16–17), this "rule of colonial difference" became increasingly articulated in terms of perceived racial differences between colonizer and colonized. Caste differences,

PATRICIA AHMED ET AL.

too, were characterized in terms of race during direct rule, a view spurred on by anthropological surveys employing dubious methods (e.g., anthropometry; Christian, 2019, p. 175; Jenkins, 2003, pp. 1,148–1,149). H. H. Risley (1908/1915, pp. 273–277) presented a racial hierarchy of caste based on fieldwork and traditional Brahmanism (Christian, 2019, p. 175). Therefore, the governmentality perspective situates the creation, deployment, and enumeration of social categories within a larger program of colonial domination.

Similarly, Said (1978, pp. 72, 123) described orientalism as an anatomical and enumerative exercise that particularized and atomized local information, which was then reconstituted scientifically into official knowledge. Enumeration was a particularizing and divisive strategy. For example, Anderson (1983/2006, pp. 168–169) suggested that while colonial powers did not often construct new ethnic-racial categories, the state's systematic quantification of these identities crystallized previously fluid markers of social difference. Thus, gazetteers, anthropological studies, censuses, and other forms of official information divided colonial populations into manageable parts that could be distilled into official knowledge easily exploited by colonial powers (Dirks, 1996, p. ix; Said, 1978, p. 123). Hence, orientalist knowledge paved the way for what armies, administrations, and bureaucracies would later do on the ground (Said, 1978, p. 123). Inden (1990/2000, pp. 1, 5; review in King, 1999, pp. 90–92) similarly argued that creating knowledge of the other was an essentializing exercise that denied colonial subjects the ability to order their world.

These arguments can be applied to British direct rule. Colonial officials erroneously viewed Hinduism and, by extension, caste, as a key organizing principle (Bates, 1995, p. 229). Official recognition of these institutions effectively made them "real" (Cohn, 1987, p. 230; reviews in de Zwart, 2000, p. 246, and King, 1999, pp. 92–94, 116). For example, military enlistment, post-EIC, was limited to "marital castes/races" (e.g., Gurkhas, Pathans, Sikhs) deemed to be loyal, skilled warriors by virtue of their lineage (Chowdhry, 2013, p. 717; Rand & Wagner, 2012, p. 234). The 1871 Criminal Tribes Act went further, designating certain castes and tribes as "criminal," prompting widespread stigmatization of them (Kamble et al., 2023, pp. 3–6; Verghese, 2016, p. 1,623).

Major policy initiatives – both social- and resource-related – justified Crown rule; numerical data were exploited in the interest of disciplining colonial officials and the local population (Appadurai, 1993, pp. 319–320). Appadurai (1993, pp. 318–319) asserted that the official quantification of caste linked certain groups with social and moral differences, thus providing justificatory and disciplinary capabilities for direct rule. For Dirks (2001, p. 7), the "colonial leviathan" constructed caste as the "measure of all things social" in two ways: by framing caste both as an important marker of tradition and as a key instrument of knowledge and power. Enumeration of caste categories in the all-India census proved instrumental in this respect (Dirks, 2001, pp. 9, 14, 16).

In sum, the governmentality approach suggests that colonial states gathered copious amounts of data on their subjects, and the state then used this information for colonial domination. The orientalism approach implies that colonial states broke down and enumerated subjects in terms of social differences

244 *Historical Trajectories*

as part of a divide-and-conquer strategy. However, both state-driven approaches arrive at the same conclusion: Colonial officials appropriated previously existing fluid, if not dubious, social categories and turned them into instruments of domination through official processes of enumeration. Thus, under direct British rule, caste emerged as a key instrument to subdue and control the Indian population.

Society-Driven Enumeration

Nevertheless, states simply cannot impose identities on subjects (de Zwart, 2000, p. 246). De Zwart (2000, p. 238) argued that such a position afforded colonial regimes too much power: If imperial administrators invented a social structure and convinced generations of people that this structure was real, this would constitute "a remarkable feat of social engineering." This sentiment is echoed by the "subaltern" school, which likewise suggests that state-centered approaches often deny Indians (especially nonelite Indians) agency and subjectivity (R. Guha, 1997, p. 3; O'Hanlon, 1988, p. 196; Prakash, 1994, p. 1,478; Spivak, 1988, pp. 280–281). Furthermore, from this perspective, British direct rule drew on previous historical periods. For example, EIC understandings of Indian society came from native informants who endorsed constructs, such as caste, which served the latter's interests (U. Chakravarti, 1998, p. 48; Frykenberg, 1993, p. 534; Viswanathan, 2003, p. 37; review in Gelders & Balagangadhara, 2011, p. 103). Caste categories carried over into direct rule and informed colonial policy (Parsons, 1999, pp. 54–55, 57–58). To gain information during direct rule, Crown officials likewise, in keeping with previous rulers (Sultans, Mughals, EIC), gathered and organized information, assisted by key native groups, including Western-educated clerks and administrators, who possessed both inside knowledge and administrative skills (Seal, 1968, pp. 8–9; 1973, pp. 331–332; see also review in Chakrabarty, 2000, p. 9).[2] Therefore, in this view, local economic and class imperatives influenced colonial understandings of native social institutions, such as caste, during the EIC and direct rule periods.

Interactive (State and Society) Enumeration

Our interactive approach has been directly applied to the Indian case, but only in passing (Emigh et al., 2021, pp. 13–16). However, it can be applied to the Indian case by showing, first, that direct rule drew knowledge from previous historical periods and, second, that the effects of information gathering during direct rule stemmed from the interactions of state and social actors. First, like the society-centered perspective, this interactive approach draws on a longer time frame to show that British direct rule depended on previous EIC actions. C. A. Bayly (1988/2006, pp. 5–6, 155–158; 1996, p. 8) argued that EIC administration and knowledge of India was shaped by Indian gentry, scribes, rural resistance, and Brahmanical influence. Relatedly, Raj (2000, pp. 120–121) asserted that EIC knowledge emerged from accommodation and negotiation between colonial state and native social actors, producing novel forms of knowledge. Under direct rule, colonial administrators used this knowledge to promote hybrid (Indian and British) institutions to legitimize their rule, but this also concretized tensions between Hindus and Muslims (Parsons, 1999, pp. 56–58).

Second, existing categories, such as caste, were transformed as result of state–society interactions. S. Guha (2003, p. 149) critiqued state-centered accounts that assumed that the British extracted revenue and labor from previously "homogenous and isolated" colonial subjects. The EIC, and later the British state to an even greater degree, carried out these processes by honing into various statuses embedded within existing social hierarchies, enhancing the significance of caste in the process (S. Guha, 2003, pp. 149, 156–163; Jaffrelot, 2000, pp. 757–758; Peabody, 2001, p. 841). The British Indian census was pivotal in this regard as it contained detailed caste listings (Jaffrelot, 2000, pp. 757–758). Various groups mobilized and formed caste associations to pressure colonial officials to elevate their caste in the census (Carroll, 1978, pp. 233–234; Jaffrelot, 2000, pp. 757–758; Jenkins, 2003, pp. 1,150–1,151).

Furthermore, direct rule could not be sustained solely on military might and thus relied heavily on the cooperation of key native groups (Copland, 2001, pp. 5–6, 10–11). The Crown controlled about one-third of the territory of the Indian subcontinent; the rest consisted of princely states (Copland, 2001, pp. 7–8). Colonial officials created alliances with Indian princes: The latter provided military support to the British on the condition of being left to rule in peace (Copland, 2001, p. 8). This further connected British rule to Indian tradition, as princes were considered to have descended from god-kings (Copland, 2001, p. 8). Nonetheless, this system of parallel rule weakened the colonial state's monopoly of violence due to its limited presence in substantial areas of India (Sakstrup, 2023, pp. 7–8). State power also rested partly on the exploitation of caste divisions by extending and withholding favors to or from rival castes or making administrative decisions that favored one group over another (Carroll, 1978, p. 234; Copland, 2001, pp. 9–10). For example, "reservation" policies reserved some Indian civil service positions for *Dalits* (so-called "untouchables"; Fuller & Narasimhan, 2010, p. 477).

HISTORICAL TRAJECTORIES LEADING TO INFORMATION GATHERING UNDER BRITISH DIRECT RULE

Thus, while the state-driven arguments suggest that the direct rule censuses had dramatic effects, the society-driven and the interactive approaches cast doubt on this interpretation. In addition, state-driven claims about the effects of information gathering during direct rule often lack temporal evidence in two ways. First, they rarely provide specific evidence that could provide "before" and "after" measures of information gathering to show that it had some particular effect during direct rule. Second, they rarely consider long-term historical trajectories of British direct rule information gathering, so they do not always account for the EIC or pre-British colonial periods, when state–society interactions were likely most influential in shaping later, India-wide censuses (de Zwart, 2000, p. 238; Parsons, 1999, p. 58; Raj, 2000, pp. 120–121; B. Singh, 2022, p. 269; Smits, 2008, pp. 13–14; Spodek, 2013, p. 55). Thus, key controversies emerging from empirical studies of direct rule in India may underestimate the extent to which, if any, native categories, information-gathering techniques, or native informants existed before British direct rule and thus influenced direct rule British activities (C. A. Bayly, 1988/2006, pp. 5–6, 155–158; 1996, p. 8). To examine the long-term historical trajectories of state–society information gathering, we start much further back in history. The Indian case is particularly interesting because there were many historical waves of colonialism before the European ones. Furthermore, we explicitly apply our theoretical perspective to an analysis of information-gathering arguments: While we have categorized scholarship as taking a society-driven or interactive approach, it does not necessarily explicitly consider our three key relationships (lay categories, information intellectuals, and power) important to understanding long-term historical trajectories of information gathering.

To do so, we return to these key relationships. First, in each period, we consider the lay categories. To what extent was caste used as a category of social difference by social actors and in what institutions (S. Guha, 2003, p. 155; Peabody, 2001, p. 819)? Second, what information intellectuals translated these lay categories into official ones (Bellenoit, 2017, pp. 1–2; Raman, 2012a, pp. 2, 8)? Third, what was the power relationship between these state and social actors (U. Chakravarti, 1998, p. 48; Viswanathan, 2003, p. 37)? It is important to consider whether social actors pressed state actors to take up the information collecting, or whether state actors demanded that the information be collected. Fourth, in each period, we also try to assess the outcome of attempts at information gathering. What official information was collected, and was it applied in social and state institutions to some transformative effect? Finally, we answer these questions in the context of our examination of historical trajectories of information gathering, so we consider how these patterns changed over the long durée. These orienting questions help us explore whether the historical trajectories correspond to the state-driven, society-driven, or interactive information-gathering perspective.

These four orienting questions also provide us the historical backdrop to the censuses of British direct rule. That is, in general, did the British introduce new techniques with transformative effects (state driven), did they borrow from pre-existing categories (society driven), or was there an interplay between British officials and the Indian populace (the interactive perspective)? A state-centered approach suggests that British administrators, during direct rule, deployed novel and obscure caste categories to order and subjugate the population. These categories, deployed in censuses, had transformative effects. It also suggests that state actors developed and deployed categories of official information gathering with relative ease. If this is the case, we should find little evidence of the collection of information about caste in the historical periods leading up to Crown rule, and, where it was collected, it should not have been transformative. A society-driven approach suggests that caste categories were widely used, even before direct British rule, translated into legal/official categories by information intellectuals, and deployed without controversy. If this is the case, the record should show a seamless transition, in terms of these categories, between successive regimes. The transformative effects of caste categories would be evident mostly where social actors pressed state actors to take up these categories and incorporate them into their administration. Finally, an interactive approach would imply a high degree of state–society interaction with respect to colonial enumeration. If this is the case, we should find that historical trajectories – including prior legacies of literacy, numeracy, and information gathering; lay categories; information intellectuals' interventions; and power relations – interact dialectically with state and social interests to create effective and transformative enumeration projects.

DATA AND METHODS

We analyze three time periods to tease out the historical development of official information gathering in India. Our sources include early Vedic/post-Vedic sources such as the Vedas, *Śutra*s, and *Smriti*s, which shed light on how early Indian society and culture affected subsequent periods; travelogues composed by early foreign visitors; and various administrative reports (*Nāmāh*s, EIC statistical reports, etc.). We supplement these data with key secondary sources. We use historical narrative – frequently used in comparative historical sociology – to understand processes and events unfolding over time to produce a particular outcome. Narrative allows us to explore and explicate trajectories or patterns that explain how and why information gathering took particular forms (Abbott, 1992, p. 428; Aminzade, 1992, p. 462; Griffin, 2007, p. 4; Lange, 2013, p. 43).

First, we examine the pre-Vedic–Gupta period to gain insight into early Indian society–state interactions with respect to information gathering. In early Harappan society, this phenomenon likely was absent, as there is little indication that nation-state-like entities existed (McIntosh, 2008, p. 90; SarDesai, 2008, p. 22). Early Vedic polities consisted of small tribal units headed by chiefs; later Vedic polities consisted of small kingdoms and tribal republics (Prasad, 2015, p. 91; SarDesai, 2008, p. 66). Smaller polities gradually were subsumed under larger polities, giving rise to dynastic empires (e.g., Maurya and Gupta) that organized large areas of India into a single state, intensifying the interplay between state and social actors, elites, information gathering, and official classification (Thapar, 2006, p. 291). The second period, the medieval, signals a transition to Persianate rule over large areas of South Asia by Afghan-Turkic invaders. Early Sultanate regimes were bureaucratized and information intensive; the Mughals represented the most sophisticated information gathering and record keeping prior to British colonialism. In the third period, the EIC became increasingly involved in politics and territorial governance and needed information for administrative purposes. In each period, we explore the presence of caste categories and the extent to which they reflected state and social interests and their interactions. To do so, we

248 *Historical Trajectories*

answer the orienting questions concerning lay categories, information intellectuals, the relative power of state and social actors, and historical trajectories, and the outcomes outlined above.

OFFICIAL INFORMATION GATHERING

Pre-Vedic Through the Gupta Period (ca. 3300 BCE Until 700 CE)

Information Gathering and Its Social Uses

Indian society supported information gathering over thousands of years. Some institutions date back to 3300 BCE along the Indus and Saraswati Rivers, in the absence of formal governance (Green, 2022, pp. 2, 14; McIntosh, 2008, p. 90; SarDesai, 2008, p. 22).[3] Artifacts suggest commercial transactions used complex, highly standardized weights and measures, calculated with decimals (Avari, 2007, p. 45; Ghanta & Mukherjee, 2020, p. 12). Excavations have revealed time and space measurements and intricate, mathematically based civil planning (Avari, 2007, p. 46; Ghanta & Mukherjee, 2020, p. 12). Written, yet-to-be-deciphered, inscriptions date back to 3000–2700 BCE (Avari, 2007, pp. 32, 43, 50–51).

Caste, or some approximation of it, may date back to Indus Valley Civilization (3300–1300 BCE; Bhattacharya, 1990, p. 641). Karve (1961, pp. 57–58) asserted that caste-like groups existed in Harappan society, citing evidence of occupational residential segregation that mirrored later caste segregation.[4] Incoming Indo-Aryans adapted this social structure, creating three top tiers for themselves (Brahmin, Kshatriya, and Vaisya) while lumping indigenous *Dasas* into the bottom tier (Sudra; Karve, 1961, p. 57; review in Berreman, 1967, p. 353). Kosambi (1944, pp. 247–248), alternatively, proposed that some Vaisya and Sudra groups derived from indigenous Indus Valley tribes and clans and assimilated into the Indo-Aryan caste structure (reviews in Habib, 2008, p. 87 and Thapar, 2008, pp. 44–45). He asserted that Brahmins originated from a mixing of Indus Valley and Aryan priests, citing ancient references to Brahmins of indigenous origin (*dashya-putra brahmana*) (Kosambi, 1965/1975, pp. 102–106; Thapar, 2003, p. 122; 2008, p. 45). Furthermore, no analogous priestly classes emerged in other contemporaneous Aryan societies (Kosambi, 1965/1975, p. 99; review in Deshpande, 2008, p. 176; cf. Thapar, 2003, pp. 64–65).[5]

The Vedic period (ca. 1700–600 BCE) commenced with the migration of Indo-Aryans into South Asia (Avari, 2007, pp. 60, 64). Most knowledge of this period derives from ancient literature due to a dearth of archaeological evidence (Avari, 2007, p. 69; Keay, 2000, pp. xvii–xviii; Vyas, 1967, p. 1). Classical texts were originally transmitted orally due to Brahmanical wariness of the written word (Fleming, 2016, p. 32; Joshi, 2018, p. 87; Lo Turco, 2013, p. 85). This proscription only applied to the upper castes; thus, scribes were often drawn from an indigenous, non-Aryan tribe, the Ambasthas, later assimilated as Kayasthas (Bellenoit, 2014, p. 886; Lo Turco, 2013, p. 85; Talbot, 2012, p. 360; Thapar, 1971, p. 429). Over time, however, writing and scribes (*lekhaka*) grew in importance (Lo Turco, 2013, p. 86; Visvanathan, 2014, pp. 33–37; Vyas, 1967,

PATRICIA AHMED ET AL.

pp. 163–164). Early mentions of scribes appear in the *Vishnu Sutra* (*The Institutes of Vishnu*, ca. 300 BCE–1000 CE/1900, p. 46–48), the *Yajnavalkya Smriti* (ca. 300–500 CE/1918, pp. 214–218), and the *Harsacharita* (Das, 1980, p. 940; Jolly, 1900, p. xxiv). Denoting scribes as Kayasthas dates to at least 171–172 CE, as scribes coalesced into occupational castes (Visvanathan, 2014, p. 37). The Kayasthas remained an important scribal group throughout Indian history.

Early Vedic texts (ca. 1500 BCE) indicate the use of a regularized decimal system (Plofker, 2009, pp. 13–14). Sophisticated geometric techniques guided the construction of religious structures, as prescribed in later Vedic texts, including the *Sata-Patha-Brahāmana* and the *Śulva Sutrā*s (*Satapatha-Brâhmana*, 1000–600 BCE/1897, pp. 1–149; see also Plofker, 2009, pp. 16–29; Puttaswamy, 2000, pp. 409–421; Sridharan, 2005, pp. 3–6).[6] Rough population estimates (ca. 1500 BCE) are found in the *Puranas* (ancient Hindu texts), though the numbers were likely inflated (R. B. Martin, 1981, pp. 61–62; Shembavnekar, 1952, p. 84).

Early Vedic polities consisted of a few major and many smaller tribal units headed by chiefs (Prasad, 2015, p. 91). Circa 1000 BCE, Indo-Aryan tribes expanded their political and cultural influence vis-á-vis the indigenous population, forming small kingdoms (*rajan*s) and tribal republics (*gana*s) (SarDesai, 2008, p. 65). In the former, there were early overlapping caste interests. Rulers of these kingdoms usually were Kshatriya, their ministerial cabinets staffed by Brahmins (SarDesai, 2008, p. 61). Over time, larger kingdoms swallowed up smaller ones, creating the need for specialized administrators and functionaries (*Ratnin*s, or "king's jewels"), including tax collectors and treasurers (*Saṃgrahītṛ*) (Prasad, 2015, p. 112; SarDesai, 2008, p. 66). Tax collection became more formalized (S. K. Sharma, 2012, p. 214; U. B. Singh, 1998, p. 15). Per the *Dharmasūtra of Gautama* (Gautama, ca. 600–200 BCE/1999, p. 95): "Farmers shall pay one-tenth, or one-eighth, or one-sixth of their produce. ... there is a tax of one-fiftieth on cattle and gold. ... a duty of one-twentieth on merchandise, and one-sixtieth on roots, fruits, flowers, medicine, honey, meat, grass, and firewood." Other *Dharmasūtra*s exempted scholars, women, students, disabled persons, and Brahmins from taxes (Āpastamba, ca. 450–350 BCE/1999, p. 70; Vasiṣṭha, ca. 300 BCE–100 CE/1999, pp. 251, 301). Population information was likely gathered and reported orally by a petty official (*gopa*), who knew the names, numbers, and occupations of small sections of households in each town (Shembavnekar, 1952, p. 84).

Caste may reflect "racialized" differences between light-skinned Indo-Aryans and dark-skinned *Dasas*, since *varna* (generally translated as caste) meant "color" in some contexts (Ayyar & Khandare, 2013, p. 75; Chandel, 2018, p. 357; Ghurye, 1932/1969, p. 46; Mukherjee, 1988, pp. 23–24; cf. Thapar, 2003, pp. 13, 112). The four-caste (*varna*) typology was first mentioned in a *Rigvedic* (ca. 1500–1200 BCE) work, the "Hymn of Man" (*Purushasukta*) (Mukherjee, 1988, p. 24). The hymn describes the origin of the four castes from the primal man Purusha: "The Brahmana ... is the mouth of Purusha. ... Kshatriya ... is created as the arms of defence. ... The Vaishya is the thighs. ... [T]he Shudra ... bears the burden of the human family as the legs" (Rigveda, ca. 1500–1200 BCE/2013, p. 875).

This myth established the precedence of the priestly class: Brahmins were created first and were considered to constitute the mouth, head, or foremost

250   *Historical Trajectories*

component of society (*Artharva-Veda Saṁhitā*, ca. 1200–1000 BCE/1905, p. 934; B. K. Smith, 1994, p. 34). *Varna* appeared in subsequent contemporaneous texts following this first mention (Mukherjee, 1988, p. 24), legitimating caste and Brahmin superiority with "canonical" authority (B. K. Smith, 1992, p. 106; 1994, pp. 32–36; Thapar, 2003, pp. 9–10; review in Prasad, 2015, pp. 124–125).

For example, Brahmins were likened to gods (*Artharva-Veda Saṁhitā*, ca. 1200–1000 BCE/1905, p. 639; *Satapatha-Brâhmana*, 1000–600 BCE/1897, p. 59–60). The *Śata-Patha-Brahāmana* (*Satapatha-Brâhmana*, 1000–600 BCE/1897, p. 338–339) further stated that "there is no thing greater [than the Brahmin]; ... the greatest, becomes the highest among his own people. ... and ever higher will be the descendants that spring from [the Brahmin]." Thus, early caste categories plausibly were tied to high caste interests.

Caste boundaries were likely reinforced by the *Manusmṛiti* (ca. 100 CE), an influential legal text that promoted the *varna* system (S. Bayly, 1999, p. 13). The *Manusmṛiti* reiterated the caste origin myth and provided detailed descriptions of duties (*dharma*) by caste (Manu, ca. 100–300/1999, pp. 74–75, 133–137). It also prescribed caste purity through endogamy: Mixing castes created "imperfect" castes (Manu, ca. 100–300/1999, p. 8).

The creation of "outcaste" groups bolsters the notion of caste as a mechanism of elite control. References to so-called "untouchables" (*cāṇḍāla*s) appear late in the Vedic period (Thapar, 2003, p. 154). The *Dharmasūtra*s disparaged this group in various ways. For example, Vedic recitation was suspended in villages if a corpse or *cāṇḍāla* was present, and ancestral offerings were ruined if viewed by a dog or *cāṇḍāla* (Āpastamba, ca. 450–350 BCE/1999, p. 18; Gautama, ca. 600–200 BCE/1999, pp. 105–106). It was sinful to touch, look at, or speak to a *cāṇḍāla*, and evil Brahmins would be reborn as *cāṇḍāla*s (Āpastamba, ca. 450–350 BCE/1999, p. 70). The shift to an agrarian economy and urbanization intensified caste stratification and Brahmanic control circa 800–600 BCE (U. Chakravarti, 1993, p. 581).

The foregoing describes the emergence and idealized (from the point of view of Brahmin ascendancy) purposes of an ascription-based *varna* system. Yet, sources indicate some fluidity. A character in the *Rāmayāṇa* epic, Viśhvāmitra, is transformed through intense asceticism (*tapas*) from Kshatriya to Brahman (Sathaye, 2015, pp. 2–3; Vyas, 1967, p. 67). However, other evidence of fluidity in Vedic texts is sparse and inconclusive, given their Brahmin authorship; strict rules ensured the pre-eminence of the sacerdotal caste (B. K. Smith, 1994, pp. 28, 32, 36).

Gradually, large areas of India become unified under Mauryan rule (321 BCE–184 BCE) into a more complex polity (Avari, 2007, p. 106; R. Chakravarti, 2016, p. 1–2; Thapar, 2006, p. 304). Writing and literacy became more common: For example, state edicts were carved into various pillars and rock formations during Ashoka the Great's rule (268–232 BCE) (Kosmin, 2014, p. 42). Xuanzang, a Chinese traveler visiting during this period, noted that the area of every kingdom, province, and principality had been ascertained in ancient India (Shembavnekar, 1952, p. 85).[7] Scribes gained political relevance and professional status. Royal service was limited to those with "knowledge of all conventions" who were "quick in composition and have good handwriting" (Kauṭilya, ca. 300

PATRICIA AHMED ET AL.

BCE/1992, p. 213). Census-taking was linked with good governance as stressed by royal advisor Kauṭilya (ca. 300 BCE/1992, p. 220; R. B. Martin, 1981, p. 62; Nambiar, 1981, p. 7) in his statecraft treatise, *Arthaśāstra* (ca. 300 BCE). Chandragupta Maurya's (321–297 BCE) state systematically registered births and deaths in the capital of Pātaliputra, likely for informational and tax purposes (V. A. Smith, 1904, pp. 120–121). Six groups of administrators ran Pātaliputra's bureaucracy (Kosmin, 2014, p. 42). Officials used village population registers, generated by paid accountants, who gathered data on occupation, age, caste, income, and household expenditures (Das Gupta, 1972, pp. 419, 421; Durand, 1977, p. 265; Kauṭilya, ca. 300 BCE/1992, p. 220).[8] Other ancient texts (ca. 400–600 CE) indicate that Indian statesmen remained preoccupied with quality intelligence gathering (C. A. Bayly, 1996, p. 12).

The significance of caste extended beyond the religious realm, as indicated by visitors to India during this period. A Greek diplomat, Megasthênes (ca. 310 BCE/1877, pp. 7, 40–44; Arrian, ca. 150 CE/1877, p. 209), visiting the court of Chandragupta Maurya circa 304–303 BCE, cited the Indian caste system in his travelogue, *Indica*, though he noted seven, not four major castes (see also Bosworth, 1996, p. 113; Ghurye, 1932/1969, p. 1–2). Megasthênes's (ca. 310 BCE/1877, pp. 43–44, 85, 86; Arrian, ca. 150 CE/1877, p. 212) account supported earlier Vedic pronouncements related to caste and caste endogamy.

Caste was also cited in the classical Gupta period (320–520 CE) and beyond in the writings of Chinese pilgrims visiting India (ca. 399–695 CE). A monk, Fâ-Hien(ca. 414/1886, pp. 38, 45, 47, 55–56, 61, 78), traveling in India from 400 to 415 CE (Beal, 1869, p. vii), mentioned Brahmins, Vaishyas, and *cāṇḍāla*s (outcastes) in his diary. Watters (1904, p. 168) noted that Xuanzang, who resided in India from 629 to 645 CE, acknowledged caste divisions:

There are four orders. ... The first ... the Brahmins ... keep their principles ... strictly observing ceremonial purity. The second ... the Kshatriyas ... has held sovereignty for many generations. ... The third ... the Vaiśyas ... barter commodities and pursue gain. ... The fourth ... the Śūdras ... toil at cultivating the soil. ... The members of a caste marry within the caste.

Another pilgrim, I-Tsing (ca. 689/1896, p. 182), while in India (671–695 CE), wrote: "The Brahmans are regarded throughout the five parts of India as the most honorable (caste). They do not ... associate with the other three castes." Thus, outsiders noted the use of caste.

Emergent states aspired to gather household-level information on caste (*varna*), occupation, and other indicators, as well as village-level characteristics, such as the number of water tanks and livestock (Bhattacharya, 1990, p. 642; J. K. Ghosh et al., 1999, p. 14; Kauṭilya, ca. 300 BCE/1992, pp. 220, 222; Nambiar, 1981, p. 7). Kauṭilya (ca. 300 BCE/1992, p. 499; J. K. Ghosh et al., 1999, p. 14) advocated the validation of official data by spies, who verified information such as individuals' incomes, prices, land, tax assessments and remissions, agricultural output, and the caste and profession of families.[9]

State and social actors' interests aligned along caste lines, albeit in limited ways. Kayastha scribes parlayed their growing importance into higher status, though their placement (Brahman, Kshatriya, etc.) in the caste system varied regionally (Gupta, 1983, pp. 195–196; Leonard, 1978, p. 12; Thapar, 2018, p. 133). The symbiotic relationship between Kshatriyas (the kingly caste) and Brahmins continued in many areas of India (Prasad, 2015, p. 119). Kshatriyas needed Brahmins to establish and maintain rule, as the latter exercised the rights of coronation, legitimation, and advice (Chandel, 2018, pp. 358, 360; Lo Turco, 2013, pp. 88–89; Subramaniam, 2009, p. 60; Thapar, 1984, p. 790). Brahmins, in turn, relied on rulers for patronage and support for their high social status (Dayma, 2006, p. 160; Lo Turco, 2013, pp. 88–89; SarDesai, 2008, pp. 66–67). Mutual interdependence fostered the formation of a Brahmin-Kshatriya (*Brahma-Kṣhatria*) power elite (Dayma, 2006, p. 160; Prasad, 2015, pp. 119, 131–132, 145; SarDesai, 2008, p. 67).

Social and State Uses of Caste

We return to our orienting questions. Our first question asked about lay categories, and, in particular, to what extent caste was used as a category of social difference by social actors and in what institutions. Our evidence suggests that caste was used as a category of social difference during this period. Although scarce, writings about everyday life, such as travelers' reports, indicate that caste was an established part of society. Some sources indicate that caste may have been fluid (Sathaye, 2015, pp. 2–3; Vyas, 1967, p. 67). Caste also appeared in religious documents. While it is difficult to discern from existing evidence, religious rites prohibiting the presence of certain groups suggest that caste played some role in social identity. In addition, caste seems to have played some role in social control. It appears that upper status groups used caste to maintain social control (e.g., higher castes over *cāṇḍāla*s). Our second question asked whether and to what extent information intellectuals translated these lay categories into official ones. Scribes emerged as information intellectuals who were able to translate caste into official information-collecting activities. Third, while we lack detailed evidence about power relationships, given the thin historical record, upper-caste interests and state rule seem to have become intertwined later during this period, as seen in symbiotic relationships between Brahmin priests and Kshatriya rulers. Fourth, we assessed the outcomes of information gathering by asking what information was collected and whether it was applied in social and state institutions to some transformative effect. We note that during this period, caste was used in state records, including censuses and tax documents. The distinctions appear in legal documents (various *Śastra*s, etc.) as well. However, we have no evidence that this information collection had any transformative power or changed the nature of the category of caste.

Finally, we try to assess the historical trajectory of information gathering. We note that the lay categories of caste and basic features of literacy and numeracy seem to predate official information gathering. They were established perhaps as early as 3300 BC. The roots of caste seem to have been located in religious, occupational, or ethnic and racial differences. States also began to collect official information perhaps as early as circa 1500–800 BCE. They collected information for taxation, often through local or locally knowledgeable officials and scribes,

PATRICIA AHMED ET AL. 253

who could translate that information into official records. These scribes pressed for more political power based on their position as information collectors. These differences were incorporated into the state structure, plausibly by the *Manusmṛiti*, a legal text written around 100 CE that reinforced caste, and this may have had social consequences. There is little evidence that the enumeration per se affected changes in consciousness or identity, though clearly caste, though still fluid, was increasing in importance.

In sum, this pattern of information gathering was primarily society driven: The lay categories of caste were translated into official information categories by scribes. Scribes were essential to state actors, who lacked the capacity to collect the information on their own. State actors then took up these categories into their governing practices, which in turn probably affected the social structure (although we have no direct evidence during this period). There is little evidence that state actors themselves devised these categories, or that enumeration itself affected categories of caste. Thus, during this period, the historical trajectory was strongly shaped by socially driven patterns. However, there was considerable interaction between the state and social actors over the collection of information about caste.

Medieval Period (ca. 700–1700 CE)

Information Gathering and Its Social Uses

Indian political development after 1000 CE was strongly influenced by successive waves of Muslim invaders, culminating in the establishment of regional sultanates and, late during this period, the strong, consolidated Mughal state, which monopolized force in large areas of India (Eaton, 2019, pp. 13, 35; Richards, 1997, pp. 206–207).[10] Both political systems exploited native scribal elites for information gathering and to establish and staff more bureaucratized modes of governance, creating a unique fusion of Persian and Sanskritic administrative models (Eaton, 2019, pp. 13, 35). The earlier sultanate model, which included ranked and salaried bureaucracies linked with state land revenue (*iqta'*) and military systems, dated back to Mahmud of Ghazni's occupation of Punjab (ca. 1033 CE). Economic, political, and social favors emanated from the ruler to his subjects (Ahmed, 2016, p. 6; Peabody, 2003, p. 3). In early medieval Indian states (both Hindu and Muslim), strength was most concentrated within the center and adjacent territories and waned in more remote areas of a given polity (Jackson, 1999, p. 87; Stein, 1985, p. 394). The Delhi Sultanate, for example, consisted of a cluster of military strongholds and taxed agrarian hinterlands, taking the form of a nexus of several directly and indirectly administered regions (Ahmed, 2016, pp. 1–2).

Sultanate rule adapted Hindu administrative systems and benefited from the cooperation and services of local dignitaries and scribes (Eaton, 2019, pp. 17, 135, 155; Raman, 2012a, p. 11).[11] Information was essential to the functioning of the sultanates. Anafasy Nikitin (1985, p. 27), a Russian traveler (ca. 1450 CE), noted Hindu (*kâfir*) scribes working for the sultan of Bidar (Bahami Sultanate). Native officials and clerks became proficient in Persian (used in state bureaucracies) and the *insha'* (courtly writing) style (Eaton, 2019, pp. 115–116; Haider, 2011, pp. 268, 270). Initially, the state kept all records in Persian; over time, scribes recorded local business in regional vernaculars as well (Bellenoit, 2017, p. 34; Eaton, 2019, p. 135; Raman, 2012a, p. 11; Welch et al., 2002, p. 16). Central authorities established local sources of knowledge, initially at the subdivisional (*pargana*) level (Kulkarni, 2017, p. 325). A 14th-century Arab traveler, Ibn Baṭṭūṭa, noted that in the Delhi Sultanate, every 100 villages were assigned a headman and an accountant treasurer who provided needed data (S. Guha, 2013, p. 147). Similar officers carried out these duties on the west coast (S. Guha, 2013, p. 147).

Though detailed accountings of official information gathering during the early medieval period are scarce, evidence suggests that it did occur. Kúfi (1900/2008, p. 152) noted ruler Muhammad Kasim's census of all merchants and artisans taken in eighth-century Sind. Certain taxes, such as the *usher* (imposed on Muslim land holders) and *jizya* (imposed on non-Muslims), implied mechanisms of religious and caste differentiation since many sultans exempted Brahmins from the *jizya* (S. Guha, 2003, p. 150; Jackson, 1999, p. 286; Mahajan, 1991/2018, p. 293; Moosvi, 2011, pp. 5–6).

Various indigenous institutions, including India's legacy of popular literacy and numeracy, greatly facilitated state information gathering. While literacy rates among the lower Indian castes and classes remained low, India was otherwise a highly literate society during this period (C. A. Bayly, 1996, pp. 36–37, 39–40). Ultimately, paper records became the preferred form of testimony in adjudications and as a source of official information (C. A. Bayly, 1993, p. 11; 1996, p. 41). Official documents and orders were transported daily, along with private letters, by a dense network of runners and camel-riding mail carriers (C. A. Bayly, 1993, p. 11; 1996, p. 40). The status of scribes and other administrative workers increased significantly by the late medieval period (Alam & Subrahmanyam, 2010, pp. 394–395).

Furthermore, state and local interests aligned along caste lines, as most Hindu officials were higher status (e.g., Kayastha, Khatri, and Brahmin) (Haider, 2011, p. 266), though these alliances were often limited. In northern India, Kayasthas provided many of the mundane requirements of sultanate courts (O'Hanlon, 2013, pp. 776–777). In the Deccan sultanates, local officials and scribes tended to be Brahmin; later Kayastha migrants vied for these positions (S. Guha, 2010, pp. 506–508; Kulkarni, 2017, pp. 325–326; O'Hanlon, 2010, pp. 576–578; 2013, pp. 775, 777). Brahmin, Vaidya, and Kayastha scribes in Bengal rose in prominence, given their high educational attainment and proximity to political power (K. Chatterjee, 2010, p. 448). Many scribal families served subsequent rulers for generations (K. Chatterjee, 2010, pp. 452–453).

While early Muslim conquests were violent, sultans typically neither questioned nor interfered much with the local social order. Rather, most sultans tolerated and accommodated Hindu religion and culture in various ways (Avari, 2013, p. 71; Eaton, 2019, p. 16; Elius et al., 2020, pp. 10–11).[12] Hindus were granted protected status (*dhimmi*) in exchange for payment of the *jizya* (Jackson, 1999, pp. 281–282). Thus, caste differences remained somewhat relevant, as noted by foreign visitors. For example, Persian scholar Al Bīrūnī (1910a, pp. 100–101; 1910b, pp. 236–238), writing during the reign of Mahmud of Ghazni (ca. 1030 CE), noted the four-*varna* system and duties incurred by each caste; he also noted the existence of *cāṇḍāla*s. Marco Polo (ca. 1300/1958, p. 277), visiting India in the 13th century, told of the province of Lar, the original geographical location of the Brahmans. He noted that the Brahmans were distinguished by an emblem consisting of a thick cotton cord tied around their torsos, across their chests, and under their arms (Polo, ca. 1300/1958, p. 277). The Venetian *Nicolò* Conti reported that Brahmins were of "superior cultivation" and "distinguished by greater sanctity of life and manners" (Bracciolini, ca. 1439–1448/1857, p. 25). The Bolognese traveler Ludovico di Varthema (1510/1863, p. 142), visiting India in the 16th century, echoed these observations: "These two last classes of people ... may not approach either the Naeri or the Brahmins within fifty paces. ... and when they pass through ... they always go crying out with a loud voice ... in order that they not meet ... the Naeri or the Brahmins."[13]

However, caste was not always specified in terms of the *varna* system (i.e., Brahman, Kshatriya, Vaishya, Sudra). Al Idrīsī (1145/1867, p. 76), an Arab geographer exploring India (ca. 1100 CE), noted seven Hindu castes: the Sákriya (kingly caste), the Brahmans (religious caste), the Kshatriya (warrior caste), the Shárduva (laborers), the Basya (artisans), the Sabdáliya (singers), and the Zakya (musicians). These different interpretations of caste speak to its fluidity (Boivin, 2005, p. 228; Dirks, 2001, pp. 19–42; Jaiswal, 1997, p. 7; Sundar, 2000, p. 117). They also indicate a popular tendency to conflate *varna* with *jati* (subcaste); eventually, the two would become indistinguishable in many contexts (Penumala, 2010, p. 407).

Late medieval information gathering intensified with the rise of Mughal power. The Mughal Empire (ca. 1526–1721 CE), founded by Zahir-uddin Muhammad Bābur in 1526, emerged as one of the largest and strongest premodern colonial states, ruling a population of over 100 million and a vast territory (Richards, 1993, pp. 1, 6, 206–207). The Mughal state was centralized and intrusive, able to project power substantially beyond its core lands (Moosvi, 2014, p. 236). By 1690, the polity ruled over most of the subcontinent, raising taxes, maintaining political stability, and monopolizing force (Richards, 1997, p. 206).

Mughal information gathering was expansive. Mughal emperors prized knowledge and were renowned for their sophisticated spying and data-gathering systems (C. A. Bayly, 1993, pp. 29–30; 1996, pp. 10, 12). Population and other data using *khana shumari*s (household registers) gathered information comparable to that prescribed earlier by Kauṭilya (ca. 300 BCE/1992, pp. 220, 222). The Mughals conducted extensive cadastral surveys (*zabt*) to assess taxes (Richards, 1993, p. 85). The cadastral surveys mirrored future colonial information-gathering endeavors: Field workers gathered data meticulously and systematically. The data were then subjected regularly to quality checks during collection and tabulation (Richards, 1993, p. 83). In keeping with the sultanates, the Mughals used high-caste Hindus to gather, collate, and disseminate official information (K. Chatterjee, 2010, p. 456; Kinra, 2010, pp. 557–558). Many recruits served prior administrations and exhibited high degrees of occupational adaptability by seizing these new opportunities (K. Chatterjee, 2010, pp. 456–457; Haider, 2011, p. 267). Local scribes and administrators were in high demand by Mughal officials in Bengal; their numbers increased greatly within imperial administration (K. Chatterjee, 2010, p. 459). Kayastha scribes were regarded highly by Mughal administrations, having already mastered courtly writing and documentation skills (Bellenoit, 2014, pp. 883, 885). These talents were parlayed into various official positions, including registrars (*qanungo*s), revenue accountants (*shomarnavi*s), and surveyors (Bellenoit, 2014, p. 883).

The Mughals adapted existing technologies into their political and administrative culture (Fisher, 1993, p. 46). Innovations included the employment of news and information writers (*akhbār nawīs*) to gather and collect specific types of official information (Fisher, 1993, p. 45; Sah, 2019, p. 293). Emperor Akbar (1542–1605 CE) similarly created an elaborate system of court diarists (*wāqi'a nawīs*) to record official acts, words, and events of his reign (Fisher, 1993, p. 47). The diarists recorded official appointments, salaries, tax assessment, marriages and births, and other vital data from various state and local officials (Fisher, 1993, p. 47; Sah, 2019, pp. 293–294; for a detailed list of data, see Ibn Mubārāk, 1891, pp. 258–259). These detailed accounts reflected the Mughals' need to preserve important data with precision (Fisher, 1993, p. 48).

Imperial genealogies, histories, and various official data were collated into books (*nāmah*s) documenting the reigns of successive Mughal emperors. The *Bābur-nāmah* (The *Bābur-nāma* ca. 1500 CE) details information germane to the royal court: battles, other events, and royal edicts (Bābur, ca. 1500/1922, pp. 455–457, 463–466). It also contains a survey of indigenous flora and fauna and an accounting of revenues for each district (*sarkar*) under Mughal control (Bābur, ca. 1500/1922, pp. 488–514, 521).

The most famous of these works, the *Akbar-Nāmah*, compiled by Ibn Mubārāk, extensively documents Emperor Akbar's reign in the 16th century. Ibn Mubārāk was an ambitious collector of official information; as Jarrett (1891/1978, p. vi) noted, "no details, from the revenues of a province to the cost of a pine-apple, from the organization of an army . . . to the price of a curry-comb, are beyond his microscopic and patient investigation." The *Ain-i-Akbari*, the third volume of the *Akbar-Nāmah*, is noted for its breadth of information (Blochmann, 1873, p. iii; Gascoigne, 1971, pp. 99–100). Volume 1 of the *Ain-i-Akbari* details, for example, official prices of gems of given weights and qualities, the average prices of essential foodstuffs, prices of perfumes, wages of construction workers, prices of building materials, salaries of army officers, and the number of soldiers and elephants under their command (Ibn Mubārāk, 1873, pp. 15–16, 62–65, 66–67, 75–76, 225–227). Volume 2 of the *Ain-i-Akbari* details the geography, peoples, and natural resources of the 12 provinces (*subah*s) under Akbar's control (Ibn Mubārāk, 1891, pp. 115–418). It shows the revenue generated by each district (*sarkar*) and subdivision (*mahal*) within each province (Ibn Mubārāk, 1891, pp. 115–418). It likewise presents the number of military personnel (infantry, cavalry, elephant) per province (see various tables in Ibn Mubārāk, 1891, pp. 115–418) and in some instances the caste of households by subdivision (see, for example, the districts of Behar, Bhadrak, and Ilahabas; Ibn Mubārāk, 1891, pp. 143, 153–154, 161). Volume 3 of the *Ain-i-Akbari* (also called the "Ethnography of Hindustan"; Ibn Mubārāk, 1894, p. 18) describes contemporaneous Hindu and Muslim communities in detail.

PATRICIA AHMED ET AL.

Thus, the Mughals clearly knew of the Hindu *varna* (caste) system. As Ibn Mubārāk (1894, p. 114) noted:

> The Hindu philosophers reckon four states ... which they term *varna.* 1. *Bráhmana.* 2. *Kshatriya.* ... 3. *Vaiśya.* ... 4. *S'údra* [*sic*]. ... the first of these classes was produced from the mouth of Brahma ... the second from his arms; the third, from his thigh and the fourth from his feet.

Ibn Mubārāk (1894, p. 115) described the duties of the three highest castes as well as that of the Shudras: to serve the upper castes and "wear their cast-off garments and eat their leavings." He summarized caste marriage rules, the conditions leading to rebirth into higher or lower castes, and other caste-related institutions (mythical origins, traditional occupations, etc.) (Ibn Mubārāk, 1894, pp. 115–119, 225–226). He also documented the fines levied for caste infractions (Ibn Mubārāk, 1894, pp. 267–268). For example, if a Shudra slandered a Brahman, "he is fined one hundred *dáms,* a Bráhman reviling a S'údra [*sic*] pays six-and-a-quarter" (Ibn Mubārāk, 1894, pp. 267). He also documented caste-appropriate religious training, dress codes, purification rituals, and food consumption (Ibn Mubārāk, 1894, pp. 271–281, 293–298, 308–310). These caste-based policies reflected the Mughals' assimilation of Brahmanical ideology in exchange for the latter's support, rather than an attempt to alter the existing status quo (Bahuguna, 2011, pp. 354–355).

Official information gathering was not limited to the Mughals during this period. For example, a wealth of official information was gathered by Munhata Nainsi (ca. 1665–1772/1969a, pp. 1–352 for Jodhpur; ca. 1665–1772/1969b, pp. 214–288 for Siwana) between 1658 and 1664 for the kingdom of Marwar in Rajasthan and reported in the *Marwar ra Pargana ri Vigat* (*Account of the Districts of Marwar*). The *Account* presented both narrative and statistical information about Marwar's capital, Jodhpur, its surrounding district, and six adjoining districts (*parganas*) (Nainsi, ca. 1665–1772/1969a, pp. 353–450 for Sojhat; ca. 1665–1772/1969b, pp. 37–213 for Merta; Peabody, 2001, p. 825). The account detailed each administrative unit, with a historical narrative and relevant data (Nainsi, ca. 1665–1772/1969a, pp. 1–352 for Jodhpur; ca. 1665–1772/1969b, pp. 37–213 for Merta; Peabody, 2001, p. 825). The lists generally included gross revenue statistics, statement of district headquarters' affairs, descriptions of frontier areas, and enumerations of every village (Nainsi, ca. 1665–1772/1969a, pp. 1–352 for Jodhpur; ca. 1665–1772/1969b, pp. 214–288 for Siwana; Peabody, 2001, p. 825). Nainsi's (ca. 1665–1772/1969a, pp. 391–392; ca. 1665–1772/1969b, pp. 9, 83–86, 223–224) census included a caste-wise enumeration of households for the districts of Phalodi, Merta, Siwana, Pokaran, and Sojhat (see also Peabody, 2001, p. 825, for Merta).

Social and State Uses of Caste
We return to our four orienting questions. First, with respect to lay categories, during this period, written texts clearly indicate social differences based on caste, which seemed most prominent in the religious context. Muslim rulers and

travelers pointed out these social differences. Caste appeared somewhat fluid in this period as there were different caste groups noted by different travelers. Evidence suggests that caste was used for social control, given restrictions on behavior as noted in the diaries of foreign visitors. Second, with respect to information intellectuals, scribes remained information intellectuals who adapted lay categories for information gathering. Third, with respect to power relations, evidence suggests that caste interests aligned with those of the state, as Hindu administrators and information gatherers tended to be higher caste (Brahmin, Kayastha, etc.), and that their interests were incorporated into the information gathering. Caste was recorded for tax rolls and population enumerations in household registers, used by both Hindu and Muslim rulers.

Fourth, with respect to information-gathering outcomes, Mughal information gathering was highly successful and plentiful, and caste seems to have been linked to identity in terms of documents collected. However, we lack evidence that it was linked to the documents administratively after collection, or that the documents fundamentally transformed caste categories. During this period, caste was still fluid, as evidenced by the different groups reported by different travelers. However, despite this fluidity, it seems to have become increasingly socially salient, as there were increasing distinctions among social groups. The Mughals greatly intensified information gathering, drawing on local Hindu scribes and informants to collect information by drawing upon enduring indigenous structures. They collected taxes and other information in great detail. Yet, there is little evidence that this information reinforced caste or that enumeration changed the categories of social actors or state bureaucracies or state structure. Perhaps the clearest effect of information gathering was to solidify the status of scribal castes as information collectors. Instead, this period suggests an intensification of social uses of caste, as well as states' uses of information intellectuals to collect data, but little cross effect between the information gathering and the conceptualization of caste.

Finally, we assess the historical trajectory. During this period, the interactive pattern of information gathering emerged more strongly than in the previous period. Building on the indigenous information-gathering structure, the Mughals were able to intensify collection efforts. The Mughals were dependent upon local scribes to collect information, primarily for taxation, but they were able to systematize its collection. However, the pattern of information gathering with respect to caste seems to have remained society driven, as the Mughals, under the auspices of their strong colonial state, seem to have collected this information about caste that was socially available, but this information gathering did not alter caste.

British East India Company

Information Gathering and Its Social Uses
The British occupation of India was initiated under the auspices of the EIC. The EIC obtained a monopoly of South Asian trade and territorial possessions via a royal charter granted by Queen Elizabeth I on December 31, 1600 (Huttenback, 1966, p. 1; Keay, 1991, p. 14). Additional royal charters granted during the 17th

century permitted the EIC to enact laws, constitutions, and ordinances to manage its trading settlements (Sen, 2002, p. 5; Shaw, 1887, pp. iii–xviii). The 1657 charter, granted by Charles II, bestowed military functions upon the EIC, allowing it to "fortify and colonize any of its establishments and to transport to them settlers, stores and ammunition" (Keay, 1991, pp. 128–129).

Over time, the EIC became increasingly embroiled in Indian politics to protect its economic interests, which were vulnerable because of the decline of the Mughal Empire, various local intrigues, and competition from other Europeans (C. A. Bayly, 1988/2006, p. 3; Lyall, 1894/1968, p. 48; St. John, 2012, p. viii). EIC administrators implemented ad hoc policies that increased their political influence (Sivramkrishna, 2014, pp. 803–804; St. John, 2012, pp. 11–12). The Company gradually acquired the administration of police, justice, and revenue collection in many parts of India, incrementally instituting techniques of colonial governance (Kalpagam, 2000, p. 48).

EIC rule became formally established in 1768, following the defeat of Mughal forces at Plassey and Buxar in 1757 and 1764, respectively (Fisher, 1993, p. 54; Michael, 2007, p. 78; Stern, 2008, p. 254).[14] The victory conferred the EIC *diwani* status in Bengal, that is, the right to gather land taxes and other revenue. Over time, the Company expanded its fiscal reach to newly acquired Indian territories (Nogues-Marco, 2021, p. 154). Subsequently, the EIC emerged as the dominant political and military power in India (St. John, 2012, p. viii).

The EIC, unlike the Mughal Empire, was a notably weak ruler. While the EIC effectively operated as a state, it managed its Indian territories though an "awkward dual sovereignty" (Raman, 2018, p. 977). Part of the EIC's sovereignty derived from Parliament's recognition of it as a chartered company. The employees of the company owed allegiance to the British Crown. But the EIC's sovereignty in India did not derive from Britain but instead from grants "received or extracted from Indian rulers" (Cohn, 1996, p. 58). This meant that Company rule relied upon local, not British, precedent, as neither British common law nor royal precedent applied to its acquisition and administration of Indian territories (Raman, 2018, p. 977). Ultimately, the issue of the EIC's land claims remained unresolved despite the search for ancient constitutions (Raman, 2018, p. 977). The "principle of indirect rule" exemplified this situation of dual sovereignty. It allowed the Company to maintain effective power in areas where it had assumed revenue collection while still formally acting as a local agent of the weakened Mughal Empire. The EIC achieved this by recognizing the nominal sovereignty of "puppet princes," whom the EIC itself had often a hand in installing (Sen, 2012, p. 231). The local populations residing in these kingdoms remained under the authority of the prince, who retained a degree of "residual sovereignty" (Sen, 2012, p. 237). Thus, brute force could not establish the EIC's full sovereignty in its Indian territories vis-à-vis certain native powers (Sen, 2012, p. 237).

A growing wariness of the Company's issues with corruption prompted a series of Parliamentary Acts to limit the EIC's power.[15] First, the office of governor of Bengal was replaced by the office of governor-general of India, a position appointed by the Crown (East India Company Act, 1772/1899, pp. 8–9; Edney, 1997, p. 8), The governor-general exercised authority over all political

260   *Historical Trajectories*

and military affairs in the Company's territories. Second, a Board of Control was established to oversee and, as appropriate, veto decisions and actions of the EIC's board of directors (East India Company Act, 1784/1899, p. 21; Edney, 1997, p. 8). This legislation marked the EIC's transition from a mercantile corporation to a territorial power, albeit with Crown oversight (Edney, 1997, p. 8; Seth, 2012, p. 234). The Company's hold on India abruptly ended following the Great Rebellion of 1857, which produced hundreds of British casualties.[16]

Land taxation evolved out of complex state–society negotiations. EIC officials, citing expediency, initially drew upon existing tax systems to generate revenue with modifications geared towards increased efficiency (Bellenoit, 2014, pp. 872, 876–877; House of Lords, 1830, p. 151; Husain & Sarwar, 2012, p. 16; Travers, 2004, p. 518). Changes were made in consultation with local administrators and rising elites, and the latter's wealth and influence rose with Company power (Husain & Sarwar, 2012, p. 24). Thus, EIC officials manipulated existing systems advantageously, privileging local hierarchies aligned with colonial interests.

During the late 18th and early 19th centuries, the Company's territories grew dramatically (Michael, 2007, p. 78). The EIC drew expeditiously upon existing models of governance (mostly Mughal), with modifications geared towards enhanced efficiency (Alamgir, 2006, pp. 420–421; St. John, 2012, p. 11). Information was key to securing and maintaining power, and EIC officials used their deep pockets to tap into India's existing information networks (C. A. Bayly, 1993, p. 42). Company innovations included the intensification of existing bureaucracy and enhanced record keeping, characterized by organized, indexed, referential, and taxonomically ordered information (Bellenoit, 2017, p. 134). The EIC's quest for the accumulation and archiving of copious amounts of information prompted colonial India to be labeled the "British *Kagaz Raj*" (Paper Rule) and a "government of writing" (Bellenoit, 2017, pp. 1–2; Raman, 2012a, pp. 2, 8).

The EIC, however, lacked the personnel, linguistic, and cultural competencies required for effective governance (Alamgir, 2006, pp. 420, 433; Raj, 2000, p. 121; St. John, 2012, pp. 21–22). Initially, the British presence was no more than a few hundred civilians and few thousand military personnel; even at the height of the British Empire, British numbers amounted to around 20,000 civilians, which was inadequate to administrate their Indian territory without significant assistance from native staff (Raj, 2000, p. 121). Thus, as was the case with the earlier Sultanate and Mughal regimes, it formed mutually beneficial alliances with local officials, administrators, and scribes to facilitate Company rule (Raj, 2000, p. 122; St. John, 2012, pp. 21–22). As in the medieval period, these linkages were formed along caste lines. Native collaborators and assistants often came from the ranks of high-status scribal groups who had served prior rulers, Brahmins and Kayasthas prominent among them (Bellenoit, 2014, pp. 882, 887; 2017, pp. 39, 67; A. Ghosh, 2003, p. 31; Raman, 2012a, p. 46; St. John, 2012, pp. 96, 103).

The Crown noted the utility of these native personnel. The House of Lords' Select Committee on the East India Company noted that various classes of experienced natives, supervised by a European officer, conducted land assessment surveys (House of Lords, 1830, p. 151). It further added that several "natives have been appointed, on comparatively high salaries, to the judicial and to the revenue offices" and acknowledged that the native officials' knowledge of local procedures and languages enhanced administrative efficiency (House of Lords, 1830, p. 180). This sentiment was echoed in a letter to Nathaniel Smith, director of the EIC, from the governor-general of India, Warren Hastings (in office from 1774–1785; 1784/1785, p. 13), who wrote: "Every accumulation of knowledge ... especially ... obtained by social communication with people over whom we exercise a dominion founded on ... conquest, is useful to the state." This knowledge was all-inclusive: traditional law, taxation, natural history, antiquities, local customs, and general living conditions (Raj, 2000, p. 122).

Alliances with scribal and other local elites facilitated the Company's formal inventories of its territories, which dated back to at least 1687 (Walby & Haan, 2012, p. 305). Political power increased the EIC's thirst for knowledge. Hastings believed that drawing up Domesday Book-like works of EIC territories was key to successful governance (Raj, 2000, p. 122). Thus, the Company quickly embarked on a mission to explore and demarcate the territory it controlled (Michael, 2007, p. 78). It undertook numerous cadastral, route, and topographical surveys to improve tax assessment, as well as administrative and military capabilities within Company-held territories (B. Chatterjee, 2021, p. 2; Edney, 1997, pp. 77–112; Markham, 1871, pp. 39–41, 42–43, 58–67; Michael, 2007, p. 83; Sanjeev, 2020, p. 126).

The EIC likewise enumerated its Indian territories and commissioned local officials to gather these data (S. Guha, 2003, p. 156). For example, officials often gathered data using local household registers (*khana shumari*) (Buchanan, 1833, p. 67; Peabody, 2001, pp. 831–832). These instruments gathered statistics on various topics, including the number of houses, families, household head's caste, occupation and religion, age and gender of household members, number of ploughs, looms, water tanks, and other public works present in each location (Buchanan, 1833, p. 67). Thus, information-gathering techniques and the information gathered itself reflected existing practices (Peabody, 2001, p. 823).

EIC population surveys typically were localized (e.g., village, *zamindari* [feudal estate], city, district, and presidency[17] levels). Statistical data were often gathered in conjunction with topographical, trigonometrical, and revenue surveys (Phillimore, 1945, p. 146; 1958, p. 233). However, professional surveyors found this task burdensome; thus, after 1836, the Board of Revenue deployed native "statistical *mootsuddies*" (accountants) to enumerate populations (Phillimore, 1958, p. 233). The EIC accrued population statistics in disparate ways. Assorted censuses, albeit of varying accuracy, were conducted.[18] Other types of counts (e.g., houses, ploughs, or consumption) were used when the population could not be reliably surveyed or if a district official deemed indigenous enumerators to be untrustworthy (Buchanan, 1928, pp. 117–119).[19] These data were multiplied by locally derived group means, such as average number per household, to estimate the population (Buchanan, 1833, pp. 67–68). Alternatively, desired statistics were provided by a knowledgeable local informant, such as a *tehlsidar* (revenue collector); district revenue officers, in turn, visited the site to

262   *Historical Trajectories*

personally verify and amend, as necessary, the provided information (Office of Registrar General, India, 1985, p. 380).

The earliest extant EIC census was conducted in 1789 in the Bengal, Bahar (Bihar), Orissa, and Benares provinces at the urging of Lord Cornwallis, the governor-general of India at the time (R. M. Martin, 1837, p. 250).[20] The data were reported for men, women, and children (R. M. Martin, 1837, p. 251). Another census, covering the same territories, was conducted in 1820 and was based on the number of villages and houses found in each district (R. M. Martin, 1837, p. 255). This enumeration again expanded upon the previous one, gathering information on categories of interest. Religion was categorized in terms of "Hindoo," "Mussalman" (Muslim), and "Parsee" (R. M. Martin, 1837, pp. 255, 353–354). Nationality was broken down into English, Portuguese, "Parsee," Jews, Americans, "Moors," "Hindoos," Malays, and Chinese, though this overlapped with some religious categories (R. M. Martin, 1837, p. 262). More detailed occupation data were gathered for the city of Benares (R. M. Martin, 1837, pp. 365–366).

The EIC gradually moved towards synchronous censuses (e.g., North-West Provinces [1853] and Punjab [1855]), as per directives from the Board of Revenue (Christian, 1854, p. 10; Madras Presidency, Board of Revenue, 1866, pp. 341–342; Government of India, 1856, p. 4). The 1850 guidelines required presidency censuses to be taken on a fixed date; village officers would enumerate rural areas; larger towns were divided "into convenient sections" entrusted to a particular officer (Madras Presidency, Board of Revenue, 1866, p. 341). Collectors made advance preparations to ensure systematic enumeration. Desired data included sex, number of children, number of houses, number of people/families per household (broken down by religion), and agricultural versus nonagricultural occupation (Madras Presidency, Board of Revenue, 1866, pp. 341–342). The instructions further noted that a memo on caste – included at the foot of the return – would enhance the value of the statistical returns, though it was not an "essential element of the General Return," for the sake of simplicity (Madras Presidency, Board of Revenue, 1866, p. 342).

Official information was collated into district reports and statistical memoirs and distributed to key local officials for administrative purposes (e.g., Markham, 1871, pp. 39–43, 44–56, 81–86). It was also gathered into encyclopedic gazetteers for public consumption. These works organized data in terms of geographical units: all India ("Hindoostan" in earlier versions), "independent" kingdoms, principalities, provinces, cities, towns, and districts (Hamilton, 1815, pp. vii–xv; examples in Thornton, 1854, pp. 2–38). As the area increased in size, the data provided increased in complexity. Data included size, location (latitude and longitude), population characteristics (size, religion, caste, and phenotype), geography (rivers, mountains, weather, etc.), local history, and revenue returns (Hamilton, 1815, pp. vii–xv, 157–158; Thornton, 1854, pp. iv, 92–100, 116–119).

Caste data initially were reported unevenly since EIC officials were unsure of its social significance. For example, Francis Buchanan (1833, p. 100), a prominent surveyor, noted that the extreme variation of caste throughout India proved that caste "did not proceed from any general law," but rather reflected regional occupational structure defined by local Brahmins. Other officials found native enumerators' inclusion of caste into enumeration vexing, as they were confused as to what it actually was (Walby & Haan, 2012, p. 303). Other administrators felt compelled to report this information when presented with long, detailed lists of castes and subcastes gathered by native enumerators (Peabody, 2001, pp. 830–832). Thus, early colonial knowledge (including that of caste) drew upon existing native discourses reflecting local politics that the British initially barely understood (Peabody, 2001, p. 819).

Despite early official confusion, caste became recognized as key to Indian social structure by various EIC administrators and European observers. S. Bayly (1999, p. 44) traced the rising social significance of caste to the 18th century, when caste became increasingly linked with an "uneasy synthesis" of three distinct occupational forms: the kingly warrior, the service provider (scribes, priests, etc.), and settled men of worth (merchants, tillers, etc.), and a growing tendency to generalize others into these categories. The EIC's reliance on service providers (scribes, etc.) and settled men of worth (especially merchants for capital investment) likely reinforced these differences.

The significance of caste was enhanced further by research conducted by orientalist scholars deployed to India during the EIC period. This scholarship was informed largely by ancient religious and legal texts that espoused the four-tiered caste system and Brahmin supremacy, a selection greatly biased, no doubt, by the Brahmins assisting these scholars (S. J. Brown, 2009, p. 306; Jogdand et al., 2016, p. 558; O'Hanlon, 2017, p. 434). Colonial officials viewed data gathering as a scientific enterprise; this stance may have created what looked like objective facts out of questionable notions about pre-British colonial Indian society (Ludden, 1993, pp. 261, 267–268). Finally, official use and institutionalization of these data enhanced their epistemological authority (Ludden, 1993, p. 261).

The growing relevance of caste was evident in the writings of EIC administrators and observers. Peter Percival (1854, p. 34), a missionary and linguist deployed to India, believed that the most remarkable feature of Hindu society was its division into "four ... castes – the sacerdotal, the military, the industrial and the servile." He further noted that caste demanded special attention, given the belief that it was divinely ordained and a fundamental principle of Hindu polity (Percival, 1854, p. 34). *The East India Gazetteer* discussed the pre-eminence of the Brahmin caste, along with various caste-based proscriptions (exogamy, dietary rules, etc.; Hamilton, 1815, p. 411). This work also detailed caste divisions in various parts of India (Hamilton, 1815, pp. 132, 216, 225–227, 232–233).

Scottish commentator Leitch Ritchie (1848, p. 154) likened caste to "cement" holding Indian society together. F. Warden (1833, p. 15), responding to an inquiry by the House of Commons regarding EIC affairs, stated that "Hindoo" social structure had been "stationary since the age of Menu [Manu]," even in the face of foreign occupations. He cited administrative policy that maintained caste as "the most efficacious instrument for controlling the moral habits of Hindus" (Warden, 1833, p. 20). F. C. Brown (1838, p. 421), responding on behalf of the EIC to concerns raised by the Board of Control, concluded that "the abolition of all the laws which ... mark the impure castes from the pure and ... by upholding the Pariah to a level

264   *Historical Trajectories*

with the Brahmin ... [will] destroy the whole fabric of Hindoo society.. The impracticability of the design is only exceeded by its enormous mischievousness." These examples show a growing official concern with caste.

Caste became a powerful construct. The EIC was so careful not to offend native caste-related prejudices that the "convicts in the East Company's gaols are allowed to preserve its distinction," since prisoners could take on traditional caste duties and were allowed to prepare their own caste-compliant meals (India as it is, 1858, p. 222; see also Indian Law Commission, 1844, p. 80). Colonial laws likewise reflected caste concerns. For example, the actions of fathers based on Hindu or Muslim rules and laws of caste were not deemed crimes, even if the practices violated British laws (*The Law Relating to India*, 1841, pp. 51, 123, 678).

Other laws codified dietary proscriptions: An individual who adulterated the food of another to render it unsuitable for the latter's caste was subject to fines of 50 rupees and 200 rupees for a first and second offense, respectively (S. J. Brown, 2009, p. 306; Jogdand et al., 2016, p. 558; O'Hanlon, 2017, p. 434). The EIC further enjoined the Indian Law Commissioners to periodically suggest "beneficial alterations" to courts, policing, and laws regarding caste (*The Law Relating to India*, 1841, p. 424).

Social and State Uses of Caste

We return a final time to our orienting questions. First, with respect to lay categories, caste was clearly used by social actors. The British seemed initially confused by it, but they soon learned it was widespread. Caste seemed tied to social identity as it was linked to other social categories (such as parent, household, occupation, etc.). Caste was used as a mechanism of social control in social and state institutions. Fines, for example, were levied against supposed caste violations. Court systems, policing, judicial procedures, and laws became tied to them. Second, scribes remained key information intellectuals who translated key categories into the language of official information gathering. Third, with respect to power, British interests and the interests of the higher status caste groups aligned, as they had during the Mughal period. The British found that caste was used by local governments, and they followed the practice by also using it, initially for informational and limited administrative purposes. The EIC was a notably weak state actor, much weaker than the Mughal states at the height of their power, and it had to rely extensively on local power structures. The EIC thus depended on previous information-gathering structures used by the Mughals, as well as local scribes and informants, to collect information. Scribal groups as castes seem to have been reinforced through their information collection. Fourth, with respect to information-gathering outcomes, we note that the EIC collected a vast amount of information, despite its weaknesses, undoubtedly drawing on the strong pattern of interactive information gathering established by the Mughals. Still, however, we have little evidence that enumeration per se reinforced caste, or that the British used the enumeration of caste for social control (though caste itself seemed to have been used for social control).

Certainly, the British used caste as a method of divide and conquer, but it is unclear that official information gathering played a role in this.

Finally, we assess the historical trajectory. The EIC built on Mughal information-gathering efforts and expanded them. Like the Mughals, EIC officials clearly aimed for social, economic, and political control over the colonized population. However, they had a notably weak presence as EIC rule was increasingly constrained by the British Crown and agreements with Indian princes. Like the Mughals, the British relied on local information intellectuals to collect information, as they lacked the political capacity to do so. Thus, during this period, the interactive pattern of information gathering among local inhabitants and the colonial power continued, clearly building on the patterns that the Mughals had established. Notably, as in the previous period, but perhaps even more dramatically so in the EIC period, caste itself was little affected by this information gathering. The British understood it poorly and initially collected it reluctantly. Furthermore, they did not have a cultural understanding of caste – in fact, they did not know what it was at first. Nevertheless, the British believed that caste was a prominent social category and enumerated it. They also incorporated it into legal codes to prevent offending Hindus. We have no evidence that enumeration changed caste categories. Rather, the evidence suggests that patterns of caste information collection were primarily socially driven, as locals provided this information to the British. The EIC used caste for their rule, but this seemed more motivated by their desire to coopt social elites to their divide-and-conquer strategy. The British seem to have created laws based on their understanding of caste. EIC information gathering thus appeared to have little effect per se on caste, and there is little evidence that enumeration was incorporated into social institutions.

CONCLUSIONS

In this chapter, we have used historical narrative to assess the applicability of three approaches to information gathering: the state-centered perspective (Cohn, 1987, pp. 230, 250; Dirks, 1992, p. 76; 1997, p. 209; Kaviraj, 1997, p. 328), the society-centered one (U. Chakravarti, 1998, p. 48; Frykenberg, 1993, p. 534; Viswanathan, 2003, p. 37), and the interactive one (Emigh et al., 2021, pp. 13–16). We examined these perspectives in two ways. First, we examined three periods of Indian history to understand, within these time periods, whether information gathering was a state-centered process, a society-centered one, or an interactive one. We did this by examining, within each period, three underlying relationships of information gathering (lay categories, information intellectuals, and the balance of power between state and social actors). We also considered our outcome: what information was collected and whether it had a transformative effect. Finally, using these four pieces of evidence, we assessed the overall historical trajectory of information gathering within each period (state driven, society driven, and interactive). Second, we used our evidence to frame the debate about the transformative effect of India-wide censuses under British direct rule. Cohn (1987, pp. 230, 250) and Dirks (2001, pp. 7, 9, 14, 16), for example, argued that such censuses had transformative effects, linked to the strong British colonial state. Thus, they seem to support the state-centered view that information gathering, in and of itself, has a transformative social effect.

In the first period, caste is referenced in the *Rigveda* (ca. 1500–1200 BCE), predating the rise of formal Indian states. The evidence shows that the ability to conduct censuses and the use of caste categories dated back to the Mauryan period (ca. 351–125 BCE), if not earlier (Bhattacharya, 1990, p. 642; J. K. Ghosh et al., 1999, p. 14; Kauṭilya, ca. 300 BCE/1992, pp. 220, 222; Nambiar, 1981, p. 7). Foreign visitors described caste classifications in writings during this time frame, suggesting some degree of social significance (Arrian, ca. 150 CE/1877, p. 209; Megasthênes, ca. BCE 310/1877, pp. 7, 40–44). It appears to have been an attempt to legitimate Brahmin elite status using religion (B. K. Smith, 1992, p. 106; 1994, pp. 32–36; Thapar, 2003, pp. 9–10). We also note a degree of fluidity in works by native and outside observers (Arrian, ca. 150 CE/1877, p. 209; Megasthênes, ca. 310 BCE/1877, pp. 7, 40–44, 209; Sathaye, 2015, pp. 2–3; Vyas, 1967, p. 67). Our evidence does not suggest that the enumeration of caste itself had any particular influence, but we acknowledge that we have little evidence during this time period.

While societal-level factors (elite interests and religious institutions) were influential early on, over time, information gathering became increasingly informed by state–society interactions. Early Indian rulers (mostly Kshatriya) often patronized Brahmin priests in exchange for legitimation of their rule (Chandel, 2018, pp. 358, 360; Lo Turco, 2013, pp. 88–89). State workers, such as scribes and administrators, began to coalesce along caste lines (Brahmin, Kayastha, etc.), giving rise to closed networks of officials who monopolized the gathering and organization of official information (Haider, 2011, p. 266). This gave rise to a strongly interactive historical trajectory around information collection per se (K. Chatterjee, 2010, p. 456; Kinra, 2010, pp. 557–558).

This state–society interactive dynamic was evident in the regimes started by Muslim invaders, who would have been unfamiliar with caste (sultanates and the later Mughal Empire, ca. 700–1700 CE). Yet, caste influenced some state policies: Several rulers excused Brahmins from paying the *jizya* tax levied on non-Muslims, and household registers included information on caste (Jackson, 1999, p. 286; Mahajan, 1991/2018, p. 293; Moosvi, 2011, pp. 5–6). Caste was also noted by several Arab and European visitors to India during this period (Al Bīrūnī, 1910a, pp. 100–101; 1910b, pp. 236–238; Polo, ca. 1300/1958, p. 277). Furthermore, the above-mentioned groups of local officials learned Persian and the *insha'* style of courtly writing and transitioned to serving the new rulers, preserving their caste-based hold on these services (Eaton, 2019, pp. 17, 135, 155; Raman, 2012a, p. 11). However, the use of caste classification in terms of official policies and governance appears to be limited to taxation and descriptive purposes. We have no evidence that its enumeration had a transformative effect.

We see a state–society interaction around the collection of information likewise continuing during the early EIC period. The EIC, initially trade oriented, became increasingly drawn into local political intrigues to protect its economic interests, leading to the annexation and control of territories well beyond the confines of their original factories (C. A. Bayly, 1988/2006, p. 3; Lyall, 1894/1968, p. 48; St. John, 2012, p. viii). Company administrators realized that they needed knowledge about Indian society to fully exploit and tax their new acquisitions. Native administrative and scribal elites, who had previously served the Mughal regime, quickly learned English and offered their services to the new regime (Raj, 2000, p. 122; St. John, 2012, pp. 21–22). Tax assessment and information gathering initially followed local conventions. Household register forms were used to gather official information (Buchanan, 1833, p. 67; Peabody, 2001, pp. 831–832). Interestingly, many EIC officials found the caste categories (often broken down into multiple subcastes) on these registers bewildering, as they were neither interested in nor explicitly requested this information (Walby & Haan, 2012, p. 303). Over time, however, colonial administrators came to attach more significance to caste (S. Bayly, 1999, p. 4).

These changing official stances on caste occurred within the context of intensifying interactions between EIC officials, orientalist scholars, and Indian elites. The Company sought capital to fund its expansion from local bankers and merchants, expanding the power and influence of these caste groups and, by extension, caste itself (St. John, 2012, p. 11). Land surveyors often gathered information on local caste distinctions, which appeared in statistical memoirs and district reports, for administrative purposes (Phillimore, 1945, p. 146; 1958, p. 233). Scholars (and other observers) who were deployed to gather, analyze, and record data on Indian history, culture, and society relied heavily on Brahmin informants (S. J. Brown, 2009, p. 306; Jogdand et al., 2016, p. 558; O'Hanlon, 2017, p. 434). The latter provided materials and information that supported Brahmin social superiority and the caste system more generally. The results of these inquiries, however biased, led the EIC to create legal codes that reinforced further caste distinctions (S. J. Brown, 2009, p. 306; Jogdand et al., 2016, p. 558; O'Hanlon, 2017, p. 434). Again, however, we find little evidence that the census categories per se had transformative effects.

Thus, with respect to our three key relationships of information gathering (lay categories, information intellectuals, and power), we show that the lay categories of caste gained importance, that scribes were key information intellectuals who translated caste into official information-gathering categories, and that they often supported their own power through collaboration with state officials. With respect to our outcome, we showed that information gathering increased over time. In fact, the collection of information did not depend on state strength, as the Mughals, though ruling through a strong state, collected less information than the EIC, which ruled through a much weaker one. Instead, the collection of information was strongly shaped by rulers' abilities to capitalize on, and develop, the interactive patterns of information gathering of previous rulers.

With respect to historical trajectories of information gathering, our historical narrative shows that information gathering developed over thousands of years. We argue that the first period suggests a society-driven pattern, slowly replaced by an interactive pattern starting in the second period. State and social actors had participated in collecting information for a long time, facilitated by scribal castes who collected information for a variety of states and state actors. These information intellectuals, in our framework, had a key relationship with state actors (Emigh et al., 2016a, pp. 25–26). While they were perhaps subordinate to the state actors, nevertheless, the state actors did not have enough power or resources to collect information without them (Raj, 2000, p. 121). Thus, they were dependent upon their help to do so. This cooperation between scribes and state officials developed over thousands of years (Bellenoit, 2014, pp. 883, 885; Lo Turco, 2013, p. 85; Talbot, 2012, p. 360).

Our historical narrative also suggests that caste itself was altered. Over time, it seemed to have become more explicit, more widespread, and entangled in more institutions. The evidence suggests both that the relatively strong Mughal state merely assimilated caste and that the relatively weak EIC one initially did not fully appreciate it (Bahuguna, 2011, p. 354; Peabody, 2001, p. 823–824; Walby & Haan, 2012, p. 303). However, these colonial states eventually realized that they could implement a divide-and-conquer strategy by supporting local elites over nonelites. The colonial powers thus incorporated caste into their political and legal practices (F. C. Brown, 1838, p. 421; Ibn Mubārāk, 1894, pp. 267–268; *The Law Relating to India*, 1841, pp. 51, 123, 678). It is perhaps through these practices, and not enumeration itself, that caste became solidified. In fact, information gathering around caste per se remained quite society driven. State officials took up social caste categories because they allowed them to rule more efficiently (Bahuguna, 2011, pp. 354–355; Warden, 1833, p. 20). And this assumption of caste itself seems to have formed a historical trajectory whereby successive waves of colonial powers used caste to implement their own divide-and-conquer strategy. However, we also note that we have no evidence that caste was altered by the enumeration of caste per se. It is, of course, possible that this occurred and that we lack the evidence to show it.

Finally, our analysis also provides an important historical backdrop to the British direct rule censuses. It shows that the use of caste to collect information was certainly not novel to British direct rule or even to EIC company rule for that matter. We showed that there was a historical trajectory, based on a strong pattern of interactive information gathering about caste, that developed quite early in Indian history and certainly during Mughal rule. Local elites collaborated with state actors to collect this information (Bellenoit, 2014, pp. 882, 887; 2017, pp. 39, 67; K. Chatterjee, 2010, pp. 456–457, 459; A. Ghosh, 2003, p. 31; Haider, 2011, p. 267; Raman, 2012a, p. 46; St. John, 2012, pp. 96, 103). The British, under direct rule, capitalized on thousands of years of information gathering and, in particular, on interactive information gathering that occurred during the latter two periods (Mughal and EIC). Thus, this practice emerged from a long historical trajectory.

What appears novel to the British direct rule case, then, is the claim that censuses per se had transformative effects (Anderson, 1983/2006, pp. 168; Appadurai, 1993, pp. 318–320; Bhagat, 2001, pp. 4,352–4,353; Cohn, 1996, p. 8; Dirks, 2001, pp. 9, 14, 16; Jaffrelot, 2000, p. 757). We found no evidence during the earlier time periods that enumeration per se transformed caste. What then, does our evidence suggest for this claim about British direct rule? Several scenarios are possible. First, it is possible that the British direct rule censuses per se did not have a transformative effect. Much of the evidence is weak and tangential for the transformative effects of censuses during British direct rule. The evidence is generally based on general descriptions of the use of census and other official data but lacks comparative evidence (e.g., where and when it was, or was not, collected and the outcomes) or temporal evidence (e.g., to show that outcomes occurred only after categories in the census or other official documents changed) (Emigh et al., 2020, p. 299). While it is clear that the British used caste as part of their divide-and-conquer strategy both during the EIC period and during direct rule, the censuses during direct rule may have had little effect per se. This pattern would be continuous with our evidence for the EIC period, suggesting that information gathering per se had little transformative effect.

Second, it is possible that the direct rule censuses did have this transformative effect (Cohn, 1987, pp. 230, 250; Dirks, 2001, pp. 7, 9, 14, 16), but if they did so, this effect was indeed novel, as it was missing during earlier periods. The British, drawing on the long trajectory of information gathering per se, may have been able to use information gathering per se as a transformative strategy; furthermore, the information-gathering trajectory may have shifted from being mostly society driven to state driven during British direct rule. This happened, for example, in the Italian case: A long history of interactive information gathering shifted to a state-driven one (Emigh et al., 2016b, pp. 109–110, 204). In this sense, Cohn (1987, pp. 230, 250) and Dirks (2001, pp. 7, 9, 14, 16) may be correct that the direct rule censuses were different from earlier ones in that they were transformative, whereas previous ones were not. If this is true, perhaps British direct rule information gathering was state centered (and transformative).

However, our long durée historical evidence casts doubt on the state-centered interpretation that the strength of British direct rule, in and of itself, created transformative census categories. And, in particular, it casts doubt on the state-centered perspective that colonial states per se used information gathering to control their populations. The strong Mughal state, also a colonial power, for example, though it collected considerable amounts of information, was not able to create transformative categories. And the EIC, also a colonial power though a much weaker state than the Mughal Empire, collected even more information, probably because it also capitalized on the previously established pattern of state and society interaction. Much of the raw material for British direct rule censuses, including the categories, the information-gathering apparatus, and the cooperation between state and social actors, had existed for thousands of years. Thus, much of the effect of the direct rule censuses derived from this interactive pattern. Obviously, more research is needed to assess more directly whether – or not – British direct rule and the strength of its state transformed information gathering. In addition, more research is needed to specify exactly what transformations occurred from information gathering itself, and what transformations occurred from more general strategies of divide and conquer that did not rely on information gathering. However, our evidence suggests that even if information gathering shifted from interactive to state centered during this period, it was only because the British, during direct rule, were able to capitalize on the centuries-long interactive patterns of information gathering that preceded them.

In sum, we argue that the state-centered perspective, in and of itself, is insufficient to explain the transformative effects of British direct rule censuses. While this case is often taken as the prima facie one to show that strong colonial states impose official categories that transform social ones (Cohn, 1987, pp. 230, 250; Dirks, 2001, pp. 7, 9, 14, 16), we cast doubt on this argument. Instead, we argue that it is equally plausible that British direct rule capitalized on centuries of a strong pattern of interactive information gathering, based in state and society cooperation (Bellenoit, 2014, pp. 882, 887; 2017, pp. 39, 67; A. Ghosh, 2003, p. 31; Raman, 2012a, p. 46; St. John, 2012, pp. 96, 103). This interactive pattern, we argue, may have allowed the shift to direct British rule – which also perhaps introduced more purposefully interventionist population censuses explicitly designed to change the population – to create transformative censuses (if indeed they were transformative) (Emigh et al., 2016b, pp. 12–13). Furthermore, we showed that information gathering, in the long run, can be socially driven (the first historical period we examined) as well as interactive (the second two historical periods we examined). Long durée historical periods are therefore needed to assess these patterns – not just research that starts when any particular state decides to collect a census.

ACKNOWLEDGMENTS

We thank Juan Wang for her comments and Michelle Marinello and Johanna Hernández-Pérez for their research assistance funded by a UCLA Faculty Senate Grant and the UCLA Social Sciences Dean. A previous version of this paper was presented at the SSHA Annual Conference in Washington DC in 2023.

NOTES

1. We note here that while Anderson's (1983/2006, pp. 163–164) specific argument about censuses is state centered, the overall thrust of his work is not. Indeed, his central claim about nationalism is that it arose from a set of deep-seated social processes: the emergence of vernacular languages, the rise of commercial exchange, and the technology of printing (Anderson, 1983/2006, p. 46). Thus, the thrust of his work is very much against the dominant state-centered perspective, even though he seems to have adopted such a view in his analysis of colonial censuses.

2. Native recruits to the Indian Civil Service, established post-EIC, initially came from long-serving scribal and administrative castes (e.g., Brahmin, Kayastha, and Baidya; Fuller & Narasimhan, 2010, p. 477; Grewal, 2016, p. 604; Lee, 2017, p. 203). Their numbers declined in the 1920s and 1930s, following the Crown's introduction of "quotas" to increase lower caste representation within the Indian Civil Service (Fuller & Narasimhan, 2010, p. 477).

3. There is no archaeological evidence (palace ruins, etc.) that supports the existence of a ruling elite in Harappan civilization (Green, 2021, p. 170; McIntosh, 2008, p. 90; SarDesai, 2008, p. 22).

4. Archaeological and DNA evidence also suggests that caste may have originated in the Indus Valley, or at least among indigenous Indians, independently of Indo-Aryan migrants (Baig et al., 2004, p. 459; Bidner & Eswaran, 2015, p. 143; S. Sharma et al., 2009, p. 54).

5. Iranian-Aryans, who were closely related to Indo-Aryans, may have had an analogous caste-like system (*pishtra*) comprising priests, rulers, and producers; however, these groupings were likely more class-like in nature (Frye, 1948, p. 232; Jaiswal, 1991, p. 42; Sam & Aryanpour, 2014, pp. 110–111; cf. Avari, 2007, p. 74; Bouglé, 1971, p. 42).

6. The spelling of our references exactly reproduces the original texts. These spellings, as well as their underlying transliterations, may differ from current ones.

7. Due to differences in transliteration from Mandarin, Xuanzang is also known as Hieun Tsiang, Hieun-tsang, Yüan Chuāng, and Yüan Chwang (e.g., Beal, 1906, p. xviii; Sastri, 1939/1972, p. 2; Watters, 1904, p. xi).

8. It is possible that enumeration continued, but that records did not survive the hot, humid climate or were destroyed by later invaders (Das Gupta, 1972, p. 419). Nonetheless, Risley and Gait (1903, p. v) noted that "making periodic estimates of the [Indian] population is of very old standing." Indeed, many early indigenous efforts to gather official data were so elaborate that they often mirrored those of British colonial officials (C. A. Bayly, 1996, p. 21).

9. These information categories foreshadow those in the household registers (*khana shumari*) used by later Moghul, Maratha, and British regimes, as will be discussed in the following sections.

10. These political entities were so named because they were ruled by a sultan, a Persian title for a ruler viewed as both universal and supreme, occupying an infinite sovereign space (Eaton, 2019, p. 14).

11. This was also true of earlier Muslim regimes, such as the one established by Muhammad Kasim in Sind (Gidumal, 1900/2008, p. 4; Kúfí, 1900/2008, pp. 152–153; Moosvi, 2011, p. 4) in the eighth century CE. See Kulkarni (2017, pp. 321–330) for a detailed discussion of the Deccan sultanates.

12. This approach was likely pragmatic as intolerance would be unwise, given the overwhelming Hindu majority (Alam, 1989, p. 52; Eaton, 2019, p. 54).

13. Other mentions of the high status of Brahmins during this period include Abd-er-Razzāk (ca. 1450/1857, pp. 23, 36, 40), Ibn Baṭṭūta (1353/1994, pp. 795, 811–812), and Kúfí (1900/2008, pp. 36, 122, 124).

14. Brenner (1993, p. 48) suggested that monarchs granted the EIC charters partly in exchange for performing diplomatic and political functions for the Crown overseas. Over time, the EIC effectively functioned as a state (Bose & Ramraj, 2020, p. 287; Burke, 1788/1834, pp. 291–292; Macaulay, 1833, p. 20; Menon, 2016, pp. 151–152; Mulligan, 2018, p. 42; Seth, 2012, p. 232; Stern, 2007, p. 1; 2008, p. 283). A 1793 British ruling, in the case of *Nabob* (a corruption of the Urdu word *nawab*, a type of Muslim ruler) *of the Carnatic v. East India Company*, essentially recognized a treaty negotiated between the Company and the *nawab* as an agreement between two sovereigns (Mulligan, 2018, p. 51). Keay (1991, p. xix) thus argued that the EIC was not simply a forerunner to Crown rule, given the Company's eventual role as an "all-conquering force in Indian politics."

15. Following the British victory at the battle of Plassey, corruption became rampant among Company officials as they looted and stripped Bengal's assets, previously the richest Mughal province (Robins, 2012, p. 4; Stagl, 2012, p. 106). The Crown and the general public found ostentatious displays of wealth by *nabobs* (*nouveau-riche* EIC traders) and officials, such as Lord Clive, increasingly disturbing (Lawson & Phillips, 1984, pp. 226, 228). George Gray (1766/1775, p. 118), a former EIC official, responding to testimony given by Lord Clive, noted: "Whatever they [Clive and others] are possessed of has come to them as presents, plunder, or such means as Lord *Clive* [original emphasis] has declared, in a military capacity, '*Vivitur ex rapto*' [One lives out of plunder (Ovid)]."

16. Afterward, the British Crown assumed direct control of the EIC's Indian territories until India won independence in 1947.

17. A presidency was a large base of operations under the EIC's political and military control (Lawson, 1993, pp. 65–66).

18. See, for example, the reports and accounts of Dacca and Fureedpore in 1792 (Bengal and Agra Annual Guide and Gazetteer, 1842, p. 280), Trinevelly District in 1801 (Office of

272   *Historical Trajectories*

the Registrar General, India, 1989, p. 191), Benares in 1803 (Office of the Registrar General, India, 1989, p. 405), Canara in 1807 (Baber, 1833, p. 423), North Konkun from 1819 to 1821 (Office of the Registrar General, India, 1985, p. 314), Surat District in 1815 (Office of the Registrar General, India, 1985, p. 327), Ahmedabad from 1820 to 1826 (Office of the Registrar General, India 1985, p. 281), and Kaira from 1820 to 1826 (Cruikshank, 1853, p. 135).

19. Examples include reports for 1752 Calcutta (Mitra, 1954, p. 5), 1807–1808 Dinajpur District (Buchanan, 1833, pp. 67–68), 1809–1810 Purnea District (Buchanan, 1928, p. 119), 1809–1810 Rongopoor District (Buchanan, 1928, p. 119), 1811 Furruckabad (Office of the Registrar General, India 1985, p. 457), and 1816 Jaipur/Dhoondar (Office of the Registrar General, India, 1985, p. 37).

20. Other smaller scale EIC enumerations likely took place but, prior to 1756, many official EIC records did not survive the harsh climate, paper-eating white ants, or, as in the case of Calcutta, military sieges (Mitra, 1954, p. 5).

REFERENCES

Abbott, A. (1992). From causes to events: Notes on narrative positivism. *Sociological Methods & Research, 20*(4), 428–455.

Abd-er-Razzāk. (1857). Narrative of the voyage of Abd-er-Razzak, ambassador from Shah Rukh, A.H. 845, A.D. 1442. In R. H. Major (Ed.), *India in the fifteenth century: Being a collection of narratives of voyages to India in the century preceding the Portuguese discovery of the Cape of Good Hope, from Latin, Persian, Russian, and Italian sources* (pp. 1–49). Hakluyt Society. (Original work written ca. 1450).

Ahmed, F. F. (2016). *Muslim rule in medieval India: Power and religion in the Delhi Sultanate*. I. B. Tauris.

Al Bīrūnī, M. ibn A. (1910a). *Alberuni's India. An account of the religion, philosophy, literature, geography, chronology, astronomy, customs, laws and astrology of India about A.D. 1030* (Vol. 1; E. C. Sachau, Trans.). Kegan Paul, Trench, Trübner. (Original work written ca. 1030).

Al Bīrūnī, M. ibn A. (1910b). *Alberuni's India. An account of the religion, philosophy, literature, geography, chronology, astronomy, customs, laws and astrology of India about A.D. 1030* (Vol. 2; E. C. Sachau, Trans.). Kegan Paul, Trench, Trübner. (Original work written ca. 1030).

Al Idrīsī, M. (1867). Early Arab geographers. VIII. Nuzhatu-L Mushtak of Al Idrisi. In H. M. Elliot & J. Dowson (Eds.), *The history of India as told by its own historians. The Muhammadan period* (Vol. 1, pp. 74–93). Trübner. (Original work written 1145).

Alam, M. (1989). Competition and co-existence: Indo-Islamic interaction in medieval north India. *Itinerario: Journal of Imperial and Global Interactions, 13*(1), 37–60.

Alam, M., & Subrahmanyam, S. (2010). Witnesses and agents of empire: Eighteenth-century historiography and the world of the Mughal *munshī*. *Journal of the Economic and Social History of the Orient, 53*(1–2), 393–423.

Alamgir, A. K. (2006). "The learned Brāhmen, who assists me": Changing colonial relationships in the 18th and 19th century India. *The Journal of Historical Sociology, 19*(4), 419–446.

Aminzade, R. (1992). Historical sociology and time. *Sociological Methods & Research, 20*(4), 456–480.

Anderson, B. (2006). *Imagined communities: Reflections on the origins and spread of nationalism* (Revised ed.). Verso. (Original work published 1983).

Āpastamba. (1999). The Dharmasūtra of Āpastamba. In P. Olivelle (Ed. & Trans.), *Dharmasūtras: The law codes of Āpastamba, Gautama, Baudhāyana, and Vasiṣṭha* (pp. 3–73). Oxford University Press. (Original work written ca. 450–350 BCE).

Appadurai, A. (1993). Number in the colonial imagination. In C. A. Breckenridge & P. van der Veer (Eds.), *Orientalism and the postcolonial predicament: Perspectives on South Asia* (pp. 314–339). University of Pennsylvania Press.

Arrian. (1877). The first part of The Indika of Arrian. In J. W. McCrindle (Ed. & Trans.), *Ancient India as described by Megasthenês and Arrian; being a translation of the fragments of the Indika of*

PATRICIA AHMED ET AL.

Megasthenês collected by Dr. Schwanbeck, and of the first part of the Indika of Arrian (pp. 175–217). Thacker, Spink & Co. (Original work written ca. 150 CE).

Artharva-Veda Saṁhitā (Books VIII–XIX). (W. D. Whitney, Ed. & Trans.): Vol. 8. *Harvard oriental series* (C. R. Lanman, Ed.) (1905). Harvard University. (Original work written ca. 1200–1000 BCE).

Avari, B. (2007). *India: The ancient past: A history of the Indian sub-continent from c. 7000 BC to AD 1200*. Routledge.

Avari, B. (2013). *Islamic civilization in South Asia: A history of Muslim power and presence in the Indian subcontinent*. Routledge.

Ayyar, V., & Khandare, L. (2013). Mapping color and caste discrimination in Indian society. In R. E. Hall (Ed.), *The melanin millennium: Skin color as 21st century international discourse* (pp. 71–95). Springer.

Baber, T. H. (1833). (3.): Answers of T. H. Baber, Esq. In *Public: Appendix to the report from the Select Committee of the House of Commons on the affairs of the East-India Company, 16th August 1832, and minutes of evidence* (Vol. 1, pp. 421–448). J. L. Cox and Son.

Bābur, Z. M. (1922). *The Bābur-nāma in English (Memoirs of Bābur)* (Vol. 2; A. S. Beveridge, Trans.). Luzac. (Original work written ca. 1500).

Bahuguna, R. P. (2011). The ideological–political role of Brahmans in later medieval India. *Proceedings of the Indian History Congress, 72*(1), 353–359.

Baig, M. M., Khan, A. A., & Kulkarni, K. M. (2004). Mitochondrial DNA diversity in tribal and caste groups of Maharashtra (India) and its implication on their genetic origins. *Annals of Human Genetics, 68*(5), 453–460.

Bates, C. (1995). Race, caste, and tribe in central India: The early origins of Indian anthropometry. In P. Robb (Ed.), *The concept of race in South Asia* (pp. 219–259). Oxford University Press.

Bayly, C. A. (1993). Knowing the country: Empires and information in India. *Modern Asian Studies, 27*(1), 3–43.

Bayly, C. A. (1996). *Empire and information: Intelligence gathering and social communication in India, 1780–1870*. Cambridge University Press.

Bayly, C. A. (2006). *The new Cambridge history of India. Indian society and the making of the British Empire* (Pt. 2, Vol. 1; G. Johnson, C.A. Bayly, & J. F. Richards, Eds.). Cambridge University Press. (Original work published 1988).

Bayly, S. (1999). *The new Cambridge history of India. Caste, society and politics in India from the eighteenth century to the modern age* (Pt. 4, Vol. 3; G. Johnson, C. A. Bayly, & J. F. Richards, Eds.). Cambridge University Press.

Beal, S. (1869). Preface. In *Travels of Fah-Hian and Sung-Yun, Buddhist pilgrims, from China to India (400 AD and 518 AD)* (pp. vii–xiii; S. Beal, Trans.). Trübner.

Beal, S. (1906). Introduction. In H. Tsiang, *Si-Yu-Ki: Buddhist records of the western world* (Vol. 1, pp. ix–xxii; S. Beal, Trans.). Kegan Paul, Trench, Trübner.

Bellenoit, H. (2014). Between qanungos and clerks: The cultural and service worlds of Hindustan's pensmen, c. 1750–1850. *Modern Asian Studies, 48*(4), 872–910.

Bellenoit, H. (2017). *The formation of the colonial state in India: Scribes, paper and taxes, 1760–1860*. Routledge.

Berreman, G. D. (1967). Caste as social process. *Southwestern Journal of Anthropology, 23*(4), 351–370.

Bhagat, R. B. (2001). Census and the construction of communalism in India. *Economic and Political Weekly, 36*(46/47), 4352–4356.

Bhagat, R. B. (2003). Role of census in racial and ethnic construction: US, British and Indian censuses. *Economic and Political Weekly, 38*(8), 686–691.

Bhagat, R. B. (2006). Census and caste enumeration: British legacy and contemporary practice in India. *Genus, 62*(2), 119–134.

Bhattacharya, D. (1990). The Mandal Commission in a historical and statistical perspective. *Proceedings of the Indian History Congress, 51*, 641–648.

Bidner, C., & Eswaran, M. (2015). A gender-based theory of the caste system of India. *Journal of Development Economics, 114*(May), 142–158.

Blochmann, H. (1873). Preface. In A. F. Ibn Mubārāk (Ed.), *The Ain i Akbari* (Vol. 1, pp. iii–vii; H. Blochmann, Trans.). Asiatic Society of Bengal.

Boivin, N. (2005). Orientalism, ideology and identity: Examining caste in South Asian archaeology. *Journal of Social Archaeology, 5*(2), 225–252.

Bose, N., & Ramraj, V. V. (2020). *Lex mercatoria*, legal pluralism, and the modern state through the lens of the East India Company, 1600–1757. *Comparative Studies of South Asia, Africa and the Middle East, 40*(2), 277–290.

Bosworth, A. B. (1996). The historical setting of Megasthenes' *Indica. Classical Philology, 91*(2), 113–127.

Bouglé, C. (1971). *Essays on the caste system* (D. F. Pocock, Trans.). Cambridge University Press.

Bourdieu, P. (1994). Rethinking the state: Genesis and structure of the bureaucratic field. (L. J. D. Wacquant & S. Farage, Trans.). *Sociological Theory, 12*(1), 1–18.

Bracciolini, P. (1857). The travels of Nicolò Conti, in the East, in the early part of the fifteenth century, as related by Poggio Bracciolini, in his work entitled "Historia de varietate fortunæ." Lib. IV. In R. H. Major (Ed.), *India in the fifteenth century. Being a collection of narratives of voyages to India, in the century preceding the Portuguese discovery of the Cape of Good Hope; from Latin, Persian, Russian, and Italian sources* (pp. 3–39). Hakluyt Society. (Original work written ca. 1439–1448).

Brenner, R. (1993). *Merchants and revolution: Commercial change, political conflict, and London's overseas traders, 1550–1653.* Cambridge University Press.

Brown, F. C. (1838). 1. East India slavery: Answers to questions circulated by the Board of Control in August 1832. In *Returns: Slave trade, East India and Ceylon* (pp. 416–423). (publisher not identified).

Brown, S. J. (2009). William Robertson, early orientalism and the *historical disquisition* on India of 1791. *Scottish Historical Review, 88*(2), 289–312.

Buchanan, F. H. (1928). *An account of the district of Purnea in 1809–10.* Bihar and Orissa Research Society.

Buchanan (Hamilton), F. (1833). *A geographical, statistical, and historical description of the district, or Zila, of Dinajpur, in the province, or soubah, of Bengal.* Baptist Mission Press.

Burke, E. (1834). Trial of Warren Hastings, Esquire: Third day, 15th February, 1788. In *The works of Edmund Burke: With a memoir* (Vol. 3, pp. 285–307). George Dearborn. (Original work published 1788).

Carroll, L. (1978). Colonial perceptions of Indian society and the emergence of caste(s) associations. *Journal of Asian Studies, 37*(2), 233–250.

Centeno, M. A. (2002). *Blood and debt: War and the nation-state in Latin America.* Pennsylvania State University Press.

Chakrabarty, D. (2000). *Subaltern studies* and postcolonial historiography. *Nepantla: Views From South, 1*(1), 9–32.

Chakravarti, R. (2016). Mauryan Empire. In J. M. McKenzie (Ed.), *The encyclopedia of empire* (pp. 1–7). Wiley Online Library. https://onlinelibrary.wiley.com/doi/book/10.1002/9781118455074

Chakravarti, U. (1993). Conceptualising Brahmanical patriarchy in early India: Gender, caste, class and state. *Economic and Political Weekly, 28*(14), 579–585.

Chakravarti, U. (1998). *Rewriting history: The life and times of Pandita Ramabai.* Kali for Women.

Chandel, N. (2018). Varna: A historical review. *RESEARCH REVIEW International Journal of Multidisciplinary, 3*(6), 357–362.

Chatterjee, B. (2021). Founding empire: James Rennell and the eighteenth-century survey of British Bengal. *XVII–XVIII: Revue de la Société d'études anglo-américains des XVIIe et XVIIIe siècles, 78*, 1–15. https://doi.org/10.4000/1718.8375

Chatterjee, K. (2010). Scribal elites in sultanate and Mughal Bengal. *Indian Economic and Social History Review, 47*(4), 445–472.

Chatterjee, P. (1993). *The nation and its fragments: Colonial and postcolonial histories.* Princeton University Press.

Chowdhry, P. (2013). Militarized masculinities: Shaped and reshaped in colonial south-east Punjab. *Modern Asian Studies, 47*(3), 713–750.

Christian, G. J. (1854). *Report on the census of the north west provinces of the Bengal Presidency, taken on the 1st of January, 1853.* Baptist Mission Press.

Christian, M. (2019). A global critical race and racism framework: Racial entanglements and deep and malleable whiteness. *Sociology of Race and Ethnicity*, *5*(2), 169–185.

Cohn, B. S. (1987). *An anthropologist among the historians and other essays*. Oxford University Press.

Cohn, B. S. (1996). *Colonialism and its forms of knowledge: The British in India*. Princeton University Press.

Copland, I. (2001). *India 1885–1947: The unmaking of an empire*. Pearson.

Cruikshank, J. (1853). Reports on the portions of Duskroee Purgunna situated in the Ahmedabad and Kaira collectorate. In *Selections of Records of the Bombay Government. No. X* (pp. 129–140). Bombay Education Society's Press.

Das, B. (1980). Kayasthas and Karanas in Orissa – A study on inscriptions. *Proceedings of the Indian History Congress*, *41*, 940–944.

Das Gupta, A. (1972). Study of the historical demography of India. In D. V. Glass & R. Revelle (Eds.), *Population and social change* (pp. 419–435). Edward Arnold.

Dayma, Y. (2006). Structure of legitimation under the early Kadambas. *Proceedings of the Indian History Congress*, *66*, 155–166.

Deshpande, A. (2008). Caste and diversity in India. In J. B. Davis & W. Dolfsma (Eds.), *The Elgar companion to social economics* (pp. 171–187). Edgar Elgar.

Dirks, N. B. (1992). Castes of mind. *Representations*, *37*, 56–78.

Dirks, N. B. (1996). Foreword. In B. S. Cohn (Ed.), *Colonialism and its forms of knowledge: The British in India* (pp. ix–xvii). Princeton University Press.

Dirks, N. B. (1997). The policing of tradition: Colonialism and anthropology in southern India. *Comparative Studies in Society and History*, *39*(1), 182–212.

Dirks, N. B. (2001). *Castes of mind: Colonialism and the making of modern India*. Princeton University Press.

Durand, J. D. (1977). Historical estimates of world population: An evaluation. *Population and Development Review*, *3*(3), 253–296.

East India Company Act, 1784. (1899). In H. W. C. Carnduff (Ed.), *A collection of statutes relating to India, in two volumes. Up to the end of 1870* (Vol. 1, pp. 21–31). Office of the Superintendent of Government Printing. (Original work published 1784).

Eaton, R. M. (2019). *India in the Persianate age: 1000–1765*. University of California Press.

Edney, M. H. (1997). *Mapping an empire: The geographical construction of British India, 1765–1843*. University of Chicago Press.

Elius, M., Khan, I., Nor, M. R. M., Muneem, A., Mansor, F., & Zulkifli Bin Mohd Yusoff, M. Y. (2020). Muslim treatment of other religions in medieval Bengal. *SAGE Open*, *10*(4), 1–14. https://doi.org/10.1177/2158244020970546

Emigh, R. J., Ahmed, P., & Riley, D. (2021). *How everyday forms of racial categorization survived imperialist censuses in Puerto Rico*. Palgrave Macmillan.

Emigh, R. J., Riley, D., & Ahmed, P. (2016a). *How societies and states count:* Vol. 1. *Antecedents of censuses from medieval to nation states*. Palgrave Macmillan.

Emigh, R. J., Riley, D., & Ahmed, P. (2016b). *How societies and states count:* Vol. 2. *Changes in censuses from imperialist to welfare states*. Palgrave Macmillan.

Emigh, R. J., Riley, D., & Ahmed, P. (2019). Toward a sociology of knowledge of land surveys: The influences of societies and states. *Journal of Historical Sociology*, *32*(4), 404–425.

Emigh, R. J., Riley, D., & Ahmed, P. (2020). The sociology of official information gathering: Enumeration, influence, reactivity, and power of states and societies. In T. Janoski, C. de Leon, J. Misra, & I. W. Martin (Eds.), *The new handbook of political sociology* (pp. 290–320). Cambridge University Press.

Fâ-Hien. (1886). *A record of Buddhistic kingdoms: Being an account by the Chinese monk Fâ-Hien of his travels in India and Ceylon (AD 399–414) in search of the Buddhist books of discipline* (J. Legge, Trans.). Clarendon Press. (Original work written ca. 414).

Fisher, M. H. (1993). The office of Akhbār Nawīs: The transition from Mughal to British forms. *Modern Asian Studies*, *27*(1), 45–82.

Fleming, B. J. (2016). The materiality of South Asian manuscripts from the University of Pennsylvania MS. Coll. 390 and the Rāmamālā Library in Bangladesh. *Manuscript Studies: A Journal of the Schoenberg Institute for Manuscript Studies*, *1*(1), 28–51.

Foucault, M. (1977). *Discipline and punish: The birth of the prison* (A. Sheridan, Trans.). Vintage Books. (Original work published 1975).

Foucault, M. (1991). Governmentality (P. Pasquino, Trans.). In G. Burchell, C. Gordon, & P. Miller (Eds.), *The Foucault effect: Studies in governmentality with two lectures and an interview with Michel Foucault* (pp. 87–104). University of Chicago Press. (Original work published 1978).

Foucault, M. (2007). *Security, territory, and population: Lectures at the Collège de France 1977–1978* (M. Senellart, Ed.; G. Burchell, Trans.). Picador. (Original work published 1978).

Frye, R. N. (1948). Review of *Feuerpriester in Kleinasien und Iran*, by S. Wikander. *Harvard Journal of Asiatic Studies, 11*(1/2), 230–239.

Frykenberg, R. E. (1993). Constructions of Hinduism at the nexus of history and religion. *Journal of Interdisciplinary History, 23*(3), 523–550.

Fuller, C. J., & Narasimhan, H. (2010). Traditional vocations and modern professions among Tamil Brahmans in colonial and post-colonial South India. *Indian Economic & Social History Review, 47*(4), 473–496.

Gascoigne, B. (1971). *The great Moghuls*. Jonathan Cape.

Gautama. (1999). The Dharmasūtra of Gautama. In P. Olivelle (Ed. & Trans.), *Dharmasūtras: The law codes of Āpastamba, Gautama, Baudhāyana, and Vasiṣṭha* (pp. 74–126). Oxford University Press. (Original work written ca. 600–200 BCE).

Gelders, R., & Balagangadhara, S. N. (2011). Rethinking orientalism: Colonialism and the study of Indian traditions. *History of Religions, 51*(2), 101–128.

Ghanta, S., & Mukherjee, S. P. (2020). An overview of mathematical evolution in Indus Valley civilization (3500–2500 BC). *GRD Journal for Engineering, 5*(3), 12–16.

Ghosh, A. (2003). An uncertain "coming of the book": Early print cultures in colonial India. *Book History, 6*(1), 23–55.

Ghosh, J. K., Maiti, P., Rao, T. J., & Sinha, B. K. (1999). Evolution of statistics in India. *International Statistical Review, 67*(1), 13–34.

Ghurye, G. S. (1969). *Caste and race in India*. Popular Prakashan. (Original work published 1932).

Gidumal, D. (2008). Introduction. In *The Chachnamah: An ancient history of Sind, giving the Hindu period down to the Arab conquest* (M. K. Fredunbeg, Trans.; pp. 3–8). Sani Hussain Panhwar. (Original work published 1900).

Gill, M. S. (2007). Politics of population census data in India. *Economic and Political Weekly, 42*(3), 241–249.

Government of India, Foreign Department. (1856). *Selections from the records of the Government of India. (Foreign Department.) No. XI. Report on the census, taken on the 1st January 1855, of the population of the Punjab territories. Papers connected with the administration of Mysore*. Thos. Jones.

Gray, G. (1775). To the Right Honorable *Lord Clive*, President and Governor, &c., Council at *Fort-William*. In W. Bolts (Ed.), *Appendix to considerations on India affairs: Part II* (Vol. 3, pp. 118–119). J. Dodsley, G. Robson, J. Almon, Jefferies and Faden, P. Elmsly, W. Owen, T. Evans, Brotherton and Sewell, & Richardson and Urquhart. (Original letter written 1766).

Green, A. S. (2021). Killing the priest-king: Addressing egalitarianism in the Indus civilization. *Journal of Archaeological Research, 29*(2), 153–202.

Green, A. S. (2022). Of revenue without rulers: Public goods in the egalitarian cities of the Indus civilization. *Frontiers in Political Science, 4*, 1–19. https://doi.org/10.3389/fpos.2022.823071

Grewal, I. (2016). The masculinities of post-colonial governance: Bureaucratic memoirs of the Indian Civil Service. *Modern Asian Studies, 50*(2), 602–635.

Griffin, L. J. (2007). Historical sociology, narrative and event-structure analysis: Fifteen years later. *Sociologica, 1*(3), 1–17.

Guha, R. (1997). *Dominance without hegemony: History and power in colonial India*. Harvard University Press.

Guha, S. (2003). The politics of identity and enumeration in India c. 1600–1900. *Comparative Studies in Society and History, 45*(1), 148–167.

Guha, S. (2010). Serving the barbarian to preserve the *dharma*: The ideology and training of a clerical elite in peninsular India c. 1300–1800. *Indian Economic & Social History Review, 47*(4), 497–525.

Guha, S. (2013). *Beyond caste: Identity and power in South Asia, past and present.* Brill.

Gupta, C. (1983). The writers' class of ancient India – A case study in social mobility. *Indian Economic & Social History Review, 20*(2), 191–204.

Habib, I. (2008). Kosambi, Marxism and Indian history. *Economic and Political Weekly, 43*(30), 85–88.

Haider, N. (2011). Norms of professional excellence and good conduct in accountancy manuals of the Mughal Empire. *International Review of Social History, 56*(S19), 263–274.

Hamilton, W. (1815). *The East India Gazetteer: Containing particular descriptions of the empires, kingdoms, principalities, provinces, cities, towns, districts, fortresses, harbours, rivers, lakes, &c. of Hindostan, and the adjacent countries, India beyond the Ganges, and the eastern archipelago; together with sketches of the manners, customs, institutions, agriculture, commerce, manufactures, revenues, population, castes, religion, history, & c. of their various inhabitants.* John Murray.

Hastings, W. (1785). To Nathaniel Smith, Esquire. In C. Wilkins (Ed. & Trans.), *The Bhăgvăt-Gēētā or dialogues of Krēēshnă and Ărjöön; in eighteen lectures with notes* (pp. 5–16). C. Nourse. (Original letter written 1784).

House of Lords. (1830). *Report from the Select Committee of the House of Lords appointed to inquire into the present state of the affairs of the East India Company, and into the trade between Great Britain, the East Indies and China; with the minutes of evidence taken before the committee.*

Husain, M. H., & Sarwar, F. H. (2012). A comparative study of *Zamindari,* Raiyatwari and *Mahalwari* land revenue settlements: The colonial mechanisms of surplus extraction in 19th century British India. *IOSR Journal of Humanities and Social Science, 2*(4), 16–26.

Huttenback, R. A. (1966). *The British imperial experience.* Harper & Row.

I-Tsing. (1896). *A record of the Buddhist religion as practiced in India and the Malay archipelago (A.D. 671–695)* (J. Takakusu, Trans.). Clarendon Press. (Original work written ca. 689).

Ibn Baṭṭūṭa. (1994). *The travels of Ibn Baṭṭūṭa: AD 1325–1354* (Vol. 4; H. A. R. Gibb & C. F. Bennington, Eds.; C. Defrémery & B. R. Sanguinmetti, Trans.). Hakluyt Society. (Original work written 1353).

Ibn Mubārāk, A. F. (1873). *The Ain i Akbari* (Vol. 1; H. Blochmann, Trans.). The Baptist Mission Press (for the Asiatic Society). (Original work written ca. 1589–1596).

Ibn Mubārāk, A. F. (1891). *The Ain i Akbari* (Vol. 2; H. S. Jarrett, Trans.). The Baptist Mission Press (for the Asiatic Society). (Original work written ca. 1589–1596).

Ibn Mubārāk, A. F. (1894). *The Ain i Akbari* (Vol. 3; H. S. Jarrett, Trans.). The Baptist Mission Press (for the Asiatic Society). (Original work written ca. 1589–1596).

Inden, R. B. (2000). *Imagining India.* Indiana University Press. (Original work published 1990).

India as it is–India as it may be. (1858). *British Quarterly Review, 27*(53), 202–244.

Indian Law Commission. (1844). *Copies of the special reports of the Indian Law Commissioners.* House of Commons.

Jackson, P. (1999). *The Delhi Sultanate: A political and military history.* Cambridge University Press.

Jaffrelot, C. (2000). Sanskritization vs. ethnicization in India: Changing identities and caste politics before Mandal. *Asian Survey, 40*(5), 756–766.

Jaiswal, S. (1991). Varna ideology and social change. *Social Scientist, 19*(3–4), 41–48.

Jaiswal, S. (1997). Caste: Ideology and context. *Social Scientist, 25*(5–6), 3–12.

Jarrett, H. S. (1978). Preface. In H. S. Jarrett (Trans.) and J. Sarkar (Ed.), *The Āīn-i-Akbarī by Abū'l-Fazl 'Allāmī: A Gazetteer and administrative Manual of Akbar's Empire and past History of India* (Vol. 2., pp. i–viii). Royal Asiatic Society. (Original work published 1891).

Jenkins, L. D. (2003). Another "people of India" project: Colonial and national anthropology. *Journal of Asian Studies, 62*(4), 1143–1170.

Jogdand, Y. A., Khan, S. S., & Mishra, A. K. (2016). Understanding the persistence of caste: A commentary on Cotterill, Sidanius, Bhardwaj and Kumar (2014). *Journal of Social and Political Psychology, 4*(2), 554–570.

Jolly, J. (1900). Introduction. In *The Institutes of Vishnu [Vishnu Śutra]* (J. Jolly, Ed. & Trans.; pp. ix–xxxvii). Charles Scribner's Sons.

Joshi, D. (2018). Translating orality: Pictorial narrative traditions with reference to *Kaavad* and *Phad. Cankaya University Journal of Humanities and Social Sciences, 12*(1–2), 85–98.

Kalpagam, U. (2000). The colonial state and statistical knowledge. *History of the Human Sciences, 13*(2), 37–55.

Kamble, R. A., Kumar, R., & Chowdhury, A. R. (2023). "Ostracized by law": The sociopolitical and juridical construction of the "criminal tribe" in colonial India. *History and Anthropology*, 1–21. https://doi.org/10.1080/02757206.2023.2204866

Karve, I. (1961). *Hindu society: An interpretation*. Sangam Publishers.

Kauṭilya. (1992). *The Arthashastra* (L. N. Rangarajan, Ed. and Trans.). Penguin Books. (Original work written ca. 300 BCE).

Kaviraj, S. (1997). Religion and identity in India. *Ethnic and Racial Studies, 20*(2), 325–344.

Keay, J. (1991). *The Honourable Company: A history of the English East India Company*. HarperCollins.

Keay, J. (2000). *India: A history*. Atlantic Monthly Press.

King, R. (1999). *Orientalism and religion: Postcolonial theory, India and the "mystic East."* Routledge.

Kinra, R. (2010). Master and *munshī*: A Brahman secretary's guide to Mughal governance. *Indian Economic & Social History Review, 47*(4), 527–561.

Kosambi, D. D. (1944). Caste and class in India. *Science & Society, 8*(3), 243–249.

Kosambi, D. D. (1975). *An introduction to the study of Indian history* (2nd ed.). Popular Prakashan. (Original work published in 1956).

Kosmin, P. J. (2014). *The land of the elephant kings: Space, territory, and ideology in the Seleucid Empire*. Harvard University Press.

Kúfi, A. (2008). *The Chachnamah: An ancient history of Sind, giving the Hindu period down to the Arab conquest* (M. K. Fredunbeg, Trans.). Sani Hussain Panhwar. (Original work published 1900).

Kulkarni, G. T. (2017). The Hindus as part of the administrative system of the Deccani Sultanates (1347–1686 AD). *Proceedings of the Indian History Congress, 78*, 321–332.

Kumar, M. (2004). Relationship of caste and crime in colonial India: A discourse analysis. *Economic and Political Weekly, 39*(10), 1078–1087.

Lange, M. (2013). *Comparative-historical methods*. Sage.

Lawson, P. (1993). *The East India Company: A history*. Longman.

Lawson, P., & Phillips, J. (1984). "Our execrable banditti": Perceptions of nabobs in mid-eighteenth century Britain. *Albion: A Quarterly Journal Concerned with British Studies, 16*(3), 225–241.

Lee, A. (2017). Redistributive colonialism: The long-term legacy of international conflict in India. *Politics & Society, 45*(2), 173–224.

Leonard, K. I. (1978). *Social history of an Indian caste: The Kayasths of Hyderabad*. University of California Press.

Lo Turco, B. (2013). Propagation of written culture in Brahmanical India. *Scripta: An International Journal of Codicology and Palaeography, 6*, 85–93.

Ludden, D. (1993). Orientalist empiricism: Transformations of colonial knowledge. In C. A. Breckenridge & P. van der Veer (Eds.), *Orientalism and the postcolonial predicament: Perspectives on South Asia* (pp. 250–278). University of Pennsylvania Press.

Lyall, A. (1968). *The rise and expansion of the British dominion in India*. Howard Fertig. (Original work published 1894).

Macaulay, T. B. (1833). *A speech of T. B. Macaulay, Esq. M.P. on the second reading of the East-India Bill, in the House of Commons, 10th July, 1833. From Hansard's Parliamentary debates* (Vol. 18; 3rd series). T. C. Hansard.

Madras Presidency, Board of Revenue. (1866). *The standing orders of the Board of Revenue from 1820 to 1865* (R. A. Dalyell, Ed.). William Thomas.

Mahajan, V. D. (2018). *History of medieval India (Muslim rule in India): Sultanate period and Mughal period* (M. Bhatnagar, Revisor). S. Chand. (Original work published 1991).

Manu. (1999). *Manusmṛti with the "Manubhāṣya" of Medhātithi. Discourses I and II* (Vol. 3, Pt. 1; Ganganath Jha, Trans.). Motilal Banarasidass Publishers. (Original work written ca. 100–300).

Markham, C. R. (1871). *A memoir on the Indian surveys*. W. H. Allen.

Martin, R. B. (1981). Bibliographic notes on the Indian census. In N. G. Barrier (Ed.), *The census in British India: New perspectives* (pp. 61–72). Manohar.

Martin, R. M. (1837). *The British Colonial Library: Vol. 8. History of the possessions of the Honourable East India Company* (Vol. 1). Whittaker & Company.

McIntosh, J. R. (2008). *The ancient Indus Valley: New perspectives*. ABC-CLIO.

Megasthênes. (1877). The fragments of the Indika of Megasthenés. In J. W. McCrindle (Ed. & Trans.), *Ancient India as described by Megasthenés and Arrian; being a translation of the fragments of the Indika of Megasthenés collected by Dr. Schwanbeck, and of the first part of the Indika of Arrian* (pp. 3–174). Thacker, Spink & Co. (Original work written ca. 310 BCE).

Menon, M. (2016). Medicine, money, and the making of the East India Company state: William Roxburgh in Madras, c. 1790. In A. Winterbottom & F. Tesfaye (Eds.), *Histories of medicine and healing in the Indian Ocean world: The medieval and early modern period* (Vol. 1, pp. 151–178). Palgrave Macmillan.

Michael, B. A. (2007). Making territory visible: The revenue surveys of colonial South Asia. *Imago Mundi, 59*(1), 78–95.

Mitra, A. (1954). *Census of India 1951* (Vol. 6, Pt. 3). Manager of Publications.

Monten, J. (2014). Intervention and state-building: Comparative lessons from Japan, Iraq, and Afghanistan. *The Annals of the American Academy of Political and Social Science, 656*(1), 173–191.

Moosvi, S. (2011). The medieval state and caste. *Social Scientist, 39*(7–8), 3–8.

Moosvi, S. (2014). Mughal administration in rural localities. *Studies in People's History, 1*(2), 231–236.

Mukherjee, P. (1988). *Beyond the four varnas: The untouchables in India*. Indian Institute of Advanced Study.

Mulligan, M. (2018). The East India Company: Non-state actor as treaty-maker. In J. Summers & A. Gough (Eds.), *Non-state actors and international obligations: Creation, evolution and enforcement* (pp. 39–59). Brill Nijhoff.

Nainsi, M. (1969a). *Marwar ra Pargana ri Vigat* (Pt. 1). Rajasthan Prachyavidya Pratishthan. (Originally written ca. 1665–1772).

Nainsi, M. (1969b). *Marwar ra Pargana ri Vigat* (Pt. 2). Rajasthan Prachyavidya Pratishthan. (Originally written ca. 1665–1772).

Nambiar, M. V. U. (1981). *Census of India 1981: Series – 10: Kerala: Paper 1 of 1981: Provincial population totals*. Census of India.

Nikitin, A. (1985). *Afanasy Nikitin's voyage beyond three seas: 1466–1472* (S. Apresyan, Trans.). Raduga Publishers.

Nogues-Marco, P. (2021). Measuring colonial extraction: The East India Company's rule and the drain of wealth (1757–1858). *Capitalism: A Journal of History and Economics, 2*(1), 154–195.

Office of the Registrar General, India. (1985). *Census of India 1961: Report of the population estimates of India: 1811–1820: India* (Vol. 3, Pt. B; D. Bhattacharya, Ed.). Government of India.

Office of the Registrar General, India. (1989). *Census of India 1961: Report of the population estimates of India: 1801–1810* (Vol. 2; D. Bhattacharya, Ed.). Government of India.

O'Hanlon, R. (1988). Recovering the subject: *Subaltern studies* and histories of resistance in colonial South Asia. *Modern Asian Studies, 22*(1), 189–224.

O'Hanlon, R. (2010). The social worth of scribes: Brahmins, Kāyasthas and the social order in early modern India. *Indian Economic & Social History Review, 47*(4), 563–595.

O'Hanlon, R. (2013). Contested conjunctures: Brahman communities and "early modernity" in India. *The American Historical Review, 118*(3), 765–787.

O'Hanlon, R. (2017). Caste and its histories in colonial India: A reappraisal. *Modern Asian Studies, 51*(2), 432–461.

Pant, R. (1987). The cognitive status of caste in colonial ethnography: A review of some literature on the NorthWest provinces and Oudh. *Indian Economic & Social History Review, 24*(2), 145–162.

Parsons, T. (1999). *The British imperial century, 1815–1914: A world history perspective*. Rowman & Littlefield Publishers.

Peabody, N. (2001). Cents, sense, census: Human inventories in late precolonial and early colonial India. *Comparative Studies in Society and History, 43*(4), 819–850.

Peabody, N. (2003). *Hindu kingship and polity in precolonial India*. Cambridge University Press.

Penumala, P. K. (2010). Sociology of Hinduism. In B. S. Turner (Ed.), *The new Blackwell companion to the sociology of religion* (pp. 407–430). Wiley-Blackwell.

Percival, P. (1854). *The land of the Veda: India briefly described in some of its aspects, physical, social, intellectual and moral, including the substance of a course of lectures delivered at St Augustine's Missionary College, Canterbury.* George Bell.

Phillimore, R. H. (1945). *Historical records of the Survey of India: Eighteenth century* (Vol. 1). Surveyor General of India.

Phillimore, R. H. (1958). *Historical records of the Survey of India: 1830–1843: George Everest* (Vol. 4). Surveyor General of India.

Plofker, K. (2009). *Mathematics in India.* Princeton University Press.

Polo, M. (1958). *The travels of Marco Polo* (R. Latham, Trans.). Penguin Books. (Original work written ca. 1300).

Prakash, G. (1994). Subaltern studies as postcolonial criticism. *The American Historical Review, 99*(5), 1475–1490.

Prasad, R. U. S. (2015). *The Rig-Vedic and post-Rig-Vedic polity (1500 BCE–500 BCE).* Vernon Press.

Puttaswamy, T. K. (2000). The mathematical accomplishments of ancient Indian mathematicians. In H. Selin & U. d'Ambrosio (Eds.), *Mathematics across cultures: The history of non-Western mathematics* (pp. 409–422). Springer Science+Business Media, B.V. Kluwer Academic Publishers.

Raj, K. (2000). Colonial encounters and the forging of new knowledge and national identities: Great Britain and India, 1760–1850. *Osiris, 15*(1), 119–134.

Raman, B. (2012a). *Document Raj: Writing and scribes in early colonial South India.* University of Chicago Press.

Raman, B. (2012b). The duplicity of paper: Counterfeit, discretion, and bureaucratic authority in early colonial Madras. *Comparative Studies in Society and History, 54*(2), 229–250.

Raman, B. (2018). Sovereignty, property and land development: The East India Company in Madras. *Journal of the Economic and Social History of the Orient, 61*(5–6), 976–1004.

Rand, G., & Wagner, K. A. (2012). Recruiting the "martial races": Identities and military service in colonial India. *Patterns of Prejudice, 46*(3–4), 232–254.

Richards, J. F. (1993). *The new Cambridge history of India: The Mughal Empire* (Pt. 1, Vol. 5; G. Johnson, C.A. Bayly, & J. F. Richards, Eds.). Cambridge University Press.

Richards, J. F. (1997). Early modern India and world history. *Journal of World History, 8*(2), 197–209.

Rigveda (Vol. 1; T. Ram, Trans.). (2013). Vijaykumar Govindram Hasanand. (Original work written ca. 1500–1200 BCE).

Risley, H. H. (1915). *The people of India* (W. Crooke, Ed.; 2nd ed.). Thacker, Spink & Co. (Original work published 1908).

Risley, H. H., & Gait, E. A. (1903). *Census of India, 1901: India: Report* (Vol. 1, Pt. 1). Office of the Superintendent of Government Printing.

Ritchie, L. (1848). *A history of the Indian empire and the East Indian Company from the earliest times to the present. Together with accounts of Beloochistan, Affghanistan, Cashmere, Thibet, the Burman Empire, Sian, the Malay peninsula, the Chinese Empire, Japan, Australia, S. Africa, etc. Comprehending their history, religions, laws, manners and customs, commercial resources, etc.* (Vol. 1). W. H. Allen.

Robins, N. (2012). *The corporation that changed the world: How the East India Company shaped the modern multinational.* Pluto Press.

Rose, N., O'Malley, P., & Valverde, M. (2006). Governmentality. *Annual Review of Law and Social Science, 2,* 83–104.

Sah, R. S. (2019). Mughal state and the information system: 1556–1707. *Indian Historical Review, 46*(2), 292–309.

Said, E. W. (1978). *Orientalism.* Vintage Books.

Sakstrup, C. (2023). When strength becomes weakness: Precolonial state development, monopoly on violence, and civil war. *Comparative Political Studies, 56*(14), 2131–2164.

Sam, B. M., & Aryanpour, B. (2014). The origin of social classes, profession and colour in the Indo-European societies and ancient Persia. *Journal of Anthropology and Archaeology, 2*(1), 109–127.

Sanjeev, T. (2020). Surveying and producing the frontier in nineteenth century Manipur: Challenges and practices. *Asian Ethnicity, 21*(1), 122–136.

SarDesai, D. R. (2008). *India: The definitive history*. Westview Press.

Sastri, K. A. N. (1972). *Foreign notices of South India from Megasthenes to Ma Huan*. University of Madras. (Original work published 1939).

Sathaye, A. A. (2015). *Crossing the lines of caste: Viśvāmitra and the construction of Brahmin power in Hindu mythology*. Oxford University Press.

Scott, D. (1995). Colonial governmentality. *Social Text, 43*(Autumn), 191–220.

Seal, A. (1968). *The emergence of Indian nationalism: Competition and collaboration in the later nineteenth century*. Cambridge University Press.

Seal, A. (1973). Imperialism and nationalism in India. *Modern Asian Studies, 7*(3), 321–347.

Sen, S. (2002). *Distant sovereignty: National imperialism and the origins of British India*. Routledge.

Sen, S. (2012). Unfinished conquest: Residual sovereignty and the legal foundations of the British Empire in India. *Law, Culture and the Humanities, 9*(2), 227–242.

Seth, V. K. (2012). The East India Company: A case study in corporate governance. *Global Business Review, 13*(2), 221–238.

Sharma, S., Rai, E., Sharma, P., Jena, M., Singh, S., Darvishi, K., Bhat, A. K., Bhanwer, A. J. S., Tiwari, P. K., & Bamezai, R. N. K. (2009). The Indian origin of paternal haplogroup R1a1* substantiates the autochthonous origin of Brahmins and the caste system. *Journal of Human Genetics, 54*(1), 47–55.

Sharma, S. K. (2012). Public finance in ancient India: Reflections on taxation and revenue in Kautilya's *Arthashastra*. *Indian Journal of Political Science, 73*(2), 209–220.

Shaw, J. (1887). *Charters relating to the East India Company from 1600 to 1761: Reprinted from a former collection with some additions and a preface*. R. Hill at the Government Press.

Shembavnekar, K. M. (1952). The population of ancient India (500 BC to 100 AD). *Annals of the Bhandarkar Oriental Research Institute, 33*(1/4), 83–96.

Singh, B. (2022). The revolt of 1857 reasons of genesis: A study. *EPRA International Journal of Multidisciplinary Research, 8*(10), 269–272.

Singh, U. B. (1998). *Administrative system in India (Vedic age to 1947)*. APH Publishing.

Sivramkrishna, S. (2014). From merchant to merchant-ruler: A structure–conduct–performance perspective of the East India Company's history, 1600–1765. *Business History, 56*(5), 789–815.

Smith, B. K. (1992). Canonical authority and social classification: Veda and *varṇa* in ancient Indian texts. *History of Religions, 32*(2), 103–125.

Smith, B. K. (1994). *Classifying the universe: The ancient Indian varṇa system and the origins of caste*. Oxford University Press.

Smith, R. S. (1985). Rule-by-records and rule-by-reports: Complementary aspects of the British imperial rule of law. *Contributions to Indian Sociology, 19*(1), 153–176.

Smith, R. S. (2000). Between local tax and global statistic: The census as local record. *Contributions to Indian Sociology, 34*(1), 1–35.

Smith, V. A. (1904). *The Early history of India from 600 BC to the Muhammadan conquest, including the invasion of Alexander the Great*. Clarendon Press.

Smits, K. (2008). John Stuart Mill on the antipodes: Settler violence against Indigenous peoples and the legitimacy of colonial rule. *Australian Journal of Politics & History, 54*(1), 1–15.

Soifer, H., & vom Hau, M. (2008). Unpacking the *strength* of the state: The utility of state infrastructural power. *Studies in Comparative International Development, 43*(3–4), 219–230.

Spivak, G. C. (1988). Can the subaltern speak? In C. Nelson & L. Grossberg (Eds.), *Marxism and the interpretation of culture* (pp. 271–313). Macmillan Education.

Spodek, H. (2013). City planning in India under British rule. *Economic and Political Weekly, 48*(4), 53–61.

Sridharan, R. (2005). Mathematics in ancient and medieval India. In G. G. Emch, R. Sridharan, & M. D. Srinivas (Eds.), *Contributions to the history of Indian mathematics* (pp. 1–29). Hindustan Book Agency.

Stagl, J. F. (2012). The rule of law against the rule of greed: Edmund Burke against the East India Company. *Rechtsgeschichte – Legal History, 20*, 104–124.

Stein, B. (1985). State formation and economy reconsidered: Part one. *Modern Asian Studies, 19*(3), 387–413.

Stern, P. J. (2007). Politics and ideology in the early East India Company-State: The case of St Helena, 1673–1709. *Journal of Imperial and Commonwealth History, 35*(1), 1–23.

Stern, P. J. (2008). "A politie of civill & military power": Political thought and the late seventeenth-century foundations of the East India Company-State. *Journal of British Studies, 47*(2), 253–283.

St. John, I. (2012). *The making of the Raj: India under the East India Company.* Praeger.

Subramaniam, V. (2009). Indian legacy of bureaucracy and administration. In A. Farazmand (Ed.), *Bureaucracy and administration* (pp. 53–64). CRC Press.

Sundar, N. (2000). Caste as census category: Implications for sociology. *Current Sociology, 48*(3), 111–126.

Talbot, C. (2012). Justifying defeat: A Rajput perspective on the Age of Akbar. *Journal of the Economic and Social History of the Orient, 55*(2/3), 329–368.

Thapar, R. (1971). The image of the barbarian in early India. *Comparative Studies in Society and History, 13*(4), 408–436.

Thapar, R. (1984). Légitimation politique et filiation: Le *varna kshatriya* en Inde du nord [Political legitimation and filiation: The *Kshatriya varna* in northern India]. *Annales. Économies, Sociétés, Civilisation., 39*(4), 783–797.

Thapar, R. (2003). *The Penguin history of early India: From the origins to AD 1300.* Penguin Books.

Thapar, R. (2006). The Mauryan Empire in early India. *Historical Research, 79*(205), 287–305.

Thapar, R. (2008). Early Indian history and the legacy of D D Kosambi. *Economic & Political Weekly, 43*(30), 43–51.

Thapar, R. (2018). Revisiting Max Weber's religion of India. *Max Weber Studies, 18*(1), 122–139.

The Bengal and Agra annual guide and gazetteer for 1841 (Vol. 2, 3rd ed.). (1842). William Rushton.

The Institutes of Vishnu [Vishnu Śutra] (J. Jolly, Ed. & Trans). (1900). Charles Scribner's Sons. (Original work written ca. 300 BCE–1000 CE).

The law relating to India, and the East-India Company; with notes and an appendix. (1841). Wm. H. Allen London.

The Satapatha-Brâhmana according to the text of the Mādhyandina School (Pt. 4, Books VII, IX, and X). (1897). (J. Eggeling, Ed. & Trans.). Clarendon Press. (Original date written ca. 1000–600 BCE).

Thornton, E. (1854). *A gazetteer of the territories under the government of the East-India Company, and of the native states on the continent of India* (Vol. 1). Wm. H. Allen.

Travers, T. R. (2004). "The real value of the lands": The nawabs, the British and the land tax in eighteenth-century Bengal. *Modern Asian Studies, 38*(3), 517–558.

di Varthema, L. (1863). *The travels of Ludovico di Varthema in Egypt, Syria, Arabia Deserta and Arabia Felix in Persia, India, and Ethiopia, A.D. 1503 to 1508* (G. P. Badger, Ed.; J. W. Jones, Trans.). Hakluyt Society. (Original work published 1510).

Vasiṣṭha. (1999). The Dharmasūtra of Vasiṣṭha. In P. Olivelle (Ed. & Trans.), *Dharmasūtras: The law codes of Āpastamba, Gautama, Baudhāyana, and Vasiṣṭha* (pp. 244–326). Oxford University Press. (Original work written ca. 300 BCE–100 CE).

Verghese, A. (2016). British rule and tribal revolts in India: The curious case of Bastar. *Modern Asian Studies, 50*(5), 1619–1644.

Visvanathan, M. (2014). From the *lekhaka* to the *Kāyastha*: Scribes in early historic court and society (200 BCE–200 CE). *Proceedings of the Indian History Congress, 75*, 34–40.

Viswanathan, G. (2003). Colonialism and the construction of Hinduism. In G. Flood (Ed.), *The Blackwell companion to Hinduism* (pp. 23–44). Blackwell Publishers.

Vyas, S. N. (1967). *India in the Rāmayāṇa age: A study of the social and cultural conditions in ancient India as described in Vālmīki's Rāmayāṇa.* Atma Ram & Sons.

Walby, K., & Haan, M. (2012). Caste confusion and census enumeration in colonial India, 1871–1921. *Histoire sociale/Social History, 45*(90), 301–318.

Warden, F. (1833). Answers to circular (4.): F. Warden, Esq. In *Public: Appendix to the report from the Select Committee of the House of Commons on the affairs of the East-India Company, 16th August 1832, and minutes of evidence* (Vol. 1, pp. 10–42). J. L. Cox and Son.

Watters, T. (1904). *On Yuan Chwang's travels in India: 629–645 A.D.* Royal Asiatic Society.

Welch, A., Keshani, H., & Bain, A. (2002). Epigraphs, scripture, and architecture in the early Delhi Sultanate. *Muqarnas: An Annual On the Visual Cultures of the Islamic World, 19*(1), 12–43.

Willmott, K. (2023). Colonial numbers: Quantification, Indigeneity, and the politics of fiscal surveillance. *Surveillance and Society, 21*(1), 16–28.

Yajnavalkya Smriti. (1918). In Ś. C. Vidyârṇava (Trans.), *The sacred books of the Hindus: Yajnavalkya Smriti. Mitaksara and Balambhatta: The Âchâra Adhyâya* (Vol. 21, Book 1). Apurva Krishna Bose. (Original work written ca. 300–500 CE).

de Zwart, F. (2000). The logic of affirmative action: Caste, class and quotas in India. *Acta Sociologica, 43*(3), 235–249.

INDEX

Abilities, 182
Ableism, 5–6
Absolute private property, possibility of, 195–197
Absorption strategies, 215–216
Acts and Statutes of Barbadoes (ASB), 222
Agrarian elites, 152
American federalism, 118–119
American Legislative Exchange Council (ALEC), 120–121
Anti-Bribery Convention, 53
Anti-corruption, 52–55
  campaigns, 54
  to power consolidation, 61–63
  reform, 49
Anti-system grievances, 50–51
Argentina, 141–142
  elite relations in, 149–152
  macroeconomics of inflation in, 152–157
Argentine Central Bank, 157–158, 161
Art patronage, 81
Artists, 48
Asian art, 71–72
  elite art patronage and cultural legitimation, 72–73
  ethnic differences, 76–80
  methods, 73
  patronage, 74–80
  racial differences, 74–75
Asian elites, 33–34, 72
Associação Luso-Africana Ponto nos Is (The Luso-African Association), 92
Associational power, 21, 26–27

Barbadian Catholic Irish, 217–218
Barbados, 222–226
  before 1692 Conspiracy, 222–223

after conspiracy, 224–226
Conspiracy of 1692, 223–224
pathway, 220–221
Bengal Rent Commission, 202
Black communities, 86
Black cultural capitalists, 72–73
Black Death of 1348, 14–15
Black Lives Matter Movement, 90–91
Boston Symphony Orchestra, 72
"Bread-and-butter" corruption (*see* Street-level corruption)
British East India Company, 258–265
  information gathering and social uses, 258–264
  social and state uses of caste, 264–265
Bureaucracy, 26
Bureaucratized societies, 9

Calliano, Ismael, 102–104
Capitalism, 20–21, 23, 114–115
Capitalists, 24
Cash, 24
Catholic Irish under English imperial rule, 216–220
  different majorities, different vulnerabilities, 219
  racial state in context, 219–220
  racialization of Catholic Irish, 217–218
  stagnation *vs.* success, 218
Catholicism, 217, 232
Censuses, 240
  categorization, 242
Center for Media and Democracy (CMD), 125–126
Central bank deficit, origins and continuity of, 157–159
China, 46
Classic statements of elite theory, 6

INDEX

Coalitional power, 21, 29–30
Coda, 201–202
Coercive power, 19
Cohesion, 144–146
Colonial enumeration, 242
Colonial leviathan, 243
Colonial officials, 243–244
Colonialism, 204–205
Community–union coalitions, 30
Comparative process tracing (CPT), 220
Conflict, 181
Consensuality, 22–23
Conservative elites' dominance, 125
Conspiracy of 1692, 223–224
Contemporary revolutions, 46
Contentious politics, 4–5
Control-function method, 122–124
Cooperation, 181
Corporate board interlocked networks, 151–152
Corporate coherence, 146, 159
Corporate cohesion, 142–143
Corporate political action, 115–116
Corrupted revolutions, corrupt elites to, 58–61
Corruption, 46, 48, 55
Corruption grievances, 48
   possibilities and limitations, 63–66
   and protest in Tunisia, Ukraine, and China, 64
Corruption Perceptions Index (CPI), 53
Cova da Moura project, 90–91
Credibility, 148
Crisis, 143
Cultivators (*raiyats*), 175–176, 185
'Cultivators' rights
   diminishing information asymmetry and stabilization (and enhancement) of, 200–201
   fluctuation of, 199–200
Cultural capital, 72
Cultural capitalists, 72
Cultural legitimation, 72–73

Cultural patronage, 71–72
Cultural schema, 32
Cumulative number of bans or moratoriums, 125

Decolonization, 86
   Dori Nigro, 96–99
   history, form, and sociological and artistic methodology of *Travessia* project, 90–95
   Ismael Calliano, 102–104
   Luciane De AraúJo Santos, 99–100
   Mauricio Igor, 100–102
   Porto, 95–96
   theoretical framework, 87–90
Deep democratization, 49
Democracy, 9
Democrats, 118
Depth of power, 22
Dialectical realism, 38
Diffusion effect, 127
Dillon's Rule, 126
Diminution, 199–200
Direct rule censuses in India, 241–245
   interactive enumeration, 244–245
   society-driven enumeration, 244
   state-driven enumeration, 242–244
Directionality, 23
Disruption, 28–29
Distribution of wealth, 24
Distributional conflict theories, 142–143
Dollarization, 165
Domestic social movements, 30
Dominance, 181

East India Company (EIC), 189
Economic corruption, 47
Economic elites, 146–147, 150, 152
   limited capacity of, 164–165
Economic inequality, 4
Economic liberalization, 120–121
Economic organizations, 26
Economic policy, 150
Economic power, 19, 24–25
Economic structural power, 27

Index

Economic team, 150
Education, 4
Efficiency framework, 176–177
"Elite cartels" syndromes, 49
Elites, 3–6, 34, 37, 72, 86–87, 114, 212–214
    art patronage, 72–73
    Bourdieu, 12–13
    capacities, 18
    cohesion and fragmentation in state elites, 144–146
    configurations, 5
    conflict, 113, 178–179, 1785
    current state, 17–18
    fragmentation, 148
    fragmentation of state elites, 149–150
    Lachmann, 13–17
    Michels, 9–11
    Mills, 11–12
    Mosca, 7–9
    Pareto, 7
    politics, 144–149
    power competition, 52–55
    relations in Argentina, 149–152
    theory, 3–5
    tradition of, 6–18
    transformation of classification, 213
    turnover, 145–146, 148–149
Emerging markets, 52–53
Endogenous events, 214–215
Environmental change, 4
Ethnic elites, 33–34
Ethnicity, 71–72, 212
Ethnoracial classifications, 213
Ethnoracial hierarchies, 211–216
    elite transformation of classification, 213
    elites and racial state, 213–214
    nonelite transformation of categorization, 212–213
Ethnoracially marginalized groups, 212
European–American immigrants, 213
Events

analysis, 221–232
categorization, and classification, 214–216
Catholic Irish under English imperial rule, 216–220
establishing pathways, 220–221
ethnoracial hierarchies, 211–216
method, 220–221
Exogenous events, 214–215
Exú na Álvares Cabral, 98–99

Factionalism, 148–149
Feudal elites, 114–115
Fiscal capacity, 127
Formality, 22
"Fourth generation" of revolution theory, 46
Fracking, 116–117
Fragmentation, 144–149
    in state elites, 144–146
Fragmented authoritarianism, 61–62
French Occupation of 1667, 228–229
French Revolution, 141–142

Gender, 5–6
Geopolitical polarization, 115–116
German Weimar Republic, 141–142
Global south, 52–53
Globalization, 28
"Good governance" agenda, 54
Governmentality approach, 243–244
Grievances, 46
Gross domestic product (GDP), 53

Hegemony, 8–9
Heterogeneity, 115–116
Historical change, 34–37
Historical trajectories, 245, 247–248, 265
Home Rule, 126
Hydraulic Fracking Blog, 122
Hyperinflation, 141–143, 161, 163
    elite politics, 144–149
    elite relations in Argentina, 149–152
    first wave, 159–163

institutional weakness and
distributional conflict
theories, 142–143
macroeconomics of inflation in
Argentina, 152–157
origins and continuity of central
bank deficit, 157–159
second wave, 163–166

Ideational power, 21, 30, 33
Ideological power, 19
Ideology, 10
Igor, Mauricio, 100–102
Immigration, 4
Incumbent policy elites, 145
India, 175–176
Industrial lobbying, 119–121
on state preemption, 121
Industry lobbyists, 128–130
Industry regulation, 115
Inflation, 141–142
Information gathering, 240
and social uses, 248–252
Institutional corruption, 50–52
Institutional orders, 49
Institutional theories, 145–146
Institutional weakness, 142–143
Insulation, 216
Interactive enumeration, 244–245
Intermediaries, 186
Interorganizational cohesion, 145

Korean patrons, 77

Labor unions, 30
Land, 175–176
property rights changes under early
EIC rule, 193–195
rights under early EIC rule to
permanent settlement,
193–198
surveys, 240
"Landlords" (*zamindars*), 175–176
Laws of Barbadoes (sic) (LoB), 220
League of Women for Community
Service, 72–73

Legislative competition, 126
Legitimacy, 8–9, 31
Legitimation, 73
Liberal democracy, 17
Liberalism, 51
Lobbying, 117
Lobbyists, 125
Local bans, 116–117
Local elites, 116
Lockean liberal tradition, 51
Luso-tropicalism, myth of, 88–89

Macroeconomics of inflation in
Argentina, 152–157
Market, 177
Marketplace bargaining power, 27
Marxism, 4–6
Marxist theory, 4–5, 31
Mass democracy, 12
Mass mobilization against elites,
50–52
Material power, 25
Material resources, 24–25
Maximum ability to pay (MAP),
36–37, 183–184
as common knowledge, 184
Medieval period, 253–258
information gathering and social
uses, 253–257
social and state uses of caste,
257–258
Metropolitan Museum of Art, 73–74,
80
Military power, 19
Modernization, 51
Monetary regulation account,
157–158
Monetary resources, 25
Money laundering, 52–53
Montserrat, 226–232
after French Occupation, 229–232
French Occupation of 1667,
228–229
pathway, 221
Before the 1667 French
Occupation, 226–228

Index 289

Montserratian Catholic Irish, 217–218
Museum of Fine Arts in Boston, 72

National Conference of State
Legislatures (NCSL), 122
National elites, 116
New York's Japanese community, 80
Nigro, Dori, 96–99
Non-bourgeois elites, 179
Nonagentive power, 18–19
Nonelites, 3–6, 16–17, 34, 37, 86–87,
212
transformation of categorization,
212–213

Official information gathering, 240
data and methods, 247–248
direct rule censuses in India,
241–245
historical trajectories, 245,
247–248, 265
Oligarchic tendencies, 13
Oligarchs and clans syndrome, 49, 52
Oligarchy, 10
Orange Revolution, 59
Organization, 10, 26
Organization for Economic
Cooperation and
Development (OECD), 53
Organizational assets, 25
Organizational power, 21, 25–26
Orientalism, 243–244
Outright factionalism, 148–149

Pamphleteers, 48
Panama Papers, 52–53
Pandora Papers, 57–58
Party elites, 119, 144–145
Pervasive corruption, 54
Pitt's India Act, 195
Plan Bonex, 156, 165–166
Plan Primavera, 159–161
Plural elites, 9
Poisson models, 122, 124
Policy elites, 144–145, 150

Policy incoherence in plan primavera,
159–161
Policymaking
in fragmented elites, 147–149
process, 144–149
Political corruption, 47
Political elites (*see also* State elites),
114–115
conflicts in urban-rural
polarization, 117–119
ideological orientation, 115
Political formulas, 8–9
Political legitimacy, 17
Political polarization, 115
control variables, 126–127
data, 121
dependent variables and
estimation, 122–124
independent and moderating
variables, 124–126
method, 121–127
results, 127–132
theory, 117–121
Political power, 19, 23, 26
Political process theory, 3–4
Popular sovereignty, 7
Porto, 86, 95–96
colonized roads, 96–99
Exú na Álvares Cabral, 98–99
Porto Nigro, 96–98
Porto Nigro, 96–98
Portuguese Colonial Empire, 87
Post settlement dynamics in property
rights, 199–202
diminishing information
asymmetry and
stabilization (and
enhancement) of
cultivators' rights, 200–201
fluctuation of cultivators' rights,
199–200
Power (*see also* Relational power), 4,
16, 212
combining mechanisms and
expressions of, 33–34
conceptualizing, 18–24

and economic interests in
bargaining framework,
179–181
elite, 11
resources theory, 21–22
Power/conflict approach,
177–181
economic interests, 177–178
and ideology, 177
Pre-Vedic through Gupta period,
248–253
information gathering and social
uses, 248–252
social and state uses of caste,
252–253
Preachers, 48
Primitive accumulation, 177–178
Private property, 14–15, 178–179
Privatization of land, 175–176, 178
Proletarianization of plurality of
peasants, 14–15
Property rights, 176
in colonial Bengal, 189–202
extant theoretical approaches and
explanations, 176–181
framework, 181–189
with intermediaries, 186
with intermediaries without means
of violence, 186–189
in land, 182
mechanisms and outcomes,
190–192
outcome with intermediaries
without means of violence,
187
outcome without intermediaries,
185
preconditions and empirical
implications of theoretical
framework, 189–192
sketching framework, 182–189
Status Quo Ante, 190
with undifferentiated groups,
184–185
Protest, 46
Protestantism, 7

"Pure" efficiency approach, 180

Quasi-fiscal deficit, 155–157

Race, 5–6, 71–72, 212
Racial domination, 214
Racial elites, 33–34
Racial justice, 4
Racial state, 213–214
in context, 219–220
Racialization of Catholic Irish,
217–218
Radical Civic Union, 149
Radical party, 159–160
Relational power
associational power, 26–27
coalitional power, 29–30
of elites and nonelites, 24–34
ideational power, 30–33
material resources, 24–25
organizational power, 25–26
structural power, 27–29
theory, 3–4
tradition of elite theory, 6–18
Remunerative power, 19
Republican Party, 119–120
Reputational individualism, 148
Resource mobilization theory, 3–4,
32–33
Revolution theory, 46
Revolutionary mobilization, 48–55
Revolutionary movements, 46
Revolutionary potential, 52–55
Rights, 182
Risks for industry regulation, 119
Riverbank, 78

Santos, Luciane De AraúJo, 99–100
Sexual orientation, 5–6
Social changes, 178
Social mechanisms of power, 21
Social reality, 5, 7
Social stratification, 5–6
Social types, 9
Socialism, 11
Societies, 240

"Society-centered" approach, 240–241
Society-driven enumeration, 244
Sociological institutionalists, 146
Soft colonization, 88
"Soft manners" narratives, 88
Soliciting bribes, 56
Stabilization, 143
 of Zamindars' rights, 197–198
Stagnation, 218
Stalemate, 144, 149–150, 152
State capture, 119–121
State elites, 150–152
 cohesion and fragmentation in,
  144–146
 economic and, 146–147
 fragmentation, 149–150
State legislators affiliated with ALEC,
  125–126
State preemption, 131–132
State-driven enumeration, 242–244
States, 240
"Strange immigrant" in Portuguese
  academia, 99–100
Street protests, corrupt streets to,
  55–58
Street-level corruption, 47–50
Structural power, 21, 27, 29
Sub-rulers, 186
Subcontractors, 186–187
Substitutionist ideology, 17
Sudden protest, 49–50
"Supply side" of corrupt transactions,
  53
Symbolic power, 19
Synchronic cohesion, 150

"Syndromes of corruption" typology,
  47
Systemic corruption, 47

Tax evasion, 52–53
Transitioning economies, 52–53
Transparency International, 48, 53
TRAVESSIA, 86, 90
 history, form, and sociological and
  artistic methodology, 90–95
Tunisia, 46
Tunisia Revolution (2011), 48, 55, 58
Two-stage least-square (2SLS)
  regression, 122

Ukraine, 46
Ukrainian politics, 58
United Nations Convention against
  Corruption (UNCAC), 53
Urban-rural polarization, 115–118,
  124–125
US hegemony, 15
US sociology, 11

Visibility, 22

War of attrition model, 143, 154–155
Washington Consensus, 54
White elites, 86–87
 in Portugal, 87–90
 power over social narratives, 89–90
White patrons, 75
Workplace bargaining power, 27
World Bank, 48, 53
 Stolen Asset Recovery Initiative,
  53

Printed and bound by CPI Group (UK) Ltd, Croydon, CR0 4YY
03/11/2024